Across the Great Divide

Across the Great Divide

Cultures of Manhood in the American West

Edited by Matthew Basso, Laura McCall, and Dee Garceau

ROUTLEDGE

NEW YORK • LONDON

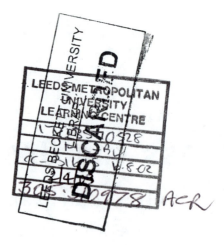

Published in 2001 by

Routledge
29 West 35th Street
New York, NY 10001

Published in Great Britain by
Routledge
11 New Fetter Lane
London EC4P 4EE

Routledge is an imprint of the Taylor & Francis Group.

Library of Congress Cataloging-in-Publication Data

Across the great divide: cultures of manhood in the American West / edited by Matthew Basso, Laura McCall, and Dee Garceau.
    p. cm.
Includes bibliographical references and index.
ISBN 0–415–92470–7 (hb.) — ISBN 0–415–92471–5 (pbk.)
    1. Masculinity—West (U.S.)—History. 2. Men—West (U.S.)—History. I. Basso, Matthew. II. McCall, Laura. III. Garceau, Dee, 1955–

HQ1090.5.W4 A37 2000
305.31'0978—cd21   00-042206

Matt Basso: For my mom and pop, Mary Basso and Lawrence Donald Basso, endlessly supportive, boundlessly generous, invariably droll "Texans."

Dee Garceau: For Davida Gordon Madden and Arthur Joseph Garceau, who set me on this trail.

Laura McCall: For my nephews, Noel and Quinn Coleman, true sons of the West.

Contents

Acknowledgments

This project began during an informal conversation at a meeting of the Western History Association in 1997. Following a panel presentation of intriguing new examinations of constructions of manhood in the American West, we discussed the need for a volume that would pull together multicultural research on gender systems, analyses of masculinity, and revisionist scholarship in western history. That conversation became this book. Along the way we have been fortunate to work with many talented scholars. Among these our thanks first must go to our contributors. Their fresh vision and original research illuminated the core themes of *Across the Great Divide,* and we appreciate their craftsmanship in seeing this volume through to completion. Thanks also to Elaine Tyler May, Dave Roediger, Alex Lubin, Erika Lee, Gunther Peck, Valerie Matsumoto, Nayan Shah, and Estelle Freedman for helping us find junior and senior scholars producing remarkable work on the cultures of manhood in the American West.

We are deeply indebted to those who read and critiqued the essays as well as those who challenged us to clarify the volume's unifying themes. Nancy Scott Jackson, Angela Smith, Betsey Jameson, Randy Rodriguez, Deirdre Mullane, and Derek Krissoff were at once astute, unsparing, and encouraging. Derek, in particular, exhibited both masterful editing skills and extraordinary patience as we worked to fine-tune the manuscript. *Across the Great Divide* is a much better book because of him.

For help negotiating the byzantine world of procuring illustrations and gaining copyright permissions we would like to thank Debra Neiswonger at the Colorado Historical Society; Joshua Shaw and Philip Cronenwett at Darmouth College Special Collections; Wallace Dailey of the Theodore Roosevelt Collection at the Houghton Library, Harvard University; Clyde Janes at the Sutro Library; Wendy Welker and Cathy Adams at the

California Historical Society; Brian Shovers and Ellie Arguimbau at the Montana Historical Society Library and Archives; Amy Boemer at the University of Minnesota's McGrath Library; Stephen Zimmer, director of the Philmont Museum and Seton Memorial Library; Susan Snyder at the Bancroft Library; Barbara Hall at the Academy of Motion Picture Arts and Sciences; Kristine Krueger at NFIS; Brian Patrick at Miramax; and Tony Clark, Durwood Ball, Brian Klopotek, and Bob Johnson. The staff at the University of Minnesota's program in American studies eased the production of this book in numerous ways. Many thanks to Betty Agee, Colleen Hennen, Ben Line, and Ana Chavier.

We would like to recognize a number of the pioneers in the field whose groundbreaking works have inspired us: Clyde Griffen, R. W. Connell, Anthony Rotundo, Mark Carnes, Vicky Ruiz, Peter Filene, Donald Yacavone, Susan Armitage, Betsey Jameson, Joan Jensen, Darlis Miller, John Faragher, Peter Iverson, Theda Perdue, Kathleen Brown, SuCheng Chan, Albert Hurtado, William Cronon, Sherman Alexie, and Michael Kimmel.

Lastly, we appreciated the spirit of candor, trust, and professionalism that buoyed our collaboration. At the outset we believed the ways we complemented each other intellectually would strengthen both *Across the Great Divide* and our own scholarship. Three years later we can confirm this judgment.

Introduction

Laura McCall

In 1882, Theodore Roosevelt arrived in Albany, New York, to begin his political career as a state legislator. The idealistic twenty-three-year-old had entered politics to make over the world but what he soon learned was that he needed to transform himself. Newspapers habitually derided Roosevelt's manhood. They called him "weakling," "Jane Dandy," "Punkin Lily," and "the exquisite Mr. Roosevelt." They ridiculed his fancy clothing and, in an obvious phallic allusion, alleged that he was "given to sucking the knob of an ivory cane."[1]

A mere five years later, TR was running for mayor of New York as "the Cowboy of the Dakotas." Before taking up what Roosevelt claimed would be permanent residence on his Dakota ranch, he granted a "final" interview to the *New York Tribune,* saying,

> It would electrify some of my friends who have accused me of repre-
> senting the kid-glove element in politics if they could see me galloping
> over the plains, day in and day out, clad in a buckskin shirt and leather
> chaparajos, with a big sombrero on my head. For good healthy exercise
> I would strongly recommend some of our gilded youth go West and
> try a short course of riding bucking ponies, and assist at the branding
> of a lot of Texas steers.[2]

Throughout his sojourn in Dakota Territory, Roosevelt sent self-promoting press releases back to New York, refashioning himself as the embodiment of iconic western masculinity. By the time he ran for mayor, few remembered his sickly childhood, his extremely genteel upbringing, or his dandified early adulthood.

Roosevelt reinvented himself at a time when standards of ideal manhood were undergoing profound change. His father had instructed him in

Victorian norms of manliness that emphasized self-restraint, chastity, sobriety, self-denial, sentiment, and delayed gratification. The youthful TR regarded his father as "the best man I ever knew. He combined strength and courage with gentleness, tenderness and great unselfishness . . . . He made us understand that the same standard of clean living was demanded for the boys as for the girls, that what was wrong in a woman could not be right in a man."[3] Nevertheless, when Roosevelt left his elegant and refined home for the bustling world of late-nineteenth-century politics, he relinquished his father's emblems of proper masculine behavior and embraced a newer ideal that stressed physical prowess, the masculine primitive, and a deliberate linkage between white supremacy and male dominance.[4] Roosevelt became a vigorous proponent of this new ideal, leading "Rough Riders" in the Spanish-American War and exhorting American men to take up "the strenuous life." In a speech before the Hamilton Club of Chicago in 1899, the cowboy–New Yorker unabashedly fused manhood and nationalism. "As it is with the individual," he thundered, "so it is with the nation. . . . When men fear righteous war, they tremble on the brink of doom." U.S. naval and commercial supremacy demanded "stern men with empires in their brains."[5]

Unlike the patrician Roosevelt, General George Armstrong Custer came of age in the "real" West of frontier Ohio. In the summer of 1876, Custer led five companies of the U.S. Seventh Cavalry into the Black Hills of Montana Territory and launched a headlong attack on a large encampment of Sioux and their allies. Every American knows what happened next. For the Native peoples, the ensuing Battle of Little Bighorn was a last-ditch defense of their shrinking homeland and disappearing way of life. Though they scored a stunning victory, it came far too late to stem the tide of white settlers and American military power that was sweeping through the West, confining Native peoples to reservations and laying railroad track to promote the expansion of Euro-American business and agriculture.[6]

George Armstrong Custer personified another fitting symbol of the masculine drive to conquer and succeed. The "Boy General," having first attained that rank as a twenty-three-year-old in the Civil War, embodied many of the qualities identified with western American manhood. He was brash, bold, articulate, and "loved war. It nourished and energized him."[7] He never stood still when he led his men in battle; in fact, the term "Custer's luck" came into common usage as the daring general developed a reputation for surviving reckless charges.[8] Custer was arrogant, vain, and ambitious, and he desperately sought wealth.[9] His hunger for personal glory knew no limits. He ignored the advice of his own scouts and officers before the fateful battle, refusing to see the truth before him.[10] Biographer Frederick F. Van de Water called him a perpetual adolescent with a passion

THEODORE ROOSEVELT, THE VERY IMAGE OF VICTORIAN BOYHOOD, JUST BEFORE HIS SECOND BIRTHDAY. COURTESY OF HOUGHTON LIBRARY, HARVARD UNIVERSITY.

THEODORE ROOSEVELT, REFASHIONED INTO THE "COWBOY OF THE DAKOTAS." COURTESY OF HOUGHTON LIBRARY, HARVARD UNIVERSITY.

for recognition and adulation,[11] while Brian Dippie has noted, "The code of the West will justify sheer idiocy so long as it is valiant."[12] Regardless, Custer's contemporaries and later aficionados lionized Custer's rash act. The admiring Frederick Whittaker claimed, "To Custer alone was it given to join a romantic life of perfect success to a death of perfect heroism."[13] His dramatic destruction on a western battlefield made his name synonymous with the martyrdom of the virile, uncompromising white man conquering the West.

The historic and mythic figure of Custer straddled the divide between glorious warrior and cruel murderer, a fine line for any masculine identity based upon the pursuit of war. Moreover, by portraying Custer's death as coming in a charge, as several nineteenth-century artists preferred to feature it,[14] rather than as a relatively passive defensive stance, the aggressive masculine initiative of the West was affirmed.

For American men, eastern men in particular, Custer filled a need for a late-nineteenth-century masculine hero. Historian Anthony Rotundo writes that industrialization and the growth of urbane leisure left many men feeling overcivilized. "Idleness and luxury" undermined men's sense of their own natures. "As [white] men of the late 19th century sought to connect themselves to primitive impulse and to define their lives in terms of passionate struggle," Rotundo surmises, "they often turned to martial ideals and images as a way to focus their vision of a manly life."[15]

Fiction and the popular imagination tested, transformed, and confirmed the masculinity of rugged valorous figures in the West. "Its heroes bore none of the marks of degraded status," wrote Henry Nash Smith. "They were in reality not members of society at all, but noble anarchs owning [sic] no master, free denizens of a limitless wilderness."[16] Such an ideology proclaimed this vast kingdom—this "virgin land"—as the ideal setting for attainment of masculinity; in this scenario, a man must be free and beholden to no other to be a true western man.[17]

These perceptions have been elaborated and defined primarily in popular fiction and movies. Lee Clark Mitchell describes the motifs by which these prevailing forms measure manhood, for "masculinity is not simply a blunt biological fact but is as well a cultural fiction that must be created," and Westerns have established a coded pictorial language to measure the manliness of their characters.[18] The Custer and Roosevelt myths conform to and exploit this code to startling effect.

Mitchell relates how "the Western can be reduced to oppositions between those who stand and those who fall down—between upright men on horseback and those whose supposedly 'natural' position is prone. The prone are always revealed in the end to be non-men (a category that generously embraces Indians, preachers, Mexicans, small children, Easterners and women)."[19] That Custer died staging a last stand exemplifies this principle. Images from 1876 to the latter half of the twentieth century consistently show Custer facing death on his feet, standing tall and fighting against the overwhelming onslaught until the last possible moment—an image of heroic masculine sacrifice that reminded his contemporaries of the gender-affirming rewards of heroic male action. The historically insupportable but widespread belief that he was the last of his men standing adds immensely to his masculine status. As Robert Utley has written, "Custer commands both universality and widely perceived symbolic association. The universality is valid, the legacy of a dramatic and controversial career capped by one of the grandest denouements in American history." Custer represents "the mysterious interaction of history, legend, and myth in the national consciousness."[20] Like him or not, everyone knows George Armstrong Custer.

These two famous lives framed a turbulent period in U.S. history. Some of the tumult stemmed from a presumed breakdown in masculine authority, but what caused this apparent crisis remains a subject of lively debate. Some cite the crucible of the Civil War, others the closing of the frontier and its attendant loss of opportunity for the self-made man. Unstable economic conditions, the emergence of giant industrial combinations, and what John Higham has described as "the sheer dullness of urban-industrial culture"[21] endangered the nonconformist entrepreneurial spirit. Working-class and immigrant men competed with middle-class men for control of the political arena. Women publicly challenged men to quit alcohol and give them the vote. In reaction to the growing sentimentalization and feminization of American culture,[22] beleaguered men responded with muscular Christianity, the strenuous life, and pseudoscientific theories that stressed the mental and physical superiority of white males. The rugged, individualistic maverick of the West became a fashionable antidote to urban malaise.

As these snapshots of Roosevelt and Custer also indicate, perceptions of the men who inhabited the American West are mired in stereotype and fantasy. "For more than a century," writes Richard White, "the American West has been the most strongly imagined section of the United States."[23] Through oral and written history, songs, fiction, art, and film, the West has been identified with mythic themes of adventure and transformation. In the legendary West, Europeans became Americans who tamed a wilderness. According to Frederick Jackson Turner and the decades of scholarship he inspired, Indians stepped on stage only when whites arrived, and women appeared as scenery rather than as actors.[24] This imagined West represented a nationalist narrative of white settlement, a tale of linear progress in which American democracy spread from coast to coast. The drama was masculine, an assumption so tacit that one social historian remarked, "No one has ever questioned, let alone analyzed, the masculinity of the frontier society. Since it is as obvious as the sun in the daytime, the subject has not been discussed."[25]

Historians of women in the American West were the first to challenge this characterization by calling for analyses of gender in a region they sardonically dubbed "Hisland." Women's historians investigated how gender systems evolved over time, explored how women's roles changed in the course of interactions among different cultures, and illustrated how western history offered vivid case studies in race relations, cultural brokerage, colonialism, and conquest.[26] In this sense, the West served as a laboratory of gender where competing systems of social organization came into contact, often generating conflict as well as consensus.[27]

After women's historians illuminated the significance of gender in the West, scholars revisited the mythic, masculine West with new questions. What was it about the American West that contributed to identification with theatrical masculine emblems like the gunfighter, the cowboy, or the Native warrior? What purposes did these constructions serve? As Mary Murphy explains, the myth of western masculinity is rooted in a belief that the West was an escape, a restorative from the trammels and turmoils of eastern life—a "therapeutic retreat" for white men like "cowboy" Theodore Roosevelt or for the scores who, for over two centuries, have been "playing Indian."[28] For most of the men in this book, however, the West was home. The western expanses represented not a temporary respite but a permanent place where men shaped or were molded by the daily rounds of work, family life, and community.

Across the Great Divide moves away from the "entrenched icons" of western historiography. The romanticization and continuing currency of iconic Western manhood personified by Roosevelt and Custer veil many struggles against colonialism, conquest, and notions of white male supremacy. Nevertheless, while contesting Custer's and Roosevelt's roles as factual and paradigmatic emblems of manhood in the West, this study does not dismiss the relevance of the myths they represent.[29] Instead, this book foregrounds both the multicultural and gendered divides of a West where real people lived, and reveals the dynamics through which idolized figures had and continue to have very real explanatory power. Indeed, one theme unifying this volume is the dialectical process by which cultures of manhood took shape, as actual residents of the American West encountered notions of iconic western masculinity.

Several essays in this volume illuminate the role of emblematic figures in underwriting a set of values that affirmed the power of a single group. Scholars of gender utilize the term *hegemonic masculinity* to describe this dominance. Hegemonic masculinity, which is not static but always in process, not only shapes images of ideal manhood; it also becomes institutionalized. Hegemony emerges through systems of human organization that allocate power, resources, and privilege. Through such entitlements, the cultural dominance of one group becomes embedded in religious doctrine, political rights, civil codes, wage structures, family organization, and sexual mores. According to R. W. Connell, hegemonic manhood is both created and reinforced by subordinating women, people of color, and homosexuals. Connell asserts, however, that ideals of hegemonic manhood fail to correspond with the actual personalities of most men. Rather, they exist as tropes, figurative images or types that reinforce "conventional" yet often unexamined wisdom about men.[30] Some men resoundingly support these models, others challenge elements of hegemonic manhood while living within its constraints, and many exist entirely outside its boundaries. The interplay between hegemonic notions of manhood and the residents of the lived West forms the first unifying theme of this volume.

Several authors explore how subaltern communities contested hegemonic manhood by disrupting and recasting white myths of western masculinity. Men in frontier settlements often encountered situations that destabilized or rendered inoperable conventional wisdoms about prototypical manhood. In these open and often unfamiliar spaces, rigid divisions of responsibility, categories of belonging, and terrains of exclusion softened. Despite the glaring instances of racism and sexism delineated in this volume, the very population who represented iconic manhood occasionally threw off the mantle and embraced alternative forms of masculinity. Ranchers and cowboys, for example, skirted between windfalls of iconic status and lingering disrepute, ultimately redefining tenets of manliness to suit their daily lives and creating new patterns of intimacy. Urban men, albeit to magnify Anglo manhood and justify imperial possession, nevertheless emulated the manly strength and courage of Native Americans. More recently, Asian writers and Native American filmmakers have refashioned the notions of "cowboy" and "Indian" in ways that reflect the experience of people of color in the American West.

Just as subordinated peoples and alternative sexualities changed the face of gender systems in the West, women were in constant dialogue with western masculinity as well. Several essays in this volume address the ways women surfaced as foils for defining an oppositional male identity. Women also appeared as symbols of rank and privilege to measure the status of men. Further, they emerged as exemplars of morality whose presence—real or imagined—outlined the boundaries of acceptable social behavior. Like their less-privileged male counterparts, women sometimes disputed and renegotiated the patterns of entitlement. The dialectical interaction among the challengers and the perceived dominators reveal larger processes of transformation woven from the economic and political contingencies of western life. In short, the real West emerges as a pluralistic region where competing notions of manhood played out in encounters among ethnic and racial cultures, classes, and genders.

The issue of national identity also loomed large. Indeed, a second theme unifying *Across the Great Divide* examines the relationship between masculinity and nationalism. As the outlines of the Roosevelt and Custer myths suggest, U.S. destiny was often expressed in masculine terms. Neither Roosevelt nor Custer were subtle on this count; both fervently believed themselves agents of American expansion and representatives of Anglo superiority. But in many cases, the relationship between manhood and nationalism was more elusive. Several of the essays herein present the norms governing male and female relationships as expressions of a hierarchical order that ultimately supported colonial ambition. Others address urban Anglo cultures of manhood that never directly confronted the concept of Manifest Destiny yet played it out through imitation of "Indian" ritual. Still another examines the role of the Federal government in shaping economic opportunity at moments and locations where occupational identity and manhood were tightly bound together. Whether men consolidated their position through domestic hierarchies, presumed a "melting-pot" identity, or contested federal control, nationalism colored western constructions of manhood. If one conclusion emerges from the exploration of these varied motifs, it is that manhood in the West, while always a complex, historically specific construct, was often mobilized in conjunction with race, class, gender, and national identity as a stratagem for defining, disrupting, or maintaining privilege.

Consider, for example, Ramón A. Gutiérrez's essay on honor and virtue in colonial New Mexico. His work constitutes not only one of the first and most provocative forays into analyses of masculinity, but also—in its role as the lead essay—provides an instructive analytic foundation for the exploration of a number of unifying themes that connect across the divides of identity and power.

In "'Tell Me with Whom You Walk and I Will Tell You Who You Are,'" Gutiérrez mines ethnographies, archaeological site studies, and collections of myths, as well as civil and ecclesiastical court records to reveal a complex system of honor and status based upon hierarchies of class and gender. In so doing, he illuminates elements of a feudal patriarchal system employed to both sanctify the reality of unequal gender relations and reinforce European racial dominance over indigenous peoples in colonial society. Honor in Spanish New Mexico was strictly a male possession whereas shame was considered intrinsic to females. Men protected and controlled the virtue of their women in order to ensure personal and familial honor and status. This ideology echoed the firm belief that God made men dominant over women, who should submit to male authority and direction regardless of class. A peasant man, for example, deferred to his aristocratic betters but, like them, could claim the masculine virtue of honor as long as his wife and daughters' reputations remained intact.

Gutiérrez's study broadens historical understandings of masculinity and power in the West by illustrating how colonial civilizations shaped western manhood. Tenets of iconic masculinity not only moved west with the Anglos but also north from Mexico into the Spanish borderlands. Moreover, through his analysis of how women's behavior framed masculine status, Gutiérrez shows how gender distinctions functioned in relation to each other, a theme that recurs in Karen Leong's and Dee Garceau's chapters in *Across the Great Divide*. Finally, Gutiérrez's examination of inter- and intra-ethnic sexual relationships illustrates the dynamic bonds among sexuality, ethnicity, and power in the construction of masculine cultures.

Susan Johnson's work on Gold Rush California references the scholarship on mid-nineteenth-century eastern manhood and suggests new approaches to understanding gender in the West. Johnson combs journals, letters, and newspapers for expressions of a masculine persona in the southern diggings. From the miners' worlds of work and leisure, the record reveals a fluid society in which normative behaviors were challenged and transformed. Sexuality and the making of manhood were illuminated not only as constructed categories but as choices tied to ideologies of gender. Populations in the mining regions were 97 percent male and ethnically diverse. Mexican, Chilean, French, Chinese, and Native peoples created a heterogeneous world that disrupted Anglo presumptions of dominance. Miners contested the meanings of manhood and many Anglo men found themselves on the defensive.

Amid this unstable social milieu, some miners eventually rejected the Victorian assumption of male dereliction in the absence of women and sought pleasure "in the constant company of men." Johnson further illuminates the cross-hatching of race, gender, and nationality within systems of hierarchy employed to order life in the diggings. Like Gutiérrez, she finds a complex dynamic of interlocking meanings through which men created interchangeable categories of subordination. In the absence of women, Anglo men in the California gold fields projected familiar gender hierarchies onto people of color and immigrants.

Gunther Peck's study of working- and middle-class men on the Comstock Lode complements Johnson's insights by delineating the critical relationship between class and the construction of masculine cultures in the West. While middle-class men confined their hazards to the comfortable halls of Virginia City's stock exchanges, working-class men not only participated in a culture of peril at their dangerous workplaces but also reveled in the risks involved in gambling and fighting. Significantly, Peck sees all of these activities as rooted in an economic imperative "predicated on enduring gender hierarchies" that involved access to the opposite sex. Working- and middle-class men, furthermore, rallied together in their use of racialized others as foils for the solidification of white masculinity. Chinese men most clearly threatened the economic and gender security of white mine workers. Conversely, Native American men, as fictionally constructed by middle-class members of fraternal organizations active on the Comstock, provided access to "an idealized past in which risk-taking and masculine hierarchies were secure and unquestioned" and thereby affirmed the authority and supremacy of middle-class men. Peck's analysis of fraternal organizations also links his work to that of scholars interested in eastern manhood,[31] while his analysis of mine workers reveals new dimensions of class recognition in the industrializing West. Peck, like Susan Johnson, addresses the harnessing of racialized myths about manhood to assert Anglo authority. His comparisons place in relief the uniqueness of western masculine cultures, the West's multicultural population within those cultures, and the construction of masculine myth.

Durwood Ball provides a similar perspective. Examining legal hangings in the New Mexico and Arizona Territories between 1864 and 1910, Ball discovers in public executions "a well-choreographed ritual of communal self-improvement." To audiences and journalists, legal strangulation signified an allegory of masculine performance and Victorian moral atonement. Spectators applauded the sinner who embraced the verdict, admitted his wrong, accepted his death sentence as just, and met his demise with stoicism and "unflappable cool." Eyewitnesses and newspaper readers alike saw a condemned man's ability to face hanging calmly as a drama of redemption and a reaffirmation of community morality.

Ball explores the nuances of reportage and public perception which, together, constructed a Western manhood that fortified Victorian concepts of self-discipline and moral integrity as hallmarks of masculinity. Those hapless victims who physically lost control fell short of the manly courage that signaled remorse and thus redemption. Convicts who displayed aggressive cockiness, sarcasm, or other forms of resistance were equally criticized by reporters. Like unmanly tears or trembling, bravado indicated a lack of contrition as well as a convict's refusal to take responsibility for his crime—the ultimate in unmanly behavior.

Not only did hangings reveal a masculinized drama of moral redemption, they also conveyed race positioning. Condemned Euro-Victorian men could, even at death's door, proclaim their superiority over women and men of color by demonstrating the reserve and self-control attributed to men of Nordic stock. Most could not lay claim to class privilege but they and the Anglo members of their communities could appropriate racial superiority. Journalists often found the manly virtues lacking in men of color, who were more likely to be described in contemporary newspapers as "brutes" with neither "refinement" nor "intelligence." On the other hand, overt resistance among minority convicts might have reflected their rebellion against the standards of the hegemonic culture by which men of color had been judged. To them, justice had not been served. At public hangings, the dramas of life, death, and moral redemption potentially obscured the twin specters of race prejudice and miscarried justice.

David Anthony Tyeeme Clark and Joane Nagel deepen these contemplations with a sociohistorical meditation on the refashioning of Anglo and Native American masculinities during the late nineteenth and early twentieth centuries. Following the battle at Peji Sla Wakapa (Little Bighorn) and in the face of rapid urbanization and industrialization, white American men feared delicacy and sentimentality. To compensate, they resurrected images of a vigorous, potent masculinity in Wild West pageants, in literature, on athletic fields, and in associations such as the Improved Order of Red Men. Whites reconstructed the "Indian" to signify masculinist colonial conquest and imperial possession and, in so doing, restored the future of white manhood "at the expense of indigenous people by robbing them of their cultural capital, infusing it with new meaning, and then using it to remake themselves as masters and masterful." As Gail Bederman has observed, "between 1890 and 1917, as white middle-class men actively worked to reinforce male power, their race became a factor which was crucial to their gender . . . . By harnessing male supremacy to white supremacy and celebrating both as essential to human perfection, hegemonic versions of civilization maintained the power of Victorian gender ideologies by presenting [white] male power as natural and inevitable."[32] This racist and masculinist stance did not go unanswered, however. Clark and Nagel conclude with twentieth-century Native American responses to white appropriation, showing how the dominant discourse is renegotiated by those with less power.

Karen Leong plumbs Congressional records, newspapers, and popular doggerel for evidence of changing attitudes toward Chinese men in the late-nineteenth-century West. She roots emerging concepts of Chinese manhood in public debate over the exclusion movement. Scholars of Chinese immigration have shown how anti-Chinese rhetoric shifted from overt racism to gendered arguments about morality and family that, in turn, shaped popular concepts regarding Chinese men. Leong elaborates and refines these insights, locating the significance of the Page Law in Anglo constructions of Chinese manhood.

During Reconstruction, when the nation was especially sensitive to issues of race discrimination, restrictions against Chinese immigration based solely on arguments of racial inferiority proved unacceptable. Exclusion advocates subsequently changed their strategy to one that could be reconciled with democratic ideals. Although race always lurked near the surface, politicians and journalists preferred to use gender as the basis for their criticism of Chinese men. In their analyses, Chinese men violated America's gendered moral order: they exploited their women as prostitutes, lacked wives and nuclear families to civilize them, and worked in such female occupational roles as servant or launderer—paid labors that threatened the livelihoods of white working-class women.

Leong's essay reveals a larger dynamic involving the political use of gender norms to assert race hierarchy, in this case to protect white dominance in the American West in general and California in particular. As Hudson Janisch observes, "If the South fought to protect white womanhood, the West fought to protect white manhood."[33] Because Chinese men allegedly failed to protect female virtue, display patriarchal family organization, or protect masculine occupational privilege, the critics judged them as "unassimilable." Leong's work is particularly innovative in its demonstration of how the dominant culture used the treatment of women as a mirror for masculinity.

Instances in which women's place was used to outline masculine status were not limited to white constructions of Chinese manhood. Women also became foils against which the American cowboy defined manliness. Cowboys, the most powerfully masculine icons of the region, have received an inordinate amount of attention in western historiography as well as in the popular imagination. Past studies typically took an elegiac tone, waxing nostalgic about a vanishing way of life, where real cowboys often appeared as exemplary masculine types: less violent, more industrious, and more wholesome, than the mythic cowboy but still tough and stoic. From Teddy Roosevelt's *The Round-Up* (1889) to David Dary's *Cowboy Culture* (1981), politicians, journalists, and historians have presented the minutiae of cowboy life in celebratory terms.[34]

Few, however, have critically examined the daily lives of range cowboys in the context of changing gender systems or class identities within the cattle industry. Dee Garceau's essay explores the connections between cowboy myth, the gendering of ranch work, and masculine occupations in the West. Garceau discovers a subculture that embraced alternatives to Victorian manhood and flourished during the era of open-range herding. In a careful analysis of cowboy narratives from the late nineteenth and early twentieth centuries, Garceau reveals a working-class subgroup who affirmed the masculine privileges of life on the margins. Unlike the middle-class patriarch of late-Victorian society, range cowboys claimed sexual license without secrecy, fraternal love without the overlay of heroic manhood, fictive marriage with prostitutes, and spontaneous cross-dressing. These mores and behaviors stood in stark contrast to bourgeois markers of respectability such as marriage, property ownership, and economic support of dependents.

Garceau further traces cowboy self-representation through the transition from open-range herding to fenced, family ranches. Here she finds a shift in both gender and class dispositions, as women's labor became part of the enterprise and middle-class values became the norm. When cowboys married and acquired property, they renounced the alternative privileges of the margins, save one: work around cattle remained gender-segregated. Women on family ranches might readily cross over into a variety of men's chores—digging irrigation ditches, pitching hay, herding sheep—but cowboys resisted the use of women as reserve labor. Consequently, work with beef cattle retained its distinctive maleness. Thus cowboys on family ranches barred women from sharing in the iconic cultural status of the legendary range cowboy. Masculine occupational identity—and its tie to the mythic cowboy—was the one vestige of privilege from a subculture that translated from the margins to middle-class respectability. Like Susan Johnson, Garceau reveals changes in masculine self-construction that encoded real labor as male and corresponded with significant economic transitions.

In another important and long-overdue shift in emphasis, Karen R. Merrill examines the other key players in cow country: the settled ranchers. Merrill describes the transformation in attitudes toward wild and domesticated animals following the disastrous winter of 1886–87,[35] which, coupled with changing culinary tastes and rationalized business practices, forced cattlemen to behave more "domestically"—more protective and nurturing—toward their herds.

From diaries, memoirs, and journalistic records, Merrill uncovers a significant story in the history of masculinity and ranching in the West. The economics of cattle ranching on the northern plains required better care of cattle and a more intimate involvement in the reproduction of livestock. Birthing and husbandry, not just fattening steers, became the norm. This transition encouraged an ethos of caretaking among ranchers which, when combined with the growing popularity of sport hunting, expanded to include certain game animals, most notably elk and deer. Truly "wild" animals, such as wolves and coyotes, found no place in this home-oriented vision. Predator destruction represented a complex weaving of the domestication of the range with patriarchal protection.

Merrill claims ranchers sought to create a "domesticated space" within the rugged terrain and harsh climate of their homes on the range. When Merrill peels back the highly masculinized image of ranching, what she finds is a complicated ethos of "family" that extended to livestock, game, women, and children. Ranchers acted not only out of duty and responsibility but to maximize profits: the concept of husbandry became a useful rhetorical tool that enabled ranchers to promote domestic virtue while keeping their eyes on the bottom line. Further, although most no longer butchered their cattle, violence prevailed in the branding, castrating, and horn burning of steers. In the final act of violence, ranchers sent their cattle to the slaughterhouse, thereby abdicating their role as "protectors who ultimately did not protect."

Although Matthew L. Basso's "Man-Power" chronologically begins where Merrill's study of ranchers ends, Basso discerns a vastly dissimilar male culture. To unearth the complex codes of manhood operating among ethnic male copper workers in Montana during World War II, Basso utilizes short stories, local newspapers, and union-management meeting records to convey these men's perspectives on the Selective Service System's process of drafting soldiers. Men comprised 65 percent of the homefront labor force and every time one of Montana's copper workers requested a deferment his community judged not only the acceptability of his behavior but also his manhood. Basso asserts that the war taught subtle lessons about the sometimes combustible, oftentimes mundane process of constructing manhood in the hypermasculine world of western copper, where the murky area occupied by deferred workers challenged more sharply defined typologies such as "soldier," "draft dodger," or "slacker."

"Man-Power" also comes to terms with one virtually unstudied facet of the process through which hegemonic masculinity gets constantly reconstructed: the power of the state. Contrary to received wisdom, World War II actually produced a crisis in manhood that had a profound effect on the relationship between white working-class men in the West and the liberal state they once championed. Basso's research deepens current investigations in feminist political philosophy on the gendering of the state as male.

Following World War II, Jack Kerouac's Beat novels captured the imagination of a generation with their portraits of a new kind of western hero—one who partly salved and partly deflected men's anxiety about their changing roles in postwar society. Kerouac's real-life friend, Neal Cassady of Denver, resembled western heroes of years past. A rootless drifter, Cassady sought work and love where he could, far outside the bounds of society and its restrictive mores. But unlike the standard cowboy stereotype, Cassady was an emotionally and intellectually complex man who read philosophy and French literature, had sexual affairs with men as well as women, and served as the inspiration for several works of Beat literature. The new image of western masculinity Kerouac created in his rendering of Neal Cassady held tremendous appeal in the 1950s and 1960s, as the old masculine heroic ideal came under fire and new images of passionate manhood took hold in the public mind.

Craig Leavitt is the first scholar to identify the strong western component in Beat literature. Although Cassady's contemporaries recognized his distinctly western flavor—Gary Snyder described him as the embodiment of "the archetypal West, the energy of the frontier, still coming down," and Lawrence Ferlinghetti believed the "West that Cassady grew up in . . . is a time and place as remote as the Gold Rush"—not one monograph seriously analyzes the western Beat phenomenon.[36] Leavitt's essay, which incorporates classic primary documents from the Beat era as well as historical analyses of American masculinity, redresses this significant imbalance.

In "All the Best Cowboys Have Chinese Eyes," Steven M. Lee examines western male images in postwar literature, specifically in the writings of three contemporary Asian American men: David Mura, Frank Chin, and John Yau. Arguing that the cowboy hero is one of the most powerful symbolic figures to embody an American national ideal, Lee contends that Asian Americans adopted and shaped the image and incorporated it into their art as well as into their personal lives. In so doing, they "disrupt the myth of national identity by revealing the gaps and fissures" inherent in the ideal. Excluded from and disillusioned by the rhetoric of inclusivity in the United States, these Asian-American artists explore and exploit the disparity between the discourses inherent in the cowboy image and the various sociohistorical forces that seek to control and define the Asian-American male. Indeed, the cowboy is so ubiquitous in U.S. culture, so ingrained in the collective consciousness, that many observers fail to recognize the extent to which this image is a cause and an effect of a nationalism that is both racialized and gendered.

Lee artfully examines the often semiautobiographical novels and plays of Mura, Chin, and Yau. David Mura, for example, recalls how his childhood play sprang full-blown from the most renowned Western television programs of the 1950s. He donned cowboy attire and mimicked the attitudes and behavior of his favorite cowboy heroes, but was "remarkably blind to the physicality of his own racialized body." When Mura eventually comprehended the "incongruities between his Asian physical features and the ideal cowboy hero," the personal and psychological trauma he experienced prompted him to articulate this disenchantment in his art. Lee's analysis of these works demonstrates how the cowboy hero lends himself to oppositional manipulation—not just assimilationist containment—by Asian-American male artists. The interrelated discourses of nationality, race, and gender define the image and confine the man.

Most modern-day Americans receive notions of western masculinity through visual representations, particularly the cinema and television. The last two essays in this collection provide dramatic analyses of masculinity in film. Brian Klopotek contrasts the simplistic image of the "Indian"—a product of the white man's imagination—with the complex and multifaceted realities facing Native communities in the late-twentieth-century West. Klopotek first traces white cinematic constructions of the symbolic Indian, a stock character who served as a foil to exalt or critique Anglo values and habits. With subtlety, he then contrasts these images with those created by Native people in three influential films: *Powwow Highway* (1989), *Grand Avenue* (1996), and *Smoke Signals* (1998).

Klopotek describes how Native American writers, producers, directors, and actors are moving away from stereotypical images of Indianness such as hypermasculinity, the regenerative value of male violence, the denigration or invisibility of Native women, and the noble but feminized savage. Rather than perpetuating representations whose purpose is to validate white masculinity, Native American filmmakers "have manipulated gender images . . . to create more recognizable cinematic images of themselves." These carefully crafted movies depict contemporary Native peoples in urban settings and recognize the vital role of women in maintaining the strength of family and community. Rather than theatrical warriors, the heroes of these films are nerds, struggling fathers, Vietnam veterans, and activists. Although motion pictures cannot adequately define all aspects of Native American masculinity, Klopotek contends they offer visions of what Native men can be as well as what Native men are not.

In "Tex-Sex-Mex," José E. Limón examines the intertwined spheres of colonialism, sexuality, and race in the conflicted social interactions between Anglo and Mexican Americans. Rather than finding a sharp dichotomy between fictional and cinematic portrayals of Mexican and Anglo women (with the dark and sensual Mexican habitually abandoned for the respectable but sexually repressed Anglo), Limón describes how Mexican women in literature and film are used to reframe masculine character.

Following the work of Homi K. Bhabha, Limón argues that the stereotype of Mexican women has always been enigmatic. In many films, Mexican women challenged and mediated the ruling power, personified by their white cowboy lovers, but they were not shown as totally subverting the arrangement until the movie *Lone Star* (1996). In John Sayles's transcendent film, the world of colonized and colonizer becomes fused in the love relationship between an Anglo man and his Mexican half-sister.

Limón's intriguing essay uses postcolonial theory to understand gender relations in modern-day Texas. By carefully analyzing paradigms about masculinity and challenging their authenticity in the contemporary West, Limón skillfully illuminates the ambiguities characteristic of western manhood. His essay reflects a promising new direction in western scholarship in which films can be reread as cultural documents that reflect and catalyze progress in gender and race relations.

Across the Great Divide introduces new perspectives about manhood in the American West, but many questions remain. What, for example, has been and continues to be the function of violence in the construction of masculinity? Is violence inherently American? Did it arise in the South or the West, in urban or rural settings? Richard Slotkin, for one, believes "violence is central to both the historical development of the Frontier and its mythic representation."[37] Although Slotkin acknowledges that Euro-Americans do not possess a monopoly on violence, distinctively American is "the mythic significance we have assigned to the kinds of violence we have actually experienced, the forms of symbolic violence we imagine or invent, and the political uses to which we put that symbolism."[38] How does the ritualized violence described in Durwood Ball's essay contrast with the lynchings of African Americans in the postbellum South?[39] Was the unrelenting violence against animals described in Karen Merrill's chapter translated into other forms of brutality? Could the western man's inability to reveal himself, as suggested by Craig Leavitt, or a man's concern about his standing among other men result in explosive rage or substance abuse? Why are the worst epithets one can hurl at a man, such as sissy or girly boy, those that question his masculinity?[40]

Boyhood provides a logical starting point for answering these questions. Elliott West's pathbreaking monograph on white children of the western frontier suggests that because busy parents had little time to direct their children's work or leisure, young men and women made their own accommodations with the country. Boys, however, confronted unique circumstances. In some settings, because of startling sex-role imbalances, men faced the prospect of having to do "women's work" as well as to never marry.[41] Gunther Peck's essay notes that in 1870 only 18 percent of the miners and 26 percent of the professional men in Gold Hill, Nevada, were married. If "marriage was a mark of full manhood," one which "completed the social identity of a male adult,"[42] could the unlikelihood of a wedded life preoccupy men with feelings of desperation or inadequacy? In settlements where men outnumbered women, did men value women more highly because they were rare? Or is that merely a pretty tradition which obscured a misogynist reality? Given the nature of frontier conditions, when men did marry, were their marriages more companionate and egalitarian? As Mary Murphy has asked, "What exactly did a man want in a wife? And what did he think a husband was supposed to be? How did a good father behave?"[43]

African-American cultures in the West require further scrutiny as well. Because race and gender in the United States reflect interlocking systems of hierarchy, the issue of masculine identity in the West is complicated by race, as several essays in this volume indicate. In an effort to redress the historic focus on a white West, scholars have begun to explore the activities of black men west of the Mississippi, including African-American mountain men, cowboys, Buffalo Soldiers, and Exodusters.[44] These studies, though not explicitly focused on gender, nonetheless indicate new directions for gender historians.

In their research on black cowboys, for example, Kenneth Porter, Philip Durham, and Everett Jones find paradoxical evidence regarding black men's position in the cattle industry. Work as a cowhand offered the opportunity for a more dignified life than that of the Jim Crow South. On the range, a hierarchy of skill prevailed in which a black cowboy earned the same wage as his white peers and drew respect for the abilities he demonstrated. On the other hand, the hierarchy of skill applied only to labor, not to management, which remained closed to black cowboys. One might rise to the position of hand, but never trail boss or ranch foreman. Moreover, black cowboys endured prejudicial treatment on long drives; often they were assigned the most dangerous tasks, such as swimming an unfamiliar river or busting the most violent bronc.[45]

Not only does this research reveal the interplay of race prejudice and meritocracy in the cattle business, it also hints at the role of gender in these configurations. Black camp cooks held an especially paradoxical position in cattle outfits. Their talents were dearly valued in an industry where good cooks attracted the finest cowhands and kept workers loyal to the crew. Yet camp cooks were feminized with the label "Old Woman" and often drawn into mascot status as entertainers.[46] Such glimpses of African-American cowboys invite closer analyses of manhood as a construct shaped by the ways black men negotiated the customs of gender and race hierarchy that colored opportunity in the West. The pathbreaking studies of Shirley Ann Wilson Moore and Quintard Taylor on African-American communities in the West, as well as Darlene Clark Hine and Earnestine Jenkins' multivolume readers on African-American manhood, indicate we are on the verge of significant breakthroughs in this area.[47]

Recent scholarship on Native American gender systems also recommends new lines of inquiry about manhood in the West. One avenue concerns the use of gender as a rhetorical strategy between competing cultures. Kathleen Brown's study of the Anglo-Algonquian gender frontier on the middle-Atlantic coast during the era of English invasion shows how Powhatans and Englishmen feminized each other during their respective efforts to assert political and diplomatic dominance.[48] In light of rhetorical distortions of gender that occurred on both sides of the cultural divide, Brown's study suggests the potential for reexamining relations between Native nations and Euro-Americans on the frontier.

Another line of investigation involves the nature of syncretic initiatives undertaken as Native men redefined their roles in response to new cultural, political, and economic pressures. Karen Anderson, Theda Purdue, and Katherine Osburn explore Native responses to the disruptions of disease, declining game populations, Christian missionaries, and Euro-American encroachment. Anderson investigates the Montagnais-Naskapi during seventeenth-century French settlement, Purdue traces the evolution of Cherokee gender systems during the early and mid-nineteenth century, and Osburn examines Southern Ute fatherhood in the late nineteenth and early twentieth centuries. Their studies illustrate how Native American men revitalized their economic roles through acquisition and control of private property or appropriated literacy to maintain their authority. Montagnais-Naskapi men, for example, adopted a French-Catholic model for patriarchal order in exchange for farmlands protected by the French from Iroquois harassment. Cherokee men replaced hunting, the deerskin trade, and warfare with commercial cotton farming, ownership of slave labor, and capitalist entrepreneurship as new arenas for masculine competition and achievement. Ute fathers utilized new skills, such as letter writing, as a means of maintaining their traditional roles as protectors and nurturers of their children. Native people's syncretic responses to new contingencies in their environment suggest new potentials for analyses of manhood.[49]

A related line of inquiry brings the concept of syncretism to other histories of the trans-Mississippi West. In a study of economic transformation among southwestern tribes during the late nineteenth and early twentieth centuries, Peter Iverson demonstrates the concept of tradition as an ongoing process of defining collective identity. Iverson found that some Native people took up cattle ranching as a way to rebuild their economies in the wake of confinement to reservations. Among the White Mountain and San Carlos Apache, for example, cattle became a new resource through which Apache ranchers could express indigenous values such as reciprocity and generosity, care of elders, pride in horsemanship, and the organization of work through kinship relations.[50] Iverson's perspectives on Native social and economic evolution invite further study of Native cultures of manhood in the West as traditions in process.

If race, ethnicity, and class are variables that complicate a gendered West, so too are environmental forces. Much of the trans-Mississippi West is situated within an arid zone that nonetheless boasts of valuable mineral deposits, fertile soil, and rich grasslands. Mid- and late-nineteenth-century mining booms, for example, proved to be volatile sites where gender roles were disrupted, challenged, and reconstructed, creating dialogue between the old and the new. In addition, the harvest of natural resources tied western locales to national and international economies. Gender systems in these settlements often reflected the political dimensions of resource extraction in the West.

The West's monumental scale and rugged beauty obscure the delicate ecosystems that characterize much of the region. Eco-feminists and environmental historians have suggested that the male desire to conquer and destroy has resulted in phenomenal environmental catastrophes. Conversely, men have often led the way in clean-up efforts, open-space preservation and, tellingly, eco-sabotage.[51] Scholars must reconcile these conflicting aspects of the male persona.

Through its reconceptualizations of gender, race, and class, *Across the Great Divide* opens new conversations about the history of manhood in the American West. Rather than regarding masculinity as a static biological fact or unchanging cultural construction, this volume illustrates the flexibility as well as the perils and promises available to the men who actually occupied the vast western expanses.

Notes

Laura McCall wishes to acknowledge Matt Basso, Dee Garceau, James Drake, and Craig Leavitt for their helpful comments on earlier drafts, and James Drake, Steve Ernst, and George Sibley for technical assistance.

1. Gail Bederman, *Manliness and Civilization: A Cultural History of Gender and Race in the United States,* 1880–1917 (Chicago: University of Chicago Press, 1995), 170. Roosevelt's new colleagues in Albany recalled how, after TR made an appearance in full dinner dress, they "almost shouted with laughter to think that the most veritable representative of the New York dude had come to the Assembly." Another assemblyman "remembered Roosevelt as being off-puttingly full of himself." See H. W. Brands, *T.R.: The Last Romantic* (New York: Basic Books, 1997), 130.

2. Cited in Bederman, 175. See also Anthony Rotundo, *American Manhood: Transformations in Masculinity from the Revolution to the Modern Era* (New York: Basic Books, 1993), 231–39; Milton Meltzer, *Theodore Roosevelt and His America* (New York: Franklin Watts, 1994); and John A. Garraty, *Theodore Roosevelt: The Strenuous Life* (New York: Harper and Row, 1967).

3. Bederman, 172.

4. See Kevin White, *The First Sexual Revolution: The Emergence of Male Heterosexuality in Modern America* (New York: New York University Press, 1993); David Roediger, *The Wages of Whiteness: Race and the Making of the American Working Class,* rev. ed. (London: Verso, 1999); and David Roediger, "The Pursuit of Whiteness: Property, Terror, and Expansion, 1790–1860," *Journal of the Early Republic* 19 (winter 1999): 579–600. Such a linkage might have been made earlier in the South. See Kathleen M. Brown, *Good Wives, Nasty Wenches, and Anxious Patriarchs: Gender, Race, and Power in Colonial Virginia* (Chapel Hill: University of North Carolina Press, 1996).

5. Theodore Roosevelt, "The Strenuous Life," in *The Works of Theodore Roosevelt* (New York: Scribner and Sons, 1926), 319–31.

6. Robert Utley writes that "no single force proved more decisive in the conquest of the Indians than the railroads. Ever the realist, General Sherman clearly understood the significance of the railroads." At the time of his retirement in 1883, he observed that the Army, the "industrious farmers and miners of lands vacated by the aborigines have been largely instrumental to that end, but the railroad which used to follow in the rear now goes forward with the picket line in the great battle of civilization with barbarism, and has become the greater cause." Quoted in Utley, *Cavalier in Buckskin: George Armstrong Custer and the Western Military Frontier* (Norman: University of Oklahoma Press, 1988), 126–27; and Paul Andrew Hutton, ed., *The Custer Reader* (Lincoln: University of Nebraska Press, 1992).

7. Utley, 36 and 205.

8. James Welch with Paul Jeffrey Stekler, *Killing Custer: The Battle of the Little Bighorn and the Fate of the Plains Indians* (New York: W. W. Norton, 1994); and James Welch, *C'est un beau jour pour mourir: L'Amerique de Custer contre les indiens des plaines, 1865–1890* (Paris: Albin Michel, 1999).

9. Utley, 155.

10. Bruce A. Rosenberg, *Custer and The Epic of Defeat* (University Park: Pennsylvania State University Press, 1974), 29.

11. Cited in Brian Dippie, *Custer's Last Stand: The Anatomy of an American Myth* (Bozeman: University of Montana Press, 1974), 68.

12. Ibid., 111.

13. Quoted in Rosenberg, 86.

14. Dippie, 34.

15. Rotundo, 251 and 232.

16. Quoted in Rosenberg, 117.

17. See Eric Foner, *Free Soil, Free Labor, Free Men: The Ideology of the Republican Party before the Civil War* (New York: Oxford University Press, 1970); and Drew R. McCoy, *The Elusive Republic: Political Economy in Jeffersonian America* (Chapel Hill: University of North Carolina Press, 1980).

18. Lee Clark Mitchell, *Westerns: Making The Man In Fiction and Film* (Chicago: University of Chicago Press, 1996), 155.

19. Ibid., 168.

20. Utley, 210.

21. John Higham, "The Reorientation of American Culture in the 1890s," in *Writing American History: Essays in Modern Scholarship,* ed. Higham (Bloomington: Indiana University Press, 1970), 79.

22. Ann Douglas, *The Feminization of American Culture* (New York: Avon, 1977).

23. Richard White, *"It's Your Misfortune and None of My Own": A New History of the American West* (Norman: University of Oklahoma Press, 1991), 613.

24. Frederick Jackson Turner, "The Significance of the Frontier in American History" (1893), in *The Frontier in American History* (New York: Holt, 1947), 1–38; Ray Allen Billington, *Westward Expansion: A History of the American Frontier* (New York: Macmillan, 1949); Martin Ridge and Ray Allen Billington,

eds., *America's Frontier Story: A Documentary History of Westward Expansion* (New York: Holt, Rinehart & Winston, 1969); and Walter Prescott Webb, *The Great Plains* (New York: Grossett and Dunlap, 1931).

25. Richard Bartlett, *The New Country: A Social History of the American Frontier, 1776–1890* (New York: Oxford University Press, 1974), 343. See also Madelon E. Heatherington, "Romance without Women: The Sterile Fiction of the American West," *The Georgia Review* 33 (fall 1979): 643–56.

26. Elizabeth Jameson and Susan Armitage, eds., "Editors' Introduction," in *Writing the Range: Race, Class, and Culture in the Women's West* (Norman: University of Oklahoma Press, 1997), 3–16; Anne M. Butler, "Through a Lens Less Turnerian: Women on the Frontier," *Reviews in American History* 17 (September 1989): 417–22; Susan Armitage, "Through Women's Eyes: A New View of the West," in *The Women's West,* ed. Susan Armitage and Elizabeth Jameson (Norman: University of Oklahoma Press, 1987), 9–18; Joan M. Jensen and Darlis A. Miller, "The Gentle Tamers Revisited: New Approaches to the History of Women in the American West," *Pacific Historical Review* 49 (May 1980): 173–213; Glenda Riley, *A Place to Grow: Women in the American West* (Albuquerque: University of New Mexico Press, Harlan Davidson, 1992); Lillian Schlissel, Vicki L. Ruiz, and Janice Monk, eds., *Western Women: Their Land, Their Lives* (Albuquerque: University of New Mexico Press, 1988); Peggy Pascoe, *Relations of Rescue: The Search for Female Moral Authority in the American West* (New York: Oxford University Press, 1990); Paula Petrik, *No Step Backward: Women and Family on the Rocky Mountain Mining Frontier, Helena, Montana 1865–1900* (Helena: Montana Historical Society Press, 1987); Sarah Deutsch, *No Separate Refuge. Culture, Class, and Gender on the Anglo-Hispanic Frontier, 1880–1940.* (New York: Oxford University Press, 1987); Sandra L. Myres, *Westering Women and the Frontier Experience, 1800–1915* (Albuquerque: University of New Mexico Press, 1982); Julie Roy Jeffrey, *Frontier Women. The Trans-Mississippi West, 1840–1880* (New York: Hill and Wang, 1979); John Mack Faragher, *Women and Men on the Overland Trail* (New Haven: Yale University Press, 1979); Dee Garceau, *The Important Things of Life: Women, Work and Family in Sweeetwater County, Wyoming, 1880-1929* (Lincoln: University of Nebraska Press, 1997); Elizabeth Jameson, "Toward a Multicultural History of Women in the Western United States," *Signs* 13 (1988): 761–91; Elizabeth Jameson, *All That Glitters: Class, Conflict, and Community in Cripple Creek* (Urbana: University of Illinois Press, 1998); Brigitte Georgi-Findlay, *The Frontiers of Women's Writing: Women's Narratives and the Rhetoric of Westward Expansion* (Tucson: University of Arizona Press, 1996); and Nancy Wilson Ross, *Westward the Women* (New York: Random House, 1944; reprint, San Francisco: North Point Press, 1985).

27. Mae M. Ngai, "The Architecture of Race in American Immigration Law: A Reexamination of the Immigration Act of 1924," *Journal of American History* 86 (June 1999): 67–92.

The mythic West has been roundly confronted in other ways as well. The idea of the West as a place of transformation endures, but concepts of frontier have shifted. Scholars now regard the West as a meeting ground of cultures, a crucible of intertribal diplomacy as well as of encounters among Native, European, and Asian Americans. See William Cronon, George Miles, and Jay Gitlin, eds., *Under an Open Sky: Rethinking America's Western Past* (New York: W. W. Norton, 1992); Donald Fixico, ed., *Rethinking American Indian History* (Albuquerque: University of New Mexico Press, 1997); Margaret Connell Szasz, ed., *Between Indian and White Worlds: The Cultural Broker* (Norman: University of Oklahoma Press, 1994); SuCheng Chan et. al., eds., *Peoples of Color in the American West* (Lexington, Mass: D. C. Heath, 1994); and Allan Bogue, "The Significance of the History of the American West: Postscripts and Prospects," *Western Historical Quarterly* 24 (February 1993), 45-68.

Eastern fascination with western men, western women, and Native Americans often transformed them into potent symbols for the dominant culture. Writers and artists peopled an imaginary landscape with idealized figures like the "cowboy" and the "Indian." Analyzing these images offers insight into the construction of national memory as well as into the power relations between dominant and subordinate cultures. Exploring how western men and Native peoples redefined such images sheds new light on processes of social change. For Native Americans, see Henry Nash Smith, *Virgin Land: The American West as Symbol and Myth* (Cambridge: Harvard University Press, 1950); L. G. Moses, *Wild West Shows and the Images of American Indians, 1883–1933* (Albuquerque: University of New Mexico Press, 1996); Paul Reddin, *Wild West Shows* (Urbana: University of Illinois Press, 1999); Robert Berkhofer, *The White Man's Indian: Images of the American Indian from Columbus to the Present* (New York: Vintage, 1978); Nancy Shoemaker, ed., *Negotiators of Change: Historical Perspectives on Native American Women* (New York: Routledge, 1995); Donna Kessler, *The Making of Sacagawea: A Euro-American Legend* (Tuscaloosa: University of Alabama Press, 1996); and Elizabeth Johns, "'From the Outer Verge of Our Civilization,'" in *American Genre Painting: The Politics of Everyday Life* (New Haven: Yale University Press, 1991), 60–99. For cowboys, see note 34.

28. Mary Murphy, "Making Men in the West: The Coming of Age of Miles Cavanaugh and Martin Frank Dunham," in *Over the Edge: Remapping the American West,* ed. Valerie J. Matsumoto and Blake Allmendinger (Berkeley and Los Angeles: University of California Press, 1999), 133–47; and Philip J. Deloria, *Playing Indian* (New Haven: Yale University Press, 1998).

29. Mary Murphy utilizes the trope of "entrenched icons" (144). Stereotypes of western men and women are articulated in Beverly J. Stoeltje, "'A Helpmate for Man Indeed': The Image of the Frontier Woman," *Journal of American Folklore* 88 (January–March 1975): 25–41. See also Barbara Meldrum, "Images of Women in Western American Literature," *The Midwest Quarterly* 17 (April 1976): 252–67.

30. See R. W. Connell, *Masculinities* (Berkeley and Los Angeles: University of California Press, 1995) and R. W. Connell, "Hegemonic Masculinity and Emphasized Femininity," in *Feminist Frontiers IV,* ed. Verta Taylor, Laurel Richardson, and Nancy Whittier (New York: McGraw-Hill, 1997), 22–25.

31. Eastern fraternal organizations are investigated in Donald Yacovone, "'Surpassing the Love of Women': Victorian Manhood and the Language of Fraternal Love," in *A Shared Experience: Men, Women and the History of Gender,* ed. Laura McCall and Donald Yacovone (New York: New York University Press, 1998), 195–221; and Mark C. Carnes, "Middle-Class Men and the Solace of Fraternal Ritual," in *Meanings for Manhood: Constructions of Masculinity in Victorian America,* ed. Mark C. Carnes and Clyde Griffen (Chicago: University of Chicago Press, 1990), 37–66.

32. Bederman, 5 and 26.

33. Hudson Janisch, "The Chinese, the Courts, and the Constitution: A Study of the Legal Issues Raised by the Chinese Immigration to the United States, 1850–1902" (J.S.D. thesis, University of Chicago, 1971), 184.

34. Theodore Roosevelt, "The Round-Up," *Ranch Life, and the Hunting Trail* (New York: Scribner and Sons, 1926), 317–40; David Dary, *Cowboy Culture: A Saga of Five Centuries* (New York: Knopf, 1981). Standard treatments of the cowboy include Joe Bertram Frantz and Julian Ernest Choate, Jr., *The American Cowboy: The Myth and the Reality* (Norman: University of Oklahoma Press, 1955); William W. Savage, Jr., *The Cowboy Hero: His Image in American History and Culture* (Norman: University of Oklahoma Press, 1979); Blake Allmendinger, *The Cowboy: Representations of Labor in an American Work Culture* (New York: Oxford University Press, 1992); Robert Murray Davis, *Playing Cowboys: Low Culture and High Art in the Western* (Norman: University of Oklahoma Press, 1992); and Bruce Rosenberg, *The Code of the West* (Bloomington: Indiana University Press, 1982). For ranching, consult Ernest Staples Osgood, *The Day of the Cattlemen* (Minneapolis: University of Minnesota Press, 1929); and Maurice Frink, W. Turrentine Jackson, and Agnes Wright Spring, *When Grass Was King: Contributions to the Western Range Cattle Industry* (Boulder: University of Colorado Press, 1956).

35. For the formidable winter of 1886–87, consult Barbara F. Rackley, "The Hard Winter: 1886–1887," *Montana* 21 (January 1971): 50–60.; Ray Allen Billington, *Westward Expansion: A History of the American Frontier* (New York: Macmillan, 1949), 596–97; and Robert F. Dykstra, *The Cattle Towns* (New York: Knopf, 1968), 149.

36. Snyder and Ferlinghetti are quoted in *The Portable Beat Reader,* ed. Ann Charters (New York: Penguin, 1992), 189–90. See also Harry Russell Huebel, "The 'Holy Goof': Neal Cassady and the Post-War American Counter Culture," *Illinois Quarterly* 35 (April 1973): 52–61. In *On The Road,* Jack Kerouac contrasts Cassady's western "criminality" with that of the East: Cassady's "was a wild yea-saying over-burst of American joy; it was Western, the west wind, an ode from the Plains, something new, long prophesied, long a-coming." Jack Kerouac, *On The Road,* (New York: New American Library, 1957), 11.

37. Richard Slotkin, *Gunfighter Nation: The Myth of the Frontier in Twentieth-Century America* (Norman: University of Oklahoma Press, 1992), 11.

38. Ibid., 13. For a discussion of the gendered foundations of violence, see Michael Bellesiles, intro-duction, and John C. Pettegrew, "Homosociality and the Legal Sanction of Male Heterosexual Aggression in the Early Twentieth Century," in *Lethal Imagination: Violence and Brutality in American History,* ed. Michael Bellesiles (New York: New York University Press, 1999). Pettegrew argues explicitly that "men are men precisely because they are violent."

39. For lynching, see Christopher Waldrop, "Word and Deed: the Language of Lynching, 1820–1953," in Bellesiles, ed., *Lethal Imagination,* 229–58.

40. Some analysts believe the deaths of Matthew Shepard in Laramie, Wyoming or the thirteen stu-dents at Columbine High School in Littleton, Colorado, in the 1990s were driven by young men's con-cerns about their standing among other men. According to JoAnn Wypijewski, every one of those boy-murderers "had been taunted as a wuss, a fag, a loser, or had been rejected by a girl." JoAnn Wypijewski, "A Boy's Life: For Matthew Shepard's Killers, What Does It Take to Pass as a Man?" *Harper's* (September 1999), 74. See also Wayne Martino, "Policing Masculinities: Investigating the Role of Homophobia and Heteronormativity in the Lives of Adolescent School Boys," *Journal of Men's Studies* 8 (winter 2000): 213–36. Screenwriter Stephen Schiff, who grew up in Littleton during the 1960s, believes the violence at Columbine sprang from the loss of place wrought by the generification of American cul-ture. In a country dotted with strip malls and the mind-numbing sameness of franchises, "the differences between things are neither prized nor scorned but simply wiped from existence." Stephen Schiff, "Children From Nowhere Can Easily Become Lost," *International Herald Tribune,* April 23, 1999.

41. Elliott West, *Growing Up with the Country: Childhood on the Far Western Frontier* (Albuquerque: University of New Mexico Press, 1989) 115, 117, and 140. See also Ruth Barnes Moynihan, "Children and Young People on the Overland Trail," *Western Historical Quarterly* 6 (July 1975): 279–94; and Elliott West and Paula Petrik, eds., *Small Worlds: Children and Adolescents in America, 1850–1950* (Lawrence: University Press of Kansas, 1992).

42. Rotundo, 115. Rotundo adds, "Men turned to women to make them whole, to provide them with means of living and being which they believed they could not provide for themselves" (132).

43. Murphy, 134.

44. Philip Durham and Everett L. Jones, *The Negro Cowboys* (New York: Dodd, Mead, 1965); William Loren Katz, *The Black West: A Documentary and Pictorial History of the African-American Role in the Westward Expansion of the United States* (New York: Simon and Schuster, 1996); William Loren Katz, *The Black West,* rev. ed., (New York: Anchor/Doubleday, 1973); Nell Irvin Painter, *The Exodusters: Black Migration to Kansas After Reconstruction* (New York: Knopf, 1976); Charles L. Kenner, *Buffalo Soldiers and Officers of the Ninth Cavalry, 1867–1898. Black and White Together* (Norman: University of Oklahoma Press, 1999); William H. Leckie, *The Buffalo Soldiers: A Narrative of the Negro Cavalry of the West* (Norman: University of Oklahoma Press, 19667).

45. Kenneth Porter, "Negro Labor in the Western Cattle Industry, 1866–1900," *Labor History* 10 (summer 1969): 346–74; and Philip Durham and Everett L. Jones, *The Negro Cowboys.*

46. Porter, 370–74.

47. Shirley Ann Wilson Moore, *"To Place Our Deeds": The African American Community in Richmond, California, 1920–1963* (Berkeley and Los Angeles: University of California Press, 1999); Quintard Taylor, *The Forging of a Black Community: Seattle's Central District From 1870 Through the Civil Rights Era* (Seattle: University of Washington Press, 1994); Quintard Taylor, *In Search of the the Racial Frontier: African Americans in the American West. 1528–1990* (New York: W. W. Norton, 1998); Darlene Clark Hine and Earnestine Jenkins. *A Question of Manhood: A Reader in U.S. Black Men's History and Masculinity,* vol. 1, *"Manhood Rights": The Construction of Black Male Hisotry and Manhood, 1750–1870* (Bloomington: Indiana University Press, 1999).

48. Kathleen Brown, "The Anglo-Algonquin Gender Frontier," in Shoemaker, ed., *Negotiators of Change,* 26–48.

49. Karen Anderson, *Chain Her By One Foot: The Subjugation of Native Women in Seventeenth-Century New France* (New York: Routledge, 1991); Theda Purdue, "Women, Men, and American Indian Policy: The Cherokee Response to Civilization," in Shoemaker, ed., *Negotiators of Change,* 90–109; Katherine M. B. Osburn, "'I Am Going to Write to You': Nurturing Fathers and the Office of Indian Affairs on the Southern Ute Reservation, 1895–1934," in McCall and Yacovone, eds., *A Shared Experience,* 245–70. See also Theda Purdue and Michael Green, eds., *The Chrokee Removal: A Brief History With Documents* (Boston: St. Martin's Press, 1995) and William C. McLoughlin, "An Alternative Missionary Style: Evan Jones and John B. Jones Among the Cherokees," in *Between Indian and White Worlds: The Cultural Broker,* ed. Margaret Connell Szasz (Norman: University of Oklahoma Press, 1994) 98–121.

50. Peter Iverson, "When Indians Became Cowboys," *Montana* 45 (winter 1995): 16–31.

51. Environmental histories include Roderick Nash, *Wilderness and the American Mind* (New Haven: Yale University Press, 1967); Max Oelschlaeger, *The Idea of Wilderness: From Prehistory to the Age of Ecology* (New Haven: Yale University Press, 1991); Patricia Nelson Limerick, *The Legacy of Conquest: The Unbroken Past of the American West* (New York: W. W. Norton, 1987); and Susan Rhoades Neel, "A Place of Extremes: Nature, History, and the American West," in *A New Significance: Re-envisioning the History of the American West,* ed. Clyde A. Milner II (Oxford: Oxford University Press, 1996). For women and the land, consult Annette Kolodny, *The Land before Her: Fantasy and Experience of the American Frontiers, 1630–1860* (Chapel Hill: University of North Carolina Press, 1984); Annette Kolodny, *The Lay of the Land: Metaphor as Experience and History in American Life and Letters* (Chapel Hill: University of North Carolina Press, 1975); Irene Diamond and Gloria Orenstein, *Reweaving the World: The Emergence of Ecofeminism* (San Francisco: Sierra Club Books, 1989); Vandana Shiva, *Staying Alive: Women, Ecology and Development* (London: Zed Books, 1989); and Carolyn Merchant, *The Death of Nature: Women, Ecology, and the Scientific Revolution* (San Francisco: Harper and Row, 1980).

"Tell Me with Whom You Walk and I Will Tell You Who You Are"

Honor and Virtue in Eighteenth-Century Colonial New Mexico

Ramón A. Gutiérrez

On a cold November night in 1726, Catharina de los Rios of Santa Fe lay sick in bed, feverish, delirious, her body totally covered with a pox-like rash. Fearing death was near and wishing to die with a clear conscience, she summoned Fray Francisco Romero, the local representative of the Inquisition, to confess her sins and to denounce herself and her paramour, Francisco Montes Vigil, for the sins of heresy, blasphemy, and the desecration of sacred images. Catharina believed her sickness was God's punishment for her *desvergonzada conducta*, her shameless conduct. The priest arrived, and Catharina recounted the following story. On several nights, some ten years earlier, she and Francisco had consumed large amounts of corn brandy and under the influence had undressed and engaged in the carnal act. At the point of ecstasy Francisco had blasphemed the name of the Almighty, uttering heretical words by shouting, "I am God and my pleasure is even better than if I were in heavenly glory." The desecration of the sacred images occurred after coitus. Francisco asked Catharina to remove the rosary and medals she wore around her neck and he placed them in her *partes vergonzozas* (shameful parts). Catharina had never confessed this *deshonor* (dishonor) because she feared reprisals from Francisco. He had told her their acts were not a sin, and if she confessed them he would have her exiled from New Mexico. Fearing him, Catharina never complained until the day she thought eternity was at hand.[1]

Ninety years later, Don Francisco Armijo arrived at the Albuquerque home of his mother-in-law, Doña María Antonia Durán, in a very agitated mood at about nine in the evening of March 12, 1816. In one hand he had his whip, in the other a knife. He demanded to see his wife, Doña María Rosalía Maestas, who had been staying with her mother while he was out of town. When his wife entered the room Don Francisco began whipping her violently. He threw her to the floor, put his foot on her throat, and with the knife cut off her braids and hair. Don Francisco hurled the braids at his mother-in-law and dragged his wife out of the house. Why such violent treatment? Don Francisco Armijo said it was "to protect my honor." He had heard that during his absence Juan García had propositioned his wife to adultery, giving her two sheep as a present and taking her in his carriage to the fiesta at Los Ranchos. For this Doña María Rosalía had brought scandal to his reputation, "because she will not live in seclusion . . . she is shameless."[2]

What do these two examples have in common? The language employed to express the most intimate violations of self-integrity is what is important here. When Catharina de los Ríos wanted to repent for the shameless conduct that had dishonored her, when Francisco Montes Vigil desecrated the Christian images by placing them in Catharina's shameful parts, and when Don Francisco Armijo complained that his wife was shameless and whipped her and cut off her hair to guard her honor, they were expressing the basic tenets of what Spaniards believed constituted a virtuous life. The nexus between personal public behavior and a social structure predicated on conquest, force, and hierarchical order was provided by honor and shame, the values that most fundamentally defined virtue in colonial New Mexico. The centrality of honor-virtue is best illustrated by contrasting the ideal with actual occurrences, particularly when honor was lost through seduction.

The Boundaries of Virtue

Honor-status, the measure of one's social standing, was an award for valorous conduct. Its maintenance over time, especially if it had been inherited from one's father through ascription, depended on honor-virtue. Honor-virtue divided the society horizontally by status groups and, within each group, determined the pecking order of persons in the status hierarchy according to reputation—that is, their reproduction of ideals of proper social conduct. The order of precedence to which peers submitted and their willingness to validate an individual's position depended upon their evaluation of the person's behavior according to established community norms. Since precedence at the upper levels of the social order guaranteed control over more resources and power, it was usually among the aristocracy and elites that the most intense conflicts over honor-virtue occurred. Vendetta and lineage feuds were typical of the fights through which upper-class men avenged sullied reputations and restored their claims to virtue.

Honor as virtue was an attribute of both individuals and corporate groups. When speaking of personal honor, it was considered a state of conscience that elevated the person's actions above reproach. If a person's intentions were honorable, it was irrelevant what others might think. This focus on intentions gave honor an aspect of personal autonomy that was displayed particularly in the desire to preside over others. Honor created social privilege; it established one's standing and prestige.[3] Such privilege was central to the hierarchical social structure of the Spanish empire. To some extent, privilege was determined by gender and class: men presided over women, aristocratic men over peasants and artisans. But within these hierarchies, the variable of honor further determined one's position. Everyone, whether man or woman, rich or poor, participated in the dance of honor—proving it, displaying it, or destroying it. Honorable aristocrats achieved higher status than their dishonored peers; honorable peasants claimed higher status than their dishonored compadres.

Honor also belonged collectively to one's family and to one's kindred as a group. "*Dime con quien andas y te dire quien eres,*" the Spanish proverb held: "Tell me with whom you walk and I will tell you who you are." The patriarch of a family or household was responsible for the actions of all his dependents. The conduct of children reflected on the father. The conduct of wives, sisters, and daughters reflected on their husbands, brothers, and fathers. Transgressions were perceived by others as signs of poor familial socialization. The honor of one reflected on all, just as the dishonor of one tarnished all.

Honor-virtue prescribed gender-specific rules of proper social comportment. Honor (*honor*) was strictly a male attribute while shame (*vergüenza*) was intrinsic to females. Infractions of behavioral norms by men compromised their honor; in women, such behavior indicated shamelessness. Honor and shame were the motivating forces behind appropriate behavior. Men demonstrated honor if they acted with *hombría* (manliness) by exerting authority over their families, displaying honesty and loyalty, and guarding the reputations of themselves and their dependents. Like men, women who acted with honesty and loyalty enhanced their own and their family's reputations.[4] But there the similarities ended. When it came to sexual morality, a strict double standard prevailed.

Women displayed shame when they were sexually pure and displayed the utmost discretion around men. *Vergüenza* brought blushes to a woman's face when lewd matters were discussed, and called for timidity around men. A woman who flouted these behavioral norms had lost her sense of shame. Men, in contrast, gained honor through sexual conquests, flirtations, and braggadocio.

Both in males and females these ethically valued qualities were rooted in sexual physiology. The *miembro*, the virile member or the penis, produced masculinity and *hombría*. Men were legally impotent without it. In 1781 Jacinta Trujillo of Abiquiu demanded an annulment to her eight-day-old marriage to Antonio Choño, because he was like a woman, "totally lacking a member." An emasculated man was referred to as *manso*, meaning meek, gentle, humble, and lamblike. *Manso* was also the word used to signify a castrated animal or person. New Mexico's Indians were conquered and made *mansos* by a technique for which Fray Nicolás Hidalgo was renowned. In 1638 the friar beat Pedro Acomilla of Taos Pueblo and grabbed him "by the member and twisted it so much that it broke in half." In a similar incident, Asensio, a Nambé Indian, did not lose his penis in his confrontation with Baltasar Baca, but his humiliation was just as emasculating. Asensio found Baca stealing four of his watermelons one day in 1743 and, when he tried to stop the thievery, Baca grabbed Asensio by the virile member and twisted it until Asensio fainted from the pain.[5]

Some Spanish men equated penis size with virility and manliness. In 1606, Gaspar Reyes found himself sick and destitute. Hoping to secure charity from the local Franciscan friars, he begged for food at their residence. A certain Fray Pedro took him in and fed him lavishly with a meal that even included wine. When Gaspar was finished eating, the friar "stuck his hand in my pants, took my virile member and wriggled it . . . and said to me, yours is small, mine is bigger." The priest then took Gaspar to his cell, where he tried to use Gaspar's posterior for a nefarious end. To be buggered was a symbolic sign of defeat equated with femininity; to bugger was an assertion of dominance and masculinity. Significantly, it was a priest who was concerned about penis size and actively tried to sodomize Gaspar. Any man who did not assert his sexuality and preferred abstinence or sexual purity ran the risk of being labeled tame, assumed castrated, and thereby lacking the necessary appendage of honor.[6]

If masculinity and honor were dependent on the virile member, femininity and shame were located in the *partes vergonzozas*. Antonia García of Santa Fe complained to the Inquisition in 1725 that Fray Francisco Romero had solicited sex from her in the confessional "with evil caresses to my shameful parts." Marcos Sánchez of Tomé savagely beat his concubine Manuela Carillo in 1793 because he had heard she was sleeping with another man. Marcos confronted Manuela about this one night and tried to force himself on her. Manuela resisted and, because she did, "he threw her to the floor, spread open her legs and scratched her shameful parts, and then he took his pouch of tobacco and emptied it on her parts and then rubbed them with dirt."[7]

The ultimate sign of female physiological purity was the intact maidenhead, an ideal perhaps only maintained by nuns, the symbolic brides of Christ, and Mary, the Mother of Christ, who conceived without the loss of her virginity. One incredulous New Mexican who dared to question Mary's purity was pursued by the Inquisition for propositions contrary to the Catholic faith. Don Francisco Paris of Santa Fe was reputed to have said of the Virgin Mary in 1804, "[A] virgin! How can she be a virgin? A woman once she conceives cannot be a virgin."[8]

If an unmarried woman lost her maidenhood, she also lost the natural and ethical qualities inhering from it. Manuela Armijo of Santa Fe in 1725 protested to the ecclesiastical judge that Juan Lovato "took my virginity and cleanliness with a promise of marriage." Lovato admitted, "It is true that I violated the virginity, purity and honesty of Manuela Armijo, but it was not with a promise of marriage."[9]

Because honor and shame were so closely tied to self-conceptions, concern over honor-virtue was often represented through body symbolism. The head, the heart, the blood, and the genitalia figured prominently when honor was discussed. A person's head was the symbol of personal and collective honor. The king's honor was exhibited through a crowned head; the honor of the bishop through his miter. Honor and deference were paid by bowing one's head, taking off one's hat, or for women by covering their heads. Decapitation was considered a most dishonorable punishment because it was believed that honor surrounded the head. Honor challenges were frequently initiated through a slap to the face. Manuel Martín of San Juan punished his daughter for bearing an illegitimate child in 1766 by cutting off all her hair. A bald head signified her shamelessness to the community. Catholic priests cut a tonsure in their hair as a sign of their vow of chastity and pledge to sexual purity.[10]

The heart was the organ through which personal desires and conscience were experienced. "I wish to marry for no other reason than to serve God and because it comes forth from my heart, without it being the result of any other motivation," said Sebastiana de la Serna of her 1715 marriage bid. Concupiscence sprang from the heart, said Fray José de la Prada. Writing the governor of New Mexico concerning the sexual laxity of his congregation, Prada complained that "their customs and heathen friskiness have sunken very deep roots into their hearts." In a sermon on lust, another friar warned his congregation of the metabolic repercussions of an unregulated heart. "It is from the heart that we must displace this monster of sensuality . . . it is the cause of so many sudden deaths, infectious disease and numerous maladies of the liver." But if a heart could be infected by lust, it was also the seat of conscience. When one's word of honor was given to another, the word was deemed sealed in the heart.[11]

Blood was the essence of life and the vehicle through which honor was perpetuated. "Stains of honor are only cleansed by blood," a Spanish aristocratic motto asserted. "Blood is the soap of honor," another proverb held. In colonial New Mexico, the racial preoccupations of the nobility were expressed through their concern for their purity of blood. To assure that their blood was not metaphysically polluted they guarded against marriage with dishonored or infamous persons—Indians and slaves. As late as 1837, Don Andrés Luján and Doña Juana Vigil of Valencia, New Mexico, expressed the belief that freedom from blood contamination was the basis of their honor. Seeking an episcopal dispensation for their proposed incestuous marriage, they argued, "Our families have always maintained themselves clean and with honor, not mixing with castes their purity of blood."[12]

Even Spanish norms regarding sexual position embodied the patriarchal social order. New Mexico's Spaniards likened the earth to females and furrows to their genitals. The germination process in which men engaged through plowing and planting was similar to the penis's function in insemination. The Latin etymology of the verb "to sow" and the noun "season" was the verb *serere*, which as a noun also meant "semen." Sexual intercourse was a fertility ritual. The phallus was like a plowshare creating furrows in the female earth. The woman, below and on her back, spread open her legs; the man, from above, inserted the penis as he would the plow into the ground for the implantation of seeds. Thomás Sánchez, the seventeenth-century Spanish theologian, in his *De sancto matrimonii sacramento*, proposed that nature itself prescribed this sexual posture: "We must first of all establish what is the natural manner of intercourse as far as position is concerned. . . . The man must lie on top and the woman on her back beneath. Because this manner is more appropriate for the effusion of the male seed, for its reception into the female vessel." The gender positioning embodied by this instruction is revealed in Sanchez's railing against the *mulier supra virum* (woman above man) coital position. "This method [of intercourse] is absolutely contrary to the order of nature," wrote Sanchez:

> It is natural for the man to act and for the woman to be passive; and if the man is beneath, he becomes submissive by the very fact of his position, and the woman being above is active; and who cannot see how much nature herself abhors this mutation? Because in scholastic history it is said that the cause of the flood was that women, carried away by madness, used men improperly, the latter being beneath and the former above.[13]

Every society prescribes the scope of behavior appropriate for each gender, and colonial New Mexican society was no different. There, the values of honor and shame defined the acceptable acts men and women could undertake. The sentiment of shame that prescribed female sexual purity was appropriate only to women. Men of honor enforced female purity in their mothers, wives, daughters, and sisters, protecting feminine purity from assault. Concurrently, though, a man enhanced his honor through the conquest of another man's woman. It was precisely in this contradiction that positioning in the honor-virtual hierarchy occurred. Precedence was determined by how well these two imperatives, female sexual protection within the family and sexual conquest over women outside the family, were reconciled.

Because God had created woman as the weaker of the sexes and rendered her helpless to the desires of men, male authority enforced through seclusion was one way to safeguard female shame and maintain the family's honor. Doña María Luisa de Aragón of Tomé expressed a correlate of this conception of the female when she lamented in 1766 that her married daughter had conceived a child from an adulterous liaison while her husband was absent in Mexico City. Doña María stated, "My daughter had that unfortunate frailty to which all of the feminine sex are exposed." Frailty to the ploys of men and the desires of flesh meant that it was necessary to seclude women to protect their virtue.

Men could win and enhance their honor through action, but a woman's virtue was a quality that could not be won, only maintained or lost. For this reason Juana Trujillo's parents kept her public contacts to a minimum. In 1705 she refused to talk to a friend she encountered in Santa Fe's plaza while running errands with her brother because "I feared that they would beat me at home particularly if my brother told my parents that he left me talking." Governor Bernardo López de Mendizábal in 1663 said he cared for the purity of his female servants by keeping them in a bedroom adjacent to his, with access only through his room. The women entered the governor's bedroom as they wished, even when Mendizábal and his wife were in bed. The male servants had strict orders that when they came to the room they should speak from the door but not enter. A friend advised Francisca de Salazar in 1702 that if she wanted to protect her daughter Juana's virginity she should keep her always behind locked doors.[14]

A double standard existed with regard to social behavior. Don Agustín Durán of Santa Fe cogently expressed the different expectations of male and female conduct. In a note to the vicar of the province on December 20, 1845, opposing the marriage of a son, José, to his sister-in-law Doña María Solomé Ortiz on the grounds of incest, Durán wrote:

> The intimate relations between the two houses; the great physical difficulties which deter the father from watching over his daughters [the father of Doña María was described as a very old and blind widower], and the familiarity between my son and Doña María, may be the cause of unfortunate consequences; were it up to me I would put an end to this so as not to cause damage, but I am forced to accept the natural facts: my son is a man and it is not possible to keep him in seclusion as a woman; this being the case, what am I to do?

Men could not be secluded because domination and conquest were essential qualities of masculinity necessary to safeguard family honor.[15]

A sexually shameless woman who dishonored her husband or her father could in no way restore or avenge her honor. Only a man could do that. The folktale "La Constancia" illustrates this point. After the protagonist Constancia loses her honor because of alleged adultery, her husband forfeits his own honor and wealth and, as punishment, throws his wife into the sea.

Washing up on Spanish shores, she transforms herself into a man, dons armor, and kills all the infidel Moors possible. Her husband's honor is avenged and restored only after Constancia's masculine displays of military prowess are rewarded by the king, who bestows upon the brave warrior honor, wealth, and the crown of the kingdom. Only in the role of a man can Constancia actively restore her honor.

Honor-virtue was militantly protected, fiercely contested, and scandalously lost. An exaggerated moral code for personal public behavior based upon honor developed among New Mexico's Spanish colonists because the social and legal institutions that normally would have ordered society were absent on this remote frontier where might was right. Add to such isolation a mobile and heterogeneous population as well as a violent and exploitative class system and the potential for disorder increased. In this volatile setting, Spanish colonists believed that maintenance of honor-virtue reinforced hierarchy and cohesiveness. Proper familial government, demonstrations of personal and familial worth, and maintenance of one's position through appropriate behavior were accepted as forces of order in Spanish New Mexico.

New Mexican colonists cherished their consensus regarding what sorts of behaviors were virtuous and honorable. Men of the nobility and landed peasantry alike were concerned for their personal and familial repute. They judged honor by how well they resolved the contradictory imperatives of domination (protection of one's womenfolk from assault) and conquest (prowess gained through sullying the purity of other men's women). They worked at minimizing affronts to their own virtue so as to keep their honor-status intact. Female seclusion and a high symbolic value placed on virginity and marital fidelity were inseparable from these goals.

Yet only in aristocratic households, where servants and retainers abounded, could resources be expended to ensure that females were properly restrained and protected. The maintenance of virtue among aristocratic females was possible only because Indian and *genízaro* (slave) women could be forced or persuaded to offer sexual service. Slaves were dishonored by their bondage, lacked familial ties to the community and could therefore be abused without fear of retaliation. As one friar lamented in his 1734 report to the viceroy, Spanish New Mexicans justified raping such women by saying that "an Indian does not care if you fornicate with his woman because she has no shame."[16]

The landed peasantry prized honor-virtue just as much as the nobility because it signified participation in the values and ideals of Spanish society. No matter how lowly the peasant, he prided himself on being a Spaniard and thereby a player in the game of honor. Like men of the nobility, his sport was the conquest of Indian and *genízaro* women; his boast, the ability to maintain the purity of his own women. Manuel Alvarez, the United States Consul in

Santa Fe, astutely observed this phenomenon in 1834 when he wrote, "the honorable man (if it is possible for a poor man to be honorable) has a jewel in having an honorable wife."[17]

The peasantry undoubtedly had to reconcile gender prescriptions with the exigencies of production and reproduction. The required participation of all able household members at planting and harvest meant that there were periods when constraints on females of this class were less rigorously enforced. Juana Carillo of Santa Fe admitted as much in 1712 when she confessed enjoying the affections of two men her father had hired for spring planting. In households where men were frequently absent, such as those of soldiers, muleteers, shepherds, and hunters, cultural ideals were also necessarily less rigidly enforced. Women married to such men supervised family and home for large parts of the year, staved off Indian attack, and cared for the group's public rights, thus illuminating how difficult it was for them to lead sheltered and secluded lives. Indeed it was not uncommon to hear these women lament because they had been assaulted, raped, or seduced while their husbands or fathers were away from home.[18]

Seduction: The Conflict between Status and Virtue

The preceding discussion of what honor and shame meant to men and women was culled largely from civil and ecclesiastical court cases. Such conflictive situations established the definition of the ideal, and just how far it could be pushed before the authorities responded. Seductions illustrate how honor was won and lost through access to female sexuality and clarify how the honor code functioned in action.

Seductions in colonial New Mexico followed a rather standard pattern. A young man would begin courtship by gaining the attention of a girl, sending her flowers or love notes, serenading her, or simply giving her affectionate glances from a distance, a wink and smile at a dance. After she was sufficiently knowledgeable of his attraction and had reciprocated with trust, he would usually take advantage of the confidence and, by promising marriage, would satisfy his desires. The discovery of the illicit sexual act was likely only if pregnancy resulted, or if the man reneged on his promise and tried to marry someone else. In that case, a range of actions was possible depending on the particular circumstances and the status of the individuals involved. The seducer, the seduced woman, and the parents and families of both had differing and sometimes contradictory interests to protect. Each acted to enhance, preserve, or recoup his or her honor.

When a young women was seduced she was considered shameless. Her shamelessness dishonored her father and family as a whole. The verdict of public opinion about the family's reputation and honor depended on the father's riposte. The absence of a response to affront was dishonorable and socially negative. However, if a man admitted his weakness and humiliation and did not contest the defilement of his property and his honor, he became a cuckold in the community's eyes.

The most desirable way for a father to restore his honor and that of his sullied daughter was to demand marriage. If the seducer kept his word of honor and married the woman, the honor-virtue that she left exposed through seduction was thereby restored. If no one publicized the matter, the reputation of the woman and the honor-status of her family did not decrease. For example, María del Rosario Martín of San Juan discovered in 1785 that she had been impregnated by her amour Mariano Sánchez. María pleaded passionately before the ecclesiastical judge, for her parents were dead, that in justice Mariano should fulfill his promise of marriage. She recounted how one of Mariano's brothers had also seduced, impregnated, and under parental counsel abandoned a woman. María rightfully feared that "it can be presumed that his father wants to do with me as he did with the already mentioned daughter-in-law, and seeing that I must protect my honor and that of my family, and if this matter is not resolved not only will I remain dishonored, but it is also possible that my brothers will take my life, an attempt they have already made." Bowing to ecclesiastical and familial pressure, Mariano finally married María.[19]

When the social distance between a man and his pregnant lover was too great, the maintenance of family honor-status was deemed of more importance than restoring the honor-virtue of the woman through marriage. The marriage of an aristocrat and a peasant woman could only bring dishonor upon his family, for marriage was a sign of equality. Mexican clerics inquired of the Crown in 1752 what their policy should be when seduction occurred between partners of widely disparate status. The response came in an order stating:

> If the maiden seduced under promise of marriage is inferior in status, so she would cause greater dishonor to his lineage if he married her than the one that would fall on her by remaining seduced (as when for instance a Duke, Count, Marquis or Gentleman of known nobility were to seduce a mulatto girl, a *china*, a *coyota,* or the daughter of a hangman, a butcher, a tanner), he must [not] marry her because the injury to himself and his entire lineage would be greater than that incurred by the maiden by remaining unredeemed, and at any rate one must choose the lesser evil . . . for the latter is an offense of an individual and does no harm to the Republic, while the former is an offence of such gravity that it will denigrate an entire family, dishonor a person of pre-eminence, defame and stain an entire noble lineage and destroy a thing which gives splendor and honor to the Republic. But if the

seduced maiden is of only slightly inferior status, of not very marked inequality, so that her inferiority does not cause marked dishonour to the family, then, if the seducer does not wish to endow her, or she justly rejects compensation in the form of endowment, he must be compelled to marry her; because in this case her injury would prevail over the offence inflicted upon the seducer's family for they would not suffer grave damage through the marriage whereas she would were she not to marry.[20]

Competition for honor-virtue was limited to persons of equal status. Thus the refusal to challenge someone of a much higher or much lower state was honorable because of the recognition of these disparities. Such opponents often had their day in court. An affronted father recognized his powerlessness to respond to the pique of a more formidable adversary, or admitted his frustration in dealing with a *genízaro* plebian who showed utter disregard for honor. The only hope for redress in such cases was through the legal system. Differences in status and power were obvious when in 1775 the chief constable of Santa Cruz, militia captain Don Salvador García, as legal representative for his son Esteban, appeared to arbitrate an agreement with a lowly farmer Gregorio Martín, who represented his daughter Josepha. Esteban had tarnished the honor and reputation of Josepha and now refused to marry her. Martín demanded of García some sort of compensation to restore the honor of the family and of his daughter. After considerable jockeying, García agreed to pay Martín 150 pesos, provided Josepha place no obstacle to any marriage Esteban might later contract. The parties were satisfied, and an agreement was signed. In a very similar 1725 Santa Fe case, Juan Lovato paid Manuela Armijo 200 pesos to help restore her honor, lest she appear a dissolute woman.[21]

The honor of the male seducer was quite a different matter. He could and often did marry the woman he defiled to make good on his word and to restore her honor. But men who had no intention of marrying the women they seduced contested their virtue. One ploy was to admit the obvious: a pregnancy had resulted from illicit sexual activity, but no promise of marriage had been given.[22]

Indeed the burden of proof in seduction cases was always upon the woman and her family. She had to produce witnesses who would testify to her betrothal, her good conduct, and her virginity. If witnesses to the betrothal did not exist, the woman at the very least had to produce the *prenda*, the gift ritually exchanged between lovers as an outward sign of their intention to marry. The *prenda*, often a rosary, a religious medallion, or small piece of jewelry, was given great importance by the courts because after such a gift had been presented, a maiden felt secure in submitting to the sexual desires of her husband-to-be. Then, even if she became pregnant from premarital intercourse, the impending marriage would save her from any public dishonor or scandal. The exchange of *prendas* made it more difficult for the male to renege on his word, though as the evidence indicates, not impossible.

Juana Luján of Santa Fe complained to Fray Manuel Moreno in 1702 that Bentura de Esquibel had taken her honesty and virginity. She wept over the loss of honor and recounted the events of her seduction. Asked for concrete proof of a word of marriage, Juana presented the *prenda*, a silver image of Our Lady of Guadalupe that Bentura had given her. When Juana Padilla discovered she was with child in 1777, she told the local priest how she had allowed herself to be conquered by the carnal appetite of Gregorio of Isleta Pueblo. She demanded he keep his promise of matrimony assured with the exchange of a rosary. Gregorio denied all and explained, "it is true that she gave me a rosary but it was not given as a *prenda*, she gave it to me because I did not have one, and she told me, take this rosary so that the devil does not take you, but she did not say it was a *prenda*." Gregorio vowed he had no desire to make Juana his wife. He was a footloose man with no intention of settling down. Neither woman ever got the marriage they wanted, but neither were their seducers completely free from responsibility. Juana Luján was awarded 200 pesos "because Bentura Esquibel tarnished her honor." Gregorio was forced to pay Juana Padilla two black shawls for her dishonor.[23]

For men, seduction, aside from fulfilling sexual urges, was an opportunity to exhibit their virility. Since women were pawns in the honor system, their spoliation afforded men boasting material to enhance their own reputations. Preeminence in this value schema was achieved not only through the accomplishment of an act, but through public recognition of that act as a feat. An affront, if not personally or publicly perceived as such, could hardly bring insult or elevate one's status, so gloating publicly of a power to use and manipulate women was common. José Salazar of Albuquerque displayed great braggadocio in 1766 explaining to his friends how he had fifteen illicit acts of intercourse with María Rosa Chávez:

> When a table is placed before you, who will not eat. It is true that as a man I solicited her, she admitted me and I ruined her, but not now or ever will I marry her even though they may quarter me; my spirit has been very deeply chilled by the fact they have demanded that I marry her, and even though they may put me in the stocks up to my neck, I will never marry her.

Proof of betrothal was not produced, and José never married María.[24]

A second strategy of avoiding responsibility for a seduction was to impugn the woman's reputation. Here the man admitted his promise and sexual contact, but claimed that his refusal to marry was based on the fact that he had not found the woman a virgin. The contradictory aspects of honor surfaced in these instances. On the one hand, a father and sons exhibited honorable conduct by aggressively protecting the sexual shame of their womenfolk, placing great value on premarital virginity and marital fidelity. On the other hand, male honor was also secured and enhanced through displays of potency, notably the corruption of other men's women. So the logical ploy in such seduction cases was for a man to argue that he wanted to marry a bride of virtue and good repute; that the woman had been easily seduced, evidence of her sexual laxity; and that she was already lacking the flower of her body when they copulated. The law only punished the seduction of a virgin; others, particularly widows, abandoned women, and *genízaros* were considered sport for the prowess of men. Thus, if the seducer could produce witnesses concerning the female's promiscuity he most certainly would avoid punishment for his conduct.

"Human frailty was the cause of my dishonor," explained Juana Rodríguez in 1705, in response to Sebastian Luján's accusation that she was "a woman of the world who had no honor." Sebastian had proposed marriage to another woman. When Juana heard of this she quickly asked the local priest to impede it, claiming that she had a previous promise. Juana sobbingly told Santa Fe's ecclesiastical judge how on the September feast of the Virgin Mary, while home alone, Luján conquered her:

> When I entered into the house to put away some hides, he followed in after me . . . and when I wanted to exit, he would not let me, and three times he solicited my flower with a promise of marriage, and just as we frequently played together, he began to play with me on this occasion, and he solicited his pleasure, but as a woman I resisted, and he told me that my resistance was a sign that I was not a virgin, finally I admonished him not to leave me dissolute and then consented freely to his pleasure and let him deflower me.

María de las Nieves watched all this through a crack in the door and later found Juana weeping and cleaning her genitals with a blood-soaked cloth. Maria asked her what had happened, and Juana explained how Sebastian had taken her virginity and pleaded "for the love of God do not tell my mother or any other person."

Sebastian Luján on his behalf presented Calletano Fajardo who testified that he personally had had "dry loves" (anal sex) with Juana and had heard her say that Francisco Perea had deflowered her with a promise of marriage. Luján responded to the charges against him, saying:

> That I violated the said Juana Rodríguez with a promise of marriage is false. I did not lie to her nor will I deny that as . . . a man I wooed her, she consented to my pleasure, and she could easily have asked me for a

prenda as a sign of any promise. When I had the act with her I found that she no longer had the flower of her body. And the testimony by the witness on Juana's behalf that she saw us copulate and later found Juana crying and cleaning herself could have been done to solace her evil. For if she had the audacity to embrace a single man she most certainly could have reached similar extremes with others. . . . She is at fault in this case for she roams the streets alone at night, going from house to house.

Luján presented enough evidence to impugn Juana Rodríguez's sexual purity. Luján was allowed to marry Juana Trujillo, leaving Juana Rodríguez destitute and dishonored.[25]

Similarly, when Juana de Guadalupe in 1705 tried to impede the marriage of Antonio de Belásquez to Juana Rodríguez because of a prior promise to her, Belásquez responded,

> I made love to the said Juana de Guadalupe after having known that she treated illicitly with Juan Antonio Ramos, the Indian Mariquite, Zhacambe, and many others who I will not mention so as not to become a bother. This being the case, I entered into the ranks just like the rest of them without having given her a promise of marriage as she alleges. It would be of very grave consequence to wish to enter into the state of matrimony with a person who roams in the fashion I have just described. And besides that, if she gives me legitimate proof that I deflowered her and gave her a promise of marriage, I will immediately do whatever you, reverend father, decide. For if the said Juana de Guadalupe had shame and respect for the ecclesiastical tribunal, she would not have the audacity to expose her honor to public scrutiny only to remain totally defamed. If I owed her anything, I am a Christian and as such would act according to the laws of conscience . . . but in this matter she appears to be acting more under the influence of her mother than of her free will, and as such, I am convinced that this appears to me more dementia than justice.

Juana dropped her opposition to the marriage when confronted with her less than proper past. She said she no longer wished to marry Belásquez "because I fear a bad life with him, because of his threats, and because of the mistreatments I have already experienced . . . and I fear, as he has already warned me, that he will treat me not as his wife but as his slave." Instead, Juana demanded that her honor be indemnified. Belásquez refused. He had not taken Juana's honor and felt alms were inappropriate in the case. "As a man I had her single and free by the same luck that others have had her," he explained.[26]

Reputation was a public evaluation of how well a person personified the ideals of the honor code. Just as it was in the self-interest of men to have their sexual feats and prowess proclaimed, it was also to the benefit of women and particularly of their fathers and brothers to keep the knowledge of any frailty as secret as possible. In this task they often had the help of parish priests, who felt a primary responsibility for protecting the virtue of women and attenuating public scandal. To have it known that a daughter had been seduced and lost her virginity was to significantly alter her symbolic value on the marriage market. Familial resources could be severely taxed by marrying such a woman. If a father was going to secure her an honorable husband, a generous dowry had to be offered that adequately remunerated the male for the acceptance of a spoiled woman. If the ability to economically counterbalance the loss of virtue did not exist, parents might have to consent to someone of a lower status becoming their son-in-law, or face the possibility of their daughter never marrying.

For this reason village gossip was a significant force to contend with when attempting to minimize the impact of affronts to one's honor. Alameda's constable, Don Cleto de Miera, understood this when in 1805 he wrote to Governor Real Alencaster relating the details of the seduction of his daughter María de las Nievas Miera y Pacheco by Josef Trujillo. Don Cleto protested that Josef "denigrates my person by the mere act of saying, [as he has] repeated on two occasions, that my daughter has become pregnant because of her unruly habits. [This] young man talks too much and without restraint causing prejudice to my honor." Several persons urged Josef to marry María, but he refused. When María bore his child, the parish priest summoned Josef so that the illegitimacy could be resolved prudently. Josef stood firm in his resolve. When the ecclesiastical judge ordered María and Josef punished for their behavior, Josef fled to seek the governor's aid. María was placed in a good Christian home as a punishment and a warning to other girls lest they fall prey to the weaknesses of the flesh. Trujillo was finally apprehended and charged with ravishment in the civil courts. Despite her punishment, María appears to have been innocent of sexual initiative, much less voluntary sexual surrender. She described her deflowering as a rape:

> Trujillo, availing himself more of absolute force than of promises or
> gifts, deflowered my virginity without even the least bit of my consent,
> adding to this the countless pleas which I made of him, but which
> were finally useless and had no other result than to quiet the fact of my
> ravishment, not so much because he was concerned for my honor, but
> so that his crime would not be discovered. I was effectively silenced
> because on no occasion are women who enjoy the state of virginity per-
> mitted scandal or involvements. Trujillo took my virginity and now
> states in his affidavit that I have bad and unruly habits. I was silenced
> and would have remained silent to protect my honor and that of my

parents, but time finally displayed my disgrace with a pregnancy from the said rape, and because of this my parents finally charged me to declare, not without substantial shame, that: the said Josef Trujillo (and none other) raped me in the manner I have described. My father reproached the young man shortly after my declaration, without scandal, the parish priest did the same, without publicizing it; and because Trujillo's conscience bothered him because of this crime, and realized he could suffer some prejudice for his infamy, or better, he realized that he was going to be apprehended, he fled.

Not surprisingly, María had soured on the idea of marriage to Josef and only wanted proof of Trujillo's allegation that she was a woman of bad habits. If he could not prove this, he deserved the sternest punishment possible. Trujillo's defense was pointless and rambling. His most damning comment was that he had seen María outside her father's home alone at night. He proved nothing. Although Trujillo was apparently guilty, the final pages of this court docket are missing and so the verdict remains unknown. María de las Nieves, however, appears never to have married.[27]

Village gossip was always a powerful force in the regulation of social behavior. Its circulation was quick and its repercussions wide. Just as known dishonors lowered one's status in the eyes of the community, reputed peccadillos did too. In the folktale "La Constancia," José María, Constancia's husband, was dishonored not because Constancia had committed adultery with the vagabond (she did not), but because José María believed what he had been told about his wife's behavior. Similarly, Don Francisco Armijo whipped his wife, María, in 1816 because he had heard she had been propositioned to adultery while he was out of town. In neither case was the woman asked if the charges were true. The husbands were more concerned about what everyone else thought. Thus individuals had to be constantly on guard to exhibit conduct befitting their sex, as well as vigilant that no one maliciously tarnished their reputations.

Anxiety for reputation prompted Doña María Manuela de la Luz Romero to sue Mariano Baca in 1767. Baca, a half-breed of very low status and "depraved habits," had been telling people he had seduced Doña María, an Albuquerque aristocrat, and was intent on redeeming her through marriage. Doña María appeared before the civil court and charged Baca with slander. "I am an honest and sheltered maiden. The good upbringing and prudence with which my parents raised me is publicly known in Albuquerque. They have given no one cause, either because of their acts or mine, to defame my honor or that of my parents." She demanded that Mariano be punished for tarnishing the virtue that honorable and well-bred maidens customarily guarded with great care. To prove that Mariano's allegations were false, Doña María went to the home of Albuquerque's ecclesiastical notary, Joseph Hurtado de Mendoza, on April 21, 1767, accompanied by Bárbara Benavides, a respected midwife from Atrisco, and a friend, Gertrudis Montoya, to ask that the notary witness a gynecological examination that would establish Doña Maria's virginity. The notary agreed to certify the proceedings in the presence of his wife, his sister, Bárbara Benavides, and Gertrudis Montoya. Mendoza attested,

> I examined [Doña María] visually with the four women. . . . Bárbara, the midwife, placed the second finger of her right hand in the narrow concave of her genitals and could penetrate no further than the tip of the said second finger, entering only as far as the middle of the nail . . . for this reason it is indisputable that she is a virgin and the slander which has been voiced is false.

When the justice in Durango, Don Antonio Lavendera, reviewed the case, he was furious at the notary's participation in the exam. "This notary has shown himself dishonest, of depraved habits and poor upbringing," Lavendera wrote. "He should be aware that such exams and reviews are only tolerated among the most immoral; and even more amazing is the fact that a woman who claims to be so honest and sheltered would let herself be examined in such manner." For this nefarious certification Lavendera ordered Hurtado placed in the pillory for one hour. Mariano Baca's punishment was left to Governor Pedro Fermín de Mendinueta, who ordered him tied to the gibbet, given one hundred lashes, and sentenced to one year in jail. The governor hoped that such a severe punishment would deter other low-status men from besmirching the honor of aristocratic maidens and forcing them to undergo such scandalous exams to recover their reputations. The governor further ordered the constable of Albuquerque to publicly proclaim on the next major feast day that the rumors that Mariano Baca had circulated about Doña María were totally false.[28]

However, once false information had been disseminated by word of mouth, it was often difficult to amend. A public declaration was hardly an adequate way of restoring one's honor. Gossip spread like wildfire, and often blazed beyond containment. María Rosalía Madrid of Santa Cruz was the victim of such pernicious innuendo. In 1813, when she called on Francisca Córdova to borrow a tub, Francisca asked her about the broken promise of marriage with which she was trying to stop the betrothal of José Fresquis. "I was extremely shamed and went home crying to tell my father Don José Ignacio Madrid," said María. The story was a total fabrication. Nonetheless, it had been circulating for six months before she heard of it. Don José Ignacio Madrid was livid over the slur to his family's honor and had Francisca Córdova, her husband, Miguel Barela, Joseph Manuel Guillén, and José

Fresquis jailed to determine who had been circulating such a lie. Guillén told the court that he had learned of the matter from his wife, who said the information came from Ramón Cárdenas:

> Cárdenas said that it had been told to him by Simón Bernal, and Bernal said that the wife of José Manuel Guillen had told him . . . the flames of this hell then jumped to Juan Josef Esquibel, and the flames continued to rage into a burning inferno, landing next on the daughters of Josef Maestas who told the said Esquibel, and still not extinguished, this artificial fire landed on José del Carmen Fresquis who was the person who told my wife the story when we went to a wake.

The case ended when José Fresquis admitted that he had had no relation with María and that the charge of a broken promise of marriage had been launched not by María Rosalía Madrid, but by a woman from Truchas. He vowed to correct this grave misunderstanding, but by then the damage had been done.[29]

Public reputation, a peer evaluation concerning one's reproduction of ideal values of virtuous social conduct, was ultimately the source of an individual's right to precedence. To determine a person's position on the vertical hierarchy of honor-status, aristocrats and peasants alike evaluated the honor-virtue of members of their status groups. If an aristocrat was deemed virtuous, his family and kin would gain precedence before those persons deemed dishonored. The same held for the landed peasantry. The virtuous peasant was ranked above the corrupt. Of course, because honor-status was largely ascribed and honor-virtue achieved, the most vice-ridden aristocrat always enjoyed more honor-status than the most virtuous peasant. Similarly, the most corrupt peasant enjoyed more honor than the Indians and *genizaros*, who had no honor.

The status hierarchy that was established in colonial New Mexico and that regulated social relations until the beginning of the nineteenth century was a Spanish monarchical tool used to reward those groups who had expanded the realm. Honors, as well as the concept of honor as a moral code, were elements of a feudal patriarchal ideology employed by the state to bolster its own power, to legitimate the rewards it granted to persons for service to the monarchy, and to sanctify the reality of unequal power relationships in society. Embedded in this ideology was the belief that God's earthly and natural design made men dominant over women and that females should submit to male authority. Conquest, domination, and protection of dependents were hallmarks of male excellence; they were qualities that maintained the patrimony and perpetuated an honored image of self and family over time.

Notes

1. Archivo General de la Nacion-Inquisicion (AGN-INQ), Mexico City, Mexico, 1726 757-25:167–72.

2. Spanish Archives of New Mexico (SA) 1816, 18:579–603.

3. Julian Pitt-Rivers, "Honor," in *International Encyclopedia of the Social Sciences* (New York: Macmillan, 1968), 505.

4. J. Caro Baroja, "Honor and Shame: A Historical Account of Several Conflicts," in *Honor and Shame: The Values of Mediterranean Society*, ed. J. Peristiany, (Chicago: University of Chicago Press, 1965), 81–137; Julian Pitt-Rivers, "Honour and Social Status," in Peristiany, 21–77; Alfonzo García Valdecasas, *El Hidalgo y El Honor* (Madrid: Revista de Occidente, 1948), 137–264; Americo Castro, *De la edad conflictiva: Crisis de la cultura Española en el siglo XVII* (Madrid: Taurus, 1972); J. Davis, *People of the Mediterranean* (London: Routledge and Kegan Paul, 1977), 89–100.

5. AGN-INQ 1638, 388-22:440-42; SA 1743, 8:133–45.

6. Archives of the Archdiocese of Santa Fe—Loose Documents (AASF-LD) 1781, 52:569; AGN-INQ 1606, 368:140-42; Julian Pitt-Rivers, *The People of the Sierra* (Chicago: University of Chicago Press, 1966), 21–77.

7. Testimony of Manuela's mother. AGN-INQ 1726, 757-26:167–72; SA 1793, 13:357-58.

8. AGN-INQ, 1804, 1382-190: no number. The method by which the Virgin Mary conceived was the subject of considerable debate among medieval theologians. It was generally believed that the Holy Spirit entered Mary's body through some unnatural route. The learned consensus was that impregnation had occurred through the ear. See Edmund Leach, "Virgin Birth," *Proceedings of the Royal Anthropological Institute* (1966): 39–49. The most comprehensive study of the different meanings the cult of the Virgin Mary has assumed over time is Marina Warner, *Alone of All Her Sex: The Myth and the Cult of the Virgin Mary* (New York: Knopf, 1976). Several anthropologists have studied the cult of the Virgin of Guadalupe in Mexico to determine the ways in which native Indian culture and Spanish culture have been fused to form this national symbol. See Eric Wolf, "The Virgin of Guadalupe: Mexican National Symbol," *Journal of American Folklore* 71 (1958): 34–139; J. Lafaye, *Quetzalcoatl and Guadalupe: The Formation of Mexican National Consciousness, 1531-1813* (Chicago: University of Chicago Press, 1976). Victor Turner brilliantly analyzes the political use of the various devotions to the Virgin Mary during Mexican independence in "Hidalgo: History as Social Drama," in *Dramas, Fields, and Metaphors: Symbolic Action in Human Society* (Ithaca, N.Y.: Cornell University Press, 1974), 98-155. Attempts to interpret the Virgin Mary as a Jungian archetype can be found in E. Neumann, *The Great Mother: An Analysis of the Archetype* (New York: Pantheon Books, 1955); and E. Stevens, "Marianismo: The Other Face of Machismo in Latin America," in *Female and Male in Latin America*, ed. Ann Pescatello (Pittsburgh: University of Pittsburgh Press, 1973), 90–101. Charles Boxer, *Mary and Misogyny: Women in Iberian Expansion Overseas, 1415-1815* (Libon: Livros Horizontes, 1975) examines the syncretisms that developed when Spanish culture expanded into Latin America and Asia, focusing specifically on women.

9. AASF-LD 1725, 51:955, 962.

10. SA 1766, 9:943; Julian Pitt-Rivers, *The Fate of Shechem or the Politics of Sex* (Cambridge: Cambridge University Press, 1977), 23.

11. AASF-DM (*Diligencias Matrimonials*) 1700, 61:209; SA 1805, 15:617; AGN-RH (*Real Hacienda*), 29-8:2.

12. AASF-DM 1837, 76:586–90.

13. Tomás Sanchez, *De sancto matrimonii sacramento* (Antwerp, 1607), quoted in Jean-Louis Flandrin, "Contraception, Marriage, and Sexual Relations in the Christian West," in *Biology of Man in History*, ed. Robert Forster and Orest A. Ranum, (Baltimore, MD: The John Hopkins University Press, 1975), 37–38.

14. Pitt-Rivers, the *People of the Sierra*, 53; AASF-DM 1766, 62:619; AASF-DM 1705, 60:383; AGN-INQ 1663, 594:244; AASF-DM 1702, 60:272.

15. AASF-DM 1845, 79:288.

16. AGN-INQ 1734, 854:253–56.

17. Manuel Alvarez Papers—notebook. Deposited at the Coronado Room of the University of New Mexico's Zimmerman Library (Albuquerque, New Mexico).

18. AASF-LD 1712, 51:735–58; AASF-DM 1702, 60:270; SA 1816, 18:579; AASF-DM 1705, 60:376.

19. AASF-DM 1785, 64:618.

20. "Dictamen de Dr. Tembra acerca de la consulta que se hizo sobre si el Cura o cualquier juez eclesiástico puede o debe impedir los matrimonios entre consortes desiguales, celebrados ya esponsales o con juramento de cumplirlos, sin consentimiento paterno," Mexico 1752, legajo 18, 701, Biblioteca Nacional (Madrid), Manuscritos de América, quoted by Verena Martínez-Alier, *Marriage, Class, and Colour in Nineteenth-Century Cuba* (Cambridge: Cambridge University Press, 1974), 101.

21. SA 1775, 10:868-72; AASF-LD 1725, 51:952–64.

22. AASF-DM 1736, 62:183–90.

23. AASF-DM 1702, 60:274; AASF-DM 1777, 63:610.

24. AASF-DM 1776, 62:514–15.

25. AASF-DM 1705, 60:376, 378, 381, 385. SA 1750, 8:963–77; AASF-LD 1775, 52:463–64; SA 1805, 15:1038–39. Other cases not mentioned in the text but that conform to the same patterns are AASF-DM 1705, 60:428; AASF-DM 1777, 63:609-11; AASF-LD 1823, 54:600–2.

26. AASF-DM 1705, 60:365, 367.

27. SA 1805, 15:597, 602, 605.

28. SA 1767, 10:4, 8, 23, 24. The role of women as gatherers and repositories of information and gossip has been studied as a form of female power within the domestic sphere. See S. Harding, "Women and Words in a Spanish Village," in *Toward an Anthropology of Women,* ed. Rayna R. Reiter (New York: Monthly Review Press, 1975), 283–308; Frederick G. Bailey, ed., *Gifts and Poison: The Politics of Reputation* (New York: Schocken Books, 1971); Larissa Alder Lomnitz and Marisol Pérez Lizaur, "The History of a Mexican Urban Family," *Journal of Family History* 3 (1978): 392–409.

Similar gynecological examinations were performed, albeit without male supervision, to determine if other women were virgins. When Antonio Román Sánchez and Manuel Chaves, both from Isleta, claimed in 1775 to have seduced maidens, Father Junco brought the local midwife to examine the girls. The maidenheads of both women were intact. The midwife certified that the men had lied. For defaming the women, Antonio and Manuel were placed in the stocks. AASF-LD 1775, 52:457–68.

29. SA 1813, 17:698, 690–91, 702–23, 63:610.

Bulls, Bears, and Dancing Boys

Race, Gender, and Leisure in the
California Gold Rush

Susan Lee Johnson

For a good many men who went to California after 1848, the notion of a "social" history of the Gold Rush would have been a contradiction in terms. For them, "society" was one of the very things the diggings lacked. Angus McIsaac said it well on Christmas Day in 1852 when he lamented, "This day I . . . thought of my situation here in this wild mountain hamlet and the very few pleasures it is adapted to afford deprived of social society & of mingling with . . . tender hearted friends." Other men modified "society" differently: "good society," "congenial society," the "sweets of society," the "pleasures of home and its society," "quiet home comfort and the society of friends."[1] But however they modified it, they found it missing in the Sierra Nevada foothills and themselves the poorer for its absence.

In describing California as devoid of society, Anglo-American and European men invoked a peculiarly nineteenth-century middle-class notion of "the social," one in which the influence of white women and their per-ceived attributes was axiomatic. "The social" was thought to revolve around familial, relational, and community concerns, around human interaction and connectedness. At the same time, women were thought to constitute a kind of glue that held families, relationships, communities—indeed, society—together. "The social," in this womanly construction, was an antidote to the manly anomie that increasingly characterized a changing economic milieu in which individual men were forced to "make themselves." It was no wonder, then, that life in the mines, where the population was ninety-seven percent male, provoked male nostalgia for that intricate mosaic of meaning seem-ingly embodied in female friends and relatives, a mosaic men felt themselves incapable of piecing together on their own.[2]

But Anglo men's nostalgia took on a special meaning in California's Southern Mines. Gold Rush immigrants imagined the Sierra Nevada foothills as broken up into two regions: the Northern Mines, the diggings located in the drainage of the Sacramento River, and the Southern Mines, the diggings located in the drainage of the San Joaquin River. The Southern Mines were the destination of disproportionate numbers of non-Anglo-American immigrants to the diggings, and the homeland for Native peoples collectively known as Miwoks. So in the south, the absence of Anglo women was matched by the presence of large numbers of Miwoks, Mexicans, Chileans, French, and, later, Chinese. Of these, only the Miwok population included roughly as many women as men, though Mexican women accompanied their menfolk to the diggings in noticeable numbers, and handfuls of Chilean and French women and, later, Chinese and Anglo-American women lived in the larger camps and towns.[3]

J. D. Borthwick, a Scottish artist and writer, described the difference between the Northern and Southern Mines this way:

In the north, one occasionally saw some straggling Frenchmen . . . , here and there a party of Chinamen, and a few Mexicans. . . . The southern mines, however, were full of all sorts of people. There were villages peopled nearly altogether by Mexicans, others by Frenchmen; in some places there were parties of two or three hundred Chilians forming a community of their own. The Chinese camps were very numerous; and besides all such distinct colonies . . . every town of the southern mines contained a very large foreign population.

Nevertheless, for many Anglo immigrants, this presence equaled an absence of "good" and "congenial" society. As one miner complained, "The society I think is not as good here as farther north, there is fewer families. Where men have their wives and children and settle down everything looks and *is* better than where the population is of the transient unsettled kind."[4]

These transient, unsettled people, however, turned the diggings into a grand field for human interaction and connectedness, not only in the ways they organized labor but also, and perhaps particularly, in the ways they occupied themselves during their leisure hours.[5] Of course, notions of labor and leisure were in flux in the nineteenth century, particularly in industrializing areas such as the northeastern United States. There, as wage work and accompanying notions of time discipline began to replace older labor systems, the distinction between work and leisure was becoming more pronounced.[6] But even Gold Rush immigrants who came from industrializing areas found themselves plunged into largely preindustrial work patterns in the diggings. Whether they came from industrializing areas or not, all immigrants in the mines were part of the global movement of people, goods, and capital that accompanied the proliferation of market economies and the colonial ambitions of North Atlantic nations in the nineteenth century, and, given this context, all immigrants participated in marking mining labor as the "work" of the Gold Rush.

But people in all Gold Rush communities, immigrant and Indian, sought both diversion from the business of producing material life and spiritual sustenance to enable that business or to give it meaning: they sang and prayed, they gambled and got drunk, they danced to one another's drumming or fiddle-playing and cheered at bull and bear fights. Leisure, defined loosely to include both diversion and sacred practices, was often a contested terrain upon which goldseekers drew boundaries that separated them into opposing camps—camps divided by different notions of what constituted appropriate behavior in a disproportionately male "social" world. Still, the twain did meet; polyglot peoples bartered for companionship at fandango houses, Chilean and French men met at Mass, and Anglos and Mexicans sat cheek by jowl over games of chance. Meanwhile, some Spanish- and French-speaking women created a market for heterosocial pleasures that became key in redistributing Gold Rush wealth and in challenging Anglo notions of what would *count* as "society." Indeed, whenever a miner cut loose and stopped working, someone else started—a *matador*, a preacher, a woman at her gaming table. The worlds of labor and leisure, then, were bound together.

Opposing labor to leisure, of course, obscures the extent to which the two terms and the social practices they represent depend on one another for meaning. The leading term, labor, and the social practices it represents generally take precedence in studies of mining rushes, given the predominance of men among the migrants and the prevalence of cultural constructions of labor as male.[7] No historian could deny the central importance of mining labor to life in the Sierra foothills after 1848. But in mining—a new occupation for many but one most identified as suitable for men—immigrants found a daily practice in which to ground a sense of themselves as appropriately gendered. Leisure, by contrast (along with reproductive labor such as cooking, sewing, and laundering), proved a site in which oppositions such as male/female and white/nonwhite were thrown into disarray. So here the focus is on leisure because it was a key site in which gendered and racialized meanings got made, unmade, and remade during the Gold Rush. When immigrant men laid down their picks and shovels, they found that the oppositions which created both social order and social relations—that is, society—back home were all out of kilter in California.[8]

This, of course, was especially true of Anglo-American men, who assumed postures of domination in an expanding nation-state that had just acquired continental breadth, and who were best positioned to reap the benefits of the emerging class system that accompanied industrialization (though many would fail miserably in their efforts to achieve middle-class status, and others would contest the emerging class system itself). For such men, the

Gold Rush created a kind of crisis of representation, because so much of what they imagined as society was unavailable or unrecognizable in California, and what was within reach did not look suitably social. How, then, would they make sense—for themselves, for each other, and for folks back home—of what they did find and see and touch in the diggings? Posing the question in this manner is not meant to suggest that Gold Rush participants who were not Anglo and male were somehow accustomed to life in the mines. However familiar the rise and fall of the foothills might have been to Miwok women and men, for most participants, a gold rush was something new under the sun. Nor does the question mean that the representational practices of such peoples were unaffected by the upheaval of the Gold Rush. But few Miwok, Mexican, Chilean, French, and Chinese in California conflated their daily lives with a project of national expansion and economic growth infused with notions of progress and "manifest destiny." All, however, would be touched—some violently—by the will to dominance of those for whom such conflations came easily.

For Miwok people, for example, the Gold Rush was about invasion on an unprecedented scale, despite earlier contact with Spanish Mexicans on the California coast and white fur trappers coming west over the Sierra Nevada. Miwok responses to conquest were many, from armed resistance, to petitions on their own behalf, to the assimilation of gold digging into women's gathering activities, to retreat from the foothills up into the mountains.[9] When they laid down the woven baskets they used to pan for gold and the weapons they used to fight off the invaders, though, Miwoks worked to represent their new situation by incorporating symbols of conquest into customary ceremonies. Key among these was one called the *pota* ceremony, a commemorative gathering that reminded participants of unnatural or unusual deaths, generally by violence or witchcraft, within a lineage group. Much of this ceremony involved relatives of the deceased dancing around vertical poles to which were attached effigies of murderers or others held responsible for the death; dancers attacked the effigies with arrows, clubs, and knives.[10]

In August 1855, white immigrant Alfred Doten attended a Miwok *pota* ceremony on the south fork of the Cosumnes River, where he saw Miwoks dancing around a flagstaff that supported not only the customary effigy but a U.S. flag as well. An English-speaking Miwok explained to Doten that this ceremony recalled an earlier time when a neighboring group of Indians had come to a festival, but brought with them "a kind of poison" that made the local people ill. Medicine men learned the nature of the poison, however, and could now prevent the sickness; the ceremony was held "in commemoration of the time of the poisoning." The effigy on the flag pole, then, probably represented the bearers of the sickness that had afflicted local Miwoks years ago. The dance was a way of remembering.[11]

If Doten asked about the meaning of the U.S. flag that waved above the effigy, perhaps he got no answer. If he did, he chose not to record it either in his diary or in an account he sent to his hometown newspaper, the *Plymouth Rock*. But something about the proximity of the flag and the effigy troubled him. He noted the presence of both effigy and flag in his diary ("Old 'Santiago's' tribe was ... dancing about a flag staff, with the stars and stripes flying at the top, and a small effigy of a man hung by the neck"). But his *Plymouth Rock* article ignored the effigy altogether, portraying the dance as an innocent romp around the star-spangled banner ("the Cosumnes tribe were dancing around a pole about twenty feet high, with a small American flag flying at the top"). Doten's discomfort may have been well-placed. Items hung on poles in *pota* ceremonies (generally effigies and bear hides that also represented killers) always became objects of derision and violence.[12]

Given this, the act of dancing around a U.S. flag during a *pota* ceremony was, at best, no compliment. The incorporation of the flag into the customary practice of attacking effigies suggests an understanding of the U.S. conquest as something of an altogether different order than other tragedies that had beset Cosumnes Miwoks, tragedies that could be represented adequately by effigies of those who brought death by foul means. And, indeed, while this *pota* ceremony commemorated an earlier time of loss, sickness and death were everywhere in the summer of 1855 as well. Just two days before Doten attended the ceremony, for example, a Native boy whom area white men called Jack—who had been adopted, abducted, or otherwise taken in by two of Doten's friends—had died after "slowly wasting away with consumption." Miwok women in the area, including the boy's aunt, loudly mourned the child's passing. Likewise, the day after the *pota* dance, elders brought several sick children to healers who gathered for the ceremony, in hopes of saving them from Jack's fate.

With death all around—no doubt occasioned by disease and hunger as much as by overt violence—the 1855 *pota* ceremony looks like evidence of a new means of representation, whereby a flag stood for a people who took what they wanted in the name of a nation. The crisis of representation, then, was Doten's: he could not find a way to communicate what he had seen along the Cosumnes River to *Plymouth Rock* readers without challenging their understanding of the national project of westward expansion. Nor could he explain it to himself, even if he noted privately the proximity of effigy and flag. Miwoks found the flag's presence compatible both with collective memory of an earlier period of suffering and with the losses of the present time. For Doten, the link between death and the flag was unrecognizable, or perhaps unspeakable.[13]

While dances such as those performed in the *pota* ceremony were central to Miwok spirituality, few other Gold Rush participants incorporated dance into spiritual observances. For most this reflected Christian distinctions between body and soul, in which the bodily intensity of dance seemed a threat to religious rectitude. This is not to say that practicing Christians did not dance, but rather that dance and worship for them fell into profane and sacred domains, respectively. In the sacred domain resided church services and other religious rites performed by clergy, as well as private and informal spiritual observances such as prayer, bible-reading, and hymn-singing. Catholic and Protestant immigrants alike re-created these familiar rituals in the diggings.

The majority of Catholic Gold Rush participants, particularly Mexicans, Chileans, and French, were concentrated in the Southern Mines. Indeed, two of the three established Catholic churches in the diggings were located in southern towns.[14] When J. D. Borthwick visited the tent that served as a church in San Andreas, he found the interior strikingly spare, with the exception of an altar, which was draped with colored cloth and covered with candlesticks, "some of brass, some of wood, but most of them regular California candlesticks—old claret and champagne bottles." Closest to the altar stood a number of Mexican women, and behind them the church was filled with Mexican men, except for Borthwick and a few curious Anglo-Americans standing near the door. Suddenly, though, two of the Anglos— "great hulking fellows," Borthwick called them—swaggered in, making it clear "that their only object was to show supreme contempt" for the service. Borthwick himself, a native of Scotland, had little sympathy for Anglo-American impudence. Thus when the Mexican congregation and their French priest dramatized that impudence, Borthwick was gleeful: "the entire congregation went down on their knees, leaving these two awkward louts standing in the middle of the church as sheepish-looking a pair of asses as one could wish to see."[15]

Here the crisis of representation belonged less to Borthwick or the Mexican churchgoers than to the "great hulking fellows" who tried to disrupt the Mass.[16] That disruption was, in effect, an attempt to define the meaning of the service—that is, as a foolish exercise of piety on the part of a benighted, dark-skinned people and their foreign spiritual father. When the congregants fell to their knees, the sacredness of the space was restored, and the Anglos momentarily lost their power to establish meanings. While Mexican (and French) resistance to Anglo dominance in the diggings took overt and purposeful forms outside of Mass, this intervention into the control of definitions was probably unconscious—yet no less effective for being deployed in the course of everyday habits.[17] Still, while Borthwick enjoyed the contest of meanings, his own sense of order was disrupted by other aspects of the scene he observed. He claimed, for example, that the Mexican churchgoers spent the rest of the Sabbath gambling. For Borthwick, this accentuated the proximity of the sacred and the profane in California—altar candles in champagne bottles, obnoxious American louts standing in a roomful of prayerful Mexicans, prayerful Mexicans leaving Mass for the gaming tables.

Indeed, these kinds of juxtapositions were especially troubling to certain Protestant argonauts, for whom the Gold Rush itself was a site of moral ambiguity. That ambiguity arose in part out of a discursive shift in the meanings of white middle-class manhood in the industrializing United States, in which self-control became one of the hallmarks of manliness.[18] Two aspects of Gold Rush life ensured that questions about male restraint would assume increased relevance in California. First, there was the means by which most men earned a living. Elsewhere men might find greater congruence between their own experience as economic actors and the notion that success, increasingly defined as the accumulation of capital, resulted from hard work and prudent plans. Mining—that is, placer mining, which was not industrialized—gave men cause to dispute that belief. For one, the average daily yields of white miners declined precipitously over the course of the Gold Rush. In addition, though few made a fortune in California, those who did relied as much on luck as hard work. Placer mining exaggerated the economy's capriciousness to such an extent that men could seriously question the value of self-control.[19]

Second, the physical absence of white women—and their discursive presence—contributed to debate over male restraint. At the time of the Gold Rush, northeastern Anglo-American women and men were enacting the transformation of domestic life that accompanied industrialization. That shift included a new emphasis on the sentimental heterosociality of the privatized home, which required for its realization men's diligent exercise of self-control, and women's application of superior moral sensibilities.[20] In the diggings, then, battles raged over whether or not white men had either reason or ability to practice restraint when apart from their collective better half. Was the discursive presence of women alone enough to encourage self-control?

In the absence of women, many aspiring middle-class white men from the Northeast turned to organized Protestant worship for support in their efforts to stay on the moral high road in California. Finding that support, however, was often no simple task. Sometimes trouble arose due to the physical distance to the nearest church.[21] For other men, it was not only miles that separated them from worship. Timothy Osborn wrote twice in his diary that he would gladly walk five miles on the Sabbath, if he could find but one minister in the mines who had "enough of the true Christian spirit." His complaint may have been disingenuous, however, because when he moved down to Stockton, the bustling supply town for the Southern Mines, which boasted a number of established churches, Osborn still proved a restless soul. He tried attending the Methodist Episcopal services there, but spent as much time in his diary describing the "*low* necked dress" of a young woman in the congregation, Miss Isbell, as he did the sermon and music. By the end of the month, not even Miss Isbell could lure Osborn back to Sunday worship, as he noted in his diary, "there is but little inducement for one to sit an hour upon anything but an easy seat and be bored with a dull stereotyped sermon." For New England boys like Osborn, the thrill of the profane had it hands down over the tedium of the sacred. Indeed, the eve of the following Sabbath found Osborn and a male companion window-peeping at a young French woman of "fair proportions" as she undressed for bed.[22]

While there is ample evidence that many Protestant men worked hard to keep themselves, as one fellow put it, "*within sight* of the straight & narrow path," there is equally ample evidence that keeping that path even within their peripheral vision was a constant struggle in California.[23] Worrying white men were surrounded by others who, as another miner put it, had learned to "roll sin as a sweet morsel under the[i]r tong[ue]s."[24] For those who had, notions of sin gave way to the sweetness of Gold Rush pleasures, especially card playing, strong drink, and easy sex. But documenting these often relatively private leisure practices is not easy. The men who generated the primary sources most apt to shed light on the dailiness of pleasure-seeking in the mines were also the men most likely to have internalized Protestant moral codes that discouraged men from keeping a written record of their indulgence in cards, liquor, and sex. Those few who did used a variety of narrative strategies to explain the relationship of their behavior to their larger sense of themselves as white, Protestant-raised American men who were struggling to become part of the emerging middle class. Three examples illustrate some of the different ways in which such men confronted the crisis of representation the Gold Rush wrought: the diaries of Alfred Doten, from Plymouth, Massachusetts; of John Doble, from rural Indiana; and of Timothy Osborn, raised in Edgartown, Massachusetts (on Martha's Vineyard), but emigrated from New York City.

Of the three men, it was Alfred Doten who most reveled in what many experienced as the moral ambiguity of the Gold Rush. Although he sang temperance songs during his sea voyage to California, once in the diggings Doten rarely advocated self-control. The sheer number of terms he used to describe his drinking patterns, for example, indicates how central liquor quickly became in his life. One day he might write that he had been on a "bender" or a "tall spree," on another that he had been "tight," or "wild," or "obscure," or, more to the point, "infernally drunk."[25]

Doten's diary also includes reference to sexual encounters with both Miwok and Mexican women, and to a contemplated encounter with a light-skinned black woman.[26] For instance, Doten detailed the visit of two Miwok women to a store he was tending, an older woman and a young mother with a baby in tow. Doten claimed to have wooed the younger woman with presents and taken her into his tent, where he was "about to lay her altogether," when the older woman burst in and "gave the young gal a devil of a blowing up." Doten was convinced the younger woman appreciated his attentions: "She didn't get cross at all but gave me a slap in the face and ran away laughing." Meanwhile, the older woman shook her fist at Doten and gave him a piece of her mind in her native language, as Doten returned her fire, "cussing her in good round English." As the women left, Doten pleaded with his would-be sexual partner in Spanish to come back to the store alone when she could. She replied that she would try, though there is no evidence that she ever returned.[27]

Doten's diary, then, offers one reading of his encounter with the young Miwok mother, a reading in keeping with the meaning-making strategies of white men who gave themselves with some enthusiasm to the moral peril of the Gold Rush. But other readings are possible, if elusive in evidential terms, and must be ventured for historical situations such as this, where so much was at stake for all involved—even the future of customary ways of living, thinking, and being in the world. Without information about sexual practices among nineteenth-century Miwoks, one can but guess at what this encounter meant to the women involved.[28] Perhaps Doten was right in assuming that the younger woman was a willing partner thwarted only by the older woman's intervention. Then again, maybe the two women were of like mind, and their visit was an elaborately planned ruse to trick a white man out of some trade goods but deny him the payment—in sexual favors—he expected. Or perhaps Doten's advances were unwanted, the young woman's laughter when she broke free of his embrace a way of mocking the failed assault, and her parting promise a ploy to discourage him from tracking her down later.

Whatever the encounter meant to the women, the meaning for Doten is clear enough. Doten thought himself "quite a hunk of a boy," and he hated for anything to dampen his ardor. On his twenty-first birthday, for example, he saluted himself, "Hurrah old man how's your *crotch rope*," and then complained because a cold kept him "not in a condition to enjoy it." Enjoying it, it seems, was somehow easier with women he presumed would not bring their moral authority to bear upon him. While Doten maintained a chaste correspondence with a white sweetheart back home and politely pursued a young white woman in Calaveras County, his relationships with women of color were shorn of the trappings of courtship, or, as he satirically put it, "happy hearts, fluttering gizzards, honey sugar." Such relationships he pursued with a vengeance until September 7, 1855, just a few weeks after he attended the Miwok *pota* ceremony. While prospecting that day, Doten was crushed from the waist down by a cave-in. He was partially paralyzed for a time, and even a month later, though he had begun to take a few steps, he noted "no feeling in my crotch yet." By December, still lame, he left the diggings for good.[29]

John Doble was more ambivalent than Alfred Doten about mining camp life, and thus provides a second example of the ways white men negotiated the phantom "society" of Gold Rush California. There is no evidence that Doble was sexually active with women; indeed, he frowned on the kind of behavior Doten took in stride.[30] In fact, Doble was quite comfortable with the homosociality of the diggings. His relationship with James Troutman is a case in point. Nothing affected Doble more deeply than Troutman's untimely death, after a brief illness, in September 1853, nine months after the two moved in together in the town of Volcano. The day Troutman died, Doble wrote in his diary: "Now am I again alone the only heart that I have found that beat in unison with mine suddenly torn from me." Doble's description of the heart that "beat in unison" with his own is especially instructive: "I have never met a Man in life as generally respected as was Jim . . . he was entirely clear of all the Vices for which *Cal* is so noted he used strong drink in no form . . . he made use of no profane Language at all." The bond between the two men at first seems curious, because Doble himself was hardly "clear of all the Vices" for which California was notorious. But Doble's misgivings about these habits ran deep, and his friendship with Troutman marked a period of intense efforts at self-reformation.[31]

John Doble's particular weakness was gambling. From the start, he disapproved of the practice. After a night of poker, Doble confessed that he had "a love for that game" even though he knew that "Money thus gained is of no Value." He thought he ought to quit. He did not. After a long losing streak a few months later, Doble finally won a dollar and a half. Again he thought he should quit: "If I can resist the temptation I surely will now henceforth & forever." He could not. For six months he played only for liquor, but then joined another cash game. This time, he wrote in his diary, he was "determined to quit the evil practice of Gambling." He may or may not have kept his resolve, but he recorded no more gambling in his diary. By that time, he had lived with Jim Troutman for three months, and his commitment to learning habits of restraint was at an all-time high. For Doble, then, in contrast to Doten, seasons of indulgence brought seasons of regret. Troutman's death six months later shook Doble, but never again did he give in to temptation as he had during his first months in California.[32]

Timothy Osborn, a third miner who dared keep record of his flirtation with vice in California, followed neither Doble's trajectory of earnest self-reformation nor Doten's antipathy toward the strictures of middle-class manhood. Osborn's self-representation did not read as a triumph of the forces of good over those of evil or as a devil-may-care embrace of dissipation. Instead, his was a delicate oscillation between propriety and the pull of illicit pleasures. This back-and-forth motion takes literal shape in the way that Osborn chose straightforward prose to describe most daily concerns in his diary, and more coy and allusive language to refer to situations fraught with moral ambiguity. Sometimes not even allusion was obscure enough, though, and then Osborn abandoned conventional writing altogether, substituting shorthand in its place, as he did when describing his window-peeping at the naked French woman in Stockton. Osborn also used shorthand to record private, though less morally questionable, musings about white women back home on Martha's Vineyard—kissing was a favorite subject in these passages.[33] But the remainder of the coded entries refer quite explicitly to Osborn's curiosity about sex and the opportunities the Gold Rush offered him to indulge it.

Mining along the Merced River in 1850, Osborn lived and worked in close proximity to Miwoks. He frequently remarked at Miwoks' scant clothing, taking special interest in the women's bare breasts. He acknowledged that his curiosity "was exercised rather more freely than strict propriety would allow under other circumstances," but insisted that the women's *"modesty did not seem to suffer much."* All of this Osborn recorded in his diary with just a hint of moral inhibition. But in shorthand Osborn indicated that his exercises went beyond observation. He had heard, he wrote, that Native women, like animals, had "certain times for seeking the man." And his own experience inclined him to believe this pernicious bit of white wisdom: "I have seen Indian girls, who, when they were 'in heat,' would fondle around you and in every possible way would ask you to relieve them, while at other times it would be an impossible thing to get your own wishes gratified." Like Doten's description of his attempt to "lay" a young Miwok woman, Osborn's reflections were steeped in dominant discourses regarding Native women's "animal" proclivities. Such discourses precluded other readings of Miwok sexual practices in the context of conquest: for example, Miwok women might have had their own reasons for wanting sex at one time and not at another; some Miwok women might have welcomed intimacy with white men, for whatever reason, while others abhorred the thought; and some white men might have appealed to a Miwok woman while others repelled her.[34]

Despite this indication that Osborn may have had sex with Miwok women, most often he seems to have gratified his own wishes by conjuring up scenes in his own mind. While mining along the Merced, Osborn's favorite spot to dream was in a hammock of Peruvian netting that he rigged up beneath an oak tree. Here, Osborn would nap or read or let his thoughts drift to women back home.[35] He may also have masturbated. In one diary entry, his description of cigar smoking in the hammock seems full of double entendres. The entry begins with Osborn "smoking away . . . at a third rate 'short six,'" and imagining women he knew walking to church. In no time the diarist finds himself taking a pleasure "in the curling smoke of an ordinary 'long nine' which the unpracticed do not know." Osborn himself must have been practiced, because he knew that a smoker was a contented man who, "impotent of thought, Puffs away care." At other times, Osborn counted on sleep to bring him contentment. Once, for example, an afternoon nap delivered up a dream about a young woman in Mexico City who was wealthy, worldly, and "over-anxious to see 'Los Etados Unidos.'" Osborn was equally anxious to show her *estadounidense* valor. With sweet regret, however, he noted in his diary, "Had I not awoke by the cry of 'supper!' I should have gratified her."[36]

Even in their dreams, then, the sights and scenes of the Gold Rush haunted Anglo-American men, disrupting the ways in which they had imagined the world was ordered, showing them that such conventional terms of ordering required, at the very least, refinement in California. As the diaries of Doten, Doble, and Osborn suggest, different men negotiated this crisis of representation differently. Some tried to ignore it, projecting "social" disorder onto cultural "others"—Mexican gamblers or Miwok prostitutes, for example—collapsing race and culture into questionable leisure practices. Men such as Doten, Doble, and Osborn, however, located themselves in the very belly of the beast, and struggled to represent themselves—wholeheartedly or ambivalently, with or without a trajectory of self-reformation or dissipation—as aspiring middle-class white men in a world where constructions of gender, class, and race were unfamiliar and in flux.

And it was not only in the private pursuit of pleasure described by men like Osborn that Gold Rush participants faced this crisis of representation; such men were also relentless in their search for companionship. Both heterosocial and homosocial ties flourished in California, but the paucity of women along with cultural constructions of male needs and desires meant that for many men, contact with women was at a premium. Women knew this. In fact, the small number of non-Native women in the Southern Mines—(in 1850, maybe 800 in an enumerated immigrant population of more than 29,000) occupied an extraordinary position in what quickly became a multiracial, multiethnic market for male-female interactions.[37]

This is not the same thing as saying prostitutes abounded in the diggings. A smug Anglo man like Enos Christman living in a predominantly non-Anglo town like Sonora might claim that the women there were "nearly all lewd harlots," but even he knew the situation in Sonora was more elaborately alluring. On any given Sunday he might attend an auction, a bullfight, a circus, or an exhibition of "Model Artists" (with naked women posing), and then he might go to a dance house, a gambling hall, or a fandango. No matter where he went, part of what he paid for was often, quite simply, proximity to women. Not that sex itself was not for sale—it was. But men would lay down gold dust for far less. Christman himself, after a long Sunday working in the local newspaper office, for example, drank wine with a friend and then rushed uptown to spend his earnings at a fandango, "looking at the Americans dancing with the Mexican señoritas." No doubt the dancing Anglos were willing to pay a little bit more.[38]

Dance halls, sometimes called fandango houses, flourished in the Southern Mines and the supply town of Stockton.[39] And although Mexican and Chilean men frequented them to dance with their own or each other's countrywomen, the halls were not havens from Anglo-American hubris. Alfred Doten and his drunken companions, for example, took the occasion of the Fourth of July in 1855 to march into Fiddletown playing "Yankee Doodle" on fife and drum. They stopped at the "Spanish dance hall" there to dance, then marched downtown and "up again into the dance hall, three times around inside" and then paraded out of town. Like the impudent display of the two Anglo men in the San Andreas tent that served as a Catholic church, this march through the "Spanish dance hall" in Fiddletown is another instance in which Anglos attempted to regain control over meaning-making in the Southern Mines. Ethnic social spaces such as the fandango house might be permitted in the diggings—and patronized by Anglos—but men such as Doten and his friends made sure that the recent Anglo-American conquest of Mexican California (completed in 1848) and the dominance it implied would remain fresh in the minds of all Gold Rush participants.[40]

By far the greatest variety of fandango houses and gambling saloons in the Southern Mines was in Sonora, a town established by Mexican miners well before the flood of immigrants from the United States and Europe arrived in late 1849. One resident of Sonora, a Canadian-born merchant named William Perkins, left behind an especially rich account of social life there. The Sonora that Perkins described encompassed an unparalleled Gold Rush world of heterosocial leisure. Or so it seemed to the men who participated in it; for the women of Sonora, it was also a world of work. Moreover, it was a world of work stratified by race and national origin. According to Perkins, "A lady's social position with white gentlemen was graduated by shades of color, although we would sometimes give the preference to a slightly brown complexion, if the race was unmixed with the negro." The "social position" Perkins referred to was that of mistress: Chilean, Mexican, and French women all could make their way in Sonora by attaching themselves to men who had made some money in the diggings. Perkins's characterization of the differences between Spanish- and French-speaking women who cohabited with men says a great deal about how Anglos came to terms with the presence of females who did not fit comfortably into the category of "women" upon which such men's understanding of "the social" rested. In response, Perkins felt compelled to create new typologies of women, new hierarchies of gender, race, and ethnicity. For example, Mexican and Chilean women met Perkins's approval because they, "even in the equivocal position of mistress," maintained a certain dignity, while French women did not. French women's chief sin, it seems, was their love of money. By contrast, according to Perkins, "the spaniard" would not allow men "a glimpse of interested motives." Now disinterestedness was hardly a useful trait in a gold rush, and so it seems likely that Spanish-speaking women simply made sure that Perkins could not read their motivations. And undoubtedly, more than one Mexican or Chilean woman benefitted from his romantic naivete.[41]

Part of what distinguished French from Mexican and Chilean women in Perkins's eyes was that the former tended bars and gambling tables, while the latter did not. While Spanish-Mexican women in New Mexican towns such as Santa Fe might run saloons, in California, Spanish- and French-speaking women seem to have filled different niches in the Gold Rush market for heterosociality: French women watched over bars and gaming tables, while Mexican women sold prepared foods. Mexican women gambled too, but only French women oversaw men's winnings and losings, for which Perkins dubbed them "the forms of angels in the employ of Hell."[42]

Like many men, Perkins imposed a moral hierarchy on a market in which he was a willing consumer, and from first to last, he held the French, Mexican, and Chilean women of Sonora responsible for emptying men's pockets and tempting their weak natures. That French women earned Perkins's special disapprobation (and his patronage, too) no doubt reflected the means by which they emptied those pockets. As mistresses of gaming tables, French women put Anglo men's control of their own resources at risk. This potential loss of control mocked dominant definitions of manhood, in which manly restraint was supposed to coexist in a symbiotic relationship with womanly moral sensibilities. Here, in California, were whole new species of women, living and working not alongside emerging bourgeois neighborhoods—as, for example, prostitutes did in cities like New York—but at the very center of Gold Rush society, with few middle-class, Anglo women physically present to contest newly sexualized, racialized, and commercialized notions of womanhood.[43]

Given how hard men like Perkins worked to develop ways of ordering this new world, ways to make sense of this new situation, it is no wonder that the eventual arrival of middle-class Anglo women in the Southern Mines was disconcerting. As Perkins put it, "It is too much to expect from weak male human nature in California, that a man ever so correctly inclined, would prefer the lean arm of a bonnetted, ugly, board-shapen specimen of a descendant of the puritans, to the rosy cheeked, full formed, sprightly and elegant spaniard or Frenchwoman."[44] Having struggled to find new ways of representing gender relations that could accommodate the presence of Miwok, Mexican, Chilean, and French women, now Anglo men had to locate Anglo women in an altogether new discursive field. So in spite of white men's frequent complaints that the mines lacked the "sweets of society," not a few such men paradoxically bemoaned the arrival of increasing numbers of Anglo women in California.[45]

And that was not all. For along with the Gold Rush world of heterosocial amusement men such as Perkins described, there emerged—not surprisingly, given the demographics—a homosocial terrain of leisure as well. Indeed, beneath male complaints about the absence of "society" in California, there often ran an undercurrent of pleasure taken in the constant company of men. It was not so much that goldseekers fit into neat categories of those who preferred either the homosocial or the heterosocial—though a few, no doubt, did—but rather that the meaning of "social" life in the diggings was hotly contested.

The tension exhibited itself even in a single text by an individual Gold Rush participant. On the one hand, German goldseeker Friedrich Gerstäcker could remark at the "perfectly social body" that he and his fellow miners constituted in Calaveras County—"a little world of ourselves, in closest neighborhood and amity, eating, working, and sleeping together, and not caring more for the world around us, than if it did not exist." On the other hand, when he reflected on the long-range potential of California, he insisted that "social life" would come about there gradually, "principally by and through the presence of the gentler sex." Benjamin Butler Harris went so far as to applaud the "superior society" of the mines, made up as it had been of "people culled from every race and nation . . . [a] varicolored, and Babel-tongued group . . . free in every sense, standing on an equal plain, a nobility whose title was *manhood*." In a world where dominant constructions of gender were disrupted by the physical absence of white women, what was it about the new socialities of the mines that prompted such romantic memories? After all, as a New York friend reminded Timothy Osborn one Sunday when the men in camp dressed up for one another, "Ah! Tim, this isn't going up Broadway with a pair of bright eyes by your side."[46]

Nonetheless, men in California sometimes had bright eyes for each other. John Marshall Newton, for one, was unafraid to be caught looking. He recalled that one of his partners, a tall Dane named Hans, was "one of the most magnificent looking young men I ever saw." He had "massive shoulders and swelling muscles" that stood out "like the gnarled ridges of an oak tree." Newton remembered himself as a slight, soft-hearted boy who "yearned intensely for a friend" and who at first had so much trouble handling heavy mining tools that he often fainted from exertion. The magnificent Dane, then, was a perfect partner, because when Newton could not budge a boulder with a crowbar, he recalled, "Hans would . . . thrust me aside, take hold of the stone . . . and throw it out of the pit."[47]

Such differences in age, strength, and inclination could contribute to a cross-gendering of men's relationships with one another—so much so that the term "homosocial" itself becomes inadequate to describe those relationships. At Howard Gardiner's camp on the Tuolumne River, for example, one "handsome youngster" was christened "Sister Stilwell" because of his "fresh complexion, lack of beard, and effeminate appearance." Reveler Alfred Doten made an even more tantalizing reference in one of his diary entries, which describes a Sunday fandango with visiting Chileans that led to an expedition across the Mokelumne River to a store kept by a man named Brooks. When Doten returned home that night, he noted in his diary, "There is a Chileno *hermaphrodite* camped near Brooks' store."[48] To date, the historical record offers up no further clues about Brooks's neighbor. S/he could have been a cross-dressing man, or a passing woman, or someone with unusual genitalia. Whatever qualified h/er for Doten's designation of "hermaphrodite," s/he seems not to have kept it to herself. S/he was, in other words, a public "hermaphrodite"—someone everybody "knew" to be anatomically female or male but who cross-behaved; or someone everybody "knew" to have, for example, what nobody could easily recognize as a clitoris or a penis, testicles or a vagina. Whatever s/he had or whatever s/he did, s/he was known for miles around, and no one—least of all Alfred Doten—seemed especially troubled by h/er presence.[49]

Perhaps this is because Brooks's store on the Mokelumne and Gardiner's camp on the Tuolumne were not isolated sites of cross-gender gymnastics in the diggings. Not every ravine had a "Sister Stilwell" or a Chilean "hermaphrodite," but most saw men coming together in novel ways on a daily basis. In this, the prevalence of dance in the diggings was key.[50] J. D. Borthwick, for example, described a ball he attended at Angel's Camp, a largely Anglo town. There, a fiddle and a flute provided the music, and the fiddler led the dancers through their steps, singing out "Lady's chain," or "Set to your partner," or, a favorite call, "Promenade to the bar, and treat your partners." At Angel's Camp, lancers were special favorites—sets of five square dances for several couples, each one of the sets in a different meter. "The absence of ladies," Borthwick noted, "was a difficulty which was very easily overcome." All agreed that every man "who had a patch on a certain part of his inexpressibles" would be a woman for the night, indicating just how successfully Gold Rush demographics and contests for meanings had unsettled normative notions of gender. Meanwhile, a Scottish boy spelled the men from their lancers for a time by performing the Highland fling. After a quarter of an hour the boy retired to the bar, where, Borthwick noted, "if he had drunk with all the men who then sought the honor of 'treating' him, he would never have lived to tread another measure."[51]

J. D. Borthwick's rendering of a Gold Rush ball. Courtesy of the Bancroft Library, University of California, Berkeley.

Did the "gentlemen" see their "ladies" home, or the "men" their "boys"? The Gold Rush occurred in a period when sex between men was generally considered a sin or vice, but not an indicator of a particular identity or sense of self.[52] In this context, most Anglo letter and diary writers would have been just as wary about keeping a record of sexual contact with other men as of drunkenness, gambling, or, for that matter, nonmarital sex with women. Indeed, one of the few unambiguous extant records of sex between men in the Southern Mines occurs not in a letter or diary but in the divorce proceedings of Hanna and Jeremiah Allkin of Calaveras County. Hanna, who joined Jeremiah in California after he had been there for some time, divorced her husband in part because he brought men into their home for "purposes of buggery."[53]

But ambiguous records abound. Alfred Doten, never one to tiptoe around what some thought of as vice, habitually noted the individual men with whom he spent the night. Once he took in a friend, James Flynn, remarking, "We slept together at my house." Flynn stayed only a few days, though a week later Doten was referring to him as "Jimmy, my little partner." In that same diary entry Doten wrote that he had "slept . . . all night" with a "Dr. Quimby." Doten could make life in the camps sound like a game of musical beds. One night he wrote, "Moody and John Spicer went down to the ranch—Newt came down and passed the evening with me—slept here," and the next, "Newt and Moody stopped at the Gate—Young slept with John—I slept in the house alone for the first time."[54]

Moody and John, Newt and Moody, John and Young, Doten and Newt, Doten and Jimmy, Doten and Dr. Quimby—we cannot know what transpired when beds in the diggings were thus occupied. Certainly bed-sharing was a common practice in the nineteenth-century United States, perhaps particularly in frontier areas, and it would be foolhardy to suggest that bed partners commonly shared sexual pleasures.[55] But Doten and his friends bedded down together in a particular setting, one characterized by the presence of curious young men and lonely husbands, by close dancing and hard drinking, by distance from customary social constraints and proximity to competing cultural practices. In this context, it would also be foolhardy to suggest that Jeremiah Allkin was the only man in the Southern Mines who ever reached for a friend in the heat of the night.

This, then, was the Gold Rush world that some white men complained deprived them of "good," "congenial," or simply "social" society. Although it was abundantly clear that connections of all sorts flourished in the diggings, Anglo men did not always know how to represent those connections, which often failed to follow customary rules for negotiating oppositions that constituted the realm of the social. For such men, the absence of white women and the overwhelming presence of Miwoks, Mexicans, Chileans, and French upset the gendered and racialized oppositions upon which notions of social relations and social order rested: male/female, white/nonwhite, sacred/profane, even labor/leisure. Indeed, the profusion of California letters, diaries, and reminiscences written by Anglos is itself evidence of the crisis of representation the Gold Rush wrought.

Of course all Gold Rush participants had to renegotiate their usual modes of representation in California, where everything from the natural environment to demographics to local economies were strange and unstable. Just as Anglos could march into a Mexican dance hall playing "Yankee Doodle," as if to give their personal stamp of approval to the Treaty of Guadalupe Hidalgo, so too, for example, could Miwok dancers represent their understanding of the politics of conquest in customary *pota* ceremonies. But the *crisis* of representation—the profound disordering of conventional oppositions and conventional hierarchies—may have been peculiar to Anglo-American men in California, who in situation after situation found their power to establish meanings in jeopardy. These were, after all, the people in whose favor industrialization and westward expansion were supposed to work. But for all their faith in these processes, white men found unanticipated discursive contests in California, contests with material consequences.

These material and discursive contests were nowhere brought into sharper relief than in such popular leisure practices as gambling and blood sports.[56] In the Southern Mines, games of chance such as monte and bloody spectacles such as bull-and-bear fights reflected Gold Rush enmities that were rooted in the will to dominance of some Anglo-American men in the diggings, enmities that were played out simultaneously on a broader stage where expulsion from mining areas, excessive taxation, and paramilitary campaigns plagued Miwok, Mexican, Chilean, and French Gold Rush participants.[57]

Gambling was far and away the chief entertainment in the diggings. Games of chance took on a special significance in a setting like California, where they shared with the primary economic activity, placer mining, elements of unpredictability and irrationality.[58] Then, too, in an intensely multiethnic, multiracial place such as the Southern Mines, gambling could also expose deadly faultlines in communities bent on digging what was thought of as cash from the earth. In popular games such as monte, a pastime of Mexican origin, as well as faro, an Anglo-American favorite, gamblers ostensibly competed not with one another but with the "bank" managed by the man or woman who dealt the cards. Even though the games' design did not entail direct competition between players (as mining did not between miners), jealousies over big winnings at the monte table (as over high yields in the diggings) could foster ill will. Fear of cheating (as of unfair advantage in the mines) also ran rampant; no man wanted the deck stacked against him.[59] Indeed, no other activity in the diggings, aside from mining itself, provoked as much rancor as gambling.

Leonard Noyes, who in 1851 worked near Murphys Camp in Calaveras County, probably exaggerated when he remembered, "Every Sunday someone was shot in a Gambling den and often times during the week." As if it was part of the same thought, however, he went on to describe the "loss of life" occasioned by "quarels about [mining] claimes." In this, he suggested the symbiosis between mining and gambling as well as their common progeny: "every one was compelled to be on the Fight enough to take his own part."[60]

An incident that took place near Murphys in 1851 helps to illustrate how monte, the game of choice in the Southern Mines, could make bad blood boil. Noyes recalled that Mexicans had "quite a camp" at Indian Gulch that year, just north of Murphys. The camp boasted three tent stores, one of them kept by a Chilean named José María and his wife. Two Anglo gamblers, Hugh O'Neil and Dick Williams, opened a monte table at María's tent, where in the space of a couple days eight or ten Mexican and Chilean men "lost all their dust." O'Neil claimed that he overheard the men plotting in Spanish to murder the Anglos and reclaim the ten-thousand-dollar monte bank. So when a scuffle broke out and the Anglos thought the Mexicans and Chileans were robbing the bank, O'Neil ripped through the back of the tent with his knife and ran off with what money he could grab. Williams met a different fate; as Noyes heard it, a Mexican man put a knife through the gambler's chest. That was all it took for Anglos to tell a familiar Gold Rush tale: "by daylight everybody was out having been told the Mexicans had raised and were murdering all the Americans in Indian Gulch."[61]

A story started this way and told by Anglos tended to move inexorably toward a predictable denouement, and so it was that fifty or sixty Anglos rushed into Indian Gulch that morning, a dozen of them intent on holding a makeshift inquest and the rest hungry for quick revenge. The supposed murderers were long gone, and so the mob turned to a dark-skinned Chilean man (perhaps of African descent) who, along with his white wife, kept a boardinghouse where the Mexican monte players took their meals. Noyes recalled that he and the handful of Anglos committed to a more orderly form of vigilantism pleaded with the others to let the Chilean man go. In the end, the more vengeful Anglos prevailed, forcing the Chilean to run up a hill while they opened fire on him, killing him instantly. When his wife "burst forth in a tirade of curses," the Anglos set fire to her tent. Next the mob went after José María and his wife, at whose store Williams and O'Neil had set up their monte table. Both husband and wife were nearly hanged. Again the calmer minority of Anglos interceded, arguing that María was "a very nice Gentlemanly Chilano" who had begged for his life in English. Noyes and his comrades won this debate, perhaps by emphasizing perceived class and race differences that distinguished the English-speaking María and the dark-skinned man who kept the boardinghouse: José María and his wife escaped lynching, though they lost everything but their lives. Then, according to Noyes, the Anglos continued their depredations at Indian Gulch, burning, robbing, and killing until they were satiated.[62]

It was striking how rapidly the death of an Anglo at the hands of a Mexican became for some Anglos the opening line of a larger story about a Mexican uprising replete with murder and mayhem. Such hysterical narrative responses to ethnic tensions in the mines indicated how fearful Anglos could be of the lack of control they were able to exert in the Sierra foothills during the Gold Rush—whether control over meanings, control over the proceeds of mining, or control over the complex interactions between the two. Indeed, when the new widow of the dark-skinned Chilean man "burst forth" with her "tirade of curses," no doubt turning the charge of murder back onto the Anglos, they burned down her tent. Contests over meanings mattered. They drew blood; they destroyed homes; they brought death.

If antagonism at monte tables could escalate quickly to bloodshed, another popular pastime in the Southern Mines dramatized Gold Rush tensions rather than playing them out on human flesh. Animal flesh did not fare as well. Like monte, bull-and-bear fighting was a Mexican cultural practice, one particularly well suited to the Sierra Nevada foothills, home to both grizzly and black bears and within trading distance of low-country *ranchos*. Bull-and-bear fights were only one of the blood sports common in the mines; Mexicans also staged

THE GRIZZLY AND HIS CAPTORS.

To Tilley & May I send this picture showing how the Spaniards Catch the Bears in Cal, you must be good children and

MEXICAN MEN CAPTURING BEAR, PERHAPS FOR A BULL-AND-BEAR FIGHT. COURTESY OF THE BANCROFT LIBRARY, UNIVERSITY OF CALIFORNIA, BERKELEY.

bullfights and cockfights. But bull-and-bear fights were clear favorites among goldseekers of many descriptions—Mexican, Anglo, and French, to be sure, and perhaps others as well. Indeed, during the early 1850s, almost every good-sized camp in the Southern Mines had a wooden arena surrounded by tiers of seats where both bull-and-bear fights and bullfights were held.[63]

Bulls were the real crowd pleasers, enjoying as they did a special relationship to notions of manhood among Spanish-speaking peoples. Indeed, in California, at least, bullfights in particular seemed quite conducive to gender play, constituting a kind of liminal space in which attributes of manhood could be extracted from larger constellations and claimed by anyone willing to look a bull in the eye. At Sonora, for example, Enos Christman watched as a stunningly dressed Mexican woman entered the arena. In an intricate dance, she parried with her foe until, at an opportune moment, "she plunged the sword to the hilt into the breast of the animal." A shower of silver dollars fell at her feet, and the cheer of the crowd was deafening. Likewise, J. D. Borthwick attended a bullfight at Columbia where it had been announced that Señorita Ramona Pérez would be *matador*. In this case, however, the woman turned out to be an exquisitely cross-dressed man, who made short order of the bull and then ran out of the arena, "curtsying, and kissing her hand" to the audience. As for the bull-and-bear fights, Mexican women thronged to them, hollering and laughing and waving handkerchiefs along with the other spectators, whom one observer described as men of "all sizes, colors, and classes such as California, and California alone, can bring together." Such audiences gasped as the fight began, often with a charge by the bull that was met by a snout-crushing chomp of the bear's teeth.[64]

Another observer, J. D. Borthwick, himself an artist as well as a writer, romanticized the human diversity of the arenas, representing it as a riot of color, turning spectators into spectacle. Borthwick's description of an 1852 bull-and-bear fight at Mokelumne Hill began with the two fiddlers—"a white man and a gentleman of color"—who played while the crowd gathered. The arena itself, he thought, was "gay and brilliant," and the "shelving bank of human beings which encircled the place was like a mass of bright flowers." There were the blue, white, and red miners' shirts; the men's bronze faces; the variegated Mexican blankets; the guns and knives glancing in the sun; the red and blue French caps; and always, the "Mexican women in snowy-white dresses." The bear seemed a dull brute, but Borthwick's bull was a gorgeous beast, "of dark purple color marked with white . . . . his coat . . . as smooth and glossy as a racer's." Once the fight began, however, the purple and white, the bronze and blue, and the glint of steel all dissolved into crimson. The bull's nose turned "a mass of bloody shreds," and a red flag taunted a bear brought low. While it began as a celebration of human diversity, Borthwick's depiction of the bull-and-bear fight now took an ominous twist—the circle of bright human flowers blanched by the animal carnage within the ring.[65]

Some representations dispensed with romantic images altogether. At Mokelumne Hill, for example, proprietors advertised an upcoming event throughout the area on placards that read:

WAR! WAR!! WAR!!!
The celebrated Bull-killing Bear,
GENERAL SCOTT
will fight a Bull on Sunday the 15th inst., at 2 p.m.
at Moquelumne Hill.

General Winfield Scott, then a Whig presidential candidate, had led the invasion of Mexico in 1847, taking fourteen thousand U.S. troops from Veracruz into Mexico City in what proved the decisive campaign of the war. Like a bull-and-bear fight held in Sonora—where the bear was christened "America"—the Mokelumne Hill event, while rooted in Mexican cultural practices, took on particular Gold Rush meanings.[66] Still, in the 1850s, a bear probably did not need to be called "America" or "General Scott" for Anglo/Mexican tensions to be invoked. Bull-and-bear fights called to mind not only the association of bulls with Spanish-Mexican culture, but also the recent Bear Flag Rebellion of pre-Gold Rush Anglos against Mexican rule in California. In that conflict, a grizzly bear and a lone red star graced the flag of the short-lived Anglo "California Republic."

In bull-and-bear fights, then, enemies could meet in the ring again and again, spectators could place bets on the action, and the outcome of the contest, now freighted with ethnic and national as well as gendered meanings, could change from one Sunday to the next. All over the Southern Mines, events like this drew goldseekers from their diggings, dealers from their gaming tables, even some preachers from their makeshift pulpits. Perhaps the unpredictable endings of bull-and-bear fights and the mutual high spirits of the spectators provided some relief from the relentless tensions of life in the mines. But in the end, those tensions were reproduced in the spectacles, which themselves became representational just as surely as the practices of writing letters and diaries, attacking effigies (and flags), assigning gender by means of a patch on a pair of pants, or marching into a dance house playing patriotic tunes. Such contests over meanings in California revolved around a central question: Who would own the rush for riches in the Sierra foothills? Coming as it did at a pivotal moment in the course of industrialization, westward expansion, and class formation, the Gold Rush seemed to Anglo-American men an opportunity whereby they might secure for themselves dominant positions in the emerging social order. Once in the Southern Mines, however, such men found that the absence of white women and the presence of Native peoples, Latin Americans, Europeans, and, later, East Asians confounded their notions of what constituted "good" and "congenial" society. The crisis of representation that necessarily followed erupted with particular force across the terrain of leisure. There, the boundaries of the social—the boundaries that make meaning—blurred, transmogrified, and reconstituted themselves again and again in the Southern Mines, with different consequences for different Gold Rush participants.

Notes

Many people have given me helpful comments on partial written or spoken versions of this work, including Betty Louise Bell, Nancy Cott, William Cronon, Ann Fabian, Douglas Flamming, Camille Guerin-Gonzales, María Teresa Koreck, Howard Lamar, David Montgomery, and Mary Murphy, as well as audiences at the Ninth Berkshire Conference of Women, 1993; the Second Annual California Historical Society Conference, 1993; the American Culture and Latina/Latino Studies Brown Bag Series, University of Michigan, 1994; the History Faculty Colloquium, University of Michigan, 1994; and students in both graduate and undergraduate seminars at the University of Michigan, 1993. *Radical History Review* provided four enormously helpful anonymous readers' reports in record time, and Collective member Yukiko Hanawa not only helped me to organize my responses to these reports but also helped me to realize just whose representational practices were in crisis here.

1. Journal entry, December 25, 1852, Angus McIsaac Journal, Beinecke Library, Yale University, New Haven (hereafter cited as Beinecke Library). For brief quotations, see Benjamin Kendrick to Father, September 25, 1849, Benjamin Franklin Kendrick Letters, Beinecke Library; Joseph Pownall to Thomas

Tharp, August 5, 1850, Joseph Pownall Journal and Letterbook, Pownall Papers, Huntington Library, San Marino (hereafter cited as Huntington Library); Journal entry, September 7, 1850, Timothy C. Osborn Journal, Bancroft Library, University of California, Berkeley (hereafter cited as Bancroft Library); Journal entry, March 27, 1851, George Allen Journals, Beinecke Library; George W. B. Evans, *Mexican Gold Trail: The Journal of a Forty-Niner*, ed. Glenn S. Dumke (San Marino: Huntington Library, 1945), 259; and Jesse Smith to Sister Helen, December 23, 1852, Lura and Jesse Smith Letters, Huntington Library. Examples of such lamentations are rife in Gold Rush personal accounts. Still, there is a less prevalent but not insignificant countertendency in the same kinds of sources for some Gold Rush participants to see themselves as involved in a different kind—for a few, even a better kind—of society. I discuss such seemingly contradictory evidence below.

2. Here I rely on the argument developed by Denise Riley in her chapter entitled "'The Social,' 'Woman,' and Sociological Feminism," in *"Am I That Name?" Feminism and the Category of "Women" in History* (Minneapolis: University of Minnesota Press, 1988), 44–66. In a less direct but no less crucial way I draw on the earlier work of U.S. women's historians such as Kathryn Kish Sklar, *Catharine Beecher: A Study in American Domesticity* (New York: W. W. Norton, 1976); Nancy F. Cott, *The Bonds of Womanhood: "Woman's Sphere" in New England, 1780–1835* (New Haven: Yale University Press, 1977); and Mary P. Ryan, *Cradle of the Middle Class: The Family in Oneida County, New York, 1790–1865* (Cambridge: Cambridge University Press, 1981). In 1850, census takers enumerated well over 29,000 non-Native people in the three counties that constitute the Southern Mines, the area studied herein. Just under 800 of these were women. See United States, Bureau of the Census, *Seventh Census of the United States: 1850* (Washington, D.C., 1853), hereafter cited as *1850 Census*.

3. In this essay, I use the term *immigrant* to describe all non-Native peoples in the Southern Mines. Calaveras, Tuolumne, and Mariposa Counties roughly constituted the Southern Mines (later, part of Calaveras County became present-day Amador County). See *1850 Census*; Rodman W. Paul, *California Gold: The Beginning of Mining in the Far West* (1947; Lincoln: University of Nebraska Press, 1965), 91–115. For an earlier social history of two towns in the Northern Mines, see Ralph Mann, *After the Gold Rush: Society in Grass Valley and Nevada City, California, 1849–1870* (Stanford: Stanford University Press, 1982).

4. J. D. Borthwick, *The Gold Hunters* (1857; Oyster Bay, N.Y.: Nelson Doubleday, 1917), 290; Jesse Smith to Sister Helen, December 23, 1852, Smith Letters.

5. On the organization of mining labor, see Paul, esp. 50–66 and 124–70. Elsewhere I elaborate on productive and reproductive labor, on leisure, and on the racial and ethnic conflicts mining engendered during the Gold Rush. See "'The Gold She Gathered': Difference and Domination in the California Gold Rush, 1848–53" (Ph.D. diss., Yale University, 1993).

6. See, for example Roy Rosenzweig, *Eight Hours for What We Will: Workers and Leisure in an Industrial City, 1870–1920* (Cambridge: Cambridge University Press, 1983), 35–40; Bruce Laurie, *Artisans into Workers: Labor in Nineteenth-Century America* (New York: Hill and Wang, 1989), esp. 84–86 and 168–70; Herbert G. Gutman, "Work, Culture, and Society in Industrializing America, 1815–1919," in *Work, Culture, and Society in Industrializing America: Essays in American Working-Class and Social History* (New York: Knopf, 1976), 3–78; E. P. Thompson, "Time, Work-Discipline, and Industrial Capitalism," *Past and Present* 38 (December 1967).

7. Here I am influenced by Joan Scott, "Gender: A Useful Category of Historical Analysis," *American Historical Review* 91, no. 5 (December 1986); and "Deconstructing Equality-Versus-Difference: Or, the Uses of Poststructuralist Theory for Feminism," *Feminist Studies* 14, no. 1 (Spring 1988).

8. I elaborate on this in Johnson, chap. 4. Many thanks to Nancy Cott and Ann Fabian for helping me clarify arguments in that chapter, and hence for assisting me in shaping this essay. Yukiko Hanawa and anonymous readers for *Radical History Review* helped me to refine these arguments even further, and for that I am very grateful.

9. See Albert L. Hurtado, *Indian Survival on the California Frontier* (New Haven: Yale University Press, 1988); and Johnson, chap. 5.

10. See E. W. Gifford, "Central Miwok Ceremonies," *Anthropological Records* 14, no. 4 (1955): 261–318, esp. 295–99; and "Miwok Cults," *University of California Publications in American Archaeology and Ethnology* 18, no. 3 (1926): 391–408, esp. 397–98; and Richard Levy, "Eastern Miwok," in *Handbook of North American Indians,* vol. 8, *California,* ed. Robert F. Heizer (Washington, D.C.: Smithsonian Institution, 1978), 398–413, esp. 410–12.

11. Alfred Doten, *The Journals of Alfred Doten, 1849–1903,* 3 vols., ed. Walter Van Tilburg Clark (Reno: University of Nevada Press, 1973), 1: 238, 239–42.

12. Ibid., 1: 238, 239 (Doten's *Plymouth Rock* articles are reprinted along with his diary in these edited volumes); and Gifford, 295–99.

13. Doten, 1: 237, 240. Many thanks to Yukiko Hanawa for helping me rethink my interpretation of this event.

14. William Hanchett, "The Question of Religion and the Taming of California, 1849–1854, Part I," *California Historical Society Quarterly* 32, no. 1 (March 1953): 49–56.

15. Borthwick, 298–99. Compare Benjamin Butler Harris, *The Gila Trail: The Texas Argonauts and the Gold Rush Trail*, ed. Richard H. Dillon (Norman: University of Oklahoma Press, 1960), 144. Harris describes a drunken Anglo comrade who threatened to tear down the Catholic church at San Andreas.

16. Thanks again to Yukiko Hanawa for helping me to reinterpret this event.

17. On overt and purposeful forms of resistance, see Johnson, chaps. 1 and 5.

18. See, for example, Charles E. Rosenberg, "Sexuality, Class, and Role in Nineteenth-Century America," *American Quarterly* 35 (May 1973): 131–53; E. Anthony Rotundo, "Learning about Manhood: Gender Ideals and the Middle-Class Family in Nineteenth-Century America," in *Manliness and Morality: Middle-Class Masculinity in Britain and America, 1800–1940*, ed. J. A. Mangan and James Walvin (Manchester: Manchester University Press, 1987), 35–51, and *American Manhood: Transformations in Masculinity from the Revolution to the Modern Era* (New York: Basic Books, 1993); Howard Gadlin, "Private Lives and Public Order: A Critical View of the History of Intimate Relations in the U.S.," *Massachusetts Review* 17 (Summer 1976): 304–30; G. J. Barker-Benfield, *The Horrors of the Half-Known Life: Male Attitudes toward Women and Sexuality in Nineteenth-Century America* (New York: Harper Colophon, 1976); and Clyde Griffen, "Reconstructing Masculinity from the Evangelical Revival to the Waning of Progressivism: A Speculative Synthesis," in *Meanings for Manhood: Constructions of Masculinity in Victorian America*, ed. Mark C. Carnes and Clyde Griffen (Chicago: University of Chicago Press, 1990), 183–204; and Ryan.

19. On miners' declining daily yields, see Paul, 349–52. I owe my understanding of the ambiguous place of luck in nineteenth-century perceptions of economic advancement to Ann Fabian, *Card Sharps, Dream Books, and Bucket Shops: Gambling in Nineteenth-Century America* (Ithaca, N.Y.: Cornell University Press, 1990).

20. See, e.g., sources cited note 18 above; Cott; Sklar; Carl N. Degler, *At Odds: Women and the Family in America from the Revolution to the Present* (New York: Oxford University Press, 1980); Robert L. Griswold, *Family and Divorce in California, 1850–1890: Victorian Illusions and Everyday Realities* (Albany: State University of New York Press, 1982); and Steven Mintz and Susan Kellogg, *Domestic Revolutions: A Social History of American Family Life* (New York: Basic Books, 1988). A good first look at the impact of white women's absence on white male goldseekers appears in Andrew J. Rotter, "'Matilda for Gods Sake Write': Women and Families on the Argonaut Mind," *California History* 58, no. 2 (summer 1979): 128–41.

21. See, for example, Journal entries, April 25, May 9, 16, 23, and 30, June 20 and 27, 1852, P. V. Fox Journals, Beinecke Library.

22. Journal entries, July 7 and November 17, 1850; February 2, 9, and 23, and March 5, 1851, Osborn Journal.

23. Lucius Fairchild, *California Letters of Lucius Fairchild*, ed. Joseph Schaefer (Madison: State Historical Society of Wisconsin, 1931), 186–87. For further references, see Johnson, chap. 4.

24. Journal entry, August 3, 1850, Allen Journals.

25. Doten, 1: 3–4, 84, 105, 107, 111, 112, 125, 141.

26. Reading these references is especially complicated because a relative of Doten's, after his death in 1903, saw fit to start erasing explicit descriptions of sexual activity in the fifty years of journals Doten left behind. The censor never completed the project, and hence the later diaries are filled with sexually explicit material. But the earlier volumes, which cover the Gold Rush years, are substantially altered. Still, the references mentioned remain, if in abbreviated form, and they may stand for a greater number of sexual encounters in the mines. Ibid., 1: xii-xiii, 125–26, 150, 195.

27. Ibid., 1: 125–26.

28. Most ethnographic works on Miwoks are concerned only with marriage practices, and are silent about nonmarital sex. For an overview of the meanings of Indian-white cross-racial sex in the Gold Rush, see Hurtado, 169–92, which, however, does not shed light specifically on Miwoks. Hurtado focuses on "alliances of convenience," prostitution, and forced sex. While influenced by Hurtado's careful work, I think the situation described here may allow for other interpretations as well. For an excellent analysis of sexual violence in an earlier period of California history, see Antonia I. Castañeda, "Sexual Violence in the Politics and Policies of Conquest: Amerindian Women and the Spanish Conquest of Alta California," in *Building with Our Hands: New Directions in Chicana Studies*, ed. Adela de la Torre and Beatríz M. Pesquera (Berkeley: University of California Press, 1993), 15–33.

29. Doten, 1: 75, 121, 128, 130–34, 150, 152, 195, 243–51. Marion Goldman has chronicled Doten's later life on the Comstock Lode in Nevada, and her research indicates that the old Doten was finally revived in the new mining area. See *Gold Diggers and Silver Miners: Prostitution and Social Life on the Comstock Lode* (Ann Arbor: University of Michigan Press, 1981), 51–56.

30. John Doble, *John Doble's Journal and Letters from the Mines: Mokelumne Hill, Jackson, Volcano, and San Francisco, 1851–1865*, ed. Charles L. Camp (Denver: Old West Publishing, 1962), 47, 114.

31. Ibid., 132, 178–81.

32. Ibid., 70, 83, 114, 149.

33. Journal entries, July 11 and 18, August 18 and 24, October 19, and November 16, 1850; and January 6, 1851, Osborn Journal.

34. A Miwok named Juan, for example, explained to Belgian miner Jean-Nicolas Perlot that his people tried to conceive children so that they would be born between March and June, and thus benefit in the early months of their lives from the natural abundance of spring, summer, and fall in the Sierra foothills. Jean-Nicolas Perlot, *Gold Seeker: Adventures of a Belgian Argonaut during the Gold Rush Years*, trans. Helen Harding Bretnor and ed. Howard R. Lamar (New Haven: Yale University Press, 1985), 230. See Journal entries, August 8, September 17, and October 2, 1850, Osborn Journal.

35. Ibid., Journal entries, July 7 and 11, August 24 and 25, 1850.

36. Ibid., Journal entries, September 15 and December 10, 1850.

37. *1850 Census*. By 1852, when California conducted a state census, the population in the Southern Mines had more than doubled to over sixty thousand. But male-female breakdowns are not available for all three counties in the aggregate statistics from this 1852 census, which are published in the same volume as those from the 1850 federal census. In 1860, women still made up only about nineteen percent of the population of the Southern Mines (now constituted by Amador, Calaveras, Tuolumne, and Mariposa Counties). United States, Bureau of the Census, *Population of the United States in 1860; Compiled from . . . the Eighth Census* (Washington, D.C., 1864). As one anonymous reader of this essay noted, such markets in heterosocial pleasure "flourished with full participation" by white men in the East as well—particularly, no doubt the reader means, in urban areas. What was unique about the Gold Rush was the physical absence of "respectable" middle-class white women, which meant that such "markets" could more easily become confused with "society" in the mining camps and supply centers of California. And what was unique about the Southern Mines, in particular, was a demography in which Anglo men barely constituted a majority. On markets in pleasure in the East, see Timothy J. Gilfoyle, *City of Eros: New York City, Prostitution, and the Commercialization of Sex, 1790–1920* (New York: W. W. Norton, 1992).

38. Enos Christman, *One Man's Gold: The Letters and Journals of a Forty-Niner*, ed. Florence Morrow Christman (New York: Whittlesey House, McGraw-Hill, 1930), 179, 198. On the "Model Artists," see also William Perkins, *Three Years in California: William Perkins' Journal of Life at Sonora, 1849–1852*, ed. Dale L. Morgan and James R. Scobie (Berkeley: University of California Press, 1964), 219–20.

39. Doten, 1: 92; Journal entry, January 16, 1852, John Wallis Journal, Holt-Atherton Center for Western Studies, University of the Pacific, Stockton, California; Doble, 104, 108; and Journal entry, December 30, 1850, Osborn Journal.

40. Doten, 1: 227–28 (and compare his description of the Fiddletown event to that published in the *Plymouth Rock*, which ignores the dance hall stop, 1: 232–33).

41. Perkins, 103–4, 127–28, 130–31, 161, 163, 201–2, 218, 221–23, 242–45, 268, 303–5. Elsewhere I have examined informal union among Mexican immigrant women, linking it to earlier cultural practices that proved particularly suitable in mining areas. See "Sharing Bed and Board: Cohabitation and Cultural Difference in Central Arizona Mining Towns, 1863–1873," in *The Women's West*, ed. Susan Armitage and Elizabeth Jameson (Norman: University of Oklahoma Press, 1987), 77–91. For a useful critique of this essay, see Antonia I. Castañeda, "Women of Color and the Rewriting of Western History: The Discourse, Politics, and Decolonization of History," *Pacific Historical Review* 61, no. 4 (November 1992): 501–33, esp. 512, n. 21.

42. Perkins, 161–62, 218–19, 242–43, 269, 268. On Santa Fe, see Deena J. González, "La Tules of Image and Reality: Euro-American Attitudes and Legend Formation on a Spanish-Mexican Frontier," in ed. de la Torre and Pesquera, 75–90.

43. For the comparison to New York, see Gilfoyle.

44. Ibid., 243, 251–52, 314. Perkins made this remark in response to the arrival of the wife of Lewis Gunn, a doctor and publisher of the *Sonora Herald*, in 1851. See also Christman, 187; Borthwick, 314–15. For the perspective of the "descendant of the puritans," see Lewis C. Gunn and Elizabeth Le Breton Gunn, *Records of a California Family: Journals and Letters of Lewis C. Gunn and Elizabeth Le Breton Gunn*, ed. Ann Lee Marston (San Diego: n.p., 1928). As this collection of family papers makes clear, the white woman who arrived in Sonora, Elizabeth Gunn, descended from both English and French immigrants, hence her maiden name, Le Breton.

45. See, for example, Doble, 89–90; Perlot, 246; and my elaboration in Johnson, chap. 4.

46. Friedrich Gerstäcker, *Narrative of a Journey round the World* (New York: Harper and Bros., 1853), 236–37, 251; Harris, 112–13; and Journal entry, August 4, 1850, Osborn Journal. Compare Borthwick, 351.

47. John Marshall Newton, *Memoirs of John Marshall Newton* (n.p.: John M. Stevenson, 1913), 34, 36, 48.

48. Howard C. Gardiner, *In Pursuit of the Golden Dream: Reminiscences of San Francisco and the Northern and Southern Mines, 1849–1857*, ed. Dale L. Morgan (Stoughton, Mass.: Western Hemisphere, 1970), 216; Doten, 1: 116.

49. See Judith Butler's reading of Michel Foucault, ed., *Herculine Barbin, Being the Recently Discovered Memoirs of a Nineteenth Century Hermaphrodite*, trans. Richard McDongall (New York: Colophon, 1980) in *Gender Trouble: Feminism and the Subversion of Identity* (New York: Routledge, 1990), 93–106. On passing women in this period, see San Francisco Lesbian and Gay History Project, "'She Even Chewed Tobacco': A Pictorial Narrative of Passing Women in America," in *Hidden from History: Reclaiming the Gay and Lesbian Past*, ed. Martin Duberman, Martha Vicinus, and George Chauncey, Jr. (New York: Meridian/Penguin, 1989), 182–94; and the chapter entitled "Passing Women: 1782–1920," in *Gay American History: Lesbians and Gay Men in the U.S.A.*, ed. Jonathan Katz (New York: Thomas E. Crowell, 1976), 209–79.

50. See, for example, Journal entries, December 19 and 25, 1849, William Miller Journal, Beinecke Library; and Doten, 1: 122, 167–68, 192.

51. Borthwick, 303–4.

52. See the synthesis of scholarship on this point in John D'Emilio and Estelle B. Freedman, *Intimate Matters: A History of Sexuality in America* (New York: Harper and Row, 1988), 121–30.

53. See Hanna Allkin v. Jeremiah Allkin (1856), Case No. 84, Box 103, District Court Cases, 1856–1861, Calaveras County Court Records, Calaveras County Museum and Archives, San Andreas, California (hereafter cited as Calaveras County Archives).

54. Doten, 1: 68–69, 75, 103, 108, 109, 127, 173, 174, 205, 213, 218.

55. Compare John Mack Faragher, *Sugar Creek: Life on the Illinois Prairie* (New Haven: Yale University Press, 1986), 153–54; Martin Duberman, "'Writhing Bedfellows' in Antebellum South Carolina: Historical Interpretation and the Politics of Evidence," in ed. Duberman et al., 153–68; and E. Anthony Rotundo, "Romantic Friendship: Male Intimacy and Middle-Class Youth in the Northern United States, 1800–1900," *Journal of Social History* 23, no. 1 (1989): 1–25, and *American Manhood*.

56. I have just begun to examine the sources of these practices and their contested nature in northern Mexico. See Oakah L. Jones, Jr., *Los Paisanos: Spanish Settlers on the Northern Frontier of New Spain* (Norman: University of Oklahoma Press, 1979), esp. 32, 61, 75, 106, 251. My thanks to María Teresa Koreck for initial conversations on this subject, and for her own work in progress on northern Mexico, which will complement some of the interpretations developed herein. See "Popular Sub-Versions in Northern Mexico: From Colonists to Colonized to Revolutionaries" (Ph.D. diss., University of Chicago, 1994).

57. For elaboration, see Johnson, chaps. 1 and 5.

58. See Ann Vincent Fabian, "Rascals and Gentlemen: The Meaning of American Gambling, 1820–1890" (Ph.D. diss., Yale University, 1982), 53–59, and more generally, *Card Sharps, Dream Books, and Bucket Shops*.

59. My thanks to William Cronon for helping me to clarify this argument.

60. Leonard Withington Noyes Reminiscences, Essex Institute, Salem, Massachusetts, transcription at Calaveras County Archives, 57.

61. Ibid., 53–37. On Anglo narratives of victimization by Mexicans, see Johnson, chap. 1.

62. Noyes, 53–57. Compare Doten, 1: 98–104.

63. Noyes, 51; Doten, 1: 88; Christman, 199–200; and Journal entry, November 7, 1852, Fox Journals.

64. Christman, 199–200; Borthwick, 276–85, 336–37; Hinton Rowan Helper, *The Land of Gold: Reality versus Fiction* (Baltimore: Henry Taylor, 1855), 116–30, esp. 124; Perkins, 273–77; and Frank Marryat, *Mountains and Molehills; or Recollections of a Burnt Journal*, ed. Robin Winks (1855; Philadelphia: J. B. Lippincott, 1962), 131. A key difference between Clifford Geertz's Balinese cockfight, on the one hand, and California bull-and-bear fights, on the other, is women's participation in the latter and the liminality that participation signals in the realm of Gold Rush gender relations. See "Deep Play: Notes on the Balinese Cockfight," in *The Interpretation of Cultures* (New York: Basic Books, 1973), 412–53, esp. 417–18, n. 4.

65. Borthwick, 276–83.

66. Ibid.; and Marryat, 131.

Manly Gambles

The Politics of Risk on the Comstock
Lode, 1860-1880

Gunther Peck

During his tour of the great silver mines of Virginia City, Nevada, in 1876, journalist and geologist Eliot Lord was both impressed and horrified by the "cool" detachment of Cornish miners as they risked their lives underground in pursuit of hard currency. Lord was particularly fascinated by the daring of one Cornishman who fell into a shaft thirteen hundred feet deep only to emerge unscathed minutes later "by an astonishing combination of coolness, strength, and luck." As he climbed out of the pit, the Cornishman remarked matter-of-factly, "By the bloody 'ell. If I hadn't caught hold of the pumpbob nose, I'd a been scattered all abroad." Lord used such anecdotes to paint a portrait of the Cornish miner as a dispassionate gambler who daily wagered his financial and bodily assets, whether in games of blackjack above ground or in earning wages underground. Wrote Lord, "The miners' fondness for gambling leads them to regard the possibility of death . . . as a risk that every gamester must face, and they stake their lives on the cost because they consider the chances in favor of their preservation."[1]

Like many middle-class professionals in the nineteenth century, Lord considered gambling to be immoral and blamed miners' high mortality rates and enduring financial insecurity upon their penchant for taking risks.[2] Determining which forms of risk were morally acceptable and manly had become crucial to middle-class men's ongoing project of self-definition in the nineteenth century.[3] In this respect, Lord's description of all wage-earning men as gamblers tells us more about his own struggle to define legitimate gain and manhood than it does about working-class notions of masculine risk-taking. Yet Lord's was an ambivalent moralism, tinged as it was with admiration for the miner's heroism and manly "coolness." From Lord's nostalgic perspective as a citified eastern professional, the Cornish miner embodied admirable aspects of a heroic but vanishing manliness, long associated with the frontier, in which individual bravery and manly skill rather than market laws and machines governed the productive lives of men. If Lord condemned the manly gambles miners took every day, he also venerated their risk-taking ethos that had, so the popular frontier myth went, conquered the wilderness and brought civilization to a savage desert.[4]

But middle-class reformers such as Lord were hardly alone in struggling to create a moral economy of acceptable and manly risks.[5] Miners on the Comstock grappled with their own notions of acceptable risk, but they grounded their definitions of it and their manhood in the daily challenges of wage work and working-class solidarity. While all classes of men and women in Virginia City and nearby Gold Hill took chances, the substance and meaning of risks varied tremendously along class, gender, and racial lines. The experience of risk and the cost of failure depended a great deal on what was at stake in the gamble—a day's wages, a person's reputation, the well-being of one's family, a percentage of company profits, an arm, or a life itself. While all miners on the Comstock might have appeared equally reckless to Eliot Lord, the experience and significance of their underground gambles differed significantly for single and married miners, and for Chinese and Irish miners. Rather than being characteristic of a timeless and classless "frontier" culture, risk-taking in Virginia City sparked debates about the changing nature of work, manhood, and citizenship on the rapidly industrializing frontier.[6]

Historians of the mining West have devoted relatively little attention to the gendered and class-based geography of risk-taking because of its associations with the celebrated individualism and upward mobility of Frederick J. Turner's frontier.[7] For many western historians, "class" and the "frontier" have been, almost by definition, oxymoronic terms, despite attempts by Carlos Schwantes to reconcile the two concepts in his provocative discussion of a "wageworkers' frontier."[8] Labor historians such as Melvyn Dubofsky have understandably rejected Turner's formulation of western development and argued that the West's labor history was singularly exploitative and class-ridden.[9] Dubofsky avoided tackling the thorny problem of class on the frontier by locating the "origins" of the western working class in the frontier's disappearance after 1890.[10] This conceptual hurdle continues to confront even the most recent and sophisticated literature of the "new" western history. In their essay "Becoming West: Toward a New Meaning for Western History," for example, William Cronon, George Miles, and Jay Gitlin recognize the existence of class relations in frontier economies, but argue that "self-shaping" identities such as class emerged most forcefully in the transition from frontier to region.[11]

In this essay I examine the "problem" of class formation on the frontier by exploring the contested meanings of that quintessential frontier activity—

risk-taking.[12] The popularity of risk-taking among miners did not reflect their individualism, conservatism, or some kind of false consciousness, but rather lay at the core of a gendered and racialized sense of working-class autonomy.[13] Examining the way miners defined and took risks during the "flush times" provides an important window into the origins and varieties of working-class manhood and class consciousness on the mining frontier. Although an analysis of the contested meanings of risk could encompass nearly all of Virginia City's social groups and perhaps illuminate the relational nature of class, race, and gender formation, my aims in this essay are more modest: I will focus upon the class-based geography of risk among white male residents of Virginia City and Gold Hill as a case study of how working-class manhood on the frontier acquired meaning and definition primarily in dialogue with middle-class reformers and capitalists.[14] The first section contrasts the experience of risk for working-class miners and middle-class professionals during the 1860s as a dramatic depression refigured the nature of financial and physical risk-taking on the Comstock Lode. The second section explores the contested meanings of risk by examining how two all-male organizations—the Gold Hill Miners' Union and the Improved Order of Red Men, Pi-Ute Tribe No. 1—rationalized its consequences. The final section considers how competing middle-class and working-class notions of manhood and acceptable risk shaped the patterns of dialogue and conflict between miners and capitalists on the Comstock.

In *Roughing It*, Mark Twain vividly satirized the "speculative frenzy" that had transformed Virginia City from a barren desert into a bustling metropolis of ten thousand people between 1860 and 1865:

> Joy sat on every countenance, and there was a glad almost fierce intensity in every eye that told of the money-getting schemes that were seething in every brain and the high hope that held sway in every heart. Money was as plenty as dust; every individual considered himself wealthy.[15]

Twain realized that miners' gilded hopes were rarely fulfilled, and his comparison of money and dust anticipated the dramatic "bust" Virginia City experienced a year later, when prices on the local stock exchange plummeted fourfold in just two months. But Twain had only an inkling of the dramatic transformation in productive relations Virginia City was experiencing during the early 1860s. The stock market crash of 1864 accelerated a profound reorganization and consolidation of property ownership on the Comstock in which a few large mining companies emerged as the principal producers of silver and gold. Expensive investment requirements, a shortage of outside capital, and low stock prices forced many mining companies out of business.

Those who survived the crash, however, expanded production throughout the ensuing depression.[16] By 1865, the vast majority of miners on the Comstock Lode no longer worked above ground, but instead toiled underground for wages in large, highly capitalized mine operations.[17] Manhood for these miners would not be acquired as property owners or prospectors working their own claims, but as wage earners far below the surface of Virginia City.

The impact of the 1864 depression on the community's emerging class structure can be seen in the changing rates of occupational and residential mobility on the Comstock Lode during the 1860s. The percentage of the workforce who were miners remained relatively constant during the 1860s, averaging about 40 percent of all residents on the Comstock. Similarly, the percentage engaged in unskilled tasks, the skilled trades, and professional jobs remained roughly the same before and after the 1864 depression.[18] What changed dramatically during the 1860s were people's occupational and residential mobility. In 1862, residential persistence in Virginia City and Gold Hill was extremely low, particularly among miners; only one out of four miners remained on the Comstock a year later. In 1868, more than two out of three miners remained on the Comstock the next year.[19] In comparison to other American cities, residential turnover remained high in Virginia City and Gold Hill, but it was considerably lower than in the "flush times." Job mobility, both upward and downward, was likewise dramatically lower in 1868 than in 1862; in 1868 only one in twenty persisting residents of Gold Hill changed occupations, while in 1862 nearly two out of five changed jobs. These statistical patterns illustrate how rapidly economic categories hardened and opportunities decreased for men and women of all occupations with the onset of industrial mining on the Comstock.

Perhaps most indicative of the transformation of economic life was the increasing stratification of personal wealth and land ownership in Virginia City and Gold Hill. By 1870, a small middle class, representing one in seven residents and comprised primarily of clerks, professionals, and small proprietors, controlled over half of the community's personal wealth. Miners, by contrast, comprised 43 percent of all male occupation holders on the lode, but owned just 12 percent of the total wealth listed in the 1870 census. This stratification was partially mirrored by the patterns of home ownership in Gold Hill and Virginia City; members of the middle class were 50 percent more likely to be married and own their own homes than were miners. Perhaps the most salient and significant fact about wealth and land ownership in 1870, however, was that only 18 percent of all male occupation holders owned any property on the Comstock. By 1870, very few "capitalists" lived in Virginia City or Gold Hill; much of the community and its extracted wealth was in fact owned by the Bank of California and its superintendent, William Sharon, who lived in San Fransisco.

VIRGINIA CITY MINERS ON SHIFT. THE HEAT IN THE MINES WAS INTENSE, BUT IT WAS THE LEAST OF THE RISKS OF UNDERGROUND WORK. COURTESY OF CALIFORNIA HISTORICAL SOCIETY.

The growth of industrial mining not only transformed patterns of occupational mobility, personal wealth, and property ownership on the Comstock, but also dramatically altered the shape and meaning of risk-taking for all classes of fortune seekers in Virginia City. For miners, wagework changed, but did not eliminate, the financial insecurities of mining. Striking pay dirt as a placer miner involved a considerable degree of chance, and most claims did not supply steady forms of income. But wagework hardly gave miners a risk-free income, for although wages on the Comstock remained high—four dollars a day throughout the 1860s and 1870s—steady employment was unusual, even for skilled white miners. Changes in the value of silver and gold, falling stock prices, and financial panics frequently left miners suddenly out of work. If wagework preserved miners' financial insecurity, it also homogenized the nature of such risk. Never before had individual miners seemingly had less control over the outcomes of their daily gambles. "Luck" for the frontier wage earner no longer meant striking a rich vein of one's own ore, but rather procuring steady work at steady wages and maintaining, above all else, steady health.

Perhaps the most serious new risks that wage-earning miners took on were the occupational dangers of underground work. Fire, poisonous gas, explosions, cave-ins, and other hazards killed or injured more than nine hundred miners between 1863 and 1880, giving the Comstock Lode one of the worst industrial accident rates in the world during these decades.[20] The physical risks of placer mining—frostbite, starvation, bandits' guns—paled in comparison to the dangers of deep-lode mining. Given the fact that mining companies rarely if ever compensated workers and their families for lost wages or livelihoods, the financial consequences of these injuries were daunting indeed. All miners, no matter how skilled, learned to expect the unexpected when working underground. Sometimes even this maxim left miners ill-prepared for the fatal moment. In the winter of 1867, two men on their way to work underground in Gold Hill were killed when "a small dog accidentally happened to fall from the surface . . . knocking them off the cage and precipitating them to the bottom of the shaft."[21] Unlike the Cornish miner who caught the pumpbob nose, these two men lost the daily gamble of underground wage-work on the Comstock. Even the most agile and cool-headed miner could not anticipate, let alone calculate, the arbitrary effects of such risks.

Industrial mining also transformed the experience and meaning of risk for large mine-owners, but in ways that illustrate the class-based meanings of financial and physical risk-taking. Although mining accidents took a heavy financial toll on mine companies, no Comstock capitalists were ever killed by the daily gambles of mining and only rarely were white-collar, middle-class employees affected by mining accidents.[22] When a fire raged out of control in the Yellow Jacket mine of Gold Hill for two weeks in the spring of 1869, killing forty-two miners underground, the company experienced only a temporary halt in ore production, a financial setback that was soon calculated and rationalized in terms of temporarily reduced profits and higher stock assessments.[23]

The transformation of risk-taking along class lines was equally pronounced in financial venues such as the development of Virginia City's frontier stock exchange. In 1860, just one year after silver had been discovered in Virginia City, money was itself a scarce commodity, and most financial transactions were conducted by barter or with newly created stock certificates. Wrote Eliot Lord, "sales of claims for money were comparatively rare, but barters were incessant."[24] Placer miners and would-be capitalists alike traded stocks with one another in lieu of currency and more precise financial arrangements. With the creation of the Washoe Stock Exchange in 1862, however, the barter of mining stocks increasingly fell under the control of large stock-trading companies and banks with financial connections far beyond Virginia City. By 1863, the principal traders on the new exchange were not placer or wage-earning miners, but an expanding class of professional stock brokers with direct links to banking houses in San Fransisco and New York. Of forty official stock exchange members in 1863, twenty-five were listed in the Virginia City directory as professional brokers with addresses in San Fransisco and New York, while the remaining fifteen comprised a cross-section of Virginia City's professional community. Doctors, lawyers, notary publics, and most of the city's municipal officers, including the mayor, justice of the peace, county assessor, police and probate judges, and secretary of the school board rounded out the stock exchange's membership.[25] Many miners continued to purchase stock after the depression of 1864, but the local exchange was increasingly an arena of professional risk-taking in which few if any miners ever made the "paper fortunes" celebrated by Mark Twain.

Miners continued taking financial risks but more often did so within their own predominantly male, working-class communities.[27] Miners spent much of their leisure time placing bets in local saloons or in the streets whenever occasions arose.[27] Any physical contest, whether involving men, dogs, chickens, or bears, quickly became the focus of intense discussion and wagering on the streets above the greatest silver strike in America.[28] When two small dogs got into a fight in downtown Gold Hill in January 1867, "a crowd of more than two hundred persons gathered, all eager and excited to see whose pup would come out ahead." When one of the "pups" finally got the better of the other, money flowed freely through the crowd. Losers quickly paid the victors, whether in coin or drinks at the nearby saloon, where many soon migrated.[29] Although these contests were intensely competitive and often violent, there were few enduring winners in such affairs; today's winners were tomorrow's losers, as most "earnings" remained within the same working-class community of single men. Patterns of violence between working-class men did not make them America's "primitive rebels," for the mutualistic sensibilities that informed such contests were often predicated on enduring gender hierarchies outside the workplace, in this case affordable access to Virginia City's community of prostitutes.[30] Prize fights and gambling contests nonetheless formed important elements of an alternative working-class culture in Virginia City, one that venerated chance and limited economic gains rather than rational capital accumulation. Risks were shared in these spontaneous contests, as were their consequences.[31] Sharing risks rather than calculating or rationalizing their individual costs made one manly.

The contested meanings of manly risk-taking among working-class miners and middle-class stockbrokers were perhaps best expressed in the ways their respective fraternal organizations celebrated and rationalized risk-taking. For members of the Gold Hill Miners' Union (GHMU), the mutualistic sensibilities of working-class gambling contests informed the design and administration of the union's health benefits program. Founded in January 1867 and constitutionally dedicated to resisting the "tyrannical, oppressive power of capital," the GHMU soon pledged itself to paying the medical bills and funeral costs of every member injured or killed on the job. All of the risks and gambles underground were to be shared equally above ground. The only restriction in receiving benefits was at least two months of union membership. The financial ledger of the union between 1867 and 1870 provides a glimpse of the union's benefit program in action. Throughout these years, the union devoted the bulk of its strained resources to providing sick benefits to injured members. Miners paid monthly assessments to the union's sick fund and contributed additional amounts from their pockets at union meetings, mostly in the form of one- or two-dollar donations. Assessments and miners' donations were not clustered around Christmas or other "charitable" occasions, but were spread evenly throughout the year, reflecting the constant and demanding needs of the union's injured members.[33]

The mutualistic nature of the union's benefit program is brought into sharper relief when one considers the demographic character of Virginia City's working class. Like most miners in Virginia City and Gold Hill, members of the Comstock unions in 1870 were highly transient, only occasionally married, and usually propertyless.[33] The union's short residential requirement for membership and health benefits was ideally suited to its young, predominantly single male membership. The bulk of the union's resources was in fact directed toward providing aid to its single members rather than to married miners and their dependents. When the financial burden of paying its medical expenses threatened to bankrupt the unions in the fall of 1867, the unions resisted protecting the benefits of more permanent and settled members by lowering sick payments for all miners from ten to eight dollars a week. The benefits program was not a conservative institution, created to reward stable elements of the working class, as David Emmons found in his study of the Butte Miners' Union, but rather one that protected the health and mobility of all miners on the Comstock.[34]

The GHMU's connection to a working class that celebrated risk-taking and luck were reflected in the union's fund-raising efforts on behalf of its injured members. Like other fraternal organizations in Gold Hill, the GHMU's constitution stipulated that members had to be "men of good moral character," but only intoxication and profanity were deemed fineable offenses in the union's by-laws.[35] Prizefighting and gambling, by contrast, were morally acceptable or at least compatible with the union's mutualistic sensibilities; lotteries were central features of many union fund-raisers, as were shooting contests, card gambling, and cockfights. The birds and equipment for such activities were in all likelihood provided by James Orendorff, one of a half dozen honorary members of the union and owner of the largest and best-attended cock- and dogfighting pit in Gold Hill. By gambling together above ground, union members sought to overcome the unequal financial burdens faced by individual losers of the daily gamble underground. The union's adaptation of such popular forms of working-class leisure to its political project represented its own form of risk-rationalization, one that strengthened the mutualistic nature of risk-taking while also making its meaning potentially more oppositional.[36]

If miners' notions of manly risk-taking embodied aspects of their working-class identity, they also expressed their racialized identity as white men. Members of the Virginia City and Gold Hill Miners' Unions perceived

Chinese laborers as a grave threat to their independence, despite their demonstrated capacity for risk-taking and collective action during the great Union-Pacific railroad strike of 1867, during which thousands of Chinese workers put down their tools and demanded higher pay, an eight-hour day, and an abolition to whipping.[37] When eleven hundred of the same Chinese laborers were hired to build a railroad to Virginia City in the summer of 1869 by William Sharon, however, the Comstock unions published the following indictment of Chinese workers:

> Capital has decreed that Chinese shall supplant and drive hence the present race of toilers. . . . Can we compete with a barbarous race, devoid of energy and careless of the State's weal? Sunk in their own debasement, having no voice in government, how long would it be ere ruin would swamp the capitalist and poor man together?. . . We appeal to the working men to step to the front and hurl back the tide of barbarous invaders.[38]

This somewhat contradictory indictment of Chinese workers as both "barbarous" and "devoid of energy" was both racialized and gendered, one in which Chinese workers, rather than wage labor itself, threatened miners' independence and the civic order.[39] Chinese workers were not merely job competitors, but also embodiments of an unrepublican dependence caused by the evils of capitalism.[40] The Chinese could perform the degraded and emasculating work of laundry service, but only white miners were men enough to take the "real" gambles of underground wage work.

Risk had a sharply different shape and meaning for members of the Improved Order of Red Men, Pi-Ute Tribe No. 1, one of the most intriguing middle-class fraternal societies to appear in western Nevada. The Red Men were not in fact Paiute Indians, but a motley collection of more than fifty white stockbrokers, clerks, proprietors, and skilled craftsmen, nearly all of them married.[41] The Red Men's appropriation of Indian culture distinguished them from other middle-class fraternal groups in Nevada, but what the Red Men discovered in their mythic past was fundamentally similar. Like the Masons, the Red Men invoked an idealized past in which risk-taking and masculine hierarchies were secure and unquestioned. Some of these values were manifest in the tribe's internal structure. In order to become the Sachem or the Keeper of Wampum, a Red Man had first to acquire a hunter's degree, then a warrior's degree, and finally the chief's degree. Chiefs then became council members who elected the Sachem and the keeper of wampum and voted on whether braves became hunters or warriors became chiefs.[42]

If the Improved Order's internal hierarchy glorified a primitive and pristine world of male authority, as has been suggested by Mark Carnes, it simultaneously ritualized middle-class notions of risk and upward mobility. Promotion into the higher ranks of Red Men was something all deserving members could attain; the principal factors in a brave's promotion to hunter were prompt payment of all dues and promotional fees. Each new degree cost "five fathoms of wampum," or five dollars in gold specie.[43] Because the Red Men's cultural hierarchy was not built upon real economic competition, however, it guaranteed upward mobility to all participants willing to climb and metaphorically minimized the various risks of a capitalist economy. The Red Men's tribal structure thus preserved the attributes and signs of manly risk-taking while simultaneously eliminating some of the psychological consequences of failure.

The logic behind the Red Men's benefit program likewise revealed their attachment to middle-class notions of manhood and risk and highlighted the class-based differences between fraternal orders on the Comstock. Rather than sharing the costs of all risks equally, the Red Men sought to minimize the financial costs of sickness by making benefits proportional to one's rank and investment in the order. Although all injured members received sick pay, the order created a hierarchy of benefits, contingent upon each member's financial investment. Initiates who were sick or "unable to follow the hunt" received but five dollars a week, while chiefs received ten.[44] The order also sought to exclude individuals likely to become a drain on the tribe's financial resources. A committee on "character and fitness" checked the financial references, age, occupation, medical history, and current health condition of each applicant for membership. Men over fifty years of age, men in poor health, and men "without reputable means of support," such as gamblers, were considered high risks and excluded from the order.[45] Rather than share the financial consequences of sickness and injury, the Red Men sought to calculate its precise cost in "fathoms of wampum."

Attempts to rationalize risk in fathoms of wampum celebrated its own kind of irrationality, but the Red Men's approach to risk emblematized many of the ideological imperatives around which the middle class formed itself in the mid-nineteenth century. The Red Men's penchant for calculating the costs of benevolence was most clearly expressed by Virginia City's middle-class reformers. Conrad Wiegand, editor of the *People's Tribune*, led a crusade for the moral efficacy and efficiency of life insurance that crystallized his class's faith in the power of rational calculation.[46]

> To insure the life of one man would be a mere gambling speculation, but to insure 5 or 10 thousand lives, carefully selected, is perfectly safe . . . the rate of interest being fixed, the annual premiums can be determined to a mathematical certainty,[47] saying,

Like the Red Men, Wiegand possessed an abiding aversion to gambling and gamblers, who at least implicitly celebrated chance and irrational risk-taking. Luck and chance, ideas that the Gold Hill Miners' Union incorporated into its fund-raising activities, were anathema to the emerging system of industrial capitalism whose market laws and spirit of rational capital accumulation made gambling potentially subversive and unmanly. Peter Lynch, editor of the Gold Hill *Daily News,* exemplified this reasoning in an editorial entitled "What Is Luck?" Lynch answered his own question succinctly: "'luck' and 'ill-luck' are really a person's folly, laziness, or willful misapplication of means."[48] Like Lynch and Wiegand, the Red Men preferred to construct fraternity out of precise calculations and risk-free applicants rather than lotteries and cockfights.

If the health insurance programs of the GHMU and Improved Order of Red Men exemplified differences between working-class and middle-class manhood, they also revealed how racialized perceptions of risk were on the frontier. For the white men who were initiated into the Improved Order of Red Men, taking ritualized risks such as the initiation hunt was a racially transformative experience, in which "palefaces" became true Red Men. This process of racial crossing had its antecedents in other fraternal orders, but what is critical about the Red Men, as Philip Deloria has shown, is that they excluded Indians from these rituals of manly and racial transformation.[49] The right of racial "crossing" was reserved for white men only, as it was for white blackface actors throughout much of the country during the nineteenth century. This element of cultural power was vividly present among the Red Men of Carson City who took their lodge name from the local Paiute Indians, defeated by white soldiers just a decade before the Irish Red Men founded their tribe.[50] What is indeed remarkable about the Red Men of Nevada is how closely connected, temporally and spatially, their appropriation and homogenization of Paiute culture was to the actual military conquest of the Paiute Indians. For the Irish clerks who became warriors and keepers of wampum when the council fire was lit, the image of the fearless, risk-taking Paiute Indian affirmed their ability to be honorable risk-takers on the "frontier," despite there being little danger in these hunts and no resemblance to the actual culture of Paiute Indians.[51]

Although miners and middle-class Red Men rationalized risk in profoundly different ways, all classes of white men on the Comstock could, at celebrated moments, affirm a common identity as manly risk-takers. Paiute Indians played an important role in the construction of white manhood for both miners and middle-class professionals. This was perhaps best captured by their conspicuous role in Virginia City's Fourth of July parade of 1865. At the end of a long procession featuring several of Virginia City's fire companies and Irish ethnic societies came "a body of 27 Paiutes, mounted two by two, and led by young Winnemucca, the war chief himself, who rode barebacked with the left side of his face and clothing . . . painted with stripes of Red Ochre."[55] Here indeed was the image of a brave and fearless "Red Man" acceptable to the entire crowd of frontier enthusiasts. In his right hand, Winnemucca carried another symbol of the new risk-taking polity for which he found himself the mascot, the Paiute flag. Consisting of a reconstructed American flag with "two white arrows and a tomahawk" in place of the union stars, the flag evoked many of the risks of hunting, battle, and war that the palefaces of Carson City would soon ritualize when they became Red Men a few years later.[53] Miners and middle-class professionals alike celebrated this noble icon of risk, Winnemucca, who just five years before had been a savage antagonist to all white men in their heroic and manly struggle to conquer the West.

If images of risk provided opportunities for cross-class celebration and social harmony among white men, they also provoked dialogue between miners and capitalists over the true meaning of manly risk-taking and, by extension, of proper industrial relations. The different experience and meaning of risk to miners and capitalists prompted both conflict and cooperation between classes on the Comstock. In the fall of 1869, members of the Comstock unions temporarily blocked William Sharon's attempt to complete a railroad to Virginia City on the grounds that Chinese workers represented an unacceptable threat to miners' manhood. Yet just three weeks earlier, miners had pledged their financial support for the tunnel project of capitalist Adolph Sutro, whose enterprise would allegedly improve miners' safety underground. Whether the relationships between these charismatic capitalists and the Comstock unions were conflictual or cooperative, they revealed just how class-based the experience and meaning of manly risk-taking was for miners and capitalists on the industrial frontier.

Miners' perception of the Chinese as an unmanly threat to their independence sparked one of the sharpest confrontations between William Sharon and the Comstock Unions in Virginia City's history. When Chinese railroad workers neared completion of the railroad to Virginia City in July 1869, over three hundred members of the Comstock unions marched in military style to the edge of town and drove them from their camp. Miners refused to allow Chinese workers back to work until William Sharon signed an agreement that "barred him from employing Chinese within the limits of Virginia City and Gold Hill."[54] After signing the agreement, Sharon spoke to a crowd of 400 angry miners in Virginia City:

> We want *miners* and not Chinamen. They have no interest in the country, nor even in religion . . . and we can only employ them at menial service, inferior occupations, railroad grading, and that sort of thing.[55]

In mimicking miners' own republican criticism of the Chinese as citizenless threats to the civic order, Sharon reversed his outspoken defense of the merits of Chinese labor. In so doing, Sharon offered a concession to miners' racialized definition of manly risk-taking, one that worked to his political advantage but also placed limits on his power as an employer on the Comstock.

Sharon used his speech not merely to criticize the manhood of Chinese workers, however, but also to trumpet the providential power of capital. "There is a wrong feeling of antagonism," asserted Sharon, between miners and their employers. The interests of capital and labor were, Sharon declared, inextricably linked:

> Can there be mines or mills without capital? Is it not this very capital that pays four dollars a day to you miners?. . . Great God! Would you kill the goose that lays the golden egg?[56]

Sharon heralded the benefits that the railroad would bring to white workers in the form of reduced transportation costs, higher company profits, and higher wages. Like many nineteenth-century entrepreneurs, Sharon portrayed himself as an industrial hero whose financial investments and gambles were beneficial to the entire community, while casting his financial rival, Adolph Sutro, as an unmanly antihero.[57] "That penniless adventurer," asserted Sharon, "who does not pay a cent in taxes, wishes to make use of you to make himself rich." According to Sharon, Sutro was a man whose self-serving investments threatened miners' financial security. Asked Sharon, "How many men would the running of that tunnel employ at $4 a day, and how good is the security of your pay? I think you would rather have our paper than his."[58] In highlighting the security of his capital over Sutro's, Sharon implicitly recognized how serious miners' financial risks were, but he sought to deflect such hostility toward his "penniless" rival. Whatever their misgivings about Sharon, Comstock miners applauded his denunciation of Sutro and gave him "three rousing cheers," according to Lynch, himself an outspoken supporter of Sharon and the railroad.

The generous response of Comstock miners to William Sharon must be understood in a comparative context, however, for Adolph Sutro also received thunderous applause from Comstock unionists just three weeks before Sharon's speech. Since 1864, Sutro had unsuccessfully lobbied the federal government and bankers in San Fransisco, New York, and London for capital to begin construction on a four-mile-long drainage and ventilation tunnel underneath the Comstock Lode that would "liberate streams of wealth" from the earth.[59] When a fire razed Gold Hill's Yellow Jacket mine in July 1869, Sutro saw an opportunity to gain the financial and moral capital he so desperately needed. In September, Sutro addressed a crowd of four hundred miners at Piper's Opera House in Virginia City and called on them to buy stock in his great "cooperative association," the Sutro Tunnel Company. To the surprise of his friends and foes alike, union members heeded his exhortations and pledged to purchase fifty thousand dollars worth of stock in the project. Construction began just ten days later amid boisterous cheers, as Adolph Sutro himself took the first "swing of the pick," followed by James Phelan, president of the Virginia City Miners' Union.[60]

While William Sharon made concessions to miners' racist fears of Chinese workers above ground, Adolph Sutro adapted his oration to miners' class-based fears of physical injury.[61] "The most perfect ventilation would be insured" by the tunnel, stated Sutro, a facility that would also afford numerous exits from the Comstock mines should another fire trap miners under the surface. The broadside advertising Sutro's speech highlighted this message by portraying a beehive cross-section of two mines with workers dying in the lower levels of one for want of an appropriate exit while workers in the other escaped safely, with American flag in hand, through Sutro's tunnel.[62] Sutro described his project as the cornerstone of a "rational system of mining" that would not only improve miners' health and manhood, but also prolong the productive life of the mines themselves.

Sutro's appeal to working-class notions of manly risk-taking was as emotional as it was rational, however, particularly as he neared the conclusion of his three-hour oration. After discussing the scientific merits of his tunnel enterprise, Sutro condemned mine owners for their moral irresponsibility in the recent mine disaster, saying,

> Let me explain to you why they make you work in a foul
> atmosphere which sends half of you to your graves in the prime
> of manhood; let me show you why they allowed 42 of your miners
> to be foully murdered in the fire of Gold Hill for want of an exit
> through the tunnel; and let me show them to you in true colors,
> and hold them up to the shame, contempt, and ignominy they so
> richly deserve.[63]

Rather than blame the accident on miners' carelessness, as local newspaper editors and mine owners had done, Sutro placed the accident's onus upon the Bank of California. The antagonist in Sutro's republican morality play was not the degraded and unmanly Chinese worker, but William Sharon himself, whom he described as a "would-be-tyrant" and a "cancer on the body politic."[64] Implicit in Sutro's denunciation of Sharon was a distinction between the kinds of manly risks that miners and mine owners assumed; although Sharon frequently took financial risks in the name of the community's general welfare, such actions frequently cost miners their lives. William Sharon was, above all, a calculating capitalist, for whom miners' lives were a matter of profit and loss and whose imprudent financial risks ruined miners' physical health and "manhood."

Sutro also appealed to miners' sense of fair financial risk by attacking the Bank of California's manipulation of the Washoe Stock Exchange. Risking miners' wages on the local stock market was a no-win proposition, according to Sutro, because the Bank of California made tremendous amounts of money through its infamous "stock-jobbing" operations, keeping stock

prices artificially high or low by concealing information about the value of newly discovered ore bodies. Stated Sutro,

> A few of you make a good strike once in a while by sheer accident; that keeps up the excitement, and so you keep all gambling in stocks, paying your assessments, and in the end you will all be eaten up like the poor mouse. There is no guess work. It is a sure thing.[65]

In contrast to the Red Men and middle-class reformers, Sutro did not criticize the practice of gambling itself, but the fact that the Bank of California had changed the rules of the financial game. Sutro summed up this problem by asking miners a pointed question: "What show have you when the cards are stacked against you?"[66] Chance and luck, foundations of working-class manhood, were being destroyed by the Bank of California to the great detriment of Comstock miners.

Sutro's speech combined what seemed to be a defense of miners' traditional freedom to be risk-takers with a bold and potentially radical commitment to eliminating its negative physical and financial consequences. Sutro sought to make working-class notions of manly risk conform to the logic of his own middle-class vision of rational risk-taking: in short, to preserve the appearance of manly gambling, while minimizing its actual consequences. This combination produced a number of tensions within Sutro's speech; much of his rational system of mining, for example, incorporated the language of the speculative fever that had so recently "swept over Washoe county," as Mark Twain put it. Sutro boasted of the riches his tunnel would discover in terms that must have seemed familiar to miners accustomed to rumors of fabulous strikes:

> Were that tunnel completed today, a glorious reality, pouring out a silver stream of $40,000,000 or $50,000,000 per annum, these same capitalists who first want to eye the riches way down in the earth before they consent to invest, would be eager to enter similar undertakings and tunnelling would become the order of the day.[67]

In contrast to those literal-minded and timid capitalists, Sutro, like Sharon, portrayed himself as a true risk-taker, a man whom miners could respect and even emulate. Sutro cultivated this image by referring to himself as "an honest miner" in his speech, while on every piece of tunnel company stock he depicted himself in miners' clothing swinging a pick. Sutro's posture as a manly, risk-taking miner hardly squared with his wealthy financial background or his promises to eliminate risk, but it resonated with Comstock miners who defined their manhood, at least partially, in terms of the gambles they took daily.

If Sutro appropriated the same aspects of working-class manhood that Eliot Lord admired, he also framed his entrepreneurial ambitions in the language of labor radicalism during the Gilded Age.[68] Sutro portrayed his tunnel company as a unique answer to the vexing problems of dependence and insecurity wagework had generated on the frontier. Unlike Sharon's mining companies, which assessed stockholders the costs of investment and thus, according to Sutro, exploited "honest" working men, his tunnel company possessed only nonassessable stock. Explained Sutro, "the shares are unassailable forever so as to protect the poor men; one share is as secure as a thousand . . . . In buying a share in the concern you absolutely own it; nobody can ever assess you one cent." Buying tunnel company stock would not only eliminate financial risk, but ultimately entitle miners to collective ownership and control of the Comstock Lode itself. All financial investments in the tunnel would, according to Sutro, "be expended directly again in labor among yourselves *under your own direction* and from dependents you will become masters." Investment in the tunnel company promised miners not only a safer work environment and financial security, but a radical victory over capital itself. "It will be the most glorious triumph of labor over capital," proclaimed Sutro, a scheme that "would . . . realize the wildest dreams of the French Socialists, Proudhon, Le Blanc, and others." Capital would not be destroyed, but liberated and harnessed by working men, whose power would become, for the first time, "unlimited."[69]

In attempting to harness working-class ideologies and manhood to his tunnel project, Sutro misperceived the importance of risk to miners' gendered sense of independence and militancy. For Comstock union members, the consequences of their underground gambles could be shared among other white miners, but the risks themselves could not and perhaps should not be eliminated. Union-organized lotteries celebrated not merely chance, but miners' ability to take risks and assume responsibility for the consequences. Sutro, by contrast, sought to eliminate risk altogether, much as the Red Men sought to minimize it with their "committee on character and fitness." Sutro's claim that mine owners alone bore responsibility for preserving miners' safety suggested that miners were dependent upon their employers for something more than their four-dollar daily wage. Notions of employer liability, which had gained considerable popularity among anthracite coal miners in Pennsylvania by 1870, remained nascent at best in Virginia City because such ideas challenged Comstock miners' control over the contours of miners' health and manhood.[70] How to rationalize the financial burdens of miners' injuries, and how to control who took the manly gambles of underground wagework were questions of exclusive union purview, questions that had undergirded the unions' rise to power.

Given the grandiose nature of Sutro's claims, it is difficult not to perceive a degree of opportunism in his speech. Rarely, after all, did Sutro mention the improved safety features of his tunnel project when seeking support from middle-class and professional audiences. Instead, he emphasized the tremendous wealth the tunnel would "liberate." Middle-class critics of Sutro's tunnel scheme, such as Lynch, certainly thought he was insincere, labelling his attempt to sell miners tunnel company stock "one of the most bare-faced swindles in history."[71] Yet to infer from such evidence that Sutro had merely "duped" miners would distort the political and cultural context in which both Sutro and Sharon made their speeches to the Comstock unions. The seeming popularity of these risk-taking capitalists was not "delusional," as Anthony Wallace suggested in his study of the Pennsylvania mining community of St. Clair.[72] Rather, Comstock miners exploited their own notions of manly financial and physical risks to their advantage as a class of skilled white men, playing Virginia City's capitalists off one another whenever occasions arose. While miners applauded Sutro's denunciation of Sharon as a "cancer on the body politic" one week, they loudly cheered Sharon's excoriation of Sutro as a "penniless adventurer" the next.[74] What Sharon and Sutro offered Comstock miners was not cooptation, but concessions to different aspects of miners' own racialized and class-based understanding of manly risk-taking.

At the conclusion of his study of the Comstock, Eliot Lord remarked that mining was "the only business pursuit . . . where skill, energy, foresight, and industry, aided by ample capital, will not command a measure of success." The business of mining was a business of gambling, according to Lord, in which "ordinary economies of business management are often looked upon as petty details."[74] Lord's explanation for this was largely environmental; the geology of the Comstock Lode, with its scattered pockets of ore, made a truly "rational" or scientific system of mining nearly impossible. The existence of a pervasive ethos of risk-taking in Virginia City was thus a by-product of the land itself. Over a decade before Frederick Jackson Turner published his famous essay, Lord believed that the mining frontier had remade its inhabitants, turning one and all, miners and mine-owners, Irish and Chinese, men and women, into gamblers.

Yet if Lord accurately assessed the impact of geology on the emergence of a "speculative character" in Virginia City, he fundamentally misperceived the ideological complexity of risk on the frontier. All residents of the Comstock may indeed have gambled, but the nature and meaning of their risks varied tremendously. The experience of manly risk-taking that changed and helped define class consciousness on the industrial frontier provides one aspect of that cultural history. The emergence of a middle-class moral economy that condemned miners' penchant for risk-taking above and below ground was part of a process of class formation on the Comstock, a contest that was never fully complete nor won by the Improved Order of Red Men or capitalists such as William Sharon. The manly gambles miners assumed, however irrational to middle-class observers, were crucial to the strength and political militancy of working-class manhood in Nevada; these risks fundamentally distinguished miners from their middle-class fraternal brothers. Working-class notions of acceptable risk, rooted in the very real insecurities of underground wagework and developed above ground in saloons and union-sponsored lotteries, could lead miners to exclude non-white workers from their ranks or to support the manly gamble of a charismatic capitalist. But such actions strengthened rather than weakened miners' commitment to a working-class moral economy that celebrated mutuality, manhood, whiteness, and the power of chance.

Class, gender, and race struggles were thus critical parts of the frontier's evolution, both as a physical place and an idea. Images of risk, such as the fearless Paiute Indian, were not crude vehicles of class struggle, nor were such images "owned" by any particular class of people on the Comstock. Such images often stimulated cross-class celebrations of the frontier in Virginia City and Gold Hill, but risk-taking remained an activity that fomented considerable discussion and disagreement over the boundaries and meaning of social class and manhood on the Comstock. If class relations shaped the frontier's development, the idea of the frontier—with its mythologies of white manhood, mobility, and risk—likewise exerted a powerful effect upon the ways people thought about class relations. For wage-earning miners, the impact of the frontier was not necessarily disillusioning, as Carlos Schwantes, Melvyn Dubofsky, and Richard Slotkin have variously suggested, but also potentially empowering.[75] Miners on the Comstock were remarkably successful in establishing a tradition of frontier labor militancy—a tradition, both radical and racist, that future generations of western workers would struggle to defend as the experience and meaning of manly risk underwent continual change and redefinition.

Notes

I would like to thank Matt Basso for sheperding this essay through the publicity process, and the *Journal of Social History* for allowing it to be reprinted.

1 . Eliot Lord, *Comstock Mining and Manners*, U.S. Geological Survey, vol. 4 (Washington: G.P.O., 1883)1 405.

2 . For a discussion of the accident rates on the Comstock Lode and their causes, see Lord, 385–86.

3 . For an excellent discussion of the middle class's ambivalence toward risk-taking and gambling in the nineteenth century, see Ann Fabian, *Card Sharps, Dream Books, and Bucket Shops: Gambling in Nineteenth-Century America* (Ithaca, N.Y.: Cornell University Press, 1990).

4 . Much of Eliot Lord's middle-class veneration of working-class manliness was imbued with overtones of homoeroticism. Take, for example, Lord's description of miners' work conditions underground: "View their work! . . . The men throw off their clothes at once. Only a light breech-cloth covers their hips, and thick-soled shoes protect their feet from the scorching rocks and steaming rills of water which trickle over the floor of the levels. Except for these coverings they toil naked, with heavy drops of sweat starting from every pore" (Lord, 389). For a fine discussion of the connections between homoeroticism and cross-class relations in the Gilded Age, see Michael Moon's provocative essay "'The Gentle Boy from the Dangerous Classes': Pederasty, Domesticity, and Capitalism in Horatio Alger," *Representations* 19 (summer 1987): 87–110.

5 . Fabian, 5.

6 . The term *frontier* describes the earliest phase of Anglo-American colonization in the West during which whites, Indians, Mexicans, and blacks struggled to gain control of the land's resources. The frontier was both a process of conquest and the place where such political and economic struggles occurred. I will also discuss the frontier as an idea, particularly when examining the ideologies that defined and legitimated white people's conquest of the West. My definition of the frontier owes much to Patricia Limerick's formulation of western history in *The Legacy of Conquest* (New York: W. W. Norton, 1987), but preserves the usefulness of the term *frontier* and the important notion of process imbedded within it. I do not mean to suggest that Frederick Jackson Turner's progression from "savagery to civilization" was indeed correct. Rather, I mean to highlight the importance of historical processes—conquest and capitalism—in writing western social history. For an excellent discussion of Turner's potential use to western social historians, see William Cronon's essay "Revisiting the Vanishing Frontier: The Legacy of Frederick Jackson Turner," *Western Historical Quarterly* 18 (April 1987): 157–76.

7. See Frederick Jackson Turner, "The Significance of the Frontier in American History," in *Annual Report of the American Historical Association for the Year 1893*, 1894. Mining historian Rodman Paul rejected the cultural components of Turner's vision of western development, emphasizing instead the various roles of technology, geology, and the market. In so doing, however, Paul reified the market and tech-

nology as objective historical "facts" that defined the contours of western mining, while neglecting the social relations embodied within these terms. We know little, for example, about how different perceptions of risk influenced the economic and technological development of western mining towns. Although the scattered geography of silver and gold ore in the Comstock Lode contributed to Virginia City's "speculative mania" and cross-cultural celebrations of risk, it by no means defined how different groups of people perceived risk and struggled to rationalize its varied consequences. See Rodman Paul, *Mining Frontiers of the Far West, 1849–1880* (Berkeley and Los Angeles: University of California Press, 1963).

8 . See Carlos Schwantes, "The Concept of the Wageworkers' Frontier: An American-Canadian Perspective," in *The Western Historical Quarterly*, 18 (January 1987): 39–55. The most notable exception to this generality is Richard Slotkin's *The Fatal Environment: The Myth of the Frontier in the Age of Industrialization, 1800–1880* (New York: Atheneum, 1985), in which he argues that the frontier and capitalism have been inextricably bound together. Writes Slotkin, "the frontier myth and its ideology are founded on the desire to avoid recognition of the perilous consequences of capitalist development in the New World, and they represent a displacement or deflection of social conflict into the world of myth" (47).

9 . See Melvyn Dubofsky, *We Shall Be All: A History of the Industrial Workers of the World* (New York, 1971).

10 . See Dubofsky, "The Origins of Western Working-Class Radicalism, 1890–1905," *Labor History* 7 (spring 1966): 131–54.

11 . See William Cronon, George Miles, and Jay Gitlin, "Becoming West: Toward a New Meaning for Western History," in *Under an Open Sky: Rethinking America's Western Past* (New York: W. W. Norton, 1992), 20–21. Notwithstanding their problematic periodization of "self-shaping" identities, Cronon, Miles, and Gitlin go much further in making material processes such as "market making" and class formation central to any conceptualization of western history.

12 . Anthony Wallace's study of the mining community of St. Clair offers some constructive avenues for exploring the historical importance of risk-taking on the Comstock Lode. Wallace argues that mine owners' penchant for taking risks led them to ignore safety measures that would have greatly increased the profitability and longevity of their coal mining enterprises. In so doing, he skillfully illuminates how mine owners' "risk-seeking" ideology shaped the context of technological innovation in ways that did not conform to presentist notions of rational choice theory, market "laws," and technological efficiency. See Wallace, *St. Clair: A Nineteenth Century Coal Town's Experience with a Disaster-Prone Industry* (New York: Knopf, 1981).

13 . See Wallace's discussion of the "delusional" nature of "risk-seeking" ideologies among coal miners in Pennsylvania, in *St. Clair*, 258–61. Richard Slotkin reaches a similar conclusion about the "frontier myth" in *The Fatal Environment* (47), arguing that it was, by definition, "a deflection of social conflict," a "substitute" for real class formation.

14 . Gender and race figured prominently in the process of working-class formation on the frontier, but this essay is not primarily a study of gender and race relations in Virginia City. For a fine study of prostitution in Virginia City that sheds light on the complexities of risk for frontier women, see Marion Goldman's *Gold-Diggers and Silver Miners: Prostitution and Social Life on the Comstock Lode* (Ann Arbor: University of Michigan Press, 1981).

15 . Mark Twain, *Roughing It* (New York: Viking Press, 1984), 751–52.

16 . During the worst five months of the 1864 depression, for example, the size of the Savage Mining Company's workforce nearly doubled from 115 to 213. The consolidation and expansion of silver production on the Comstock required expensive machinery and large workforces for constructing deep shaft mines and smelting plants. Records of the Savage Mining Company, Payroll Records, Beinecke Library (BL), Yale University.

17 . See Richard E. Lingenfelter, *Hardrock Miners: A History of the Mining Labor Movement in the American West, 1863–1893* (Berkeley and Los Angeles: University of California Press, 1974): 30–32.

18. Male Occupation Holders, Gold Hill, 1870

Occupation	Number	% of Whole	Wealth	% Owning Home	% Married
Unskilled	69	26.7	$ 39	6	8
Miners	111	43.0	$ 132	18	18
Skilled Trades	40	15.5	$1,229	33	33
Professional	38	14.8	$1,698	26	26

The above figures were calculated from a one-in-ten random sample of all occupation holders in Gold Hill, Nevada. (*Ninth Federal Census of the United States Government,* 1870, Storey County, Nevada.)

19. RESIDENTIAL AND OCCUPATIONAL MOBILITY, GOLD HILL, NEVADA

Occupation	1862–1863			1864–1868[*]		
		% Persisting	% Changing Jobs		% Persisting	% Changing Jobs
Unskilled	(9)	67	56	(15)	61	0
Miners	(25)	23	22	(49)	67	4
Skilled trades	(19)	25	50	(42)	72	21
Professional	(19)	74	35	(31)	70	3
TOTAL	(72)	42	36	(137)	68	5

[*] These figures represent the average annual persistence and mobility rates between 1864 and 1868. The figures in parentheses represent the number sampled. All statistics are based on a one-in-ten random sampling of occupation holders in the Gold Hill City directories of 1862, 1863, 1864, and 1868. The occupational sampling of the city directories yields a slightly different occupational structure than does the census of 1870. The smaller percentage of miners might be due to their higher residential mobility combined with the greater thoroughness in counting of the federal census takers.

20. Eliot Lord provides a grim summary of the number of deaths and injuries on the Comstock between 1863 and 1880. Calculations from his figures indicate that 7.8 per thousand workers died underground annually in the Comstock mines. This remarkably high rate was nearly four times the fatality rate for coal miners in England and higher even than Pennsylvania's anthracite region, where 7.1 miners per thousand perished each year during the same period. (Lord, 385–86; and Wallace, 250–251.)

21. Gold Hill *Daily News*, February 2, 1867, 3.

22. Although mining accidents were common occurrences on the Comstock, few companies went bankrupt because of them, in contrast to Pennsylvania's anthracite region. See Wallace's chapter entitled "The Politics of Safety," esp. 258–61. For an insightful treatment of the consolidation and comparative stability of mine ownership on the Comstock see Paul, *Mining Frontiers of the Far West,* and Lingenfelter, *Hardrock Miners.*

23. Gold Hill *Daily News*, April 12, 1869, 2–3.

24. Lord, 73.

25. My analysis of the occupational makeup of the Washoe Stock Exchange was compiled by cross-referencing the names of its traders with their stated occupations in the city directories of Virginia City and Gold Hill. Many of the stockbrokers listed two residences in the directory, one on the Comstock and the other in San Francisco. See *First Directory of the Nevada Territory, 1862,* 306ff., and *Second Directory of the Nevada Territory, 1863,* 33–35: (Virginia City: Territorial Enterprise Printing Office, 1862 and 1863). For a better understanding of the professional and urban character of the local stock exchange, see its weekly publication *The Washoe Stock Circular,* which published detailed lists of all company stocks in San Fransisco and Nevada as well as the amount and date of all assessments levied by mining companies in the region. *The Washoe Stock Circular,* May 25, 1864, Vol. no. 3, Bancroft Library, Berkeley California.]

26. Women remained a small minority in Virginia City and Gold Hill throughout the 1860s and well into the 1870s, despite the increasing numbers of married couples in the community. In 1870, fully 84 percent of all occupation holders in Virginia City and Gold Hill were male, and 82 percent of them were single (*Ninth Census of the United States for the State of Nevada,* Storey County.)

27. Although gambling on the Comstock quickly became the stuff of western myth, descriptions of these folkloric contests were not entirely removed from the community's industrial transformation. Eliot Lord's description of gambling, for example, is flavored with references to industrial mining: "Little stacks of gold fringed the monte carlo tables and glittered beneath the swinging lamps. A ceaseless din of boisterous talk, oaths, and laughter spread from the open doors into the streets. The rattle of dice, coin, balls, and spinning markers, the flapping of greasy cards and the chorus of calls and interjections went on day and night." Gambling in Virginia City, much like the ore stamps under its streets, produced a "ceaseless din," "day and night," replete with its own "grease" and "rattling."

28. For a provocative but somewhat romanticized discussion of the competitive and mutualistic nature of working-class male culture in the mid-nineteenth century, see Eliot Gorn's "'Good-Bye Boys, I Died a True American': Homicide, Nativism, and Working-Class Culture in Antebellum New York City," *Journal of American History* 74 (September 1987): 388–410. See also Gorn's brief discussion of prize-fighting in Virginia City in *The Manly Art: A History of Bare-Knuckle Prize Fighting in America* (Ithaca, N.Y.: Cornell University Press, 1985), 174.

29. Gold Hill *Daily News*, February 2, 1867, 3.

30. For a fine discussion of working-class male violence and its connections to domestic abuse, see Pamela Haag's "The 'Ill-Use of a Wife': Working-Class Violence in Domestic and Public New York City, 1860–1880," *Journal of Social History,* 25, no. 3 (spring 1992): 447–78.

31. My distinction between "alternative" and "oppositional" working-class cultures rests on Roy Rosenzweig's discussion of the saloon and working-class mutualism in *Eight Hours for What we Will: Workers and Leisure in an Industrial City, 1870–1920* (Cambridge: Cambridge University Press 1985), 223. My analysis of the reciprocal nature of working-class gambling also owes much to the work of Ann Fabian, *Card Sharps*, 3, 142–50. For a more theoretical discussion of reciprocal economies, see Marshall Sahlins, *Stone Age Economics* (Chicago: University of Chicago Press, 1972).

32. The unions' commitment to preserving miners' health was part of its original constitution and was subsequently adopted by the Virginia City Miners' Union when it was formed on July 4, 1867. See the *Constitution, By-Laws, and Rules of Order of the Miners' Union of Gold Hill* (Virginia City: Territorial Printing Office, 1867), 1. Evidence of the financial burdens of the GHMU's health program was gleaned from the union ledger book which lists all financial transactions and income of the union, including assessments levied and benefits paid (Ledger Book of the Gold Hill Miner's Union, 1867–1870, BL).

33. A comparison of the residential persistence rates of members of the Gold Hill Miner's Union with all miners in Gold Hill in 1870 reveals little difference. In contrast to Butte, Montana, where the local union was dominated by a "stable" portion of the working class, principally home-owning miners with families, the GHMU consisted primarily of single men whose persistence rates were virtually indistinguishable from the mining population at large in 1870. For a discussion of persistence and mobility among Butte miners, see David Emmons, *The Butte Irish: Class and Ethnicity in an American Mining Town, 1875–1925* (Urbana: University of Illinois Press, 1989), 142ff.

PERSISTENCE RATES IN GOLD HILL

	Gold Hill Union Members (109)[*]	All Miners in Gold Hill(111)
% Married	26	19
% Home Owners	20	18
% Annually Persistent	68	67

[*] These statistics were compiled by cross-referencing union membership records with the federal census of 1870 in Gold Hill. Persistence rates of union members were based upon a one-in-ten sample of occupation holders in the Gold Hill City directories of 1864, 1868, and 1871.

34. Emmons, 142; For a discussion of the financial necessity of lowering union sick benefits, see Lingenfelter, 51.

35. *Constitution, By-Laws, and Rules of Order of the Miners' Union of Gold Hill*, BL, 5.

36. Gold Hill Miners' Union, Records of the Picnic Committee, September 6, 1875; Gold Hill *Daily News*, September 19, 1867, 3; and Lingenfelter, 51; My suggestion that James Orendorff, saloon proprietor and owner of Gold Hill's cockfighting pit, provided birds and equipment for union fund-raisers is based upon the fact that he possessed a remarkably close association with the union as one of only five honorary members initiated between 1867 and 1870, and one of the only nonminers in the union (Records of the Gold Hill Miners' Union, Ledger Book, 1867–1870, BL).

37. See David Montgomery's discussion of the strike in *The Fall of the House of Labor: The Workplace, the State, and American Labor Activism, 1865–1925* (Cambridge: Cambridge University Press, 1987), 67–68.

38. Gold Hill *Daily News*, July 7, 1869.

39. For a fine analysis of the economic and cultural roots of anti-Chinese racism among California miners during the Gold Rush and after, see Alexander Saxton, *The Indispensable Enemy: Labor and the Anti-Chinese Movement in California* (Berkeley and Los Angeles: University of California Press, 1971).

40. As David Roediger and Alexander Saxton have convincingly demonstrated, the specter of "wage slavery" was as much a racial threat as a problem of class. See David Roediger's *The Wages of Whiteness: Race and the Making of the American Working Class* (London: Verso, 1991), 117–19. See also Alexander Saxton, *The Rise and Fall of the White Republic: Class Politics and Mass Culture in Nineteenth-Century America* (London: Verso, 1990).

41. A complete membership list of the order was appended to its first published by-laws and constitution in 1871. See *Constitution, By-Laws, and Rules of Order of Pi-Ute Tribe No. 1, Improved Order of Red Men* (Carson City, Nev.: Carson City Printing Office, 1871), 26: BL. A cross-referencing of these names with the Virginia City directory of 1871 revealed an occupational structure very similar to the Masons:

FRATERNAL ORDER	% Professional	% Skilled	% Miner	% Unskilled
Red Men, Pi-Ute Tribe No. 1 (51)	79	19	2	0
Masons, Virginia City Lodge (32)	88	12	0	0

42. See the Red Men's *Constitution*, 4–8. For an analysis of the gendered meanings of the Red Men's initiation ceremonies, see Mark Carnes's *Secret Ritual and Manhood in Victorian America* (New Haven: Yale University Press, 1989), 98–99. Carnes argues that fraternalism was principally a gendered phenome-

non in which "fraternal ritual provided solace and pyschological guidance during young men's troubled passage to manhood in Victorian America." Carnes makes few if any distinctions between middle-class and working-class fraternal groups and consequently denigrates the importance of changing class relations in shaping this "passage." The middle-class bias of many recent studies of manhood and masculinity is explored at some length by Clyde Griffen in his "Reconstructing Masculinity from the Evangelical Revival to the Waning of Progressivism: A Speculative Synthesis," in *Meanings for Manhood*, ed. Mark Carnes and Clyde Griffen (Chicago: University of Chicago Press, 1990), 183–205.

43. Red Men's *Constitution*, 11–12.

44. Red Men's *Constitution*, 19.

45. Red Men's *Constitution*, 9.

46. For a fine analysis of the middle class's resistance and eventual conversion to the merits of life insurance, see Viviana Zelizer, *Morals and Markets: The Development of Life Insurance in the United States* (New York: Columbia University Press, 1979).

47. *The People's Tribune*, March 1870 (Gold Hill, Nevada), 20, (BL).

48. Gold Hill *Daily News*, April 9, 1867, 3.

49. Philip Deloria, "White Sachems and Red Masons," unpublished paper delivered to the American Studies Association, Baltimore, November 1991.

50. For a history of the Paiute tribe in western Nevada, see Martha C. Knack and Omer C. Stewart, *As Long as the River Shall Run: An Ethnohistory of Pyramid Lake Indian Reservation* (Berkeley and Los Angeles: University of California Press, 1984). For a folkloric account of the Paiute Indian war of 1860 and Chief Winnemucca's defeat, see Ferol Egan, *Sand in a Whirlwind: The Paiute Indian War of 1860* (New York: Doubleday, 1972).

51. For Virginia City's actual Paiute Indians, risk-taking was an activity sharply circumscribed by the racialized definitions of risk that Red Men and other middle-class white men cherished. Like the Chinese, no Paiute Indians were allowed to take the manly gambles of underground wagework. Indians were allowed to gamble what money they had in Virginia City's saloons, but they were condemned for so doing by middle-class professionals. When newspaper editor Peter Lynch saw some Paiute boys gambling on the street in 1867, he was particularly disturbed by "the earnestness with which the children of the forest entered the spirit of gambling." These children were no longer noble, but tragic figures to Lynch, incapable of ever assuming the heroic risks that "real" Paiute Indians were supposed to take. Gold Hill *Daily News*, March 29, 1867, 3.

52. *The Celebration of the 88th Anniversary of the Declaration of Independence, July 4, 1865* (San Fransisco: Francis Valentine and Company, 1865), 4–6, BL.

53. If the Paiutes in procession were aware of the restricted symbolic space they had been allotted, it also seems they understood some of its ironies and pushed these boundaries with their own figure of racial crossing. Besides Winnemucca, only one other Indian wore paint in the procession, an old man who "daubed his hair and face with white paint in a peculiar manner." Although the reporter for the *Territorial Enterprise* who wrote the parade account "did not understand the reason" for this, it suggests that the Paiutes were indeed capable of taking chances, but in ways that potentially subverted the racialized images of risk and power thrust upon them by parade planners.

54. Lord, 355–57; Gold Hill *Daily News*, July 7, 1869, 3; and Saxton, 59–60.

55. Gold Hill *Daily News*, October 7, 1869, 3.

56. Gold Hill *Daily News*, October 7, 1869, 3.

57. For a fine analysis of the industrialist as hero, see the discussion of capitalist Matthew Carey's popularity among Pennsylvania anthracite miners in Wallace, 258–61.

58. Gold Hill *Daily News*, October 7, 1869, 3.

59. For a discussion of the tunnel's "scientific" merits, see the pamphlet of Sutro's chief engineer and architect, Ferdinand Baron Richthofen, *The Comstock Lode: Its Character and the Probable Mode of Its Continuance in Depth* (San Fransisco: Town and Bacon Printers, 1866), 3, BL.

60. Joseph Aron, *History of a Great Work and an Honest Miner*, (San Fransisco, 1891), 14 BL; and Virginia City *Territorial Enterprise*, September 22, 1869, 1. Much of Sutro's speech was adopted from his recently published pamphlet, *The Sutro Tunnel Company to the Comstock Lode in the State of Nevada: Importance of its Construction and Revenue to Be Derived Therefrom*, (New York, 1866), BL.

61. Historians have noted Sutro's popularity with the Comstock unions and have correctly attributed this to his outspoken support for improving miners' safety and welfare underground. See, for example, Richard Lingenfelter's *Hardrock Miners*, which places Sutro's popularity within the context of the union's opposition to the Bank of California. See also Mary and Robert Stewart, *Adolph Sutro: A Biography* (Berkeley: Howell-North, 1962), which describes Sutro's campaign for miners' safety as a reflection of his paternal goodness. Both works treat the issue of miners' safety as a pragmatic and nonideological issue, however, and consequently did not explore the impact or significance of working-class notions of risk.

62. For a reproduction of the broadside, see George Lyman's history of the Comstock Lode, *Ralston's Ring: California Plunders the Comstock Lode* (New York: Charles Scribner & Sons, 1937), 147.

63. Aron, 14.

64. Relations between Sutro and William Sharon had not always been so antagonistic. In 1867, Sutro enjoyed the support of most local mining superintendents and the Bank of California for his tunnel enterprise. Sharon himself predicted in the winter of 1867 that "the entire world of mining engineers and engineering capitalists" would soon envy Sutro's tunnel (Gold Hill *Daily News*, January 30, 1867, 2). Sharon abruptly withdrew his support, however, when he learned that Sutro was planning to "tax" every ton of ore moved through the tunnel. When Sutro subsequently announced his plan to build a town at the tunnel's mouth that would displace the bank's milling operations in Virginia City, Sharon's hostility became elevated to a matter of republican principles. In the summer of 1867, Sharon's lawyer, Isaac Requa, stated that the "Sutro Tunnel project . . . will destroy private property." Isaac Requa, *Sutro Tunnel Remonstrance* (New York, 1867), BL.

65. Aron, 14.

66. Aron, 15.

67. Aron, 13.

68. The complex fusion of corporate and individualistic ideologies in his "cooperative" tunnel company emblematized many of the transitions middle-class American culture was experiencing in the 1860s. See Alan Trachtenberg's fine discussion of the contested emergence of the corporation in America, *The Incorporation of America: Culture and Society in the Gilded Age* (Cambridge, Mass.: Harvard University Press, 1982).

69. Aron, 15.

70. Wallace, 265ff.

71. Gold Hill *Daily News*, September 27, 1869, 2: It is difficult to surmise accurately the reaction of Virginia City and Gold Hill's small middle class to Sutro's tunnel plan. Although Sutro's "rational" system of mining was certainly rooted in a number of middle-class assumptions, Lynch's hostility to the tunnel scheme may have reflected the fact that William Sharon owned the Gold Hill *Daily News* in 1869.

72. Although Wallace successfully explored how the "risk-seeking" ideology of mining capitalists led them to ignore more economical safety measures, he analyzed risk-taking primarily as a financial activity dominated by mine owners only. How risks varied by occupation, how miners responded to a spectrum of physical and financial risks, and how their racialized and class-based definitions of acceptable risk shaped mine owners' own financial gambles remain neglected aspects of his project.

73. Gold Hill *Daily News*, October 7, 1869, 3: and Aron, 14. Miners' critical distance upon Adolph Sutro's "cooperative association" frequently manifested itself during the tunnel's nine-year construction, as miners protested Sutro's paternalistic attempts to rationalize miners' health care. When Sutro attempted to deduct the costs of a tunnel company doctor from miners' wages in 1870 and 1873, miners "remonstrated a good deal against it" and forced Sutro to adopt a voluntary risk-sharing plan. When Sutro tried to rationalize the consequences of death itself by building a cemetery near the mouth of the recently completed tunnel in 1878, union miners vehemently protested that "it would be too lonely for the poor fellow" and buried their deceased friends in Virginia City for the traditional union ceremony. Adolph Sutro, *The Sutro Tunnel: An Address Before the Bullion Club*, delivered November 6, 1879 (New York, 1879), BL Such incidents highlight the critical differences between Sutro's and miners' notions of acceptable risk and miners' success in defending their own moral economy of acceptable risks.

74. Lord, 360–61.

75. See Schwantes, "The Concept of the Wageworkers' Frontier," 40; Dubofsky, "The Origins of Western Working-Class Radicalism," 131–32; and Slotkin, *The Fatal Environment*, 47.

Cool to the End

Public Hangings and
Western Manhood

Durwood Ball

On April 21, 1861, the sheriff of San Miguel County hanged Paula Angel from a cottonwood tree outside Las Vegas, New Mexico Territory. According to court testimony, she had concealed a butcher knife, let Miguel Martin embrace her, and stabbed him to death. The all-male jury convicted Angel of murder, and Judge Kirby Benedict sentenced her to death. Consumed by the outbreak of the Civil War, no newspaper covered the hanging, and the governor overlooked or ignored commuting the death sentence.[1]

However, oral history recalls malevolence and tragedy. During the death watch, Sheriff Herrera declared his intention to execute Angel each time he passed her cell, and the tormented woman wasted away to a skeleton. On the appointed day, a hundred or so people flocked to the hanging tree. Herrera drove a kicking and screaming Angel onto the wagon bed, placed the noose around her neck, and threw the rope over a tree limb. When he cracked the whip, several men checked the horses and pleaded with him to stop. They claimed that, hanged enough in the eyes of the law, Angel ought to be spared, but the indignant sheriff swore to shoot anyone who got in his way. Stepping forth from the crowd, militia colonel J. D. Sena harangued the onlookers not to interfere, and Angel was legally hanged.[2]

Whether Herrera really prosecuted a personal vendetta is unclear from available records and accounts, but killing women, the weaker sex—legally, even—was an unmanly act in Euro-America. For women depended on the beneficence, charity, and chivalry of their men to survive and prosper. In the social bargain, women tamed their men's animal nature and civilized them for social good.[3] The residents of San Miguel County, horrified by Angel's hanging, tried to acquit their acquiescence by creating an evil sheriff and a compliant militia colonel in oral legend. Although New Mexico territorial courts had convicted numerous women of murder, governors had always commuted their death sentences. Sheriff Herrera might have vainly awaited the governor's commutation to save him from strangling a woman, albeit legally. Under Mexican rule, he could have opened the jail cell and told Angel to leave town, but the United States territorial system was much more vigilant, and Herrera may have feared Judge Benedict's prosecution for contempt.[4] The entire community hanged Paula Angel, though undoubtebly with regret and remorse.

In Victorian America, public hangings were a ritual test of manhood. Throughout Europe and the Americas, the vast majority of violent offenders were (and still are) male. Likewise, men bore the brunt of harsh sentences and legal executions for violent crimes, manslaughter and homicide specifically. Victorian America and Europe generally believed that men, innately passionate, aggressive, and licentious, were a genuine danger to the community, unless society—and men themselves—regulated their beastly instincts. A male's proscription of his savage urges was an act of manhood; society's legally strangling a murderer was a ritual of civilization. In the Victorian world, society equated civilization with manliness. At the same time, however, western judicial systems steadily eased the sentences of women convicted of murder, particularly in cases of husband killing and infanticide. Woman's inherent nature was to nurture her family and society—to give life. If she killed her husband or baby, she was considered to have been driven to insanity by spousal abuse or neglect, or desperate poverty.[5] These trends and beliefs applied equally to the far Southwest of the United States in the nineteenth and early twentieth centuries.

In the Victorian American West, a man sentenced to die by hanging was paraded before the public through the newspapers. Columnists and editors closely monitored the condemned man from the time of verdict and sentencing to the execution. Their focus was his manhood and masculinity under the strain of the ultimate male test: going to certain death. To Victorians, manliness at the threshold of death was equal to manhood in the flush of life. Seizing on a juicy story, journalists readily impugned weaklings and braggarts but extolled the man who combined moral and physical courage to create unflappable cool. The legal victim who was cool to the end admitted his guilt, embraced the verdict, accepted his fate, and calmly crossed to the other side like a good, brave man.[6]

A colloquial expression during most of the nineteenth century, the word *cool* carried two meanings. First, it connoted impertinence, impudence, and audaciousness delivered with dispassion and calm. Second, it indicated a lack of enthusiasm and ardor. However, a third definition directly related to the usage of the word here enjoyed a long history in the English language; "not heated by passion or emotion; unexcited, dispassionate; deliberate, not hasty; undisturbed, calm." The cool man was was "composed, collected, unruffled, imperturbable, nonchalant." Under stressful, tumultuous, and even terrifying conditions, he maintained his composure. His self-control was not a demonstration of cold dispassion but an exercise of manly courage.[7]

My analysis of the legal hangings in New Mexico and Arizona Territories between 1864 and 1910 includes no lynchings. No less revealing of manhood and masculinity, they are distinctly spontaneous, extralegal forms of violence, often racially motivated, a lethal exorcism of perceived social and cultural trespass.[8] Legal strangulation, however, is deliberate, state-sanctioned homicide, the culmination of the legal process. In the territorial Southwest, judicial killing was a self-conscious lesson in Euro-American civilization: the conscientious application of legal forms to strangle a bad man was a well-choreographed ritual of communal self-improvement.

During the territorial period, all hanging victims but one were male, and, indeed, males perpetrated the vast majority of assaults and murders. Both New Mexico and Arizona Territories, pining for statehood, had to tame their wild men before the United States Congress would vote them into the Union. To suppress the tumultuous, violent instincts of frontier men, Victorian society and territorial judicial codes armed courts with the power of legal retribution and moral example. In the process, they proscribed the violent impulses commonly attributed to men on the North American frontier.[9]

After the Civil War, two seemingly contradictory themes coursed through ideologies of Victorian manhood. First, through most of the nineteenth century, the respected man was self-made, sexually restrained, strong-willed, and moral—all of which added up to "strong character." Such a man proudly embraced moderation in all things: he fended off dangerous animal strength as well as embarrassing feminine weakness. His behavior and achievements in public life and the marketplace constructed his male identity. By the 1880s and 1890s Americans—men in particular—began adding a new dimension to manhood: masculinity, or the physical man. They became obsessed with bodies and passions, believing that men should be ambitious, combative, tough, aggressive, and competitive. Physical strength was equated with "strength of character." Frowned upon in antebellum America, sexual desire was gradually accepted as natural in virile males.[10] In their coverage of murder trials and public hangings, newspapermen incorporated many of these themes in their descriptions and analyses of legally charged or condemned men.

In the public-hanging ritual, the physical body became entangled with race in the evaluation of victims' manhood and masculinity. Late-nineteenth-century American men became obssessed with physical bodies and bodybuilding, and the medical sciences and pseudosciences forged links between physical proportions, virility, morality, virtue, and manliness. For instance, the American school of anthropology measured crania to divine a suite of characteristics among racial groups and tried to conclude that Anglo cranial capacity—greater than that of African Americans and other races—indicated superior intelligence. Likewise, the "science" of phrenology charted "the shape of a person's cranium" to size up personality and explain behavior. A strong jaw indicated strong moral character, while a high forehead noted intelligence. When combined, the American school and phrenology contributed to a scientific racism that championed the superiority of Anglos and "proved" the inferiority of African Americans, Mexicans, Asians, and other people of color.[11]

Racial stereotyping created inequities on the male-gender playing field. In Victorian America, Anglo-Saxon manhood was the standard by which reporters, pundits, and other observers measured the manliness in any racial or ethnic group. Men of color could and did demonstrate acceptable cool in the hanging arena, but, unlike the Anglo condemned in general, they had to overcome racial stereotypes and ethnic caricatures to achieve their manly state of grace.

Public scrutiny of the defendant's manhood began at the delivery of the verdict and sentence. His response established his behavioral baseline. During 1883, in Albuquerque, Milton Yarberry was "perfectly cool" upon his murder conviction, but his self-control evaporated at hearing the death sentence. In disbelief, his "livid" face shot "darts of malice toward the judge."[12] Two years later in Tucson, Joseph Casey projected an "unconcerned air" throughout both his trial and sentencing.[13] In 1906 in Taos, grief and tears overcame John Conley's manly self-control when the New Mexico governor refused to commute his death sentence to life imprisonment.[14] Tantrums, cavalierness, and tears were unmanly. Even the condemned man coolly accepted his peers' verdict, manfully looked death in the face, and conscientiously performed the rituals of contrition, secular and religious, that would admit or readmit him to the community of good men.

After sentencing came the death watch, usually seven to ten days of constant supervision in jail, during which the public closely observed the condemned man's moral character and physical courage. Would he improve on or backslide from his behavioral exhibition during the trial and sentencing? The community frowned on extreme behaviors—bravado, which signaled neither contrition nor remorse, or fear, which Victorian society expected from women, not men. In Taos, John Conley, a moral and physical coward, was so scared that he attempted suicide—unsuccessfully.[15] When Milton Yarberry's pale complexion received comment, he retorted, "'That may be, but I ain't sick, and I ain't scared either. Hell, I wouldn't get scared if they walked me out on the scaffold right now.'"[16] Yarberry's boast lacked moral character. In Arizona, Edwin W. Hawkins smashed dishes and rattled buckets after his conviction and sentencing but became "as quiet and docile as a man could ask" during his death watch.[17] Turning inward, Hawkins began using the death watch to rehabilitate himself—to become a man acceptable to his peers—self-restrained, strong, and Christian.

THE HANGING OF GEORGE WOODS. FRONTIER COMMUNITIES GENERALLY GATHERED FOR A LEGAL EXECUTION. PHOTOGRAPH NO. 17667. COURTESY OF ARIZONA HISTORICAL SOCIETY LIBRARY, TUCSON.

The cornerstone of moral courage was Christian faith, and the death watch was a time for legal victims to gird their souls for the final reckoning before society and God. Watched closely by the public, their private exercises of acceptance, contrition, and redemption in the shadow of certain death were less the condemnation of behavior outlawed by the legal code than the personal reinforcement of values trumpeted by the community. Some men, however, rejected the overtures of Protestant and Catholic clergy. During 1884, in Arizona, the Bisbee "murderers" refused Christian counsel: "No confessions have been made, and all maintain their innocence."[18] Unlike the raiders, Edwin Hawkins responded by adopting Father Timmermans as his "spiritual advisor."[19] Dennis Dilda converted to the Catholic faith a day before his execution but refused to see the priest the following morning.[20] The acceptance of Christianity would prepare them for the afterlife and help complete their moral profile.

The Victorian public wanted its victims to rehabilitate themselves—to restore their manliness—before going to their death, but biology and race problematized the ascent to ideal manhood. In Arizona, Zack Booth issued from a family that had "terrorized" parts of the territory for "thirty years." Rumor was that the "murderous blood" of John Wilkes Booth, Abraham Lincoln's assassin, coursed through the tumultuous Zack's veins.[21] According to Anglo pundits, racial characteristics especially handicapped blacks,

Indians, Mexicans, and other minorities. Seen as less physically and socially evolved than whites, they were prone to uncontrolled passion, rage, and sexuality. *The Daily New Mexican* reported that Santo Barela confessed to committing murder simply "because he wanted to." The writer elaborated, "When angered he was as dangerous as a wild beast, having no more discretion or care for the consequences than the most ferocious denizen of the forest."[22] Passion and aggression were sanctioned in a "socially accepted marketplace,"[23] but, in the eyes of Anglos, racial minorities were too unevolved and thus too undisciplined to apply them in proper places and ways.

Victorians linked physical character to crime. Underevolved racial minorities, Victorian pundits believed, were predisposed to violence and crime. Of Toribio Huerta, the *Santa Fe New Mexican* said, "He is a brute in appearance, has no symptoms of refinement and is evidently a half breed from the Yaqui Indian Country."[24] The reporter probably assumed that Huerta's blood combined the worst moral attributes of the Mexican and Indian races. Victorian Anglos fretted over racial miscegenation, which diluted the purity of European stock and unmanned its civilization in their eyes. Soon after Jose Ruiz's arrest, the *Albuquerque Morning Democrat*, applying phrenology to decode his face, concluded that he showed no "signs of intelligence" and that he was "a brute pure and simple."[25] According to this sober scientific analysis, biology was destiny: race condemned these two men to moral degeneracy.[26]

In the Southwest, Anglos used scientific racism to position themselves above Hispanos and Indians and to enforce white hegemony. They scorned Nuevomexicano peasants, whose ethnic roots were Spanish, Mexican, and Indian, and grudgingly accepted the Hispano aristocracy, which adamantly denied Indian blood in its veins and directly linked its families to Castillian Spain. Since the United States conquest of New Mexico in 1846, Anglo-Americans had perceived Nuevomexicano peasants as practically another Indian tribe—wild, savage, superstitious, and ignorant—the characteristics of a beast, not a man.[27] The racial inferiority of Hispanos and Indians blocked their ascent toward civilization, and, given that manhood was a condition of civilization, manliness was beyond Hispano and Indian males. Consequently, only the rule of white men would keep Arizona and New Mexico, overrun by Hispano brutes and Indian savages, from descending into chaos and ruin.

Unlike those of ethnic minorities, the bodies of some white murderers showed the promise of moral rehabilitation. Two Bisbee raiders, Dan Delaney and Tex Howard, sparked telling newspaper descriptions. A "short well built man about five feet four inches tall," Delaney bore "clear intelligent eyes, black hair, a well developed forehead" and articulated himself "in gentlemanly language." A twenty-four-year-old Texan, Howard presented "an intelligent manly face" and was called "'Handsome Tex'" by many acquaintances.[28] According to Victorian convention, Delaney and Howard strayed into a life of crime, but they still belonged to the white race, and their racial superiority opened many doors to moral regeneration.

The death watch was a final opportunity for the condemned man to admit his guilt, accept the verdict of his peers, and forgive them—key elements in his moral courage. Ironically, despite their white race and physical promise, John Conley,[29] the Bisbee raiders,[30] and Milton Yarberry[31]—white men all—forgave no one and "bitterly" maintained their innocence to the end, seemingly thinking that Anglo ethnicity entitled them to acquittal and freedom. On the other hand, some Hispano victims approached their legal doom with Catholic fatalism, repented their crimes, and consoled their peers. Dionicio Sandoval harbored "no ill" and hoped "to be forgiven."[32] Although maintaining his innocence, Demetrio Dominguez wrote, "But in this way God according to his Holy Will so decrees, and I am resigned."[33] Promising to go out a "hero," Dennis Dilda "admitted killing Deputy Sheriff Murphy, and said he was sorry for it."[34] Far from acquiescence, admission of guilt and forgiveness of peers made going to death an active, manly process for the legal victim.

Following the death declaration read by the sheriff was the death procession from the jail to the gallows. On the frontier, even when legislatures relocated executions to walled-off spaces, hanging day was a carnival that drew men, women, and children from town and countryside. Community bands played sentimental favorites, merchants plied their wares, and street vendors sold food and drink. The spectacle was a form of public theater that drove home moral and ethical lessons to the community. When the victim emerged from jail, he was jostled by crowds straining to glimpse him. Some cursed him; others wished him Godspeed. However, as the prisoner marched the path to the gallows, he bore almost iconographic power as a martyr or sacrifice to Anglo-Saxon civilization, and his death procession echoed the final walk of Jesus Christ to his crucifixion by the Romans.[35]

Representatives of Euro-American manhood shielded the victim. Leading the procession was the clergy, Protestant or Catholic, who stood for Christianity, morality, and spiritual courage. These men of the cloth had devoted their lives to controlling their passions and to helping others do the same. Ringing the condemned were the sheriff and deputies, the embodiment of law, order, and justice. Everyday, frontier lawmen plucked criminals—disorderly, immoderate, lawless men—off the streets to keep the community safe. Often controlling the crowd along the approach to the gallows was the militia or town guard. Giving up their day to maintain public order, these virtuous men stood for discipline, self-control, and physical courage. Walking at the center was the condemned, a lightning rod of manhood and masculinity, surrounded by morality, justice, and virtue, manly values advocated by the community.[36]

At the end of the death procession, the ascension of the scaffold placed the condemned man's physical courage on trial. All eyes watched to see whether his nerve faltered and whether he wet or fouled himself. In Clayton, New Mexico, Black Jack Ketchum, pugnacious and sarcastic through his trial and death watch, was "very pale as he mounted the platform, but showed no fear."[37] Of Jose Maria Martinez, a reporter for the *New Mexican* wrote, "When he came in sight of the frame, all the bravado he had shown upon his trial and afterwards, forsook him."[38] Perfecto Padilla "was so much frightened that he was hardly able to stand when the noose was placed about his neck."[39] The hanging was a warning shot to potential lawbreakers, but, instead of striking terror in the victim, legal strangulation was intended to be the culmination of his rehabilitation as a moral, law-abiding, righteous man. The ritual both held the condemned man publicly accountable for his crime and graphically reinforced standards of male behavior and manly character on the Victorian frontier.

Cockiness and arrogance, equally displeasing to the public, signaled the victim's resistance to the civilizing process and the rejection of his male peers. The *Santa Fe New Mexican* expressed unhappiness with Toribio Huerta's bold comportment: "Indeed the predominant thought seemed to be that it was his duty to show that he had no fear, and his appearance was almost that of bravado."[40] Milton Yarberry confronted his executioners on the scaffold: "'I was perfectly justified in killing both men. . . . I can point out several who know in their heart I was justified.'" As the hangman pulled the black cap over his head, Yarberry yelled, "'Well, you are going to hang an innocent man.'"[41] He died all alone, having refused to accept the judgment of his peers and embrace his community.

In contrast, many men went to their deaths with both moral and physical courage. With a rope around his neck but in perfect harmony with the crowd, Francisco Peres "shook hands with the officers and Rev. Father Gualco" before the trap was sprung.[42] Extending his "heartfelt thanks" to those persons who had blessed him with their "kindness," William Hall, from a platform in Prescott, Arizona, said, "At best life is short, and it is but a little while until we all will be on the other shore."[43] Thoroughly reformed by the time he reached the scaffold, E. W. Hawkins expressed the complete acceptance of his peers' sentence: "'Gentlemen:—I am perfectly resigned to my fate and I want you all to pray for me. I want you to pray a little word for me after it is all over. Will you? I am sorry for what I done. And I repeat, I want you to pray for me and I will pray for you in Heaven.'"[44] Displaying no "braggadocio or mock heroism," Hawkins "was as cool as a cucumber," waving "good-bye" to acquaintances in the crowd—"simply cool and calm as might be."[45] Completely rehabilitated, Hawkins could take his place among

ZACK BOOTH, HAT IN HAND, WAVING FAREWELL TO CURIOSITY SEEKERS IN GLOBE,
ARIZONA, SEPTEMBER 15, 1905. HE WAS HANGED SHORTLY THEREAFTER. PHOTOGRAPH
NO. 28197. COURTESY OF ARIZONA HISTORICAL SOCIETY LIBRARY, TUCSON.

the men of his community and ironically surpass them in manliness. With
absolute cool—equal portions of moral and physical courage—he accepted
and embraced his certain death like a heroic man.

With calm and sometimes even cheer, other legal victims also took the
hangman's noose. Having accepted his fate with dignity, William Hall "stood
the severe ordeal with great calmness."[46] "Perfectly cool" on the scaffold,
William McDowell gave "instructions regarding the rope" for a "greater
drop."[47] The *Santa Fe New Mexican* paid the good-natured James Barrett a
resounding compliment: "He showed no signs of excitement and to the last
was as cool as if he were going about the most ordinary detail of business."[48]
Viewing death as a business and the victim as one of its accountants was fitting in turn-of-the-century industrial America. In a society of divided
spheres, men occupied the aggressive and competitive world of the marketplace and politics. The criteria of manhood—spiritual calm, physical
courage, and virtue—reenforced the respect granted the "cool" victim. In
agreement on all manly principles, the spectator and the victim were united
in the cause of civilization and manhood.

In Victorian America, the public identified the American West, the
Southwest included, as a male place.[49] Manly passions, ambitions, and
aggressions—Anglo-Saxon, specifically—were critical to subduing the savage beasts and peoples of the wilderness and to beginning the process of civ-

ilizing the frontier. The American people could excuse the savagery of their citizens, even consider it manly, when their beastly acts—the slaughter of Indians or buffalo herds—served their cause. When Anglo civilization overtook the frontier and settled around them, it would reabsorb its wild whites—Joe Meek, Kit Carson, Jim Bridger, Bill Cody, and others. Unlike the Indians and most Hispanos, who were impervious to refinement and culture, these white frontiersmen would soon enough reenter civilization, marry Anglo women, and build farms or businesses, or move on to other unconquered frontiers to apply their special skills.

However, within the boundaries of civilization, savagery—white savagery, too—had no place. Untamed men were a genuine threat to economic, political, and social stability. In domestic space, women cultivated restraint and moderation in their husbands and sons, but feminine influence waned beyond the home. Men ruled the economy and politics of the public space, where, in turn, the law regulated their behavior. In business and politics, society expected aggression in a man advancing or protecting his interests, but a real man was neither selfish, reckless, nor self-destructive in public or private affairs. When his passions got away from him and he inflicted pain or violence on his home or society—when he became uncivil and unmanly— the law reined him in, and the courts tried him. If his peers convicted him, the law, representing society's best interests, exacted retribution, and the unmanly transgressor had to pay his toll, sometimes with his life.

In the case of a man sentenced to die, the public's greatest concern was not his biological life but his symbolic import. No man, not even a convicted murderer, should die in vain. From his conviction through the death watch to his execution, he had a chance to save his soul, rehabilitate himself, and reenter the ranks of good men. That process, although deeply personal, became community drama followed closely in the public record, the newspapers. Hanging in the balance was the battle between savagery and civilization, between beastliness and manhood. Every good man and virtuous woman had a stake in the struggle. If a man of color rejected the overtures of the clergy, showed no remorse for his crime, and went to the gallows with bravado and surliness, as did Toribio Huerta and Jose Maria Martinez, he simply confirmed what all the best scientists and people already knew about his race: he was a coward destined for savagery and perdition, not manhood and thus not civilization. However, if a white man marched to the gallows and spit at his peers, his defiance, a sign of private rebellion and public failure, directly challenged the community's honor, morality, and ethics, and discomfited onlookers, who hoped that his death would validate their world. At the disposal of editorialists, nonetheless, were the language and science to attribute the victim's unmanly behavior to primal instincts, small cranial capacity, bad blood, or countless other causes.

In the Victorian Southwest, the legal victim who coolly and contentedly ascended to the gallows was a triumph of manhood and civilization. His personal breakdown, struggle, and recovery became a symbolic drama with lessons for his community. As newspaper accounts reveal, the cool victim combined spiritual faith, physical courage, and virtue to face his death like a real man and to sacrifice his body for the community good. He reminded everyone that men had to control their passions and regulate themselves at work and home, and that true manhood was moderation, benevolence, charity, and public-spiritedness. No matter how badly his family or work needled him each day, the real man kept his cool and composure at all times. As he dropped through the floor, the condemned man in death reconfirmed Victorian codes of manhood and the nobility of Euro-American civilization.

Notes

1. William A. Keleher, *Turmoil in New Mexico, 1846–1868* (Santa Fe: Rydal Press, 1952), 397–99; and Aurora Hunt, *Kirby Benedict: Frontier Federal Judge*, Western Frontiersmen Series (Glendale, Calif.: The Arthur H. Clark Company, 1961), 76–77.

2. Keleher, 397–99.

3. Peter Feline, *Him/Her/Self: Sex Roles in Modern America*, 2nd ed. (Baltimore: Johns Hopkins University Press, 1986), 70.

4. Larry D. Ball, *Desert Lawmen: The High Sheriffs of New Mexico and Arizona Territories, 1846–1912* (Albuquerque: University of New Mexico Press, 1992), 158–59; and Jill Mocho, *Murder and Justice in Frontier New Mexico, 1821–1846* (Albuquerque: University of New Mexico Press, 1997), 17–18.

5. Martin J. Weiner, "The Victorian Criminalization of Men," in *Men and Violence: Gender, Honor, and Rituals in Modern Europe and America*, ed. Pieter Spierenburg (Athens: Ohio State University Press, 1998), 201–8.

6. For a list of public hangings in New Mexico and Arizona Territories, see Ball, *appendix B*.

7. For definitions of *cool*, see *The Oxford English Dictionary*, 2nd ed., prepared by J. A. Simpson and E. S. C. Weiner, vol. 3 (Oxford: Clarendon Press, 1989), 889–91; *Webster's Third New International Dictionary of the English Language, Unabridged*, pt. 1, ed. Philip Babcock Gove (Springfield, Mass: G. & C. Merriam Company, 1966); and Eric Partridge, *A Dictionary of Slang and Unconventional English*, 8th ed., ed. Paul Beale (London: Routledge and Kegan Paul, 1984), 251–52.

8. Overviews of lynching theory include Stewart E. Tolnay and E. M. Beck, *A Festival of Violence: An Analysis of Southern Lynchings, 1882–1930* (Urbana: University of Illinois Press, 1950), 17–27, and Walter T. Howard, *Lynchings: Extralegal Violence in Florida during the 1930s* (Selsinsgrove, Penn.: Susquehanna University Press, 1995), 13–25. A solid interpretive framework for lynching is Roberta Senechal de La Roche, "The Sociogenesis of Lynching," in *Under Sentence of Death: Lynching in the South*, ed. W. Fitzhugh Brundage (Chapel Hill: University of North Carolina Press, 1997), 50–52. For lynch law in the Southwest, see Ball, chap. 7.

9. Angus McLaren, *The Trials of Masculinity: Policing Sexual Boundaries, 1870–1930* (Chicago: University of Chicago Press, 1997), 114–15. See also Weiner.

10. Anthony E. Rotundo, *American Manhood: Transformations in Masculinity from the Revolution to the Modern Era* (New York: Basic Books, 1993), 3, 19–20; and Gail Bederman, *Manliness and Civilization: A Cultural History of Gender and Race in the United States, 1880–1917*, Women in Culture and Society (Chicago: University of Chicago Press, 1995), 18–19; and Feline, 70–71.

11. Joe Dubbert, *A Man's Place: Masculinity in Transition* (Englewood Cliffs, N.J.: Prentice Hall, 1979), 156; and Anthony Rotundo, "Body and Soul: Changing Ideals of American Middle-Class Manhood, 1770–1920," *Journal of Social History* 16: 24–28. The discussion of phrenology and the American school is from Ronald G. Walters, *American Reformers, 1815–1860* (New York: Hill and Wang, 1978), 156–63. The phrenological discussion also benefitted from the editorial comments of Dee Garceau, Department of History, Rhodes College, Memphis, Tennessee.

12. "Yarberry's Crimes," *Albuquerque Morning Journal*, February 9, 1883, 4, col. 3.

13. "The Death Sentence," *The Daily Star*, April 9, 1884, 4, col. 3.

14. "Conley Hears of Final Sentence," *Santa Fe New Mexican*, January 24, 1906, 1, col. 1.

15. "Conley Is Sane: To Hang Monday," *Santa Fe New Mexican*, February 1906, 1, col. 6.

16. "Attempted Escape," *Albuquerque Morning Journal*, February 8, 1883, 4, col. 3.

17. "Hawkins Has Quieted Remarkably," *Arizona Daily Star*, August 1, 1908, 7, col. 4.

18. "The Bisbee Murderers," *The Daily Star*, March 1884, 2, col. 3.

19. "Hawkins Is Facing Death Very Calmly," *Arizona Daily Star*, August 14, 1908, 8, col. 1.

20. "Dennis W. Dilda," *Arizona Weekly Journal-Miner*, 10 February 1886, 1, col. 1.

21. "Was Z. Booth of Famous Stock?" *Arizona Daily Star*, September 29, 1904, 4, col. 1.

22. "The Mesilla Hanging," *The Daily New Mexican*, May 22, 1881, 4, col. 3.

23. This idea is adapted from John Starrett Hughes, "The Madness of Separate Spheres: Insanity and Masculinity in Victorian Alabama," in *Meanings for Manhood in Victorian America*, ed. Mark C. Carnes and Clyde Griffen (Chicago: University of Chicago Press, 1990), 57.

24. "Two Hangings on Friday," *Santa Fe New Mexican*, April 23, 1901, 1, col. 4.

25. "Horrible Murder," *Albuquerque Morning Democrat*, May 28, 1898, 1, col. 5.

26. Rotundo, "Body and Soul," 24–28.

27. At the federal level, an early example of this Anglo stereotyping of Hispano lower classes is the following: Sumner to Conrad, May 27, 1852, Santa Fe, House Executive Document 1, *Annual Report of the Secretary of War,* Serial Number 674, 23–26.

28. "Death Penalty," *Arizona Daily Star*, March 29, 1884, 1, col. 2.

29. "When Will Execution Take Place?" *Santa Fe New Mexican*, February 21, 1906, 1, col. 5.

30. "Death Penalty," *Arizona Daily Star*, March 29, 1884, 1, col. 2.

31. "Attempted Escape," *Albuquerque Morning Journal*, February 8, 1883, 4, col. 3.

32. "Sandoval," *Albuquerque Democrat,* September 1906, 1, col. 2.

33. "Demetrio Dominguez—Executed at Phenix [*sic*]," *Weekly Arizona Miner*, December 3, 1880, 1, col. 3.

34. "Dennis W. Dilda," *Arizona Weekly Journal-Miner*, February 10, 1886, 1, col. 1.

35. Ball, 159–62.

36. For descriptions of death processions, see "Death Penalty," *Arizona Daily Star*, March 29, 1884, 1; "The Last Chapter," *Albuquerque Morning Journal*, February 10, 1883, 5; and "Dennis W. Dilda," *Arizona Weekly Journal-Miner*, February 10, 1886, 1.

37. "Ketchum Pays Penalty," *Santa Fe New Mexican*, April 26, 1901, 1, col. 1.

38. "The Execution of Jose Maria Martinez, at Taos," *The New Mexican*, May 21, 1864, 2, col. 2.

39. "Padilla and Ring," *Santa Fe New Mexican*, September 28, 1896, 1, col. 6.

40. "Toribio Huerta Is Hanged," *Santa Fe New Mexican*, April 26, 1901, 1, col. 2.

41. "The Last Chapter," *Albuquerque Morning Journal*, February 10, 1883, 4, col. 3.

42. "Hanging of Francisco Peres," *Arizona Daily Star*, March 29, 1884, 1, col. 4.

43. "W. H. Hall Executed," *Weekly Arizona Miner*, February 10, 1882, 3, cols. 3–4.

44. "E. W. Hawkins Executed at 2:03 P.M. in County Jail," *Arizona Daily Star*, August 15, 1908, 8, col. 3.

45. "E. W. Hawkins Executed at 2:30 P.M. in County Jail," *Arizona Daily Star*, August 14, 1908, 3, cols. 3–4.

46. "W. H. Hall Executed," *Weekly Arizona Miner*, February 14, 1882, 3, cols. 3–4.

47. "Hanging of McDowell," *Arizona Daily Star*, March 29, 1884, 1, col. 4.

48. "Eddy Execution," *Santa Fe Daily New Mexican*, September 20, 1894, 5, col. 2.

49. See Susan Lee Johnson, "'A Memory Sweet to Soldiers': The Significance of Gender," in *A New Significance: Re-envisioning the History of the American West*, ed. Clyde Milner (New York: Oxford University Press, 1996), 255–58.

White Men, Red Masks

Appropriations of "Indian" Manhood
in Imagined Wests

David Anthony Tyeeme Clark and Joane Nagel

In 1931, Hunkpapa Lakota, Moving Robe Woman, recounted a battle that took place on June 24, 1876, at *Peji Sla Wakapa* (Greasy Grass), an event remembered by most Americans today as the Battle of the Little Bighorn:[1]

> I was born seventy-seven winters ago, near [what today is] Grand River, South Dakota. . . . I belonged to Sitting Bull's band. They were great fighters. . . . I am going to tell you of the greatest battle. This was a fight against *Pehin Hanska* (General Custer). . . . Several of us Indian girls were digging wild turnips . . . [and we] looked toward camp and saw a warrior ride swiftly, shouting that the soldiers were only a few miles away. . . . I heard Hawk Man shout: *"Hoka He! Hoka He!"* (Charge! Charge!). . . . Someone said that another body of soldiers was attacking the lower end of the village. I heard afterwards that these soldiers were under the command of Long Hair (Custer). With my father and other youthful warriors I rode in that direction. . . .The valley was dense with powder smoke. I never heard such whooping and shouting. "There is never a better time to die!" shouted Red Horse. Long Hair's troopers were trapped in an enclosure. There were Indians everywhere. . . . It was not a massacre, but a hotly contested battle between two armed forces.[2]

The commentary of Wooden Leg, a young Cheyenne who fought that day in 1876, elaborates on one of the topics alluded to by Moving Robe Woman: the gendered nature of this confrontation between men. Wooden Leg recalled,

> Our war cries and war songs were mingled with many jeering calls, such as: "You are only boys. You ought not to be fighting. We whipped you on the Rosebud. You should have brought more Crows or Shoshones with you to do your fighting." Little Bird and I were after

one certain soldier. Little Bird was wearing a trailing warbonnet. He was at the right and I was at the left of the fleeing man. We were lashing him and his horse with our pony whips. It seemed not brave to shoot him. Besides, I did not want to waste my bullets.[3]

Events leading up to the American defeat at *Peji Sla Wakapa* reflected a familiar late-nineteenth-century scenario on the northern plains that began with encroachment on treaty lands by the railroads, miners, farmers, ranchers, or land speculators and progressed to federal intervention in Indian-white conflicts, militarization, suppression of native armed resistance, and removal of indigenous communities. In this case, it was rumors of Black Hills gold fed in part by an exploratory expedition organized by Custer during the summer of 1874, that sharpened already existing tensions. As white miners and settlers began pouring into the Black Hills, elected officials had to make a choice: use the army to drive the miners out of the area or use the army to protect the miners' interests from the Lakotas, whose land they were claiming and working. After the Lakotas refused to negotiate a sale or lease of the Black Hills in 1875, the year before the Custer defeat, the American president, Ulysses S. Grant, ordered his army not to enforce the provision of the 1868 Fort Laramie Treaty prohibiting non-Indians from entering Lakota territory. Indian service employees then declared a halt to treaty-guaranteed rations until the Lakotas agreed to sell.[4]

In an attempt to force the Lakotas and their allies out of much of *Paha Sapa,* the American secretary of the interior announced in December 1875 that all tribal members were required to be at the U.S. Indian agencies by January 31, 1876, or "be deemed hostile and treated accordingly by military force."[5] Many Lakotas did not recognize the intrusion of the Indian service into their internal affairs. Others did not receive this message. Even if they had heard the news and had been inclined to comply, winter weather conditions made their departure unlikely. In the American capitol, the secretary of war characterized the refusal of most Lakotas to comply with this command as an "act of war" against the United States.[6]

On February 1, 1876, government officials declared all "free" Indians, led by *Tatanka Iyotanka* (Sitting Bull) and Crazy Horse, who were not residing on reservations, to be "hostiles." The secretary of the interior asked the secretary of war to take "appropriate action." Custer's imprudent and failed assault on the Little Bighorn was part of this larger campaign to force native groups onto ever-shrinking reservations.[7]

The attention given to (some might argue obsession with) Custer's defeat generated several investigations during the late 1870s. Since then it also has motivated hundreds of scholarly monographs and articles as well as popular books and films, newsletters and enactment groups, Internet websites and links, and even action-figure playsets and Little Bighorn trading cards. The exact reasons for Custer's defeat remain a source of immense controversy and interest to this day.[8] Yet the detailed accounts provided by scholars of the Battle of Greasy Grass, along with its prelude and aftermath, continue to ignore the implication behind jeers such as "You are only boys. You ought not to be fighting." In so doing, they fail to explore the causal role of manhood in the relationship between Indian and white persons and that relationship's constitutive effect on the formation of masculine cultures.

We argue in what follows that Moving Robe Woman's words, which opened this essay, provide considerable insight into the enduring preoccupation with Custer and the battle of the Little Bighorn in the American scholarly and popular imagination. The battle of the Little Bighorn was emblematic of a simultaneous larger struggle underway in America, a conflict among men over the meaning of manhood. It is our contention that the "hotly contested battle between two armed forces" was a confrontation of masculinities enacted on the northern plains in 1876 and in the decades to follow. It was not only a battle over the control of land and resources, but a struggle that determined in many ways the definition of white manhood and the shape and content of American national and, thus, masculine identity.

To illuminate this process this chapter focuses on a large number of realist texts—memoirs, novels, and performances published or advertised as "factual" accounts—as well as ritualistic simulations enacted by boys and men, both of which reveal an emergent colonialist discourse in which white American men expropriated cultural symbols from indigenous people whom they confined on reservations. These texts further reinscribed those expropriated materials and symbols with new meanings enabling their authors and audiences to construct a masculinity into which all white men should and, they thought, could be blended to manufacture the illusion of a largely unified American national identity. In our conclusion, we further demonstrate that indigenous persons have not passively watched this process; they have struggled to reclaim their cultural capital within a larger society still appropriating "Indian-ness," and reshaped it to provide a tool of resistance and a wellspring for community revitalization.

A sizeable cast populates the following pages, but they represent only part of an even larger phenomenon. A number of these sources—the writings of Theodore Roosevelt, Frank Hamilton Cushing, and Ernest Thompson Seton, for example—will be familiar to readers, others less so. Like the gendered nature of the Battle of Greasy Grass, these texts explicitly worked to construct what Dana Nelson has termed "national manhood" through a process of expropriating native imagery.[9] Exploring this relationship between manhood and nationalism in some depth is the first step in our analysis of realist texts about Indian-white interaction.[10]

Recent historical studies of the United States argue that contemporary patterns of U.S. middle-class masculinity arose out of a renaissance of manliness in the late nineteenth and early twentieth centuries. Scholars document a preoccupation with masculine ideals of physique and behavior around the turn of the century that became institutionalized into such organizations as the modern Olympic movement, which began in 1896; Theodore Roosevelt's Rough Riders unit, which fought in the Spanish American War in 1898; a variety of boys' and men's lodges and fraternal organizations, such as the Knights of Columbus, the League of the Iroquois, and the Improved Order of Red Men, which were established or expanded in the late nineteenth century; and the Boy Scouts of America, which was founded in 1910, two years after the publication of R. S. S. Baden-Powell's influential *Scouting for Boys*.[11]

Scholars argue that at any time, in any place, there is an identifiable "normative" or "hegemonic" masculinity that sets the standards for male demeanor, thinking, and action.[12] Hegemonic masculinity is more than an "ideal," it is assumptive, widely held, and has the quality of appearing to be "natural."[13] It also serves political ends. George Mosse argues that nationalism "was a movement which began and evolved parallel to modern masculinity" in the West about a century ago. He describes modern masculinity as a centerpiece of all varieties of nationalist movements:

> The masculine stereotype was not bound to any one of the powerful political ideologies of the previous century. It supported not only conservative movements . . . but the workers' movement as well; even Bolshevik man was said to be "firm as an oak." Modern masculinity from the very first was co-opted by the new nationalist movements of the nineteenth century.[14]

Most scholars agree, identifying the late eighteenth and nineteenth centuries as the period when men used nationalism as a means of organizing local and global politics, territory, and populations.[15] Other political ideologies of that time, in particular colonialism and imperialism, also resonated with contemporary standards of masculinity.[16] Many scholars link the renaissance of manliness in Europe to the institutions and ideologies of empire.[17] John Springhall describes a middle-class English ideal of Christian manliness, "muscular Christianity," with an emphasis on sport—the "cult of games" in the public schools; he outlines how, through organizations such as the Boys' Brigades, these middle-class values were communicated to "less privileged, board school-educated, working-class boys in the nation's large urban centres." Boys from both classes served throughout the Empire in British imperial armies.[18]

In the United States, masculinity was tightly woven into two nationalist imperialist projects: Manifest Destiny, which justified and promoted westward expansion, and the Monroe Doctrine, which extended the U.S. sphere of influence to include the entire Western Hemisphere. The westward expansion of the United States that destroyed countless indigenous lives and communities during the second half of the nineteenth century proceeded at an astonishing pace, despite Custer's defeat at *Peji Sla Wakapa* in 1876. By 1903, in the annals of U.S. jurisprudence, native people were no longer independent nations capable of making treaties with the United States. Rather, they became wards of the federal government without citizenship rights.[19] The loss of sovereignty exacted an emotional toll on native individuals and exerted a disorganizing strain on native societies.[20] On the reservations there were often tremendous anxieties about basic survival, anxieties that were amplified by corrupt administrators of U.S. Indian policy. Anger, bitterness, frustration, resentment, even a sense of helplessness and futility flowed over many indigenous populations like the epidemics of earlier times.

As part of the U.S. effort to undermine what was left of the viability and sovereignty of indigenous nationhood in 1924 the U.S. Congress passed the Indian Citizenship Act, relocating native political rights and allegiances from their indigenous roots to the American state. The transfer was economic as well; in the words of Frederick Hoxie, the "campaign for equality and total assimilation had become a campaign to integrate native resources into the American economy."[21] Hoxie was right about where the campaign to assimilate Indians turned in the twentieth century, but there was more to it even than appropriating native land and resources and assimilating indigenous people. Half a century after the Lakota victory at the Little Bighorn, sixty-eight-year-old *wischasha wakon* (holy man) Black Elk echoed Moving Robe Woman's observation that the conflict between the United States and the Lakotas was not only about control of territory but also about manhood. "The Wasichus have put us in these square boxes," Black Elk told John Neihardt. "Our power is gone and we are dying, for the power is not in us any more. You can look at our boys and see how it is. When we were living by the power of the circle in the way we should, boys were men at twelve or thirteen years of age. But now it takes them very much longer to mature." In the reservations still alive in Black Elk's memory, men "were warriors at a time when boys are now like girls."[22] Colonizers were not only interested in trees and minerals, men like Neihardt, and those who read his work, also were interested in certain aspects of "Indian character" and culture thought to be useful and admirable.

This interest arose partly from fears about a fragmenting hegemonic American manhood and desires to reinvigorate and strengthen American manliness. Some reformers looked to "Indian" cultural symbols and resources as rich sources for American renewal and "nativization." In particular these Americans were attracted to—some might argue infatuated with—men like Black Elk. Gender studies scholars have documented turn-of-the-century regret at the waning potency and vivacity of middle-class American masculinity.[23] The future looked bleak to those white middle-class men who reflected on where they believed they had been and where they sensed their nation was headed at the turn of the century. As Gail Bederman notes, "Under these conditions the sons of the middle class faced the real possibility that traditional sources of male power and status, much like their sense of the western 'frontier,' would remain closed to them forever—that they would remain dainty boys instead of becoming self-made men."[24]

It was against the backdrop of this crisis of confidence in American manhood that Lakotas defeated Custer, that the still ongoing quest for an explanation for that defeat was launched, and that the subjugation of indigenous cultures was undertaken. By the 1890s, the search for ways to restore American masculine potency was already well under way. It was in their invented Indian—trapped in a remembered nineteenth century—that American men found their magic cure. American men capitalized on the modern talent for the mimetic—the ability to create endless mass-produced imitations of originals. They created their Indian, an imagined figure, to write themselves into western stories and to re-create themselves as men who dominated other men and nature.

Even in the aftermath of military defeat, land loss, and segregation on reservations, earlier imaginings of "the Indian" as a primitive but formidable adversary who stood in the way of Manifest Destiny remained largely undisturbed in the popular press and in popular theater.[25] In *The Winning of the West*, published in 1886, Theodore Roosevelt caricatured the Indian as brutal and lazy, incapable of self-motivated productive labor, but dangerous to men and cruel to women and children.[26] "I don't go so far as to think that the only good Indians are dead Indians, but I believe nine out of ten are," Roosevelt stated.[27] In his writings and speeches, Roosevelt contrasted the "virile manliness" of American men to the "brutal unmanliness" of Indians. According to Bederman, Roosevelt's "red foes were strong and terrible, cunning in council, dreadful in battle, merciless beyond belief in victory."[28] Despite native savagery and white victimization, none of Roosevelt's imagined men, red or white, was a wimp. "The men of the border," he wrote, "did not overcome and dispossess cowards and weaklings, they marched forth to spoil the stout-hearted and to take for prey the possessions of the men of might."[29]

Roosevelt's Indian was also gendered as perversely hypersexualized and aggressively manly. From the colonial era forward, these traits were common features of depictions of the imagined Indian, depictions that were sometimes eroticized. For instance, white accounts published in the late nineteenth century of native warriors and even of native captors often reflected a romantic ambivalency. June Namias analyzed dozens of those so-called Indian captivity narratives by settlers who were allegedly taken and held captive by various "Indian" groups.[30] She reports a dualism in the accounts (some admittedly fictive) of captives, a dualism captured in the contradictory term *noble savage:* "Nineteenth century captivity materials offered mixed messages for women [readers]: excitement, possible romantic bliss, but the chance of sexual harassment. The big, dark Indian was pictured simultaneously as a thrill and a sexual threat to white women and consequently a competitive sexual threat to white men."[31]

It was not only white women who had mixed feelings about native people. White men frequently sought out native women as sexual partners, and white soldiers sometimes expressed admiration for native warriors.[32] Francis Paul Prucha reports that a number of military men held positive views of indigenous people and fighters. General George Crook, defeated by Crazy Horse on the Rosebud in 1876, considered them not only physical but mental equals: "I wish to say most emphatically that the American Indian is the intellectual peer of most, if not all, the various nationalities we have assimilated to our laws, customs, and language. He is fully able to protect himself, if the ballot be given and the courts of law not closed against him."[33] Crook's contemporary, General Nelson A. Miles, articulated an assessment of native men even more telling and illustrative:

> The Indian . . . has been condemned as a malignant fiend, incapable of the better impulses of humanity and unworthy of admission to the brotherhood of man. . . . The untutored savage showed himself an apt pupil in the school of cruelty, injustice, and indiscriminate revenge. Slow to anger, he has been terrible in his wrath, pitiless in his animosity and relentless in his pursuit of revenge. . . . The art of war among the white race is called strategy or tactics; when it is practised by the Indians, it is called treachery. They employed the art of deceiving, misleading, decoying, and surprising the enemy with great cleverness. The celerity and secrecy of their movements were never excelled by the warriors of any country. They had courage, skill, sagacity, endurance, fortitude, and self-sacrifice of a high order.[34]

Unlike the "dirty and brutal" savage of Roosevelt's imaginings, Miles described an admirable adversary, someone worthy of respect, even emulation, someone who had something a white man might want, though with some reservations—a grudging admiration, a reluctant respect. There was an irony in American policies of assimilation and subjugation on the one hand, and American imaginings of Indians as strong, noble, and skilled on the other. This led to a contradictory situation in which some American reformers were busy "civilizing" indigenous people in efforts to turn them into whites, while at the same time other Americans concerned with manhood were busy emulating, or more accurately, *simulating* Indian men in an effort to revitalize Anglo masculinity. These latter Americans sought to adopt what they liked about Indian masculinity for use in building a racialized American nationalist manhood.

In these efforts at self-reconstruction, American men could discover and appropriate the alleged facts about Indian manhood from dime novels and accounts written by army officers, former pioneers, and other "experts." Disguised as unprejudiced travelers or as neutral journalists reporting the facts, these authors went to extraordinary lengths to establish themselves as impartial. Readers could find, in the words of author and self-ascribed expert on Indian affairs, Colonel Richard Irving Dodge, "entirely unbiased" accounts of "our wild Indians" and put them to work in organizations devoted to rejuvenating manliness, such as the Improved Order of Red Men or the League of the Iroquois.[35] "My position as commanding officer—'Big Chief'—and my well-known friendship for the race," the authorial voice of Colonel Dodge instructed his readers in 1883, "caused the Indians to give me more frank confidence than a white man usually obtains."[36] Another way to understand these "realist" accounts is to read them as reinventing western landscapes where hegemonic masculinity is re-created in endless struggles with Indian supermen before they were, in the minds of the conquerors, overpowered, tamed, imprisoned, and thus emasculated, on reservations.

In this light, many readers must have found Colonel Dodge's *Our Wild Indians* fascinating when they turned the pages of his 653-page tome. As the book unfolds, a tale of triumphant American manhood emerges: the text transforms a dainty little boy-child growing up in North Carolina into an increasingly formidable and wise western man, synonymously American and white. Beginning as "a small delicate lad of six years," the author disguised as child tantalizes his readers with "the thrill of horror and dismay which quivered [through] his frame" when one day he found himself "in the midst of thirty or forty stalwart, painted, feather-crowned warriors, bows in hand."[37]

Following the dainty boy's encounter with stouthearted warriors in North Carolina, readers of *Our Wild Indians* rendezvous with an army officer in Texas who imitated panic at ghosts of the Indian disguised as a cunning and artful combatant. They also relive the exploits of a reporter fronting as an anthropological observer who learned about Indian marvels and everyday life beyond the Mississippi. Readers then see the frontier West through the eyes of an imagined employ of the U.S. government who documented accounts of Indian viciousness. Finally, readers must have enjoyed the fictional formulation of an all-knowing elder statesman delivering the law to denuded shadows of those earlier "stalwart, painted, feather-crowned warriors, bows in hand," who are reduced at the end of the book to children in awe of American power. "There is no future for the Indian as Indian," Dodge declared. "But a few years ago the Indian was wild, free and independent. Now he is a prisoner of war, restrained of his liberty and confined on circumscribed areas. . . . The Indian like other men must have an object in life. . . . There is but one hope for him. . . . Tribal relations must be broken up, and the Indians individually absorbed in the great family of American citizens.[38]

Read one way, these are strange instructions coming from a career army officer whose manly vigor came at the expense of his defeated foe. Read another way, they make perfect sense. Dodge emerges from the book as the better man prepared to help those "prisoners of war" cowering on his reservation landscape. Armed with images of the vanquished and of American military might, the authorial voice, the expert, reminds his readers that "American people as a rule are brave, consequently their instincts are habitually on the side of honor and mercy. Almost everyone has manhood enough to urge him to assist the weak and helpless." In the end, the "small delicate lad of six years" had metamorphosed into a man so powerful he could feel nostalgia for the fading power of his now impotent former enemy.

Representations of the Indian as a mirror image of hegemonic masculinity also emerged in western landscapes invented off the written page. With effects similar to the simulations of the Indian offered by Roosevelt and Dodge, representations of "the Indian" in American theater were exaggerated figures deserving either brutal extermination or pity.[39] "Most people who dreamed about the west and longed after excitement and diversion from mundaneness," reports L. G. Moses, "had few places to look except to the printed page—until, that is, the appearance of the Wild West shows."[40] In these touring melodramas and outdoor pageants, men with little patience for reading could find visual images of savage threat and dramatically alluring scenes of overpowering American masculinity. On a May afternoon in 1883, Colonel William Frederick Cody, adoringly known as Buffalo Bill by his fans, led a group of Pawnees and locally recruited "cowboys" into the arena at the Omaha, Nebraska, fairgrounds. The show began, in the words of a Hartford *Courant* journalist, "with a pony bare-back riding race between Indians and went on to a climax with a grand realistic battle scene depicting the capture, torture, and death of a scout by savages; the revenge, recapture of the dead body and a victory of the government scouts."[41] Similar to spectator sports in which aggressive masculinity prevailed, Wild West shows surfaced in the years following the American Civil War as arenas where simulations of the "muscular, hardy, and stern-faced" American man defeating various lesser men were performed before enthusiastic audiences looking for, in the words of Paul Reddin, "evidence that physical prowess survived in the modern world."[42] In these theaters of American masculinity, spectators could experience, given the right cast of characters (such as Pawnees, and later Lakotas hired by Buffalo Bill), self-congratulatory fantasies about contrived "Indian wars," and could dream about futures of continued American self-importance.[43]

The white man's Indian and things thought to be Indian after the turn of the century were objects of curiosity, amazement, and exploitation that distorted and disfigured images of indigenous people in American popular culture. In their quest to bolster an endangered manhood, American men created simulations of their Indian trapped in a nostalgic frontier. In these fabricated terrains, cowboys and Indians fought it out over and over, and powerful white men emerged triumphant as masculine Americans. Americans, however, did not simply read or view such representations. They were also invited, as consumers, to reenact the stories themselves, and they accepted the invitation.

For some white Americans, the "wild"—a violent western landscape littered with the carnage of vanquished Indians—was an unattractive, perhaps even horrifying spectacle. For these men, simulating the Indian in rituals of emulation was more compelling than seeing him repeatedly killed in the theater.[44] Rather than maintain the distance of spectator, anthropologists like Frank Hamilton Cushing, for instance, immersed themselves in "Indian play" and sometimes "went native."[45] In the summer of 1882, Cushing, a physically scarred white man pictured in the ceremonial dress of the Zuni, along with his Zuni "brothers," made it into the pages of *Popular Science Monthly, Atlantic Monthly, Harper's,* and *Century Illustrated.*[46] According to the editors of *Century Illustrated Monthly Magazine,* images of "the Indian" adorned the pages of these popular magazines in order for readers to participate in the "wholesome movement . . . for the purification of American public life." Cushing had become fascinated with native cultures while doing fieldwork at Zuni, and upon his return to New York began to play Indian. As Philip Deloria describes it, Cushing "insisted upon exactitude in his costume and in his New York apartment, decorated to simulate a Zuni kiva."[47] Masquerading as Indian, Cushing surfaced in 1882 as a pre–Kevin Costner role model for educated, wealthier white men troubled by the growing potency of politically powerful immigrants.[48] Images of "the Indian" presented by Cushing and his colleagues provided reproducible models of manhood for elite easterners desiring to use things thought to be Indian to purge themselves of the enervating effects of civilization. Expiating American nationhood of its impurities and impotencies in these eastern English-language publications meant creating copies of their Indian better than the originals.

During the closing years of the nineteenth century, the period of the most brutal assimilation policies, anthropologists like Cushing went to reservations not for the purpose of exterminating indigenous cultures, but rather with the intention of documenting and consuming "noble savage" manhood. These "ideological vultures," to borrow a description from Vine Deloria, Jr., hoped to imbibe the masculine qualities of the Indian intellectually through ethnographic detail, perceptually through the photograph, ideologically through revised narratives, and experientially through Indian play.[49] This emulation of things thought to be Indian reflected what Renato Rosaldo refers to as "imperialist nostalgia," a longing for "the colonized culture as it was 'traditionally' (that is when they first encountered it). The peculiarity of colonialist yearnings is that agents of colonialism craved the very forms of life they intentionally destroyed."[50]

Cushing was not alone in his desire to become an Indian. Other white middle-class men embraced identities thought to be Indian, and anthropological work provided the materials for them to do so.[51] In addition to providing useful materials for selling eastern literary magazines and apartment decorations, imaginings about the Indian also reshaped their masculine spaces of entertainment, relaxation, and pleasure. These were the spaces where male friendships were nurtured and where threats to white male hegemony could be analyzed and expropriated, mimicked and caricatured. Examples include those who affiliated themselves and their sons with groups dedicated to the preservation of "Indian" virtues such as the Improved Order of Red Men; Ernest Thompson Seton's Woodcraft Indians, later the American Boy Scouts; and Harold S. Keltner's Y-Indian Guides, all of which barred indigenous men from membership.[52]

Seton's fantasies about Indian play, in the words of Shari Huhndorf, were "motivated by his conviction that experience in nature would endow the boys with health, moral character, and, perhaps most important, manliness. . . . Playing Indian would help boys mature properly and teach them to be men."[53] In order to make his purpose clear, Seton, occupying the role of gatekeeper to Indian play in one of his many publications, asked the father of a potential recruit if his boy was "inclined to be a sissy and afraid to play the part of a man."[54] In Seton's words, his main goal was to "combat the system that has turned such a large proportion of our robust, manly, self-reliant boyhood into a lot of flat-chested cigarette smokers, with shaky nerves and doubtful vitality."[55] The route away from sissy-ness and "doubtful vitality" in Seton's fanciful world followed an increasingly well-worn trail into "Indian country." In other words, Seton *used* the Indian to save the *white* man.

Seton introduced to a magazine-reading public in 1902 his fantasies for creating the Woodcraft Indians, "a scheme of education in outdoor life," whose model was "the ideal Indian of [James] Fenimore Cooper, perfectly embodied in Tecumseh, the great Shawnee—physically perfect, wise, brave, picturesque, dignified."[56] According to his biographer, H. Allen Anderson, Seton believed that the eastern United States was a depressingly sick copy of Europe, while the West, "because of its aboriginal tradition, was the true America."[57] Through the lens of his Woodcraft Indians, Seton encouraged his readers to imagine a primordial western landscape as a space where descent into fragility could be reversed without pulling up stakes or leaving the safety and comfort of Connecticut. His simulated western landscape in Connecticut was populated not by sturdy pioneers and fearless soldiers locked in combat with the Indian, but instead by white boys who, in his words, adopted "the best things of the best Indians."[58] In Seton's world, the "best Indians" were generic inventions—he dressed up white men and boys with adornments and embellishments expropriated from any Indian, Crow or Lakota, it mattered not as long as he deemed it representative and useful.

Reflecting on his first group of "Indian" recruits, his "Sinaway tribe," Seton breathed life into a homosocial gathering in which boys disrobed and, while he watched, swam in his lake for the purpose of working off their "animal energy" and of turning "arms white as milk" into the "brown sinewy arm of the Indian."[59] The highlight of this origin account was his storytelling in the darkness around the evening campfire, where he pontificated on the healthy standards of living embraced by his universal Indian, but "with all that is bad and cruel left out."[60]

> I told them of Indians and Plains life, gauging my stories in a steady crescendo till I had renewed the Fenimore Cooper glamour of romance, and heightened it to a blaze of glory about the Redman. . . . As I finished the tale I could feel the thrill of intense interest . . . and their regret that the noble Redmen were gone before their day.[61]

Seton imagined his inventions of "the noble Redmen," in Philip Deloria's words, as "points of entry into a magically transfiguring mimetic play for little white boys."[62] Trapping the Indian in time and place outside the boundaries of modern society, before indigenous persons forced onto reservations reminded onlookers of the negative consequences of colonialism, Seton emerged as an invented Elder able to carry forward Indian knowledges into a white present.[63]

As an effect of their being "man enough to join the tribe," by engaging in escapes to invented western landscapes, by masquerading as their exotic other, American boys and men, then and now, moved on in life to become, in Seton's words, "high-class citizens": small business owners, officers in national organizations, attorneys general, managers, and corporate presidents.[64] Playing Indian at the turn of the century reinvigorated white professional and managerial heterosexual male hegemony, pressing it into such lasting homosocial terrains as the Boy Scouts and the Y-Indian guides,[65] professional sports with Indian mascots and team names, and, more recently, the mythopoetic men's movement with its drums and elders.[66]

Indian mascots and team names have a long history in the United States. On athletic fields, beginning as early as 1897, simulations of the Indian sur-

CHARLES ALEXANDER EASTMAN DURING HIS COLLEGE DAYS AT DARTMOUTH. COURTESY
OF DARTMOUTH COLLEGE LIBRARY SPECIAL COLLECTIONS.

faced that further complicated its uses in reinvigorating and reiterating hegemonic masculinity. In the years after the American Civil War, popular sports emerged as locations where male athletes could become ritualized "Indians," where male team owners could capitalize on the Indian's marketability, and where fans could cheer or denigrate these inventions. Americans who follow baseball today are likely familiar with the Cleveland Indians and the team mascot, Chief Wahoo. This kind of imagery was visible almost from the earliest days of baseball. Following a successful athletic career at Holy Cross, the Cleveland franchise signed Louis Francis Sockalexis (Penobscot) in 1897. Sockalexis was "a massive man, with gigantic bones and bulging muscles," in the admiring words of a journalist adoring the physical beauty of the club's

ERNEST THOMPSON SETON'S ORIGINAL SINAWAY TRIBE, 1903. COURTESY OF SETON MEMORIAL LIBRARY.

recent acquisition.[67] Had everyone seen Sockalexis only in such terms, he might have had a long, noteworthy career. As it turned out, this was not the case. He became the colonizer's Indian, an abusable resource working to the psychological and material advantage of the colonizing population.

"Native Americans in baseball," according to Lawrence Hauptman, "were hardly accepted with open arms, faced frequent racial slurs, and suffered cruel indignities."[68] The exploitability of Sockalexis in the service of U.S. hegemonic manhood was immediately apparent to white men in 1897. His supposedly Indian athletic masculinity was valued as a commodity useful for selling tickets and newspapers, but devalued and denigrated as the traits of a defeated savage by fans and foes alike. When Sockalexis stepped up to bat in home games, fans assailed him with war whoops. They parodied rain and war dances thought to be Indian, allegedly performed in his honor. His teammates dubbed him "chief." When the Cleveland franchise played in an opponent's ballpark, the abuse was more vicious, with spectators actually calling for his scalp. As testimony to the contradictory and powerful place of "the Indian" in the American sporting imagination, although the Cleveland franchise was originally named the Cleveland Naps to honor a star player,

Napoleon Lajoie, after signing Sockalexis it came to be referred to as the "Indian's team." In a letter to the Cleveland franchise president in 1897, John Ward "unhesitatingly pronounced [Sockalexis] a wonder. . . . There is no feature . . . more gratifying than the fact that his presence on the team. . . will result in . . . the more significant name 'Indians.'"[69] One sportswriter wrote a poem, entitling it "Sockalexis, Chief of Sockem." Cartoonists caricatured Sockalexis in newspapers, drawing him holding a large war club and wearing a headdress with feathers. Tabloids heralded him as a direct descendant of Sitting Bull, the Hunkpapa Lakota white Americans loved to fancy as the "chief" who "massacred" Custer at the Little Bighorn.[70] Sockalexis, when he died at the age of forty-two in 1913 in Burlington, Maine, had never been west of Chicago.

Work in gender studies largely has ignored and therefore largely failed to untangle the role of the imagined Indian in strengthening U.S. hegemonic manhood. Through a series of narrative ploys, theatrical gimmicks, and artful inventions since the late nineteenth century, white men used their "Indian" to fabricate and lay claim to western landscapes as sites of white American masculine power. From these invented spaces, in the words of Roy Harvey Pearce, indigenous people "were forced out of American life and into [a controllable] American history."[71] There, in national memory, the colonizer's Indian can be found—a national liminal figure. At once symbolically central and politically excluded, the "Indian" resides at the boundaries of nationhood—a border where some immigrants become integrated and white and where others remain outside the nation, kept within storehouses of exploitable cultural capital that elide contradictions in American national ideology. Vine Deloria, Jr. noted the dangers associated with these contradictions on the eve of the American bicentennial: "Underneath all the conflicting images of the Indian one fundamental truth emerges, the white man *knows* that he is an alien and he *knows* that North America is Indian—and he will never let go of the Indian image because he thinks that by some clever manipulation he can achieve an authenticity that cannot ever be his."[72] These manipulations were and continue to be marketable commodities. People bought the renewed potency of America when they handed over money for magazines, books, theater tickets, and club memberships that rejuvenated hegemonic masculinity by simulating Indianness. In seemingly innocent acts of commodity exchange, white men restored their futures at the expense of indigenous people by robbing them of their cultural capital, infusing it with new meaning, then using it to remake themselves as masters and masterful.[73]

Fortunately such practices do not permit only cultural subjugation and appropriation; they also provide opportunities for cultural resistance, even revitalization. Even in apparent defeat, indigenous men, pioneers in a new line of defense, discovered "America" and exploited the market for things thought to be Indian. In *their* versions of Indian play, indigenous persons created landscapes populated once again by men who provided the energy necessary for believing in a future after the settler wars. Inside these indigenous texts, native people, reauthored by themselves, negotiated a reimagined western landscape populated by indigenous pioneers and word warriors, as well as a varied cast of evil and respectable white men. These reimagined indigenous pioneers embark on youthful journeys away from the familiar, thus recasting the American east-to-west fantasies of discovery and settlement—this time, by Indians of non-Indian country.

The voices defining the indigenous pioneer conjure up memories of remembered fatherly encouragement and approval. They apply warpath imagery both to reveal the cruelties of the colonizer and to reaffirm older masculine qualities of bravery.[74] "When I had grown old enough to go on the warpath there were no more wars for the Indian," a sixty-three-year-old Luther Standing Bear instructed his English-language readers in 1931, disrupting fictions of brutal savage Indian supermen with memories of a confident but scared eleven-year-old.

> I can remember when I was only a little boy wishing that I could prove to my father that I was brave too. . . . I had my chance when eleven years old. By that time the Sioux had laid down their weapons and were living a peaceful life. One day some white people came among us and called a meeting of the parents. We children did not know what it was all about, but I sensed something serious, for my father was very thoughtful for a time. Then he asked me one day if I would like to go away with the white people. . . . I consented at once, though I could think of nothing else but that these white people wanted to take us far away and kill us. . . . To me [school] meant death, but bravery was part of my blood, so I did not hesitate.[75]

Looking back on his decision to follow "the white man's trail" in 1874, Charles Alexander Eastman similarly drew strength from memories of an encouraging father telling him that going to school was "the same as if I sent you on your first war-path. I shall expect you to conquer." With his father's words pushing him forward in *From the Deep Woods to Civilization*, the teenaged Eastman throws himself into learning the white man's ways. "With all the strength of a clean young manhood" and "[having] missed the demoralizing influences of reservation life," the voice of the sixteen-year-old immigrant told its readers, "I set my heart upon the completion of a liberal education."[76]

The traveler-child as prop in these indigenous pioneer narratives draws attention away from deeper inspections of native communities. As prop, he focuses the reader's and, more specifically, the colonizer's attention away from reservations onto the transformations of the assimilating traveler on his journey into civilization. As the familiar fades into the background, emigrant narratives move from moments of departure to concentrate on memories of savage civilization populated once again with humanlike apparitions who, in Standing Bear's words, "have the thought that the Indian is a curious creature, something to be amused at."[77] Eastman, in September 1876 at eighteen years of age, for instance, was a first-year student in the preparatory department at Beloit College in Beloit, Wisconsin. Lakotas and Cheyennes had defeated Custer only weeks earlier in June. "When I went into town," the teen immigrant tells his readers, "I was followed on the streets by gangs of little white savages, giving imitation war whoops."[78]

It is at the convergence between tradition or memory, and invention, that native intellectuals and activists today sometimes take aim. As Gerald Vizenor explains, "I'm still educating an audience . . . about Indian identity. The hardest part of it is I believe [native people] are all invented as Indians. . . . The inventions have become disguises . . . [that are] not so much a breaking away as a getting back into. . . . This occurs in invented Indians because we're invented and we're invented from traditional static standards and we are stuck in coins and words like artifacts. Some upsetting is necessary."[79] Thus Vizenor envisions the imagined Indian not only as a colonial template, but also—in reinvented form coming from native imaginations—as a cultural resource. In *Prison Writings: My Life is My Sun Dance*, Leonard Peltier defends indigenous people, and what he refers to as "the Indian Way," from his prison cell in Leavenworth, Kansas. He succeeds in transforming imprisonment into a powerful metaphor of spiritual sacrifice and connection to Lakota tradition and history:

> When you grow up Indian, you quickly learn that the so-called American Dream isn't for you. For you that dream's a nightmare. . . . When I turned to one of the marshals . . . I saw . . . a mask of absolute hatred and a look in his eyes so vile that it can't even be described. . . . I swear, I saw his face and head turn into a serpent's, spitting its venom at me. . . . [Suddenly] my mind flashed with bright images of the Sun Dance, of the holy Tree of Life connecting me to the world, of the skewers being threaded into my flesh and the thongs being pulled tight until the flesh broke, freeing me. . . . Yes, this was my offering to *Tunkashila,* the Great Mystery—my flesh, my life, my very existence. They could entomb my body, but my spirit they could never touch.[80]

The battle over signifying "the Indian" was (and is) not a complete victory for white men. By both invoking and revoking the white man's Indian, indigenous people have carved out a space from which to challenge and complicate normative ideas about a racialized America in which hegemonic manhood is white.[81] The formation and maintenance of oppositional masculinities remain today the result of tensions and contradictions in ongoing conquest. Indigenous people continue to reimagine assimilation in ways that resist its unwanted consequences. They challenge mischaracterizations of indigenous character and spirituality. They expose crimes perpetrated against their people. They lament the misfortunes and celebrate the joys indigenous people experience as they move from older worlds to newer ones.[81]

Notes

We wish to thank Barry Shank, Troy Johnson, Richard Schur, and Cheryl R. Ragar for their thoughtful and helpful comments on earlier drafts of this paper.

1. On June 24, 1876, five companies of the U.S. Seventh Cavalry under the command of Lieutenant Colonel George Armstrong Custer were overpowered and routed in the valley of the Little Big Horn River by a combined force of Northern Cheyennes, Arapahos, and Lakotas, the latter led by Tasunke Witko (Crazy Horse), defending their families, who were encamped along the river. For the more conservative estimates of the number of Lakota and Cheyenne warriors in the valley of the Little Big Horn, see Robert M. Utley, *Frontier Regulars: The United States Army and the Indian, 1866–1891* (1973; reprint, Lincoln: University of Nebraska, 1984), 259. See also, more recently, Gregory F. Michno, *Lakota Noon: The Indian Narrative of Custer's Defeat* (Missoula, Mont.: Mountain Press, 1997), who is more in agreement with the substantially lower figures found in Charles Alexander Eastman, "The Story of the Little Big Horn (Told from the Indian Standpoint by One of Their Race)," *The Chautauquan* 31 (1900): 353–58; and Russell Means, *Where White Men Fear to Tread: The Autobiography of Russell Means,* ed. Marvin J. Wolf (New York: St. Martin's Press, 1995), 490. See also Paul L. Hedren, ed., *The Great Sioux War, 1876–1877: The Best from* Montana, the Magazine of History (Helena: Montana Historical Society Press, 1991), 13–14; Colin G. Calloway, *Our Hearts Fell to the Ground: Plains Indian Views of How the West Was Lost* (Boston: Bedford Books of St. Martin's Press, 1996), 134; and James Welch, *Killing Custer: The Battle of Little Bighorn and the Fate of the Plains Indians* (New York: Penguin Books, 1994).

2. Moving Robe Woman, in *Lakota Recollections of the Custer Fight: New Sources of Indian-Military History,* ed. Richard G. Hardorff (1991; reprint, Lincoln: University of Nebraska Press, 1997), 91, 92, 93, 94, and 95.

3. *Wooden Leg: A Warrior Who Fought Custer,* ed. Thomas B. Marquis (1931; reprint, Lincoln: University of Nebraska Press, 1962), 221–22.

4. Our retelling of *Peji Sla Wakapa* is constructed primarily from Hedren, John S. Gray, and Robert M. Utley, *Custer's Last Campaign: Mitch Boyer and the Little Bighorn Reconstructed* (Lincoln: University of Nebraska Press, 1993); Michno; and Welch.

5. Zachariah Taylor to the Commissioner of Indian Affairs, December 3, 1875, quoted in Welsh, 53.

6. U.S. Department of War, *Annual Report of the Secretary of War,* 43rd Cong., 2nd Sess. (Washington, D.C.: GPO, 1876), 441.

7. Shirley A. Leckie, *Elizabeth Bacon Custer and the Making of a Myth* (Norman: University of Oklahoma Press, 1993), 540.

8. W. A. Graham, *The Reno Court of Inquiry: Abstract of the Official Record of Proceedings,* intro. Brian C. Pohanka (1954; reprint, Mechanicsburg, Penn.: Stackpole Books, 1995). Charles E. Rankin, ed., *Legacy: New Perspectives on the Battle of the Little Big Horn* (Helena: Montana Historical Society Press, 1996). Brian A. Dippie, "Introduction" in Robert M. Utley, *Custer and the Great Controversy: The Origin and Development of a Legend* (1962; reprint, Lincoln, University of Nebraska Press, 1998) and Dippie, *Custer's Last Stand: The Anatomy of an American Myth* (1976; reprint, Lincoln: University of Nebraska Press, 1994) survey the scholarly literature. Issues of the Little Big Horn Associates' newsletter (established in 1967) provide historical articles and general information about Custer and others associated with the battle, period pieces and information, enactment news, and a general informational bulletin board. The Custer/Little Bighorn Battlefield Advocate Homepage, http://www.members.aol.com/CusterFact/index.html, indicates that it is "dedicated to fighting grave desecration, 'political correctness,' [antiwhite] racism, and overdevelopment at the Little Bighorn (formally Custer) Battlefield National Monument." See also http://www.garryowen.com, which contains links to action-figure playsets, newsletters such as the *Battlefield Dispatch* and *The Advocate,* and the Custer Battlefield Historical and Museum Association and the Little Bighorn Associates. See the website http://www.mt.net/~oldwest/LBH/goldsamp.htm for "Little Big Horn Trading Cards."

9 . Dana D. Nelson, *National Manhood: Capitalist Citizenship and the Fraternity of White Men* (Durham, N.C.: Duke University Press, 1998).

10. For an examination of connections between manhood and nationhood, see Joane Nagel, "Masculinity and Nationalism: Gender and Sexuality in the Making of Nations," *Ethnic and Racial Studies* 21, no. 2 (1998): 242–69.

11. See Anthony Rotundo, *American Manhood: Transformations in Masculinity from the Revolution to the Modern Era* (New York: Basic Books, 1993); Mark C. Carnes, *Secret Ritual and Manhood in Victorian America* (New Haven: Yale University Press, 1989); Gail Bederman, *Manliness and Civilization: A Cultural History of Gender and Race in the United States, 1880–1917* (Chicago: University of Chicago Press, 1995); and George L. Mosse, *The Image of Man: The Creation of Modern Masculinity* (New York: Oxford University Press, 1996).

12. Bederman; Mosse; and Robert W. Connell, *Manliness* (Berkeley and Los Angeles: University of California Press, 1995).

13. Mike Donaldson, "What is Hegemonic Masculinity?" *Theory and Society* 22, no. 4 (1993): 643–57; and David Morgan, *Discovering Men* (London: Routledge, 1992).

14. Mosse, 7.

15. See Anthony D. Smith, *National Identity* (Reno: University of Nevada Press, 1991); Samuel N. Eisenstadt and Stein Rokkan, *Building States and Nations* (Beverly Hills: Sage, 1973); Benedict Anderson, *Imagined Communities: Reflections on the Origin and Spread of Nationalism* (London: Verso, 1991); and Eric Hobsbawm, *Nations and Nationalism since 1780* (New York: Cambridge University Press, 1990).

16. See Roslyn Wallach Bologh, *Love or Greatness: Max Weber and Masculine Thinking—A Feminist Inquiry* (London: Unwin Hyman, 1990); John M. MacKenzie, "The Imperial Pioneer and Hunter and the British Masculine Stereotype in Late Victorian and Edwardian Times," in *Manliness and Morality: Middle-Class Masculinity in Britain and America, 1800–1940,* ed. J. A. Mangan and James Walvin (Manchester: Manchester University Press, 1982), 176–98; James Walvin, "Symbols of Moral Superiority: Slavery, Sport and the Changing World Order, 1900–1940," in *ibid.,* 242–60.

17. Mrinalini Sinha, *Colonial Masculinity: The "Manly Englishman" and the "Effeminate Bengali" in the Late Nineteenth Century* (Manchester: Manchester University Press, 1995); Seth Koven, "From Rough Lads to Hooligans: Boy Life, National Culture, and Social Reform," in *Nationalisms and Sexualities,* ed. Andrew Parker et al. (New York: Routledge, 1991); and Hobsbawm.

18. John Springhall, "Building Character in the British Boy: The Attempt to Extend Christian Manliness to Working-Class Adolescents, 1880–1940," in Mangan and Walvin, 52.

19. See Vine Deloria, Jr., "Congress in Its Wisdom: The Course of Indian Legislation," in *The Aggressions of Civilization: Federal Indian Policy since the 1880s,* ed. Sandra L. Cadwalader and Vine Deloria, Jr. (Philadelphia: Temple University Press, 1984); and Walter L. Williams, "From Independence to Wardship: The Legal Process of Erosion of American Indian Sovereignty, 1810–1903," *American Indian Culture and Research Journal* 7, no. 4 (1984): 5–32.

20. See, for example, Vine Deloria, Jr., "The American Indian Image in North America," in *The Pretend Indians: Images of Native Americans in the Movies,* ed. Gretchen M. Bataille and Charles L. P. Silet (Ames: Iowa State University Press, 1980), 51 and 52.

21. Frederick E. Hoxie, *A Final Promise: The Campaign to Assimilate the Indians, 1880–1920* (1984; reprint, New York: Cambridge University Press, 1989), 187, and of "The Curious Story of Reformers," in *Indians in American History: An Introduction,* ed. Frederick E. Hoxie (Arlington Heights, Ill.: Harlan Davidson, 1988), 221.

22. *Black Elk Speaks: Being the Life of a Holy Man of the Oglala Sioux,* as told to John G. Neihardt (1932; reprint, Lincoln: University of Nebraska Press, 1979), 212, 210, 211, 196, 20.

23. See, for example, Bederman; Joe L. Dubbert, "Progressivism and the Masculinity Crisis," in *The American Man* (Englewood Cliffs, NJ: Prentice Hall, 1980); Peter G. Filene, *Him/Her/Self: Sex Roles in Modern America* (Baltimore: Johns Hopkins University Press, 1986); John Higham, "The Reorientation of American Culture in the 1890s," in *Writing American History: Essays on Modern Scholarship* (Bloomington: Indiana University Press, 1978); and James R. McGovern, "David Graham Phillips and the Virility Impulse of the Progressives," *New England Quarterly* 39, no. 3 (1966): 334–55.

24. Bederman, 12.

25. For these earlier simulations, see Richard Slotkin, *Regeneration through Violence: The Mythology of the American Frontier, 1600–1860* (1973; reprint, New York: HarperPerennial, 1996); and Reginald Horsman, *Race and Manifest Destiny: The Origins of American Anglo-Saxonism* (Cambridge, Mass.: Harvard University Press, 1981), esp. 103–15.

26. "Roosevelt," according to Bederman (181), "repeatedly described Indians as brutal despoilers of women and children, invoking (like so many of his contemporaries) the ubiquitous cultural figure of the savage primitivist rapist." For antecedents of the Indian as rapist that suggest that captivity materials illuminate American anxieties about gender on the frontier and in American society, see June Namias, *White Captives: Gender and Ethnicity on the American Frontier* (Chapel Hill: University of North Carolina Press, 1993).

27. Roosevelt quoted in Herman Hagedorn, *Roosevelt in the Badlands* (1921; reprint, Boston: Houghton Mifflin, 1930), 355.

28. Bederman, 181.

29. Theodore Roosevelt, *The Winning of the West*, vol. 1: *From the Alleghenies to the Mississippi, 1769–1776* (1889; reprint, Lincoln: University of Nebraska Press, 1995), 110, 123, and 124. On Indian-hating as ideology, see Richard M. Drinnon, *Facing West: The Metaphysics of Indian-Hating and Empire Building* (1980; reprint, Norman: University of Oklahoma Press, 1997), esp. 299.

30. Indigenous people have disputed assumptions underlying these captivity narratives. See, for example, Thunder Traveling Over the Mountains (Chief Joseph), "An Indian's Views of Indian Affairs," with an introduction by William H. Ware, *North American Review* 128 (1879), 427, who asked his English-reading audience: "Can the white soldiers tell me of one time when Indian women were taken prisoner . . . without being insulted," just before pointing out that white women prisoners of war "were not insulted" by his people but instead "were treated kindly."

31. Namias, 109. See also Gary L. Ebersole, *Captured by Texts: Puritan to Postmodern Images of Indian Captivity* (Charlottesville: University of Virginia Press, 1995); and Rebecca Blevins Faery, *Cartographies of Desire: Captivity, Race, and Sex in the Shaping of an American Nation* (Norman: University of Oklahoma Press, 1999).

32. See, most recently, Albert L. Hurtado, *Intimate Frontiers: Sex, Gender, and Culture in Old California* (Albuquerque: University of New Mexico Press, 1999); Richard Godbeer, "Eroticizing the Middle Ground: Anglo-Indian Sexual Relations along the Eighteenth-Century Frontier," and Jennifer M. Spear, "'They Need Wives': Metíssage and the Regulation of Sexuality in French Louisiana, 1666–1730," in *Sex, Love, Race: Crossing Boundaries in North American History*, ed. Martha Hodes (New York: New York University Press, 1999).

33. George Crook, quoted in Francis Paul Prucha, *The Great Father: The United States Government and the American Indians* (Lincoln: University of Nebraska Press, 1984), 548.

34. Nelson A. Miles, *Personal Recollections and Observations of General Nelson A. Miles* (Chicago: Werner Company, 1896), 88 and 95; and *Serving the Republic: Memoirs of the Civil and Military Life of Nelson A. Miles* (1911; reprint, Freeport, New York: Books for the Library Press, 1971).

35. For a discussion of both white "Indian" organizations, see Mark C. Carnes, *Secret Ritual and Manhood in Victorian America* (New Haven: Yale University Press, 1989).

36. Richard Irving Dodge, *Our Wild Indians: Thirty-three Years Personal Experience among the Red Men of the Great West* (1883; reprint, New York: Archer House, 1959), v, vi. Dodge recognized that there were hundreds of indigenous nations, but that there was only one "Indian" character. See Dodge, 53, 56, and 248. For a broader discussion of representations of Indian character by U.S. army officers, see Sherry L. Smith, *The View from Officers' Row: Army Perceptions of Western Indians* (Tucson: University of Arizona Press, 1990), esp. 15–27.

37. Dodge, 30.

38. Ibid., 641, 645, and 646.

39. This was also the case for an apparently realistic art form that, upon closer inspection, forged and preserved a never-ending land of male fantasy. See Corlann Gee Bush, "The Way We Weren't: Images of Women and Men in Cowboy Art," in *The Women's West*, ed. Susan Armitage and Elizabeth Jameson (Norman: University of Oklahoma Press, 1987).

40. L. G. Moses, *Wild West Shows and the Images of American Indians, 1883–1933* (Albuquerque: University of New Mexico Press, 1996), 4.

41. Hartford *Courant* journalist, quoted in Henry Blackman Sell and Victor Weybright, *Buffalo Bill and the Wild West* (Basin, Wyo.: Big Horn Books, 1979), 135–36. See also Moses.

42. Paul Reddin, *Wild West Shows* (Urbana: University of Illinois Press, 1999), 129.

43. Last-minute rescue sequences looking back to stage melodrama and forward to epic Westerns, according to Raymond William Stedman, link the invented western landscapes of printed narratives with the visual narratives of the Wild West shows and motion picture westerns. Stedman, *Shadows of the Indian: Stereotypes in American Culture* (Norman: University of Oklahoma Press, 1982), 260.

44. The curious phenomenon of white American men "playing Indian" was nothing new at the turn of the century. See Philip J. Deloria, *Playing Indian* (New Haven: Yale University Press, 1998); and Shari Huhndorf, "From the Turn of the Century to the New Age: Playing Indian, Past and Present," in *As We Are Now: Mixblood Essays on Race and Identity*, ed. William S. Penn (Berkeley and Los Angeles: University of California Press, 1997), 184–85.

45. See, for example, Sylvia Gronewold, "Did Frank Cushing Go Native?" in *Crossing Cultural Boundaries: The Anthropological Experience*, ed. Solon T. Kimball and James B. Watson (San Francisco: Chandler Publishing Company, 1972).

46. See Frank Hamilton Cushing, "The Zuñi Social, Mythic, and Religious Systems," *Popular Science Monthly* 21 (1882): 186–92; and Cushing, "The Nation of the Willows," *Atlantic Monthly* 50 (1882): 362–74,

541–49; Cushing, "My Adventures in Zuñi," *Century Illustrated Monthly Magazine* 25, (1882): 191–207. See also Sylvester Baxter, "The Father of the Pueblos," *Harper's* 65 (1882): 72–91; and Baxter, "An Aboriginal Pilgrimage," *Century Illustrated Monthly Magazine* 24, no. 4 (1882): 526–36.

47. Philip J. Deloria, 119.

48. "Word to the Readers of the Century," *Century Illustrated Monthly Magazine* 26 (1883), 951.

49. Vine Deloria, Jr., *Custer Died for Your Sins: An Indian Manifesto* (New York: Macmillan, 1969), 95.

50. Renato Rosaldo, *Culture and Truth: The Remaking of Social Analysis* (Boston: Beacon Press, 1989), 69.

51. See, for instance, Jay Mechling, "'Playing Indian' and the Search for Authenticity in Modern White America," *Prospects* no. 5 (1980): 17–33.

52. Sherman Coolidge, an Arapaho, attempted to join the Improved Order, but was turned down. See *American Indian Magazine* 5, no. 4 (1929): 4. These peculiar practices continue today in white men's "tribes" all over the country. Sponsored by the Young Men's Christian Association, the Y-Indian Guides, for instance, in the words of the official program description, "support the father's vital family role as teacher, counselor and friend to his son." According to institutional lore, the Y-Indian Guides were "initiated" by Harold S. Keltner, St. Louis YMCA director. In 1926, apparently, Keltner organized the first tribe in Richmond Heights, Missouri, "with the help of his good friend, Joe Friday, an Ojibway Indian, and William H. Hefelfinger, chief of the first Y-Indian Guide tribe." For the official program description and a brief institutional history of the Y-Indian Guides, see http://www.ymca.net/c/1/2.html. "Keltner imbued the program with Indian traditions and trappings," according to Buzz McClain. "Sons and dads gave themselves secret Indian names, donned headbands with feathers, developed blood-curdling tribal yells, and bonded on overnight camp outs featuring quasi-educational, quasi-authentic Native American ceremonies." See Buzz McClain, "Indian Guide Camp Outs," *Dallas Child*, http://www.family.disney.go.com/Features/family_1997_09/dalc/dalc97tribes/dalc97tribes.html.

53. Huhndorf, 190, 191.

54. Ernest Thompson Seton, *The Birch Bark Roll of the Woodcraft League of America, Inc.* (New York: Doubleday, 1927), 161. See also Huhndorf, 190. An earlier version of *The Birch Bark Roll* was entitled *How to Play Indian* (Philadelphia: Curtis Publishing Company, 1903). See H. Allen Anderson, "Ernest Thompson Seton and the Woodcraft Indians," *Journal of American Culture* 8, no. 1 (1985): 46.

55. Seton quoted in H. Allen Anderson, *The Chief: Ernest Thompson Seton and the Changing West* (College Station: Texas A&M University Press, 1986), 132.

56. Ernest Thompson Seton, *Trail of an Artist-Naturalist: The Autobiography of Ernest Thompson Seton* (New York: Charles Scribner's Sons, 1940), 376.

57. Anderson, *The Chief*, 135.

58. Ernest Thompson Seton, *Boy Scouts of America: A Handbook of Woodcraft, Scouting, and Lifecraft* (New York: Doubleday, 1910), 1–2; and Seten, *Trail of an Artist-Naturalist*, in which Seton goes on to point out that "whatever is picturesque, good, and safe in Indian life, that we used" (384).

59. The image of boys swimming naked in his lake is in *Trail of an Artist-Naturist*, 380. For references to turning "arms white as milk" into the "brown sinewy arm of the Indian," see Ernest Thompson Seton, *Two Little Savages: Being the Adventures of Two Boys Who Lived as Indians and What They Learned* (1903; reprint, New York: Doubleday, 1959), 45.

60. "Like his friend Theodore Roosevelt," in the words of Seton's biographer, H. Allen Anderson, "Seton was a firm believer in the 'strenuous life,' the ideal of physical fitness based on rigorous exercise through sports and outdoor recreation to revitalize the American character." See Anderson, "Ernest Thompson Seton," 43; and Anderson, *The Chief*, 129. "The ideal life," according to Seton in another context, was "the life of an Indian with all that is bad and cruel left out." See Seton, *Two Little Savages*, 42.

61. Seton, *Trail of an Artist-Naturalist*, 380 and 381.

62. See Philip J. Deloria, 98, 103.

63. Seton's Woodcraft Indians institutionalized identities thought to be Indian through a hierarchy of "tribal" offices that included chiefs and sagamores (of various levels and purposes), wampum keepers, shamans, and dog soldiers. He designated himself Medicine Man and named himself Black Wolf because, in the words of his biographer, "he was an authority on wolves." Seton's "Indians" adopted names like Plenty Coups, Deerslayer, Tatanka, and Little Eagle. Only "Indian" names were used by Woodcraft Indians; "violators had to 'run the gauntlet' between his fellow tribesmen's legs and get slapped on the rump." See Anderson, *The Chief*, 140. Seton's boys were taught to "think Indian." Regurgitations of Woodcraft knowledges, demonstrations of physical prowess, and simulations of "Indian" dances and songs enabled boys to advance in their knowledge of Indian play.

64. Seton, *Trail of an Artist-Naturalist*, 385.

65. Like the Woodcraft Indians, Y-Indians today also move along a hierarchy of titles but, interestingly and tellingly, Y-Indian titles may be directly related to the relationship of fathers to "tribe" rather than to the individual achievements of "little braves." Also like the Woodcraft Indians, Y-Indians appear

to stage elaborate theatrical performances for indoctrinating little braves with organization knowledges like paddling canoes and drawing Indian princesses. These feats of intellectual savvy are awarded with imitation bear claws and arrowheads, fake eagle feathers, and beads. Y-Indians wear headbands and necklaces, and carry what they call "coup sticks." They hold meetings during which tally keepers take roll and wampum bearers gather dues and scouting reports, drum bearers beat drums while chiefs and little braves form circles around sacred fires, and chiefs lead little braves in repeating slogans and organizational aims.

66. For a discussion of the mythopoetic men's movement, see Michael Schwalbe, *Unlocking the Iron Cage: The Men's Movement, Gender Politics, and American Culture* (New York: Oxford University Press, 1996).

67. *Sporting Life* journalist (1897), quoted in Jay Feldman, "The Rise and Fall of Louis Sockalexis," *Baseball Research Journal* 15 (1986): 40.

68. Lawrence Hauptman, "Playing Indian," in *Tribes and Tribulations: Misconceptions about American Indians and Their Histories* (Albuquerque: University of New Mexico Press, 1995), 83 and 85. According to Hauptman, Sockalexis "was constantly insulted and even faced personal threats and racial epithets" (86).

69. John Ward, quoted in Feldman, 40.

70. Sitting Bull had been murdered at the Pine Ridge Indian Agency while being taken into custody by a reservation police officer seven years earlier in December 1890.

71. Roy Harvey Pearce, *Savagism and Civilization: A Study of the Indian and the American Mind* (1953; reprint, Berkeley and Los Angeles: University of California Press, 1988), 58.

72. Vine Deloria, Jr., "American Fantasy," in *The Pretend Indians,* xvi. See also Leslie Fielder, *The Return of the Vanishing American* (New York: Stein and Day, 1968), 75.

73. Artifacts stolen from and mass-produced photographs expropriated from hundreds of Minneconjous and Oglalas at Wounded Knee in 1890, for instance, were "affordable entertainment . . . available for leisurely consumption in parlors across America." See Christina Klein, "'Everything of Interest in the Late Pine Ridge War Are Held by Us for Sale': Popular Culture and Wounded Knee," *Western Historical Quarterly* 25, no. 1 (1994): 57–58.

74. "A Sioux boy is taught to be brave always," Standing Bear told his readers, *My Indian Boyhood* (1931; reprint, Lincoln: University of Nebraska Press, 1988), 148. "It is not sufficient to be brave enough to go to war. He must be brave enough to make personal sacrifices and to think little of personal gain."

75. Standing Bear, *My Indian Boyhood,* 156–57.

76. Charles Alexander Eastman, *From the Deep Woods to Civilization: Chapters in the Autobiography of an Indian* (1916; reprint, Lincoln: University of Nebraska Press, 1977), 31–32, 50, and 59. "My father was very proud of me to think that he could depend on me for the sake of the whole tribe" Standing Bear, similarly told himself and his readers in 1931 (*My People the Sioux,* 168).

77. Standing Bear, *Land of the Spotted Eagle* (1933; reprint, Lincoln: University of Nebraska Press, 1978), 228.

78. See Eastman, 53.

79. Neal Bowers and Charles L. P. Silet, "An Interview with Gerald Vizenor," *MELUS* 8, no. 1 (1981): 45, 46, 47.

80. Leonard Peltier, *Prison Writings: My Life is My Sun Dance,* ed. Harvey Arden (New York: St. Martin's Press, 1999), 66, 155, and 156–57.

81. See David Anthony Tyeeme Clark, "'This Warning Has Been Handed Down among My People': Evasive Indigenous Subjectivities, Native Nations, and Cultures of United States Imperialism," a dissertation (in progress) that examines the terrain of political activity and symbolic expression, which worked together to form contexts (or boundaries) for being "Indian" in a colonialist context before the hurricane of Red Power activism.

82. For a discussion of native resistance, see Paul Chaat Smith and Robert Allen Warrior, *Like A Hurricane: The Indian Movement from Alcatraz to Wounded Knee* (New York: New Press, 1996); and Alvin M. Josephy, Jr., Joane Nagel, and Troy Johnson, eds., *Red Power: The American Indians' Fight for Freedom* (Lincoln: University of Nebraska Press, 1999).

"A Distinct and Antagonistic Race"

Constructions of Chinese Manhood in the Exclusionist Debates, 1869–1878

Karen J. Leong

They are bringing plague and pestilence
In fever-laden ships,
And taking gold and silver back
On their returning trips.
They are bringing hordes of prostitutes
To ply their trade of shame,
And breeding vice and foul disease
Too horrible to name.
In fetid lanes and alleys
They are like a festering sore.
They are coming, they are coming,
Every week a thousand more.
—*Sam Booth, "They Are Coming"*[1]

Throughout the 1860s, politicians and labor leaders in California and other western states sounded the alarm at the prospect of thousands of Chinese male laborers descending like a plague, a "yellow peril," upon the United States. The image of the Chinese female prostitute proved a key rhetorical device not only in Booth's poem, but also in western states' efforts to restrict the immigration of Chinese male laborers through federal legislation. The Chinese Exclusion Act of 1882 denied entry to Chinese laborers for ten years. The first enacted piece of federal legislation to restrict immigration to the United States explicitly based on nationality, Chinese exclusion was symptomatic of heightened sensitivity to issues of race and citizenship as well as a depressed economy and labor conflicts after the Civil War. Depictions of Chinese prostitutes and the illicit sexuality associated with Chinese laborers implicated the Chinese male as immoral, uncivilized, and fundamentally unfit for American citizenship. The architects of the anti-Chinese movement and subsequent exclusion laws expanded this theme into a broad-ranging, gendered argument against the Chinese as a race. Proponents of Chinese exclusion would measure Chinese men against normative standards of Anglo-American masculinity and find them wanting.

The argument that Chinese men did not meet the ideal of Anglo-American masculinity and thus could not be virtuous republican citizens ideologically justified restricting Chinese immigrant labor. Scholars have examined how gendered arguments for exclusion relied on the image of the Chinese prostitute, yet largely have neglected complementary constructions of Chinese and Anglo-American working-class masculinity.[2] Gendered rhetoric circumvented the obstacles posed by federal constitutional law and diplomacy to states' attempts to enact anti-Chinese legislation on a racial basis. The anti-Chinese movement thus shifted emphasis from the racial threat posed by Chinese male laborers to the moral threat posed by "aberrant" Chinese gender relations. The reconstruction of racial difference as cultural difference suggested the inability of Chinese to maintain American cultural values as evidenced in the lack of a home, family, and "appropriate" relations between men and women. This strategy also allowed western state representatives to successfully situate their regional economic interests within the post-Reconstruction national discourse of race, gender, sexuality, and morality, which ultimately transcended the sectionalism of the antebellum period.

The anti-Chinese movement established itself nationally in the United States by the end of the 1870s, advocating the exclusion of the Chinese male laborer because of his fundamental difference from the Anglo-American male citizen. Perceptions that a majority of Chinese women immigrants had been forced into prostitution helped to justify the United States' rejection of Chinese manhood. Chinese men's alleged exploitation of women betrayed their lack of manhood—in this case, a failure to protect female virtue—and revealed their unsuitability as Americans. Describing the Chinese trade in women, Senator Higby of California declared in 1870, "That is their character. You cannot make citizens of them."[3] A poem printed in the *San Francisco Chronicle*, "How He Sold Her Short," told a tragic tale of a young Chinese woman, Ching Lee, who was courted by a young man in China and traveled to join him in the United States, only to be sold on arrival to another man. The poet ended this epic with a "MORAL. Now all you Chinese maidens who have lovers far away, / Be careful of your characters, and don't be led astray, / Don't leave your native rice fields to join a moon-eyed sport, / For fear you be, like poor Ching Lee, sold very badly short."[4] In 1878, a speaker in New York similarly distinguished Chinese from American men: "They consider the wife a slavish chattel; we consider her a sacred partner. . ."[5] The conclusions drawn from these images of degraded women, of "female slaves," enabled American men and women to judge Chinese standards of morality as inferior to their own.

This moral argument crystallized in the national political consciousness when, in February 1878, the House Committee on Education and Labor issued a special report addressing the question of Chinese immigration. The committee provided three reasons why the Chinese male would be an "undesirable citizen": his effect on labor, his debilitating effect on society, and his inability to assimilate. The Chinese laborer was inferior to his Anglo-European counterpart because the American laborer "shall possess courage, self-respect and independence. To do this he must have a home." Exclusionists implied that Chinese workers depressed wages to the point where property ownership became impossible. Second, the Chinese evidenced peculiar moral habits in "their treatment of women" by profiting from their sexual servitude. In other words, by organizing prostitution, Chinese men reneged on their duty as providers. Chinese women faced lives full of "privation, contempt and degradation from the cradle to the tomb." Third, Chinese men failed to establish nuclear family households. Chinese males distinguished themselves from other immigrants because "[t]hey bring with them neither wives nor families, nor do they intermarry with the resident population. . . . Mentally, morally, physically, socially and politically *they have remained a distinct and antagonistic race*."[6] All three reasons focus on the aberration of Chinese gender roles as perceived by the American public.

According to these perceptions, the Chinese male laborer failed to fulfill the gendered, cultural requirements of American citizenship. As several feminist historians have demonstrated, American citizenship relied upon and perpetuated the economic and moral dimensions of Anglo masculine identity. The American male demonstrated his independence and self-sufficiency by providing economically for his dependents—his wife and children—and upheld social morality by protecting the virtue of his dependents and others. The ability to provide for a family constituted an integral component of citizenship.[7] As Stephanie McCurry has noted in her study of antebellum South Carolina yeomen, maintaining dominance over dependents has constituted an integral yet often overlooked aspect of how republican ideology defined the independent male American citizen.[8] Increasingly after Reconstruction, citizenship was equated with a masculinity and whiteness that were maintained by policing the racial, class, and gendered boundaries of middle-class Anglo-American behavior.[9] Those males who neither formed families nor supported them thus undermined the assumed heterosexual, nuclear household basis of the national economy.

Similarly, anti-Chinese rhetoric also centered around the Chinese laborers' lack of wives, family, and homes, and the danger "inassimilable aliens" posed to the republic and its families. Without a home, a "Chinaman" had no reason to defend the country; without a family, a "Chinaman" had no reason to invest in the future well-being of the nation; without a wife, a "Chinaman" was simply barbaric and uncivilized.[10] Based on definitions of American masculinity, the "Chinaman" was no man at all. This argument developed after the mid-1870s to encompass relationships in which gender identities were central: marriage, family, and even the republic itself. In 1878, Senator Jones of Nevada succinctly explained the danger Chinese men posed by citing both their effect on wages and their responsibility for Chinese prostitutes: "They debauch our men by their virtues and our boys by their vices."[11]

Constructions of the Chinese as a race and culture alien to all things American focused upon the ways Chinese male behavior deviated from Anglo-American social norms. One magazine article described the Chinese as a "community of males, without the humanizing influences of women and children." According to this interpretation, "no such principle in the Chinese make-up as filial, connubial or any other form of affection" existed because Chinese men spent their money buying sexual favors from prostitutes as opposed to investing in their homes and families.[12] Women, as this article implies, were considered civilizing forces in American society. The lack of virtuous females offered little hope that Chinese men would change. Without their civilizing influence, Chinese men could not be expected to become true citizens. The apparent fact that most Chinese women were immoral only amplified the extent to which Chinese men were wicked and debased.

Standards of masculinity, femininity, sexuality, and morality were central to the construction of working-class Anglo-American masculinity and also defined the working-class "Chinaman."[13] Rather than solely protecting the livelihood of the white male worker and thus maintaining the rights associated with American masculinity, anti-Chinese agitators also asserted their own masculine roles as protectors of the nation's morality and families. This paralleled a similar development in the Reconstruction South where, according to Martha Hodes, the prospects of political equality and economic mobility for freedmen were expressed in fears about sexual intimacy between black men and white women, resulting in the sexualization of politics.[14] Emerging norms of sexuality and morality, then, helped to maintain a racial division between Euro-American citizenry and "others," including African-American freedmen and Chinese immigrants, at the end of Reconstruction.[15]

Further examination of the gendered rhetoric of the movement to restrict Chinese immigration illustrates how issues of sexuality and gender became integral to projections of racial difference. At this particular moment, when many Americans sought to avoid the divisive issue of racial difference in Reconstruction politics, gender norms critically expressed and contributed to the national definition of American citizenry as male and of Anglo-European descent. The image of the Chinese female immigrant as enslaved, abused, and sexually exploited provided a key means through which Anglo-American working men on the West Coast could read gender and race onto the foreign body of the Chinese male worker. By articulating their own white, American masculinity in opposition to the Chinese foreigner, they thereby claimed their own political and moral dominance within the sphere of national politics.

The Chinese question emerged on a national level at a crucial time in U.S. history. In the aftermath of the Civil War, radical Republicans sought to reshape the nation. They envisioned an ideal society based on equal rights, free labor, and the continued civilizing of the frontier. One Republican declared, "My dream is of a model republic, extending equal protection and rights to all men. . . . The wilderness shall vanish, the church and school-house will appear; . . . the whole land will revive under the magic touch of free labor."[16] Reconstruction legislated equality in terms of race and class but excluded gender.[17] Male politicians described the model republic from the very end of the Civil War and the beginnings of Reconstruction in masculine terms: the republic would include all men, who would manifest not only their destiny but also their manhood by extending the republic geographically. Women had roles in what Amy Kaplan has termed *manifest domesticity*—the civilizing efforts that accompanied the spread of free labor and government not only across the expanse of what constituted the United States, but abroad as well.[18] During radical Reconstruction, however, the gendered construction of the republic remained subordinate to the question of race that had under-lain the issue of free labor during the antebellum period.

Debates over the immigration of Chinese labor during Reconstruction revived unresolved concerns about race and the specter of slavery. Proponents of restricting Chinese labor evoked the free labor argument: Chinese wage labor would have the same effect as slavery on American labor and industry, undermining the possibility of free men to provide for their families. Opponents of restrictions, on the other hand. warned against restricting a group of immigrants on the basis of race. Indeed, opponents suc-cessfully rejected an 1869 bill that restricted the entry of Chinese contract labor and Chinese women on the grounds that the bill was motivated by race prejudice.[19] In 1869, Senator Williams proposed a bill that would deny entry to Chinese contract laborers, and would require any Chinese woman immi-grant to be accompanied by her husband or father.[20] Williams presented this secondary provision in Congress as a form of slavery on par with that of Chinese contract labor. During the open debate on this bill, Senator Pomeroy of Kansas quibbled with the largess of Senator Howard from Oregon. Pomeroy noted Howard's claims "that this [bill] is only to discriminate against a certain class; but the objection is that in that effort we discriminate against the whole. . . ." Pomeroy further disputed Howard's argument that his bill would prevent a type of slavery: "I am for the suppression of the slave trade . . . but I am not for discriminating against persons who propose to become American citizens, whether they are white or black; whether they are from China or from Africa."[21]

The agitation on the part of western states to exclude all Chinese based on race conflicted ideologically with attempts to transform the slave economy in the South to that of free labor based on the equality of all men. The passage of both the Fourteenth Amendment and the Civil Rights Bill of 1870 extended rights of equality before the law, in principle, to all naturalized or native-born peoples in the United States.[22] Some radical Republicans attempted to extend rights explicitly to Native Americans and Chinese, not solely blacks. By 1870, however, California Republicans recognized that supporting legislation granting rights to the Chinese would alienate voters and significantly erode their party's representation in that state. Subsequently, California politicians united across party lines as well as with other western representatives to ensure that the Fifteenth Amendment would not interfere with individual states' suffrage qualifications.[23]

However, western politicians who sought to exclude Chinese immigrants from America's shores still faced particularly formidable legal obstacles posed by the U.S. Constitution and international diplomacy. State laws could be overruled by both the federal and state court systems and Chinese immigrants successfully challenged many anti-Chinese laws in court.[24] The California Supreme Court and the Federal District Court ruled various state and San Francisco anti-Chinese laws unconstitutional, based largely on the 1868 Burlingame Treaty, which extended to Chinese the equal protection enjoyed by American citizens under the Fourteenth Amendment as part of a free trade and migration agreement between the United States and China.[25] California's right to self-protection was deemed subordinate to federal law in 1874, when the California Supreme Court struck down California's law prohibiting the importation of prostitutes. State protection could be ensured only by passing legislation that protected western interests on the federal level.

Meanwhile, the growing disparity between working men and industrialists resulted in class antagonism that in itself reflected norms of American manhood.[26] The self-made man celebrated by American liberal ideology demonstrated his self-sufficiency in part by his property. Working-class men in the western states feared that they might never attain this goal in the wake of the 1873 economic depression and increasing competition for jobs. During the Reconstruction era, however, their complaints—often phrased in terms of Chinese inferiority to whites—were dismissed on the whole as racist and self-seeking. One unidentified Californian complained, "It has even been asserted, and prominent men and journals in the East have repeated it, that the opposition to Chinese immigration in California is confined to a few demagogues and discontented communists."[27]

Western politicians and newspapers frequently expressed frustration that other states did not fully understand the effects of Chinese immigration. East Coast newspapers and journals regularly derided the West Coast as paranoid, reactionary, and ungrateful for the contributions of Chinese labor to the industrialization of California. *Scribner's* declared with exasperation, "In the East, the prejudice against our heathen brother John in California, seems a little unreasonable and we want more light."[28] California newspapers, in turn, deplored the "perverted condition of opinion in the East," where for months "the newspapers . . . have been filled with the grossest misrepresentations of every phase of the [Chinese] question, all proceeding from poisoned and interested sources."[29] Several newspapers reprinted commentaries from national papers concerning the reaction to the Chinese on the West Coast. West Coast papers and politicians often pointed out that if large numbers of Chinese were arriving on the East Coast the easterners would react as the West had an argument that probably contained more truth than those in the East cared to admit. The frustrated Californian suggested that the Pacific states vote on the Chinese question and that their Congressmen, "armed with these credentials, say to their brethren, of the East: 'The people of the Pacific Coast have been so far the only people exposed to Chinese immigration. They are strongly and bitterly opposed to it. . . . If they are wrong you can easily prove it. . . . Amend the treaty and confine the Chinese to the Atlantic ports. If this immigration suits you, you are welcome to it.'"[30]

What Californians perceived as an East-West polarization also involved issues of class. Newspapers outside of the West Coast frequently noted that a lower class of citizen inhabited most of California. The *San Francisco Chronicle* quoted the *Louisville Courier-Journal* claiming that the politicians were working on behalf of "the vast rabble of hoodlums in San Francisco," while the *Chronicle* itself implied that those "poisoned and interested sources" included corporations relying on cheap labor.[31] So long as they continued to dismiss the Chinese as racially inferior, laborers' demands were easily dismissed as lower-class resentment of more productive Chinese labor. By the late 1870s, however, national opinion began to accept the interpretation that the Chinese immigrating to the States were undesirables.[32] Increased attention in the national press and Congress evidenced a growing concern over Chinese immigration. This shift also reflected both the western states' greater importance in national politics and the changing rhetoric against the Chinese from issues of race to more nebulous and persuasive issues of morality and gender.[33]

West Coast representatives increasingly sought to persuade the national public that their actions were motivated not by base self-interest but by national interest. California politicians and the press consciously manipulated gendered images of Chinese in opposition to the ideal Anglo-American family unit in order to gain national sympathy and electoral support.

The policing of sexual disease, prostitution, and Chinese females proved an effective way to ultimately exclude Chinese male labor. By 1874 President Ulysses S. Grant in his annual address to Congress introduced the possibility of limiting the influx of Chinese prostitutes. Motivated by his party's viability in the western United States, Grant acknowledged the powerful images of Chinese slavery and prostitution in addressing the "problems" of the particular class of Chinese entering the United States:

> In relation to this subject I call the attention of Congress to a generally-conceded fact—that the great proportion of the Chinese immigrants who come to our shores do not come voluntarily to make their homes with us and their labor productive of general prosperity, but come under contracts with head-men who own them almost absolutely. In worse form does this apply to Chinese women. Hardly a perceptible percentage of them perform any honorable labor, but they are brought for shameful purposes, to the disgrace of the communities where settled and to the great demoralization of the youth of those localities. If this evil practice can be legislated against, it will be my pleasure as well as duty to enforce any regulation to secure so desirable an end.[34]

President Grant focused on the unfree status of both Chinese laboring men and prostitutes and its effects on American morality and productivity: unfree labor undermined the economy and political system upon which the American republic rested. If California came to rely too heavily upon Chinese contract labor, a system of unfree labor such as that in the antebellum South might result. The president implicitly appealed to the nation's conceptions of the republic, family, and female virtue. American citizens—native-born or naturalized immigrant males—constituted, protected, and perpetuated the nation; but American manhood could be weakened economically by Chinese labor and morally by Chinese prostitutes.

Western politicians, led by Horace Page and other California representatives, willingly obliged. On March 3, 1875, "An Act Supplementary to Acts in Relation to Immigration" entered the federal statutes as law.[35] The bill's purpose purportedly was to end Chinese slavery and prostitution: it required "free and voluntary immigration" from "China, Japan, or any Oriental country"; increased the fine levied on those importing contract labor; made illegal any contracting of unfree labor; prohibited the "importation into the United States of women for the purposes of prostitution"; and, lastly, denied entry to criminals or "women imported for the purposes of prostitution." Any "such obnoxious person or persons" would be returned to their own country.[36] This act, commonly referred to as the Page Act or Page Law, added a new element to Chinese immigration legislation, supplementing an 1862 bill that had attempted to halt the transportation of Chinese contract labor to the United

States. Whereas the 1862 bill withheld landing permits from ships transporting Chinese for "lewd and immoral purposes," the Page Act sought to directly prevent the importation of female prostitutes and refused entry to any woman suspected of immigrating for this purpose.[37] Significantly, this legislation established at the federal level the connection between unfree labor, prostitutes, and Chinese immigrants.

The president's strong endorsement of the issues covered in the Page Act left little room for dissent among his fellow Republicans, who traditionally opposed legislation that might discriminate on the basis of race. President Grant assumed that many Chinese immigrants entered the United States against their will, under contract to someone else who profited from their labor as workers and prostitutes. According to this widely held assumption, the bill's enactment would curtail most of the undesirable elements of Chinese immigration to the United States. Indeed, immigration officials' conviction that the majority of Chinese female immigrants to the United States were prostitutes, combined with the difficulty Chinese wives faced in proving otherwise, appear to have discouraged some Chinese women from even attempting to emigrate to the United States. As George Anthony Peffer has demonstrated, the lack of wives and families accompanying the Chinese males partly resulted from institutionalized discrimination against Chinese women immigrants by U.S. immigration officials and the Page Law of 1875.[38] The number of Chinese female immigrants to the United States significantly declined as a result of the indiscriminate enforcement of the Page Law.[39]

The Page Law of 1875 also effectively established grounds for further and broader exclusion legislation. By convincing the president and the people of the United States that a portion of the immigrants were undesirable based on moral grounds, the proponents of the Page Act opened the possibility that *all* Chinese immigrants could be categorized as undesirable. Within less than a year western politicians sought to exploit further the fears and prejudices of the American public in order to gain ready acceptance not only of the Page Act but also the necessity of revising the Burlingame Treaty.

In 1876 Senator Aaron Sargent of California spoke in favor of the resolution to renegotiate the Burlingame Treaty to allow for the further restriction of Chinese immigration. He contended that the ineffectiveness of the Page Law necessitated a policy of "general exclusion":

> The importation of females for immoral purposes is also forbidden by statute. But the law is a dead-letter, because of the impossibility of obtaining proof of its violation. And yet it is the almost universal conviction of Californians that nine-tenths of the Chinese male immigration is in violation of the former [coolie slavery], and ninety-nine hundredths of the female immigration in violation of the latter statute.

There can be no remedy but general exclusion; and the policy, justice, and necessity of that supreme measure I purpose to discuss.[40]

Senator Sargent clearly admitted he had no proof of any violations and that his argument was based on Californians' *perceptions* of these violations. Californians opposed to Chinese immigration perceived the majority of Chinese male immigrants—90 percent—as enslaved.[41] More important, they were able to persuade national opinion that these perceptions were for the most part accurate. The image of the enslaved Chinese male preempted the condemnation of racial prejudice and appealed to free labor ideology while also calling into question the fitness of Chinese men to become naturalized citizens.

Establishing a link between Chinese male labor and female sexual servitude constituted an essential part of attempts to exclude Chinese immigrants. Comparing Chinese male and female immigrants to slaves conveyed both the economic threat posed by the Chinese men and the moral threat posed by Chinese women. Perceptions of Chinese as unfree justified Americans' desires to deny them entry. Free immigration, the exclusionists argued, should be restricted to those people who came freely. As U.S. Minister to China Benjamin P. Avery explained to a Chinese diplomat who questioned the immigration restrictions on Chinese, "This system of free immigration and equal privileges has had a large share in making the United States prosperous and strong and has been encouraged and protected by very careful laws which are strictly enforced."[42]

In his legal history of Chinese immigration, Hudson Janisch observed wryly, "If the South fought to protect white womanhood, the West fought to protect white manhood."[43] The West generously extended its protection to the nation's future generations of manhood as well. Images of the "Chinaman" and the diseased Chinese prostitute converged with national concerns about the stability of American social institutions. The amoral sexuality displayed by the Chinese threatened to pollute the virtues upon which American society and civilization rested. The Congregational Churches of America adopted a resolution urging the government to revise the Burlingame Treaty and to pass measures to "prevent the importation of Chinese prostitutes, and so relieve us from impending peril to our republican and Christian institutions."[44] Urban American masculine youth especially appeared vulnerable to this threat. Testimony before the Joint Special Committee that boys seven to twelve years old visited Chinese prostitutes shocked the national audience even more than the lurid descriptions of diseased prostitutes left to die on the streets of Chinatown. The Order of Caucasians, an anti-Chinese club, warned Congress that Chinese prostitution existed in many cities and that American male youth were "enticed thither by Chinese women—and who, for a few cents, can acquire a loathsome dis-

ease, ruin their constitutions and render themselves unfit to become the pro-
genitors of a healthy and moral race."[45] Law enforcement officers, religious
leaders, and local politicians, in their testimony before Congress, assumed that
young boys were less likely to resist overt sexuality, especially at such bargain
prices. The direct correlation between the constitution of American male
youth and institutions of American society strikingly exemplifies the gendered
basis of American national identity.

Concerns about the effects of perverse Chinese sexuality on the national
body further illuminate the ideological relationships between virility and
economic health, morality and industry. The dangers of sexually transmitted
diseases graphically and concretely illustrated the danger embodied by
Chinese immigrants to the nation's morality. Wherever Chinese settled, one
editorial declared, "progress staggers and halts, industry withers, and public
morals and public decency decay and die. . . . They are the embodiment of
the plague, pestilence, famine and death."[46] Several San Francisco physicians
quoted in the San Francisco *Medico-Literary Journal* attributed such diseases
in that city to the Chinese prostitutes because they, "unlike the white women,
use no preventative measures." This article further warned that Chinese
women would spread a plague that could "sink this nation into effeminacy
and political death."[47]

Disease and immorality were physical manifestations of corruption and
vice that would not only ruin the constitutions of young men but also undermine the Constitution of the United States, which depended upon a healthy
civic life of virtuous male participants. The Chinese, claimed one pamphlet,
"corrupt the morals and undermin [*sic*] the framework of our social structure."[48] A California anti-Chinese convention memorial in 1886 explicitly
spelled out the threat to white masculinity—and thus to the nation as a
whole—posed by Chinese men. While Chinese labor thrived on low wages,

> the white laboring man, to whom the nation must, in the long run,
> look for the reproduction of the race and the bringing up and educat-
> ing of citizens to take the place of the present generation as it passes
> away, and, above all, to defend the country in time of war, is injured in
> his comfort, reduced in his scale of life and standard of living, neces-
> sarily carrying down with it his moral and physical stamina.[49]

Chinese working men and immoral Chinese women would erode the foundations of Anglo-American masculinity: work, self-sufficiency, and virility.

Discussions about the Chinese question relied upon constructions of
gender and sexuality that supported America's implicitly masculine and heterosexual national identity.[50] The virtues ascribed to Anglo-American
women increased their political visibility in opposition to Chinese males
(working women also participated in anti-Chinese demonstrations).[51] Anti-

Chinese sentiment even entertained the possibility of political franchise. If Chinese men were to gain the vote, white women's votes would be needed to "overbalance the Chinese power and give us the majority. . . . Republics and Empires have been saved through different causes, but not one yet has had the honor of having been saved by women. Well, let California have the glory of having been saved by them."[52] This appeal to American domesticity and womanhood was reminiscent of the race and gender logic expressed in the debates over the Fifteenth Amendment: when threatened by nonwhite masculinity, a common ethnic culture would transcend gender identity. Anglo-American women presumably would vote according to the same cultural values as Anglo-American men, just as Chinese men's votes would reflect their (inferior) racial and cultural identities.

Some anti-Chinese agitators sought moral protection through the American female as mother in opposition to the corrupted morality of Chinese women and the fallibility of male youth. The aforementioned article in the *Medico-Literary Journal* asked, "If it is through the Chinese women that our nation is threatened with destruction, why [do] not the American women at least raise their voices to repel them?" The article ended by appealing to mothers "to be more watchful of their sons."[53] Representing the highest virtues of Anglo-American civilization, white women had the power to protect American morality, even as their sexuality had the power to undo it.[54] The Chinese prostitute and the Anglo-American wife or mother emphasized the manhood and strength of character of American masculinity, and the "absence" of these traits in Chinese males.

By the late 1870s, anti-Chinese rhetoric shifted its primary focus from Chinese threats to morality to the ways Chinese men disrupted Anglo-American patterns of gender segregation in the workforce. After the completion of the transcontinental railroad in 1870, Chinese males increasingly competed with Anglo working men as well as women. They owned laundries and found employment as house servants. Because Chinese males apparently made few gender distinctions in the labor they performed—they did not care whether they were doing work traditionally assigned to females or males—they challenged the norms regarding accepted gendered divisions of labor in American society.

Politicians and rally speakers now warned that Chinese males threatened the economic basis of the American woman's virtue. Testimony persuaded members of the Joint Special Committee that Chinese males monopolized employment in traditionally female occupations by working for low wages, and that the "hardships resulting from these causes bear with especial weight upon women."[55] One witness testified that Anglo-American working women, who had lost their jobs at a sewing factory due to the influx of Chinese labor, could be found in places "where I presume you would not

wish your sisters, mothers, or wives to be."[56] A pamphlet comparing contemporary evils to the "greatest curse" of intemperance deplored the fact
that, although "the Chinaman" had once "filled a place and performed the
labor which was not so agreeable to Anglo-Saxon masculinity," he now
entered a domain hitherto occupied by virtuous Anglo women. As a result,
"good, honest intelligent women" were forced to "decide between a short
and wretched life of infamy and shame, or a life of starvation."[57] Chinese
male laborers blurred the gendered division of labor in western cities, economically forcing Anglo-American women into prostitution, where their
moral position would sink to that of Chinese women. The effects of Chinese
labor manifested themselves in "domestic help, where the honest, virtuous
and trustworthy females have been ousted and driven into dens of infamy
and prostitution."[58] Thus Chinese males inevitably corrupted the female sex
regardless of racial background, because they displaced Anglo-American
women from the only respectable jobs available to them.

According to exclusionists, the Chinese male's ability to work for lower
wages and in feminine occupations endangered American families. The congressional committee declared, "Family-life is a great safeguard of our political institutions."[59] This pervasive rhetoric indicates that the metaphor of
family and home was a concept accepted as normative, and that it transcended class divisions in Anglo-American society. The Anglo-American
nuclear family ensured the production of American institutions and represented a virtuous cause, one that could overshadow racist overtones. Senator
Booth of California asserted that the "source of civilization in which we live,
of the institutions we believe to be its highest outgrowth, is the family."[60] An
article in The Argonaut (1877) characterized the intricate relationships among
family, nation, and the economy:

> With us the family is not only the most sacred of our relationships, but
> is also the unit of nationality. Each family constitutes a little Republic.
> A collection of States, the nation. The nation is a collection of families.
> The "family relation" is, among our race sacredly regarded as the
> foundation of government. Society has been organized with reference
> to it. . . . The assumption that every man among us is to have a family
> and a house enters into all our calculations.[61]

The relationship of family, government, and private property—owning a
house—found expression not only in masculinity but in the primary role
assigned to males within the republic, that of citizen. Thus, the Chinese immigrants, most of whom lacked family and private property, could not be expected
to enjoy the same privileges of government protection extended to Anglo-
American males or even male immigrants from other European countries.
Representative James G. Blaine said as much in his February 1879 speech before

the Senate: "You cannot work a man who must have beef and bread, alongside of a man who can live on rice. In all such conflicts, and in all such struggles, the result is not to bring up the man who lives on rice to the beef-and-bread standard, but it is to bring down the beef-and-bread man to the rice standard."[62]

By blurring feminine and masculine roles and undermining the Anglo working male's ability to provide for his dependents, Chinese male labor threatened to expose the arbitrary division of American society into separate domains based on gender, the public, and the private, which thus far had restricted women from public political institutions, including citizenship. As leaders of the Workingman's Party complained, the Chinese "seem to have NO SEX."[63] The Chinese threat to Anglo-American manhood extended beyond economic livelihood and morality to the ideological underpinnings of American society. The Chinese laborer's willingness to do "feminine" work was perceived as unnatural, outside the gendered division of labor that reinforced masculine citizenship in American society.

As anti-Chinese rhetoric shifted to a gendered moral argument, national opinion about the Chinese question also changed. The *San Francisco Post* attributed this to a more elevated argument:

> Heretofore the anti-chinese [*sic*] agitation has been sporadic and violent in character. It assumed the tone of race antagonism—an attitude sure to arouse feeling against those who take it. When the venue was changed and the non-assimilative and aggressive attitude of this people shown towards, not only our labor, but our commerce and manufactures, our institutions and civilization, the plane of statesmanship was reached and that of bitter race hostility abandoned forever.[64]

According to the *Post*, issues of assimilation and civilization, culture and morality, transcended racism and caste prejudice. Furthermore, the argument was framed proactively: rather than reacting to perceived racial and economic threats to the American male's livelihood, American masculinity sought to protect American institutions.

Anti-Chinese rhetoric also expressed larger social tensions regarding class status, race relations, and gender and sexual norms. Cultural definitions of whiteness and masculinity became the ideological focal point for political organization nationwide: politicians seized upon anti-Chinese sentiment to mobilize political support of the working-class electorate among the developing urban areas along the West Coast. As Mary P. Ryan demonstrates, western urban politics shared a critical transformation with other urban centers nationwide. Normative definitions of race, gender, and class increasingly circumscribed American civic participation in the post-Reconstruction era. "Gender . . . provided the sexual prohibitions, codes of segregation, and rhetorical power with which to mortar the rising wall of segregation," which replaced those sectional barriers that had hitherto dominated American politics.[65] Western politicians and union leaders succeeded in developing a refined political rhetoric and strategy with which to fit a blatantly racist exclusionary argument into the larger national political trend of maintaining social order and exploiting white middle-class fears of urban disarray. [66]

Indeed, the shift from class- and race-based arguments against the Chinese from the western states to ever more sophisticated arguments for exclusion based on gender at the national level took place through trial and error between the 1860s and 1882, when Congress passed the first exclusion act. Ryan's work suggests several avenues for further analysis of the ways in which exclusion legislation was part of larger national trends. It is apparent, however, that western politicians increasingly adapted their presentation of regional concerns to the evolving concerns of the North and South to persuade northern and southern politicians of the necessity of exclusion.

The political use of gender, and the issue of sexuality associated with gender roles, emphasized the necessity of ultimately excluding Chinese as a race from America's shores. During the era of Reconstruction, a racial argument still evoked suspicion and fears of division; a moral argument based on gender and sexuality that implicitly substantiated racial difference, however, was pursued with success. [67] The race argument, or the "caste prejudice" as it was frequently referred to in Congress, found expression and subsequent acceptance within a more positive ideology affirming Anglo-American manhood.

Presuming to protect both the Chinese and Americans from slavery, western leaders could deflect criticisms of racial intolerance. On the hierarchy of race, Californians referred to the Chinese laborer as "below the most degraded specimen of the American Indian, and but very little above the beast."[68] Chinese females were the most abject of immigrants, existing in "a state of servitude beside which African slavery was a beneficient captivity."[69] Employing these comparisons enabled other regions to comprehend the West Coast situation. Many southern politicians already supported the right of California and other western states to protect their population from a Chinese invasion. The nature of the Chinese slavery argument, however, also appealed to Republicans who had worked to abolish slavery and protect the rights of newly freed African Americans but also needed political support from California voters. The resulting strategy rephrased the Chinese question as one of assimilation. This argument encompassed the ideology of equality while addressing racial and labor tensions on the West Coast.[70] Significantly, it also reinforced white masculine superiority: the Anglo-American could continue to claim paternal benevolence toward immigrants in the name of exclusion, while protecting the national body from imagined harm.

Notes

An earlier version of this essay was presented as "Gender, Race, and the 1875 Page Law" at The Repeal and Its Legacy: Conference on the 50th Anniversary of the Repeal of Exclusion Acts sponsored by the Chinese Historical Society of America and the Department of Asian American Studies at San Francisco State University, November 12–14, 1993, and printed in the conference proceedings (San Francisco: CHSA and Asian American Studies Department, SFSU, 1994).

My thanks to Mary P. Ryan, who read multiple versions of this essay and each time offered insightful critiques, and Linda Song, Margaret Pagaduan, Kimie Arguello, Marcy Sacks, and Erika Lee. I also thank Matt Basso, Laura McCall, and especially Dee Garceau, whose close readings and editing significantly shaped my revisions.

1. Sam Booth, "They Are Coming," in *The Chinese Invasion,* comp. Henry Josiah West (San Francisco: Bacon and Company, 1873). This is one stanza of the poem, most of which considers the effects of the Chinese on American labor.

2. Thomas Almaguer is one of the few scholars who has examined the development of a hierarchy of race, class, gender, and sexuality in California politics and society. His analysis of how whiteness and masculinity were constructed against the hypersexualized Chinese male and female, however, overlooks the critical role of the Page Act in this process. Mary P. Ryan's work also has examined how gender relations and sexuality were critical to urban political discourse. See Thomas Almaguer, *Racial Faultlines: The Historical Origins of White Supremacy in California* (Berkeley and Los Angeles: University of California Press,, 1994); and Mary P. Ryan, *Civic Wars: Democracy and Public Life in the American City during the Nineteenth Century* (Berkeley and Los Angeles: University of California Press, 1997), as well as Mary P. Ryan, *Women in Public: between Banners and Ballots, 1825–1880* (Baltimore: James Hopkins University Press, 1990).

3. *Congressional Globe,* February 21, 1866.

4. [D. O'C.], "How He Sold Her Short," *San Francisco Chronicle,* January 11, 1878.

5. *Daily Morning Call,* February 25, 1878.

6. *San Francisco Chronicle,* February 26, 1878 (emphasis mine).

7. See, for example, Martha Hodes, *White Women, Black Men: Illicit Sex in the 19th-Century South* (New Haven: Yale University Press, 1997); Stephanie McCurry, "Proslavery Politics in Antebellum South Carolina," *Journal of American History* 78 (1992): 1245–64; and Jacqueline Jones, *American Work* (New York: W. W. Norton, 1998).

8. McCurry, 1253 and 1259.

9. Hodes, 177.

10. This argument was popular in speeches. See, for example, *Report from the House Committee on Education and Labor,* February 25, 1878, by Senator Willis (Kentucky).

11. *San Francisco Post,* November 1, 1878.

12. "The Chinese in California," *Lippincott's Magazine* 2 (July 1868).

13. James Leroy Evans, *The Indian Savage, the Mexican Bandit, the Chinese Heathen: Three Popular Stereotypes* (Ph.D. diss., University of Texas at Austin, 1967); Lucie Cheng Hirata, "Free, Indentured, Enslaved: Chinese Prostitutes in Nineteenth-Century America," *Signs* 5 (1979): 27. Further work on nineteenth-century Chinese-American women has shown the fundamental impact of the Page Act on the formation of Chinese-American families and the community. See Judy Yung, *Unbound Feet* (Berkeley and Los Angeles: University of California Press, 1994); Sucheng Chan, "Immigration of Chinese Women under the Page Law," in *Entry Denied,* ed. Sucheng Chan (Philadelphia: Temple University Press, 1991); George Anthony Peffer, "Forbidden Families: Emigration Experience of Chinese Women under the Page Law, 1875–1882," *Journal of American Ethnic History* 6 (1986): 28–46; and Peffer, *If They Don't Bring Their Women Here: Chinese Female Immigration before Exclusion* (Urbana: University of Illinois Press, 1999).

14. Hodes, 151–71.

15. For an extended discussion of this process, see Ryan, *Civic Wars.* Ryan's ambitious comparative study of urban political culture in nineteenth-century New York, New Orleans, and San Francisco illuminates the development of each region's racial, gendered, and class politics within the larger national discourses of democracy.

16. An unidentified Republican in 1866, *Congressional Globe,* 39th Cong., 2nd sess., 118, Appendix, 78, as quoted and cited in Eric Foner, *Reconstruction: America's Unfinished Revolution, 1863–1877* (New York: Harper & Row, 1988), 235.

17. Ryan, *Civic Wars,* 297.

18. Amy Kaplan, "Manifest Domesticity," *American Literature* 70 (1998): 581–606.

19. A similar bill, proposed by James A. Johnson in 1870, also was denied because of concerns about racial prejudice. James A. Johnson, *Chinese Immigration: A Speech Made in the House of Representatives, January 25, 1870* (Washington, D.C.: Government Printing Office, 1870). Johnson proposed a joint resolu-

tion to discourage the immigration of "Chinese laborers and debased and abandoned females," and notes that Senator Williams had introduced a similar "anti-coolie, anti-harlot bill" in December 1869.

20. *Congressional Globe*, 41st Cong., 2nd Sess., Deember. 22, 1869, 299.

21. *Congressional Globe*, 41st Cong., 2nd Sess., December 22, 1869, 300.

22. Foner, 256.

23. Hudson N. Janisch, *The Chinese, the Courts, and the Constitution: A Study of the Legal Issues Raised by the Chinese Immigration to the United States, 1850–1902* (JSD thesis, University of Chicago, 1971), 184. Some politicians even requested the insertion of an exclusive clause declaring that the right to vote never was intended to apply to the Chinese or Mongolian races, but this was defeated 106 to 42 in the House. Senators Trumbull and Sumner each introduced an amendment allowing Chinese to become naturalized citizens in 1870. Both were rejected, with nearly half of the Senate not voting. See Stuart Creighton Miller, *Unwelcome Immigrant: The American Image of the Chinese, 1785–1882* (Berkeley and Los Angeles: University of California Press, 1969), 160.

24. See Charles McClain and Laurene Wu McClain, "The Chinese Contribution to the Development of American Law," in Chan, ed., *Entry Denied*.

25. San Francisco's Cubic Air Ordinance, for example, sought to limit the number of persons inhabiting a room based on cubic feet per person. See McClain and McClain.

26. Alexander Saxton, *The Indispensable Enemy: Labor and the Anti-Chinese Movement in California* (Berkeley and Los Angeles: University of California Press, 1971).

27. "The Chinese Question," in *Chinese Immigration Pamphlets*, Special Collections, Bancroft Library. University of California at Berkeley, 15.

28. *Scribner's Monthly*, January 1877, as reprinted in *San Francisco Daily Alta*, December 26, 1878. The "John" referred to is "John Chinaman."

29. *San Francisco Chronicle*, February 28, 1878.

30. "The Chinese Question," 16.

31. *San Francisco Chronicle*, January 14, 1878.

32. Gwendolyn Mink, *Old Labor and New Immigrants in American Political Development: Union, Party, and State, 1875–1920* (Ithaca, N.Y.: Cornell University Press, 1986).

33. See Saxton and Mink.

34. Message from the President, *Journal of the House of Representatives of the United States*, 43rd Cong., 2nd Sess., December 7, 1874, 12.

35. The Committee on Foreign Affairs originally introduced the Page Act to the House on February 18, 1875 with unanimous consent. Four days later, the House passed the bill. It then proceeded to the Senate Committee of Foreign Relations, which reported it to the Senate without amendment on March 3, 1875. President Ulysses S. Grant signed the Page Act into law that evening. The San Francisco newspapers merely mention the law's passage and comment no further. No records or reports remain from the committee that deliberated upon and produced this bill. See *Congressional Record*, 43rd Cong., 2nd sess., Mar. 3, 1875, 1454, 1599, and 2161; and *Journal of the House of Representatives of the United States*, 43rd Cong., 2nd sess., March 3, 1875, 487, 640, 652, and 679–80.

36. "An Act Supplementary to the Acts in Relation to Immigration," March 3, 1875, *United States Statutes at Large*, 477.

37. The Page Law was the first law to prevent women from entering the United States as immigrants on the explicit assumption that they may be prostitutes; only with the Immigration Act of 1907 would Congress authorize the deportation of foreign-born prostitutes of any race. For an extended discussion about the passage of the Page Law, its effects on the Chinese-American community, and its role in the debates on Chinese exclusion, see Peffer, *If They Don't Bring Their Women Here*.

38. Peffer, "Forbidden Families."

39. See Chan; and Peffer, "Forbidden Families."

40. Aaron A. Sargent, *Immigration of Chinese, Speech of Hon. Aaron A. Sargent, of California, in the Senate of the United States, May 2, 1876* (Washington, D.C.: Government Printing Office, 1876).

41. Almaguer, 160–62. Almaguer argues that Chinese males in service industries also were hypersexualized as threats to young women and girls, but, interestingly, these depictions did not take on the significant role of the Chinese prostitute (perhaps because they too uncomfortably paralleled racial tensions in the South).

42. Benjamin P. Avery to Prince Kung, May 28, 1878, Despatch no. 64, Inclosure I, *Despatches from United States Ministers to China 1843–1906*, vol. 38, March 31–July 31, 1875.

43. Janisch, 81. He continues, "So far did this go that legislation was proposed, making seduction by a Chinese woman of a member of the California legislature or minister 'in good standing' a criminal offense."

44. *Resolutions Adopted by the General Association of Congregational Churches of California*, *Chinese Immigration Pamphlets*, vol. 1, Special Collections, Bancroft Library, University of California at Berkeley.

45. Petition to Congress from the Chico Encampment of the Order of Caucasians, *The Pacific*, December 1877.

46. Editorial from the *Cincinnati Enquirer* as reprinted in the *San Francisco Chronicle,* January 4, 1878.

47. "How the Chinese Women Are Infusing a Poison Fate into the Anglo-Saxon Blood," reprinted from the *Medico-Literary Journal* in the *San Francisco Chronicle*, November 21, 1878.

48. Henry Josiah West, *The Chinese Invasion* (San Francisco: Bacon and Company, 1873).

49. The memorial from the anti-Chinese convention of 1886 is quoted in Samuel Gompers and Herman Gutstadt, *Meat vs. Rice: American Manhood against Asiatic Coolieism, Which Shall Survive?* Published by American Federation of Labor and printed as Senate document 137, 1902. Reprinted with introduction and appendixes by Asiatic Exclusion League.

50. Jennifer Ting, "Bachelor Society: Deviant Heterosexuality and Asian American Historiography," in *Privileging Positions*, ed. Gary Y. Okihiro, et al. (Pullman, Wash., 1995), 271–80.

51. Ryan, *Women in Public,* 163.

52. *Sacramento Record Union*, February 23, 1879.

53. *San Francisco Medico-Literary Journal*, reprinted in *San Francisco Chronicle*, November 21, 1878.

54. Ryan, *Women in Public*, 163.

55. *Report of the Joint Special Committee to Investigate Chinese Immigration*, iv.

56. Testimony of Mrs. Sophronia Swift, *Report of the Joint Special Committee to Investigate Chinese Immigration*, 246.

57. Jennett Blakeslee Frost, *California's Greatest Curse* (San Francisco: J. Winterburn & Co., 1879), 15, 18.

58. Patrick Stephen Fox, Letter to the Editor, *San Francisco Daily Mail*, November 25, 1877.

59. *Report of the Joint Special Committee to Investigate Chinese Immigration,* viii.

60. *San Francisco Chronicle*, August 12, 1878.

61. "'Caucasian' vs. 'Mongolian,'" *The Argonaut*, October 27, 1877.

62. Excerpt from the Speech of James G. Blaine in the Senate, February 14, 1879, as quoted in Gompers and Gutstadt, 22.

63. *San Francisco Chronicle*, December 28, 1877.

64. *San Francisco Post*, June 22, 1878.

65. Ryan, *Civic Wars,* 296.

66. Ryan's description of municipal attempts, through legislation and police force, to "discipline occupants of public space" in the postbellum period highlights changing expressions of masculinity in public space as well. American masculinity thus was disciplined at the same time that Chinese masculinity was disciplined (and rejected) through the ever evolving contestation and definition of American citizenship. Ryan, *Civic Wars,* 217–18.

67. This increasingly sophisticated use of gender, race, and sexuality to justify nativism would manifest itself yet again in justification of imperialism and racial eugenics toward the turn of the century. For example, see Kristin Hoganson, *Fighting for American Manhood: How Gender Politics Provoked the Spanish-American and Philippine-American Wars* (New Haven: Yale University Press, 1998), and Kaplan.

68. Memorial and Joint Resolution in Relation to the Chinese Immigration to the State of California, *Journals of Senate and Assembly of the 17th Session of the Legislature of the State of California*, vol. II (Sacramento: 1868), 3.

69. Memorial of the Senate of California to Congress of United States, April 3,1876.

70. See Mink, esp. Chap. 3, "Meat vs. Rice (and Pasta): Discovering Labor Politics in California, 1875–85."

Nomads, Bunkies, Cross-Dressers, and Family Men

Cowboy Identity and the
Gendering of Ranch Work

Dee Garceau

Cattleman Kay Luman scoffed at his sixteen-year-old daughter's offer to help with roundup and branding. Luman ran a successful livestock business in southwest Wyoming from the turn of the century through the 1920s. Already, his daughter had proven herself an able ranch hand, herding sheep, driving oxen, and harvesting crops. But Luman resisted her participation in cowcamp. "You don't know what it's like," he said. "All the ranchers send their meanest broncs up there. I don't think you can ride their horses. They have no time to be coddling you girls."[1] Though Luman's daughter proved him wrong, Kay Luman spoke for many men in the cattle industry when he discouraged women from the job. Despite the presence of female labor on ranches during this period, cowboys declared their work masculine territory. The story of why this was so reveals contests over gender and class privilege laid bare by changes in the cattle industry.

From the 1860s through 1880s, cowboys worked the open range, trailing beeves across the Great Plains.[2] The industry spread north from Texas to Montana and the Dakotas, until some 7.5 million cattle roamed these grasslands. To move herds over long distances, ranchers hired unmarried men. Bachelors accepted lower wages than married men, they could bunk together in cheap, single-sex housing and without the responsibilities of marriage, they were free to travel for months at a time.[3] To introduce women into a work culture of single men would have been impossible by late-nineteenth-century standards. Given the Victorian social mores of this period, women would have required separate housing. This would have proven too expensive at home ranches, too impractical on the trail. During the open-range era, then, cowboys lived and worked in an all-male nomadic subculture.

All this would change after the hard winter of 1886–87. That year, snows came early and stayed late. Freezing temperatures and bitter winds reached extremes. The snowpack grew so deep and so solid that cattle could not paw their way through it to forage. Overgrazing, compounded by drought during the mid-1880s, had already weakened herds. As the brutal winter hung on, thousands of cattle died of starvation and exposure. When cowboys rode out in the spring to check their herds, they found a scene they would never forget. Frozen carcasses lay piled against fences, in gullies and ravines. The dead outnumbered the living. And the live cattle were scarcely recognizable: gaunt, skeletal, more like ghosts than beeves.[4] The devastation moved cattlemen to reassess their strategies.

The winter of 1886–87 hastened the demise of open-range herding. Cattlemen reduced herd size and began to accumulate private land in order to grow winter feed. A new ethic of husbandry prevailed, best described by one Western editor who wrote, "A man who turns out a lot of cattle . . . without making provision for feeding them will not only suffer financial loss, but also the loss of the respect of the community in which he lives."[5] By the 1890s, mowing machines, hay rakes, calving barns, and fenced pastures became increasingly common features in cow country. In the decades that followed, cowboys still drove cattle from one section to another on a ranchers' spread, or herded beeves seasonally to grazing leases on public land, but the long drives of old had ended. "As time went on," said Wyoming cowboy J. M. Huston, "the country became more settled up and everything changed. . . . There were others taking up ranches in different places, [and] they kept their cattle around their ranches, feeding them hay in winter."[6] Reduced herd size, private acreage, alfalfa crops, and the new emphasis on year-round care of herds made ranching more like farming. The family ranch replaced the trail drive.

As family ranches became the norm, women's labor became integral to the enterprise. Vestiges of the nineteenth-century ideology of separate spheres shaped the way ranch families constructed their work insofar as gender-based divisions of labor were understood: the "outside work" fell to men, the household work to women.[7] "But I think most ranch women will bear me out in saying that unless the women . . . be always ready to do anything that comes along, . . . the ranch is not a success," wrote Wyoming ranch wife Mrs. B. B. Brooks in 1899.[8] Brooks's remark foretold the blurring of gendered work roles on ranches, which intensified as the twentieth century progressed. Women drove plows, harrows, and binders; dug irrigation ditches; herded sheep; and baled hay; as well as cooking and cleaning for family members and hired hands. Ranch families articulated an ethic of group partnership that normalized women's crossovers into men's work. That is, ranch women viewed their participation in men's or "outside" work as a form of service to family, a contribution to the success of the ranch.[9]

Only one type of ranch work elicited a different response from men and women alike. That was cowpunching. Narratives from the Great Plains during the first three decades of the twentieth century indicate that women ranchers who capably herded sheep, trained horses, or drove oxen were rarely called to help with cattle. Maud Wallis Traylor remembered clear gender boundaries around cattle at the Traylor family ranch in Texas during this time. As Traylor described it, ranch women could watch the beef roundup, but they never worked it: "We had our best times during round-ups. All the Traylor women would ride out to the pastures right after sun-up and watch the operations. We were expected to keep out of the way, and of course none of us thought of lending a hand."[10] Even the exceptions proved the rule. Charlotta Hartley Albert grew up at the turn of the century on her parents' isolated ranch in Horse Creek, Wyoming. The oldest two children were girls. Because her father needed a cowhand, Charlotta rode herd with him, but only until her younger brother matured enough to take her place. "I was Father's cowboy until Grover was old enough," she explained.[11] The fact that Charlotta referred to herself as "Father's cow*boy*," and that her younger brother took over as soon as he was able, reinforce the impression that ranchers saw work with beef cattle as a distinctly masculine occupation. Wyoming cowboy Edmund Randolph allowed that "some ranchers did have wives or daughters who helped with round-up from time to time," but added that "women and girls were not usually the established order."[12] Similarly, Texas cowboy C. L. Sonnichsen reported that a few ranch women liked "to get out and work stock once in a while just for the fun of it," but noted that these "tomboys" were unusual: "The neighbors of Bob Tisdale . . . speak with . . . respect of his daughter Mike, who helps on roundups and takes her part with the best of the male workers. A girl like her is the exception in cattle country, however."[13] The rare woman who worked cattle earned a masculine moniker like "Father's cowboy," or "Mike," the "tomboy."

Indeed, the few women who worked as cowhands were not accepted as women. They were incorporated into cowcamp only as quasi-men, indistinguishable from "the fellers." Elsie and Amy Cooksley's narratives illustrate this identity. In 1914, the sisters emigrated with their parents from England to Sheridan, Wyoming, to establish a cattle ranch. Ages fourteen and seventeen, Amy and Elsie herded cattle with their father. But like Traylor, Sonnichsen, and Randolph, the Cooksley sisters remarked on how unusual it was: "We were the only girls that ever rode with the roundup. I don't know why, unless it's due to the fact that Dad sent us out to take care of our own stock and we got started doing it. . . . Nobody else did."[14] Work with cattle had such a strongly gendered meaning that Elsie and Amy were accepted only as one of "the boys" by the other cowhands. Amy Cooksley said,

Well, here's an illustration. We were holding the herd one time while half the men had their dinner. We saw a lady and her daughter drive up to the wagon for dinner. When the wagon came around, sometimes the neighbors would come for a chuck wagon dinner. Our relief came out and told us we could go eat. One of the fellers said, "No way! I'm not going in there and eat with those women. I don't mind Amy and Elsie and the rest of the boys. But I'm not going in with those women."[15]

Randolph observed the same dynamic on the Herbert White ranch in western Montana during the 1920s. Two young women happened to be working roundup. "I had never seen anything like this," wrote Randolph, "they were treated exactly like the men and exchanged verbal fisticuffs with them in their own lingo. . . . There was, apparently, no thought of their being anything but good fellows."[16] Just as women on the White ranch became "fellows" when they rode herd, Wyoming ranch daughter Marie Jordan Bell veered toward "boy"hood when she worked with cattle. When Bell helped her father with roundup in southeast Wyoming shortly before World War I, her grandmother objected, convinced that the experience would masculinize Marie: "Grandma . . . scolded Mama because I was out with the boys riding. . . . She told Dad she thought he was making a boy out of me."[17] Work with cattle had become so associated with masculinity that the few women who rode herd found themselves reclassified as males—cow"boy," "fellow," "boys," or "fellers."

The masculinization of work with cattle can be attributed, in part, to the emergence of cowboy myth. Like the cattle industry itself, cowboy identity was changing. As open-range herding faded, the nomadic cowboy took root in the American imagination. By the first decade of the twentieth century, cowboy myth had been popularized in mass culture through Erastus Beadle's dime novels, traveling Wild West shows, and best-selling novels like *The Virginian*. Formerly a marginal worker, the cowboy was elevated to a masculine ideal in popular culture. These fictional cowboys rarely spent time with cattle. Rather, they chased outlaws, fought Indians, stared down bullies, and made daring rescues. The mythic cowboy became a cultural icon who symbolized honor, physical prowess, and rugged individualism.[18] Bruce Siberts, a cowboy who rode herd from the 1890s through the 1920s, wryly compared life before and after the cowboy was romanticized: "I had a liking for the girls, but when I went into town with my rough clothes on, they wouldn't pay any attention to me. . . . Owen Wister hadn't yet written his book *The Virginian* so we cowhands did not know we were so strong and glamorous as we were after people read that book."[19] Within his lifetime, Siberts saw the cowboy transformed from working stiff to hero in the American mind. And Siberts's remarks suggest that westerners themselves imbibed the myth. Cowboy myth reinforced the masculine occupational identity of raising beef, even as the reality shifted from nomadic all-male herders to men and women together on family ranches.

Work with cattle, then, stood out among ranch chores with a mystique of its own. Long after open-range herding had faded, cowboys on fenced, family ranches shared in the legendary identity of the nomadic range cowboy. The romanticization of the cowboy as an exemplary masculine type probably supported cowboys' resistance to women as reserve labor. But why discourage female participation if one needed extra cowhands? Why were female "fellers" so unusual as to merit comment? Cowboy myth does not fully explain the masculinization of this occupation on family ranches, where women had become vital members of the workforce.

To fully understand the gendering of work with cattle, one must go back to the days of open-range herding and follow cowboys through the transition to family ranching. Cowboy narratives from the late nineteenth and early twentieth centuries feature competing images of the cowboy as social outcast and the cowboy as socially respectable. Within the same narratives, one will find paeans to the freedoms of marginality, and to the rewards of respectability. These competing images, in turn, suggest that two kinds of privilege were at stake: the masculine privileges of the transient male worker, and the class privileges of the land-owning family rancher. As cowboy culture gradually embraced the middle-class respectability of settled family ranches, cowboys were loath to give up the masculine privileges associated with an all-male nomadic workforce. Hence the resistance to ranch women as cowhands.

Memoirs and folk songs from the open-range era depict an all-male culture with distinctive freedoms. Sexual license, nonmarital intimacy with women, close relationships with men, and playful cross-dressing were among the masculine privileges enjoyed by these livestock herders. In short, the long drives gave rise to a masculine subculture that thrived on alternatives to the middle-class Victorian model of manhood. Late-nineteenth-century prescriptions for manhood emphasized probity, productivity, and benevolent patriarchy. The white middle-class model of success was a prosperous businessman who married, provided for his family, and tempered his passions. Late Victorians thought that competitive individualism in the marketplace bred character, while marriage and the family "provided an institution for civilizing [men's] animal nature. In particular, the wife —the 'better half'— served as an agent of moderation, morality, and culture."[20]

Cowboys of the open range held marginal status in Victorian America. They were transient workers, skilled but cash-poor. As hired hands, they neither owned businesses nor made investments, presumably missing out on the character-building experience of competitive capitalism. Moreover, without marriage and family life, range cowboys lacked the civilizing influences of women. In 1898, former cowboy C. C. Post warned that cowboys' marginal position left them vulnerable to social and moral degradation. "The trammels of society are cast off," wrote Post, "leading to a dangerous drop into rude habits and ill-restrained language. . . . Good breeding has to be nurtured by descent and association. Coarseness may be learned in a day."[21] In the late-Victorian mind, cowboys were drifters, morally suspect and socially crude.

Cowboys may have lived on the margins during the open-range era, but they did not accept Victorian class hierarchy. In their own oral and written tradition, cowboys repositioned themselves within a hierarchy of skill suited to range life. Out on the range, a man of wealth and breeding was only a "tenderfoot," at the mercy of his betters—the able riders, ropers, and herders.[22] Neither did cowboys accept the shame implicit in Victorian moral judgments about unmarried transients. Instead, they developed alternative family structures and celebrated the freedoms of living outside the mainstream.

In lieu of the middle-class nuclear family, cowboys created distinctive relationship patterns suited to nomadic life. Unlike John Wayne and his mythic forebears, cowboys were not stoic individualists.[23] Rather, the record is poignant with their need for human companionship.[24] Outside the parameters of Victorian marriage, this need found expression in two patterns. First, cowboys paired up as sleeping partners, or "bunkies," on the range. And second, during visits to town, cowboys entered into fictive marriages with prostitutes, pair bonds that lasted longer than one night, shorter than a lifetime. Both types of relationships functioned as important sources of support and human connection for the nomadic cowboy.

Bunkies were necessary to survive cold nights on the range, where one slept in tents or under an open sky. The physical warmth of one's sleeping partner could make the difference between freezing and survival, between sleeplessness and comfort. As range cowboy Andy Adams described it, "the men usually bunked in pairs."[25] Since cowboys took turns riding night guard, it made sense for those on the same shift to sleep together. As Adams explained, this "was much better than splitting bedfellows and having them annoy each other by going out and returning from guard separately."[26]

Donald Yacavone describes an antebellum ideal of fraternal love that linked close friendships between men to a civilized existence of gentility and refinement. Fraternal love, gentility, and refinement, along with courage and moral resolution, were the hallmarks of middle-class manhood before the Civil War.[27] By the turn of the century, however, a martial model of manhood had replaced the midcentury ideal of masculine refinement. According to Anthony Rotundo, the post–Civil War generation romanticized battle as a metaphor for life, with manhood attained only through passionate struggle. Images of "primitive masculinity" proliferated as vigorous team sports, "muscular Christianity," and military service vied with the business world as sites for manly competition. This model of physical, mental, and moral duress recast fraternal love as a bond galvanized by the fires of shared struggle and risk. Urban easterners who thought of cowboys as primitive men, uncivilized but worthy of respect for their arduous work, also imagined cowboy fellowship as yet another heroic bond, enabled by the rigors of physical danger and hardship.[28]

Cowboy descriptions of their bunkies, however, were far more prosaic. Neither refined nor heroic, theses descriptions reveal a mixture of affection and annoyance, much like that between long-term married couples. Bunkies shared bedding, a physically intimate situation. Andy Adams complained that his bunkie, Paul Priest, "could use the poorest judgement in selecting a bed ground for our blankets," though Adams added that Priest "always talked and told stories to me until I fell asleep."[29] Dakota cowboy Con Price described a cowhand who got along fine with his sleeping partner except for one bad habit: "They had one bunk they both slept in and the other fellow . . . had a habit of taking a chew of tobacco in the middle of the night. As this fellow told it, 'He would spit straight up and it would fall on my face when I was asleep.'"[30] Price recalled his own year-long partnership with a fifty-five–year-old cowboy who hated the cold of the northern plains. "We nicknamed him 'Grandpa,'" wrote Price. "Between the two of us we didn't have bedding enough to pad a crutch." According to Price, "Grandpa was very cranky and was always giving me the devil for pulling the covers off of him. He would lay and moan all night, and every time I would roll over, he would holler and cuss me."[31] The two bickered over blankets through an entire season. Yet when it came time for "Grandpa" to leave, he did so with regret and affection for Price: "He came around to bid me goodbye and apologized for being so cranky. He said, 'You know, I have been sick and froze ever since I been with this outfit, but I am going to miss you when I go home."[32] Sometimes affection came without price, and bunkies simply got on well together. "Prunie Bill Evans was my dearest friend," wrote Montana cowboy J. T. Armstong. "We rode guard together and we slept together."[33] Whether odd couple or compatible friend, bunkies shared the bond of mutual reliance. In his old age, reminiscing about his bunkies and friends, Con Price wrote, "In my mind I picture each one as spokes in my wagon wheel of friendship, and I feel I have a whole, good, strong wheel."[34] Spokes in the wheel of friendship, bunkies relied on each other for warmth and human support. A cowboy's sleeping partner on the trail was his partner on night guard, his companion through the hardship and monotony of trailing cattle hundreds of miles across the plains. Bunkies, in short, were family—the cowboy's alternative family, adapted to the trail drive.

Revisionist historians speculate about cowboy sexuality, given that men lived for months at a time in the company of none but men. Cowboy myth is hypermasculine, avoiding any hint of homosexual themes.[35] Oral and written tradition created by cowboys themselves during the late nineteenth and early twentieth centuries is equivocal on the subject. From a sample of more than one

hundred cowboy songs and narratives, only two expressed homoerotic senti-ments.[36] Both were attributed to cases of mistaken identity, in which a particu-larly "fair" young man is mistaken for a woman, or vice versa. Andy Adams described a Blackfeet youth of indeterminate gender whose beauty created "a controversy over the sex of [the] young Indian."[37] Adams described the encounter as follows: "The Indian was pointed out to us across the herd, easily distinguished by beads and beaver fur trimmings in the hair, so we rode around to pass our judgement as experts on the beauty. The young Indian was not over sixteen years of age, with remarkable features"[38] Adams recalled the Blackfeet youth's refined features and the cowboys' frustration with the language barrier. Using signs, they tried to ask the Blackfeet youth whether he/she was male or female. "But the young Blackfoot paid no attention to us, being intent on watching the cows."[39] So the cowboys resorted to familiar markers of gender: "The neatly moccasined feet and the shapely hand, however, indicated the fem-inine, and when Blades and Quarternight rode up, we rendered our decision accordingly."[40] Within a few minutes, however, more was revealed:

> Blades took exception to the decision and rode alongside the young
> Indian, pretending to admire the long plaits of hair, toyed with the

beads, pinched and patted the young Blackfoot, and finally, although the rest of us, for fear the Indian might take offense and raise trouble, pleaded with him to desist, he called the youth his "squaw" when the young blood, evidently understanding the appellation, relaxed into a broad smile, and in fair English said, "Me buck."

Blades burst into a loud laugh at his success, at which the Indian smiled but accepted a cigarette and the two cronied together, while we rode away to look after our cows.[41]

Adams's narration of this event is as ambiguous as the gender of the Blackfeet youth. Blades appears more concerned with guessing correctly than with whether or not the Blackfeet youth is male or female. Neither Blades nor the young Blackfeet man seem concerned that the latter was mistaken for a woman; the two go on to "crony together" while others ride off to their posts. Was Blades making fun of the cowboys' attraction to the Blackfeet youth when he pretended "to admire the long plaits of hair, toyed with the beads, pinched and patted" the young man? If this were the case, it would suggest that homoerotic attraction was taboo, and invited derision. Or was Blades expressing his own attraction to the youth, and then deflecting it with his loud laughter? Did Adams use impersonal pronouns—"the neatly moccasined feet," "the shapely hand," "the long plaits of hair"—to distance himself from his own attraction and confusion? What of the Blackfeet youth, who appeared to take the cowboys' interest with good humor? Was he avoiding confrontation, a prudent strategy for a man of color outnumbered by white cowboys? Or was he a two-spirit person, fluent in both masculine and feminine social roles?[42] What exactly did Adams mean by the phrase "the two cronied together"? Answers to these questions elude us, for the record of such experiences is sparse.

The other expression of homoerotic feeling to surface in cowboy traditions from this period appears in the song "The Stampede," subtitled "The Cherokee Kid from the Cimmarron Strip." Attributed to Powder River Jack Lee, the introductory notes tell singers that "the following strange incident told in verse is a true story. . . . This story of the Cherokee Kid is a legend of trail days that actually happened."[43] Folklorists argue that whether the incident actually took place is beside the point; the point being that oral traditions express "psychological and cultural truths."[44] The Cherokee Kid is a young cowboy who rides with the narrator on a grueling trail drive from the Texas plains up to Kansas. In the first two verses, the narrator describes scorching sun, choking dust, and fierce electric storms that threaten to stampede five thousand unruly longhorns. In the third verse, he introduces the title character:

For numberless days we trailed the herd and by my side there rid
A buckaroo and a cowboy too, by the name of the Cherokee kid.
More like a girl with nut brown hair and waist line lithe and slim[45]

The narrator then indicates a special friendship between himself and the Cherokee Kid:

> Fifteen buckaroos trailed the herd, but the kid from the Cimarron
> would always ride close by my side or travel apart—alone.[46]

The next four verses recount a thunderstorm that frightens the herd into a stampede. The cowboys ride frantically to head off the lead cows, and in the effort, the Cherokee Kid gets trampled by a crazed steer. The narrator grabs his "little pard" from beneath the cattle, and rides him to safety, not knowing whether he is dead or alive:

> I jerked my slicker from my horse and laid him on the ground,
> I never sobbed like that before, I gently raised his head,
> and wondered why I cared so much, the little kid was—dead.[47]

As the narrator cries over his fallen friend, the Cherokee Kid stirs, and the narrator realizes that she is a woman: "He's not a boy! A woman's breast lay plain and white and bare; / The Kid's a girl, my brain's a whirl, and she's speaking to me there."[48] The Cherokee Kid confesses her love for the narrator, and the narrator responds with passion, kissing her before she dies in his arms. The closing verses honor her with a cowboy burial:

> Somewhere on the lone prairie, we laid her down to sleep,
> Where prowling wolves roam o'er the plains and mournful dirges keep,
> And where we sang 'Oh Bury me Not' to a six-gun's thundering rip,
> Out there she lies 'neath western skies—the Kid from the Cherokee
> Strip.[49]

Finally, the narrator pledges undying love for his cowboy pard who turned out to be female:

> The girl God took with the flashing eyes, my heart lies buried there,
> By the Cherokee Kid from the Cimarron Strip, with the golden nut
> brown hair.[50]

This song, like Adams's narrative of the Blackfeet youth, is rife with ambiguity. On the one hand, the narrator is attracted by the Cherokee Kid's "lithe waist" and "nut brown hair" long before he discovers her true gender. Likewise, he is passionate about his loss before discovering that his "little pard" is a young woman. These details imply homoerotic attraction. On the other hand, the narrative progression of this ballad implies that it takes a heterosexual pairing to sanction sexual passion, for only when he discovers that she is female is he free to kiss her. This suggests that heterosexual norms governed overt sexual expression. These two rare examples of homoerotic feeling in cowboy oral and written tradition raise more questions than they answer, but they are sexually charged in a way that reminiscences about bunkies were not.

If bunkies were family, and homoerotic attractions were shrouded in ambiguity, relations with prostitutes were openly sanctioned. Cowboys' oral and written tradition from the late nineteenth and early twentieth centuries celebrated the bond between range cowboys and prostitutes. Sharing outsider status as socially marginal figures, range cowboys and prostitutes developed a subculture of mutual aid and friendship. Some entered into fictive marriage with one prostitute for the duration of their stay in town. Others turned to prostitutes as nonsexual confidants, or for financial assistance.

The narrative of Teddy Blue Abbott is revealing in this regard. Abbott worked as a cowhand from 1879 through 1889, the heyday of the open range. "Prostitutes," wrote Abbott, "followed the trail herds. The madams would bring them out from Omaha and Chicago and St. Paul; you would see them in Ogallala, and then again in Cheyenne or the Black Hills."[51] Abbott described his friendships with prostitutes as follows: "In Miles City that summer [1884], I found a lot of new friends and some old ones. There was girls there that I had seen at a lot of different places along the trail. . . . I used to talk to those girls, and they would tell me a lot of stuff, . . . and they were human, too."[52] Abbott added that cowboys and prostitutes extended credit to each other, depending upon who had ready cash:

> In the spring, when a fellow was hired he would go to his girl and say: "I've got a job, but my bed's in soak." Or his saddle or his six-shooter or his horse. And she would lend him the money to get it back and he would pay her at the end of the month.
>
> . . . There was a girl called Eddie, that I took on after my pal Lily Davis left . . . she [Eddie] had just landed in Lincoln and didn't have any good clothes. . . . I had money, and I staked her an outfit. She paid it all back eventually."[53]

The terms "his girl," and "my pal" suggest relationships that reached beyond an impersonal coupling for a single night. According to Abbott, cowboys and prostitutes formed temporary partnerships, an alternative to Victorian courtship and marriage. "We all had our favorites after we got acquainted," he wrote. "We'd go in town and marry a girl for a week, take her to breakfast and dinner and supper, be with her all the time."[54] For some, it was a short step from fictive marriage to the real thing. Occasionally, a cowboy fell in love with his prostitute "wife" and legally married her.[55]

Thus cowboys pioneered alternative patterns for human relationship outside the boundaries of middle-class Victorian society. Bunkies provided companionship and physical comfort during long months on the trail. Prostitutes served as fictive wives during the weeks spent in town. In forming such relationships, the cowboy subculture disrupted Victorian judgments about marriage as a marker of adult respectability. Rather than apologize for relationships adapted to nomadic life, cowboys of the open-range era celebrated the freedoms of marginality. Abbott, for example, reveled in the sexual license enjoyed by the nomadic cowboy. He socialized with prostitutes happily and without shame. "Oh, boy, but life was good," he wrote. "Those were the days when I didn't have a care in the world. . . . the girls said I was the best-looking cowboy on the Powder River."[56] Reflecting on the sexual freedom he enjoyed as a cowboy, Abbott recognized it as a distinctly masculine privilege: "I've heard a lot about the double standard, and seen a lot of it too, and it didn't make any sense for a man to get off so easy. If I'd have been a woman and done what I done, I'd have ended up in a sporting house."[57] At the same time, Abbott noted that masculine sexual privilege found open expression only outside the mainstream. "I suppose those things [cowboy relationships with prostitutes] would shock a lot of respectable people. But we wasn't respectable and we didn't pretend to be, which was the only way we was different from some others."[58] Here, Abbott rejected the moral restrictions of the middle-class Victorian male—"we wasn't respectable and we didn't pretend to be"—embracing instead the masculine sexual privilege of the margins.

If sexual license was one such privilege, gender-bending was another. Cowboys sometimes parodied gender identity with episodes of cross-dressing. Freedom from middle-class social convention was freedom to make ribald fun of Victorian gender norms. This lay at the core of cowboy cross-dressing. Occasionally, men would take the female role socially, in order to form couples for a dance where no women were present. At these times, a cowboy dressed normally, the only feminine marker being a scarf tied to his arm to signal his place in the dance as a woman.[59] Cross-dressing, in contrast, involved one man performing for an audience of cowboys, prostitutes, and townspeople. These performances were spontaneous outbursts. They were cross-dressing as public spectacle, a focus of group hilarity, indeed, a group statement.

Dakota cowboy Ike Blasingame recalled a cowhand whose horse had plunged into the Missouri River in high water. As cowboy and horse floated downstream, the cowboy kicked off his boots, stripped to his underwear, tied his boots in his shirt, and swam for the cutbank. Meanwhile, prostitutes from a nearby brothel acted quickly to help. They hurried to the riverbank and tossed him strips of bedsheets tied together as a lifeline. He grabbed the sheets, and the prostitutes pulled him to shore. As Blasingame told it, "While his own clothes dried, they [the prostitutes] got the idea to dress him in silk petticoats and an evening gown, and introduce him as a new member of The House."[60] They pinned false curls on his head and made up his face, until "he made a very passable and well-painted Gal." Evidently he was small, and

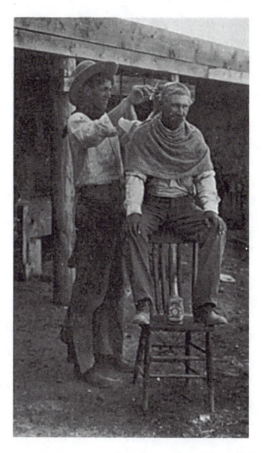

HAIRCUT FOR A BUNKIE, CIRCA 1901. COURTESY OF THE E. E. SMITH COLLECTION, LIBRARY OF CONGRESS.

"could easily be taken for one of them." The now thoroughly cross-dressed cowboy "fell right in with their fun."

> He greeted arrivals as gaily and invitingly as any of the regular Girls did. He swished his skirts and flirted; he danced and flipped his hips. . . . So well did he fit into the clothes, and so well did he act his part, he enticed several amorous gents to go upstairs to be alone with "her." When they discovered they had been taken in, they helped hook others by spreading tales of the new Gal's charms. Then every man slanted an eye "her" way, and she became the "belle of the ball."[61]

"All went hilariously well," concluded Blasingame, "and none suspected the fraud for quite a while."[62] The next day, the small cowboy put on his dry clothes and resumed life as a man, with no apparent loss of respect from his peers.

What was the meaning of such performance? In an analysis of cowboy culture that includes oral and written tradition, Blake Allmendinger argues that because they lived in all-male groups, deprived of contact with women for long periods of time, cowboys were forced to rein in their sexual appetites. Cowboy culture thus sanctioned occasional disguises that denied their gender identity in order to defuse their longing for women.[63] In light of Blasingame's account of the cross-dressed cowboy's "seduction" of men at the brothel, however, one might also argue that comic episodes of cross-dressing used humor to simultaneously express and defuse men's attraction to men. In Blasingame's episode, cowboys had opportunity both to flirt with a cross-dressed man, and to participate in the collective joke by "spreading tales of the new Gal's charms."

Allmendinger further speculates that cowboys cross-dressed as deliberate parodies of Victorian gender convention, "making light of the 'worshipped' female sex by . . . parading mock women in front of people, shocking onlookers and brooking safeguarded taboos."[64] Evidence supports this interpretation as well. On a dare spurred by another cowboy who donned women's ruffled underdrawers, Teddy Blue Abbott put on a prostitute's frilly white drawers, and the two paraded down the streets of Miles City, Montana, in full regalia. "The whole town turned out to see us," he bragged. "It turned the place upside down."[65] Similarly, Dakota cowboy Ed Lemmon recalled the time his friend Ed Comstock "wore Connie's silk dress," Connie being the "leading painted girl in Deadwood." Evidently, "Connie, in her own best silks, perched beside" Ed Comstock on a wagon. The couple, in feminine attire, wound riotously through town "with cowboys riding on both sides of the wagon," then proceeded down Main Street "on the high run, smoking up the town. Everybody in the place came out to watch."[66] Clearly both incidents were public displays, enjoyed for their shock value.

What Allmendinger does not address, however, and what stands out in all of these incidents, are the prostitutes' presence as coconspirators. In each case—Blasingame, Abbott, and Lemmon—prostitutes supplied the feminine clothing, urged the cross-dresser on, and played supporting roles in the performance. The partnership between "fancy women" and range cowboys in these performances is significant, for both groups shared outsider status in late-Victorian America. It is not surprising, then, that they might band together to mock Victorian mores. What better way to flout Victorian gender norms than to turn single males into parodies of women, in whores' clothing? In a study of California Gold Rush society, Susan Johnson refers to public disruptions of ritual behavior as contests over the power to establish meanings,[67] an appropriate paradigm for understanding these outbursts of cross-dressing. Both range cowboys and prostitutes suffered the negative judgments of mainstream society.[68] During these spontaneous displays, however, both cowboy and prostitute temporarily claimed the power to overturn social norms. Using broad parody to assault the dignity of Victorian gender convention, they challenged the sanctity of middle-class roles like wife-as-civilizer and husband-as-provider.

For all its humor, sexual license, alternative relationships, and challenge to Victorian mores, over time cowboy culture shifted with changes in the cattle industry. As family ranches gradually replaced open-range herding, cowboys traded the masculine privileges of the margins for the class privileges of the mainstream. Though vestiges of the old nomadic subculture would persist, cowboys began to upgrade their image. In 1898, when C. C. Post published his memoir *Ten Years a Cowboy*, he assured readers that "now only in the South—for instance, Arizona—is the term cowboy equivalent to desperado."[69] That same year, former cowboy W. S. James published his recollections, *Cowboy Life in Texas*, in which he tried to improve cowboys' shaky social standing by emphasizing their literacy: "Many people think the cowboy is an ignoramus as far as books are concerned," wrote James, yet "out of nine young men, the oldest in the squad being twenty-eight, who were lounging around a campfire one evening, . . . it was ascertained . . . that five out of the nine had graduated in Eastern colleges."[70] Similarly, in 1905, the National Livestock Association redeemed the cowboy's reputation in a publication called *Prose and Poetry of the Livestock Industry of the United States*. This volume excerpted statements from educated cowboy enthusiasts such as Emerson Hough and Teddy Roosevelt. Both authors represented solidly respectable late-Victorian men, and both argued that cowboys were neither morally degraded nor socially disreputable. "No other class of men ever was so unfaithfully represented," insisted Livestock Association spokesman James W. Freeman.[71] Hough waxed sentimental about the cowboy, urging readers to look beyond "the wide hat," and see "the honest face beneath it."[72]Roosevelt attributed the cowboy's roughness to his pioneer role. "The cowboy," he wrote, demonstrated "the theory of the survival of the fittest," on rugged American frontiers. In a fit of nationalism, Roosevelt proclaimed the cowboy "brave, hospitable, hardy, and adventurous . . . he prepare[d] the way for civilization." Finally, Roosevelt assured readers that from the ranks of yesterday's cowboys came today's businessmen: "There were many, even in the 'wildest and wooliest' period, who . . . kept their wits about them, saved their wages, and successfully became range-stockmen on their own account in their later years."[73] The phrase "range stockmen on their own account" elevated the cowboy to self-employed businessman, entrepreneur, a man of the owning class rather than the working class.

Like property or business ownership, marriage was another hallmark of middle-class respectability. When range cowboys became married homesteaders, they entered the middle-class world personified by "respectable" women. Relationships with prostitutes became unacceptable. In an early-twentieth-century narrative that lauded the range cowboy for his skill, loyalty, and physical endurance, Ed Randolph sided with the family rancher in rejecting prostitution. He described a hapless cowboy, Tom Bryan, who was tricked into marrying a prostitute while drunk. Abbit White, the ranch owner, "wouldn't have Tom on the ranch" when he found out.[74] Randolph spent a chapter detailing how Bryan tried to annul the marriage, and how cowboys on the White ranch sympathized with his plight. Notably, ranch woman Betty White held a central role in this story, both disapproving of the prostitute and trying to help Bryan resolve his dilemma. The episode closed with Bryan ready to dump the prostitute-wife and appreciate a respectable woman. In the last line of the chapter, Bryan gives the nod to Betty White, saying, "There's a fine little woman!"[75]

Similarly, Teddy Blue Abbott's narrative celebrated the sexual license and prostitute pals of range cowboys, only to wind up embracing marriage, respectability, and family. In 1889, Abbott married Mary Stuart, daughter of wealthy rancher Granville Stuart.[76] Abbott and his wife bought land of their own and began to farm it. "And that in a way writes the end to . . . my life on the open range," he wrote. "I wasn't a cowpuncher any more. I took a homestead, kept milk cows, and raised a garden."[77] Though Abbott "still rode and kept cattle" on the homestead, he saw marriage as a landmark that separated him from cowboy life. As befitted a property owner, he embraced the civilizing influence of a "good" woman. "I quit drinking, threw my chewing tobacco away, quit what little gambling I ever done, and started to save money," announced Abbott, sounding like a paragon of middle-class manhood. "It shows you what a good woman will do for a man," he continued. "Mary was the first decent young girl I had ever known."[78] Marriage to a good woman lifted one out of the margins and into the mainstream. Teddy Blue Abbott married up.

But the transition from the margins to the middle-class could be balky, like an ornery steer. Consider the ambivalence in Abbott's reflections on the company of respectable women:

> I'd been traveling and moving around all the time, living with men, and I can't say I ever went out of my way to seek the company of respectable ladies. We didn't consider we were fit to associate with them on account of the company we kept. . . . We were so damn scared for fear we would do or say something wrong—mention a leg or something like that that would send them up in the air.[79]

In this brief apologia, Abbott alludes to competing values that surfaced during the transition from open-range herding to family ranches. Working-class masculine privilege competed with Victorian middle-class privilege. That is,

Abbott expressed both a range cowboy's irritation with middle-class propriety ("mention a leg or something like that that would send them up in the air") and a transitional cowboy's longing for acceptance in mainstream society ("We were so damn scared for fear that we would do or say something wrong"). Other narratives echoed Abbott's discomfort with the transition from the margins to the married middle class.[80] Like Abbott's, these narratives trotted between enthusiasm for range cowboy life and affirmations of middle-class marriage and property ownership. In *Dakota Cowboy*, for example, following the ribald tale of cross-dressing with prostitutes, Blasingame insisted that the cowboy was actually very civilized. "Obscenity was frowned upon," he wrote. "Any indecent act was met with stern disapproval. Improper talk about women or lewd jokes had little part in the . . . life these men lived."[81] Even though cowboys lived and worked outdoors, declared Blasingame, "there was no reason why they must drop all habits of civilized man. Cowboys made a worthy effort to be manly, to act in accordance with what was right. . . . "[82] In narratives like these, "manliness" wavered between the masculine privileges of the margins and the class privileges of the respectable family rancher.

If homesteader-cowboys gave up the masculine privileges of the transient laborer, such as nomadism, sexual license, alternative relationships, or even cross-dressing, they held onto one remnant of those privileges as a cultural legacy of the range cowboy. That was masculine occupational identity. Once they embraced middle-class status, living and working with respectable women, homesteader-cowboys could no longer pair up with a male bunkie, befriend prostitutes, change sexual partners at will, or flout mainstream social mores with public displays of gender-bending. The only element of masculine privilege that remained on the family ranch was the gender boundary that kept women out of cowpunching, or ranked them "fellers" when they rode herd. If work with beef cattle retained a masculine occupational identity, then domesticated cowboys could claim the prestige of cowboy myth as their own, safe from appropriation by ranch women. At a time when homestead law supported female ranch ownership and the budding sport of rodeo endorsed female athletes,[83] cowboy identity stood to lose its masculine face. Cowboy myth, then, supported the masculinization of work with cattle on family ranches, and cowboys reserved the rewards of cultural iconography for men—a masculine privilege for the middle-class man.

Notes

The author would like to thank Laura McCall and Matt Basso for their helpful comments on earlier drafts. Also Bill Farr, Lois Welch, Woody Kipp, and Kath McChesney-Lape for making Missoula, Montana, a home where I could write. Their humor, support, and thoughtful conversation enlarged my vision. Jodi Allison-Bunnell, Director of the Mansfield Library Archives and Special Collections at the University of Montana; and Martha Kohl, Associate Editor at *Montana: The Magazine of Western History*, provided valuable research assistance. Loren Marshall of the Treeline Writer's Group, Troy Lawrence, and Nancy Hunt supplied indispensable technical assistance. Finally, special thanks go to Karla VanderZanden and Gary George for sharing their West.

1. Phyllis Luman Metal and Doris Platts, *Cattle King on the Green River: The Family Life and Legends of Abner Luman, a Cowboy King of the Upper Green River Valley in the Twenties* (Wilson, Wyo.: Sunshine Ranch and Friends, 1983), 126.

2. *Beeves* is a plural form of *beef,* used to refer to beef cattle.

3. Within this essay, the term *rancher* refers to the ranch owner; the term *cowboy* refers to his employees. Cowboys were hired labor. Most cowboys were landless wage workers, not ranch owners. If a cowboy made the transition to homesteading, claiming land of his own, he then became a rancher.

Interview with J. M. Huston by Josephine Jons, unpublished manuscript, WPA interview, 1938 (Cheyenne: Wyoming State Archives and Historical Department, hereafter WSAHD), MSS-1277; Charles N. Harger, "Cattle Trails of the Prairies," *Scribner's Magazine* 11 (June 1892): 738–41; Nellie Snyder Yost, *Boss Cowman: The Recollections of Ed Lemmon, 1857–1946* (Lincoln: University of Nebraska Press, 1969), 246–48; Con Price, *Trails I Rode* (Pasadena, Calif.: Trails End Publishing Co., 1947), 47–58, and 234–36; Floyd C. Bard, *Horse Wranglers* (Norman: University of Oklahoma Press, 1960), 225; and Charles Siringo, *A Texas Cowboy or, Fifteen Years on the Hurricane Deck of a Spanish Pony* (Chicago: Rand McNally, 1886), 95–102, 176–85, and 337–40. See also Blake Allmendinger, *The Cowboy: Representations of Labor in an American Work Culture* (New York: Oxford University Press, 1992), 6 and 50; and Richard White, *It's Your Misfortune and None of My Own: A New History of the American West* (Norman: University of Oklahoma Press, 1991), 222–23.

4. John Clay, *My Life on the Range* (New York: Antiquarian Press, 1961), 176–79; and White, 224–25.

5. Quoted in Ray Allen Billington, *Westward Expansion: A History of the American Frontier* (New York: MacMillan, 1974), 597.

6. Interview with Huston.

7. Dee Garceau, *The Important Things of Life: Women, Work, and Family in Sweetwater County, Wyoming, 1880–1929* (Lincoln: University of Nebraska Press, 1997), 89.

8. Mrs. B. B. Brooks, "Ranch Life on the Big Muddy," *The Daily Sun Leader,* December 22, 1899, transcribed by Mae Cody for the WPA, WSAHD MSS-3944, 1.

9. Garceau, *The Important Things of Life*, 100–102.

10. Quoted in C. L. Sonnichsen, *Cowboys and Cattle Kings* (Norman: University of Oklahoma Press, 1942), 77.

11. Helen Sargent, "Charlotta Hartley Albert," in *Tales of the Seeds-Ke-Dee* (Denver: Big Mountain Press, 1963), 351–660, esp. 354.

12. Edmund Randolph, *Hell among the Yearlings* (New York: W. W. Norton, 1955), 172.

13. Sonnichsen, 81.

14. Interview with Elsie Cooksley Lloyd and Amy Cooksley Chubb by Theresa Jordan, *Cowgirls: Women of the American West: An Oral History* (New York: Doubleday, 1984), 2–12, esp. 7.

15. Ibid., 9.

16. Randolph, 194.

17. Interview with Marie Jordan Bell by Theresa Jordan, *Cowgirls*, 24.

18. See Robert V. Hin and John Mack Faragher, "Open Range," *The American West: A New Interpretive History* (New Haven: Yale University Press, 2000), 310–29; William Savage, ed., *Cowboy Life: Reconstructing an American Myth* (Niwot: University Press of Colorado, 1993), 3–16; Robert Murray Davis, "The Virginian: Inventing the Westerner," in *Playing Cowboys: Low Culture and High Art in the Western* (Norman: University of Oklahoma Press, 1992) Robert Athearn, *The Mythic West in Twentith-Century America* (University Press of Kansas, 1986): 265–68; Robert V. Hine, "The Cowboy and the Cult of Masculinity," in *The American West: An Interpretive History* (Boston: Little, Brown, 1973); and Neal Lambert, "Owen Wister's Virginian: The Genesis of a Cultural Hero," *Western American Literature* 6 (summer 1971): 99–107.

19. Bruce Siberts, *Nothing But Prairie and Sky; Life on the Dakota Range in the Early Days*, ed. Walker D. Wyman (Norman: University of Oklahoma Press, 1954), 90.

20. Peter Filene, *Him/Her/Self: Sex Roles in Modern America*, 2nd ed. (Baltimore: Johns Hopkins University Press, 1986), 69–71, esp. 70.

21. C. C. Post, *Ten Years a Cowboy* (Denver: Thomas W. Jackson Publishing Co., 1898), 386.

22. Sonnichsen, 47; Kenneth Porter, "Negro Labor in the Western Cattle Industry, 1866–1900," *Labor History* 10 (summer 1969), 346–64, 367–68, and 370–74; and Will James, *All in the Day's Ride* (New York: Charles Scribner & Sons, 1933), 8. For an account of testing a newcomer's riding ability by giving him an ornery horse, see J. T. Armstrong, *The Big North* (Helena: Montana Historical Society Press, 1965), 30–31.

23. Herding was cooperative work; trail drives ran on a tightly choreographed routine that all hands followed. As Montana cowboy J. T. Armstrong remarked, "A good cowboy worked by the rules or he didn't stay long!" Armstrong, 34–39. See also Yost, 85.

24. Montana cowboy Teddy Blue Abbott, for example, described nursing an ailing cowboy who needed his comfort:

[O]ne of the boys with the outfit got sick and I nursed him in a hotel room until he died in my arms. . . . he did not want me to leave him a minute. . . . I hadn't been to bed all that time, only slept in a chair once in a while, because he wouldn't sleep unless he could lay his head on my arm. So I went and laid down in another room. About midnight Mr. Fuller come for me and said, "You better come now. He's asking for you." I guess he knew he was going. So I went back where he was, and he wanted to know if I would lay down beside him and let him rest his head on my shoulder. In a few minutes he mumbled something about Ethel, his sister I think, and then he was gone.

Abbott, *We Pointed Them North* (Norman: University of Oklahoma Press, 1939), 81–82.

25. Andy Adams, *The Log of a Cowboy* (Cambridge, Mass: Riverside Press, 1903; reprinted New York: Houghton Mifflin, 1927), 23. See also Price, 230 and 232; and Randolph, 118.

26. Adams, 24.

27. Donald Yacavone, "'Surpassing the Love of Women': Victorian Manhood and the Language of Fraternal Love," in *A Shared Experience: Men, Women, and the History of Gender* (New York: New York University Press, 1998), 195–221.

28. Anthony Rotundo, "Passionate Manhood: A Changing Standard of Masculinity," in *American Manhood* (New York: Basic Books, 1993), 222–46. See also Filene, 71–72.

29. Adams, 24.

30. Price, 236.

31. Ibid., 54.

32. Ibid., 56.

33. Armstrong, 45.

34. Price, 253.

35. Allmendinger, 51–56; Savage, 3–16; Davis, 3–29; Hine, 125–38.

36. For unexpurgated texts of cowboy songs, see Guy Logsdon, *The Whorehouse Bells Were Ringing, and Other Songs Cowboys Sing* (Urbana: University of Illinois Press, 1989). Logsdon compiled more than one hundred songs drawn from cowboy oral tradition. Of those that are explicitly sexual, most depict heterosexual intercourse, a few address masturbation, and one alludes to bestiality. See "The Mormon Cowboy," 38–41; "Red Light Saloon," 74–76; "Wild Buckaroo," 103–7; "Root, Hog, or Die," 140–42; "The Oaks of Jimderia," 222–23; "The Whorehouse Bells Were Ringing," 145–48; and "Old Horny Kebri-O," 235–37. Historian Clifford Westermeier found one limerick that alluded to homosexual sex as something feared by young cowboys, who occasionally suffered an older, very drunk cowboy's advances: "Young cowboys had a great fear / That old studs once filled with beer / completely addled / They'd throw on a saddle / And ride them on the rear." See Westermeier, "The Cowboy and Sex," in *The Cowboy: Sixshooters, Songs, and Sex,* ed. Charlie Harris and Buck Rainey (Norman: University of Oklahoma Press, 1976): 85–106; limerick appears on p. 93. Of the seventeen cowboy narratives surveyed for this study, only one hinted at homoerotic feeling: Andy Adams's account of the Blackfeet youth in *The Log of a Cowboy*, discussed herein.

37. Adams, 312–13.

38. Ibid., 313.

39. Ibid.

40. Ibid.

41. Ibid., 313–14.

42. Will Roscoe, "That Is My Road: The Life and Times of a Crow Berdache," *Montana: The Magazine of Western History* 40, no. 1 (winter 1990): 46–55; see also Sue Ellen Jacobs and Wesley Thomas et al., eds., *Two-Spirit People: Native American Gender Identity, Sexuality, and Spirituality* (Urbana: University of Illinois Press, 1997).

43. Jack Lee, *Cowboy Songs* (K. Ross Toole Archives, Mansfield Library, University of Montana, Missoula), 44.

44. Bruce Rosenberg, *The Code of the West* (Bloomington: Indiana University Press, 1982), 3–4; Alan Lomax, "Introduction," in *The Folksongs of North America* (New York: Doubleday, 1975), xv–xxx; Allmendinger, *The Cowboy*, 9.

45. Lee, 44.

46. Ibid.

47. Ibid.

48. Ibid.

49. Ibid.

50. Ibid.

51. Abbott, 89. For additional accounts of cowboy leisure time with prostitutes, see Price, 64; Yost,

137 and 208; and Siberts, 143–44.

52. Abbott, 89.

53. Ibid., 108 and 110–11. For additional accounts of friendship and mutual aid between cowboys and prostitutes, see Lemmon, 208 and 293.

54. Abbott, 107.

55. Ibid.

56. Ibid., 89.

57. Ibid., 107.

58. Ibid.

59. Allmendinger, 67; and Logsdon, 213.

60. Ike Blasingame, *Dakota Cowboy* (Lincoln: University of Nebraska Press, 1958), 205.

61. Ibid., 205.

62. Ibid., 205–6.

63. Allmendinger, *The Cowboy*, 51–53.

64. Ibid., 60.

65. Abbott, 111–12.

66. Yost, 209.

67. Susan Johnson, "Bulls, Bears, and Dancing Boys: Race, Gender, and Leisure in the California Gold Rush," this volume, 45–71.

68. Price, 61–62; Yost, 86 and 91–95.

69. Post, 391.

70. W. S. James, *Cowboy Life in Texas, or 27 Years a Maverick* [*sic*] (Chicago: M.A. Donohue and Co., 1989), 79–80.

71. James W. Freeman, ed., *Prose and Poetry of the Live Stock Industry of the United States,* vol. 1 (Denver: National Live Stock Historical Association, 1905), 548.

72. Hough, quoted in Savage, 162.

73. Roosevelt, quoted in Savage, 171–72 and 175.

74. Randolph, 248–68, esp. 250.

75. Ibid., 268.

76. Granville Stuart was well known in late-nineteenth-century Montana as owner of the prosperous DHS ranch. Stuart married a Cheyenne woman, with whom he had three daughters. The Stuarts raised their daughters with Victorian education and training, so that the Stuart girls were known as educated, refined women, as befitted the civilizer role. Abbott, 141–43.

77. Abbott, 207.

78. Ibid., 187.

79. Ibid., 188.

80. For accounts of discomfort around "respectable" women, see Armstrong, 32; Sonnichsen, 46; and Powder River Jack Lee, "I Aint Got No Use for the Wimmen" (K. Ross Toole Archives, Mansfield Library, University of Montana, Missoula).

81. Blasingame, 255.

82. Ibid., 255. Similarly, Floyd C. Bard wound up his narrative by extolling the joys of homesteading with his wife, Mabel. At this point in the narrative, he begins to look down on range cowboys who "ride the grub line" as somewhat beggarly. See Bard, 225–26.

83. For a discussion of homestead law and female ranch ownership, see Dee Garceau, "Single Women Homesteaders and the Meanings of Independence: Places on the Map, Places in the Mind," *Frontiers: A Journal of Women's Studies* 15, no. 3 (fall 1995): 1–26. For a discussion of female rodeo stars of the 1920s, see Theresa Jordan, "Cowgirls and the Crowd: The Early Years: Wild West and Rodeo," in *Cowgirls,* 187–236.

Domesticated Bliss

Ranchers and Their
Animals

Karen R. Merrill

"A cowboy's work, as you know, is sometimes brutal—even cruel. Often violent," wrote Western novelist and social commentator Edward Abbey. Abbey was no friend of the range livestock industry, and he never minced words. "Anyone who's taken part in gathering, roping, branding, dehorning, castrating, ear notching . . . or winching a calf from its mother knows how mean and tough and brutal it can be. And if the cowboy's mind and sensibilities have not been permanently deformed by that kind of work, he'll admit it." Abbey's point is one made by a multitude in the environmental movement, but he takes his argument one step further. The very cruelty of ranchers' work, he writes, has a profound influence on ranchers' attitudes toward other animals and the environment in which they work: "Brutal work tends to bring out the brutality in all of us. And that's probably why cattlemen, as a class (I emphasize this, as a class) tend to hate nature. Hate wildlife. Especially anything they dream might compete with their cattle."[1]

Abbey was not the first commentator to accuse western cattlemen of cruelty toward animals. After the infamous winter of 1886–87 on the high plains, when blizzards and bitter cold weather decimated cattle herds, the western livestock industry as a whole came under stinging attacks for leaving animals out on the range to fend for themselves. While such criticisms normally exempted cowboys, the working hands on ranches, they aimed particular fire at the ranchers themselves. In contrast, Abbey spares few in his condemnation, and he is clearly interested in undercutting the supposed nobility of the cowboy as a western icon, revealing his "brutality" and even venality. For Abbey, the behavior of cowboys and ranchers toward animals is not only a window on their ethical nature; it is also a window on their masculinity. "I respect real men. I admire true manliness. But I despise arrogance and brutality and bullies." The cowboy and the cattleman represent for Abbey not a "true" form of manly behavior, but a deformation of it, and their attitude toward all forms of animal life is proof. [2] They inflict pain on the animals they are supposed to care for and despise the wild animals that lie within their sight.

Abbey's writings represent a useful starting point for an essay that looks through the very window he has opened to explore how the attitudes of ranchers and cowboys toward domestic and wild animals have given a peculiar twist to masculinity in the West. Humans' relationships to animals say essential things about who we are and what we value—and about constructions of gender— but ranchers and cowboys have a far more perplexing and complicated relationship with animals than the one Abbey outlines. Moreover, to understand that relationship we must also give it a history. The crux of that history lies in the period from the late nineteenth century to the World War II, a time when ranching went from being perceived (even by many ranchers themselves) as a temporary industry in the West to one that was a settled and even defining feature of the landscape. This transformation involved a change in the way ranchers took care of their livestock and the way they understood their relationship to animals generally.[3] While cowboys will enter the picture here and there, I will focus on ranchers, because they wrote a great deal about their interactions with animals. Furthermore, because they owned the domestic animals, and they owned, controlled, or used land inhabited by predatory and game animals, ranchers' capital investments often placed them in a different relationship to animals than the one experienced by cowboys and produced a set of tensions that sparked fascinating responses.

Of course, any generalization about ranchers' written attitudes toward animals tells only part of the story. In this brief essay I do not seek the truth about ranchers' *treatment* of animals, which is far too large and varied a subject, but I aim instead to understand ranchers' changing perceptions of what their relationship to the animal world meant, and then to suggest what this awareness says about masculinity in the West. As Susan Lee Johnson has so aptly observed, the West has long been imagined as "a sort of preserve for white masculinity," and perhaps the most popular preserve *within* that preserve has been the western range, with its iconic figure of the cowboy. Indeed, the cowboy—and particularly the prototype for fictionalized cowboys, Owen Wister's Virginian—came at a time when what constituted proper behavior for manhood was in a critical transformation. The cowboy helped to articulate a host of idealized masculine traits "that focused on vigor and raw virility."[4] In contrast, ranchers occupied a more ambiguous place in the iconography of the West in the late nineteenth century, often representing the excesses of men unmoored from "civilized" society. Especially after the "Great Die-Up" of 1886–87, ranchers were popularly considered coarse and ruthless—as men and as businessmen—and few bemoaned the breaking up of the enormous ranches that had spread across the West in the 1880s.

Ranchers were keenly aware of this reputation. In the first meeting of prominent western livestock producers in 1898, for instance, the president of the organization spoke of the great need for a "new regime" in the industry that included taking better care of their animals. [5]

Ranchers' writings about animals thus reveal a vision of western masculinity that differs in fundamental ways from what is commonly associated with that popular figure, the cowboy. On the one hand, like cowboys, ranchers regaled their audiences with stories of the dangers of their occupation. The harsh weather, the rugged terrain of much ranch country, the predatory animals, and even the unpredictable behavior of their domesticated animals were all presented as challenges for ranchers to meet and overcome. On the other hand, their writings also indicate that in those challenges ranchers sought not only to control and dominate nature, but also to make a domestic space within it, which meant building real ranch homes, getting married or bringing wives to the ranch, having children, buying better breeds of cattle and sheep, and treating them well. Because they were in the business of producing domesticated animals, ranchers began looking at the animal world through the lens of the domestic. The result, by the mid-twentieth century, was that cattlemen perceived the ranch as a space of both familial intimacy with domesticated animals and as a place for provisioning wild game. More precisely, while the genre of Western film and novels during this period either masked the suffering of animals or, as Jane Tompkins notes, "schooled" audiences in the view that sympathizing with such suffering was rank sentimentality, the writings of ranchers display an increasingly freighted emotional response to animals.[6] Ranchers still sent their cattle to slaughter, but were also much more involved in the actual birthing of calves; ranchers still saw game animals like elk and deer in competition for the range's grass, but also saw themselves in the role of helping them to survive; ranchers still hoped to exterminate predatory animals, but interpreted the danger they represented in highly melodramatic ways. In all these instances, ranchers constructed their desire to dominate the animals in proximity to them as part of a domestic vision, and their manipulation was closely hitched to perceptions of themselves as caretakers.

When potential livestock owners traveled west in the late nineteenth century, they were often surprised by the absence of familiar domestic sights. Some were quite overwhelmed by the dearth of human settlement and the lack of any domestic traits in the supposedly domesticated animals they encountered. Otto Maerdian, for instance, left Illinois in 1882 for Montana, where he planned to raise sheep and various crops. After finding a little land on which to homestead, he wrote to his sister that "there are lots of tracks of wild animals" on the land. He added, "I guess that is about all there is that ever goes around it. I don't feel safe when I go there." After getting lost one day for many hours, "I was afraid to lie down in those hollows where there was nothing but trees and hills around me. I was afraid of bears and wolves or other wild beasts." Even coming upon a valley full of cattle did not soothe him. Although he figured he would not be seeing cattle if there were any bears present, "when I got where the cattle could see me, they all snorted and ran away. I felt awful lonesome in a hollow, no body around & I had a strange [i.e., new] horse." Making matters worse, the wolves "are pretty thick around here[.] [Y]ou can hear them every morning and evening."[7] For Maerdian, there was no comfort in nature and, lacking a rifle, he felt utterly vulnerable, potential prey for any predator.[8] Moreover, the domesticated species provided little comfort to him; the cattle's presence, while perhaps signifying the lack of bears, did not indicate that people were nearby. Even Maerdian's horse, because it was "strange," could not assuage his worries.

Maerdian's haplessness and anxiety contrast strongly to the reminiscences so many late-nineteenth-century ranchers published. Although they, too, remarked on the wildness of the country and the proliferation of wild animals, they tended to emphasize their dominance and, when things got out of control, their bravery. But their writings also included observations about the lack of domestication in the West, particularly when it came to their interactions with cattle. In a very typical observation, William French—who emigrated from Ireland to the United States—noted that the first time he saw the Mexican cattle he would own, "They were different from any cattle I had hitherto seen. Most of their growth seemed to have gone into their horns."[9]

The cattle of the mid- to late-nineteenth century were indeed a far different breed than those that would inhabit the range in the mid-twentieth century. The early Texas longhorns of the mid-nineteenth century, for instance, consisted at least partially of feral cattle Anglo ranchers had rounded up—the remnants from herds earlier Mexican inhabitants had owned. These cattle were put out onto "a large surface of country," wrote one observer at the time, who commented that "to hunt up and mark and brand the calves" was "no easy task."[10] But the methods of ranching at this time also underwrote the confusion over boundaries. Historian Terry Jordan describes the "Texas system" of ranching as involving a common practice, derived from both Mexico and coastal Carolina, "of allowing cattle to care for themselves year-round in stationary pastures on the free range, without supplementary feeding or protection." The result, however, was that livestock were treated with "carelessness and neglect," as there was never "any attempt to reserve special winter ranges" for them that might ensure a steady supply of food.[11]

This was the system that, with modifications, spread throughout the plains and intermountain regions before the formidable winter of 1886–87. Ranchers bought large numbers of cattle, put them on the open range, rounded them up to brand them, and then collected steers when it was time to send them off to slaughter, typically when they were three or four years old. Cattle under these conditions had a tendency to become a little wild, a trait that was already perceived in their nature: they could be quite difficult to round up and hard to control.[12] Moreover, the range country produced a continual stream of conflicts over the ownership of cattle, embodied in the form of the "maverick," which was an unbranded calf. For William French, the lack of a brand marked these animals as distinctly undomesticated, but so, too, did their behavior. When the weather was especially dry, he wrote, "some of the outlaw cattle from the hills" came to a river near his ranch. "They never approached the river except at sundown, and then only in ones or twos. They drank hurriedly, suspiciously, like wild animals, and disappeared as soon as they were full." Like hunters in the wild, French and his men observed the movements of the cattle closely, but for a very different end than that of game hunters, for "by watching for them we succeeded in putting [our] brand on many a maverick that might otherwise not have been tallied."[13]

Branding is a legal form of identification, the mark of domestication that connected the animals to individual owners and made them property under the law. But at the height of the cattle boom in the 1880s, all the branding in the West did not ensure that ranchers had succeeded in domesticating the region, and ranchers' attempts to put domesticated cattle on the range met with grave environmental obstacles. First, as investors rushed in to make a fast buck on free grass, the plains and intermountain states from Texas to the Dakotas and Montana became overstocked, and there simply was not enough grass for all the herds. More important, the Texas system could not in the long run be ecologically sustained in its northern transplantation. The Texas cattle whose genetic lines made up at least a good portion of the livestock on the plains "had never known the bite of a true continental midlatitude winter," writes Jordan, and there were indications in the 1870s and 1880s that these cattle were not adapted to the weather.[14] Calf yields were significantly lower north of Texas throughout the entire period of ranching's expansion, and on the eve of the winter of 1886–87, one writer set out to answer what had happened to the million Texas longhorns spread out across the West: "They have died of hunger; they have perished of thirst, when the icy breath of winter closed the streams; they have died of starvation by the tens of thousands during the season when cold storms sweep out of the North and course over the plains, burying the grass under snow."[15] After the winter, the devastation was too much even for some ranchers and did not revolve simply around economic loss. As Montana ranchman Granville Stuart wrote much later, in an oft-cited remark, "A business that had been fascinating to me before, suddenly became distasteful. I never wanted to own again an animal that I could not feed and shelter."[16] Such a moral response to the suffering of cattle clearly implicated ideas about their own manhood, as well: they could not protect the cattle, either as living creatures or as property, and the catastrophe proved the limits of their own control.

But more than weather stood in the way of ranchers' attempt to domesticate the range. Standing just beyond their fences were the "outlaw" beasts, and none occupied that position more fully in the West in the late nineteenth and early twentieth centuries (until its virtual extermination) than the gray wolf. Individual wolves, with reputations as particularly vicious and elusive killers, became literal outlaws—the objects of tall tales and extensive "manhunts."[17] But wolves and other predatory animals were seen generally as operating from an unsavory moral universe and deserving of any lethal and humiliating treatment.[18] In the late nineteenth century, ranchers tried to control the population of wolves and coyotes on their own, although bounty laws developed across the West in the 1870s.[19] By the mid- to late 1880s, as wolf and coyote numbers increased, the intensity of ranchers' pursuit was likened to "an industrious warfare."[20] The execution method that late-twentieth-century readers would likely find most distasteful was called "denning," and it was the one, wrote Montana rancher Elbert Bowman, "that in time did more to exterminate the wolf in our country" than either poisoning or trapping. "It was a kind of wholesale slaughter" in which the female wolf was either shot, stabbed, or dragged out and beaten with rocks. Then, often using barbed hooks, the "wolfers" (or whoever was doing the killing) would pull out and kill the pups.[21] Other forms of killing wolves had more "sport" to them, to use Theodore Roosevelt's word, and he was especially exuberant about hunting wolves with dogs. "Nothing can possibly exceed the gallantry with which good greyhounds, when their blood is up, fling themselves on a wolf or any other foe. There does not exist, and there never has existed on the wide earth, a more perfect type of dauntless courage than such a hound."[22]

Cowboys enjoyed roping wolves as well. In fact, in the first twenty-five pages of reminiscences about the XIT ranch in Texas, the former cowboys speak of roping a wolf, a bear, and a bobcat.[23] And in his story "Bullard's Wolves," Charles Russell describes how a cowboy managed to rope two wolves, both of whom were already poisoned and "stiff and staggerin'."[24] However cowboys or ranchers retell the scene, roping a wolf carried tremendous symbolic freight; the animal was yanked out of its "wildness" and often subject to what would have been considered the humiliation of being dragged from the back of a horse, like a calf.

As the sheep industry began to spread across the West in the 1890s, livestock producers increasingly called on the federal government to aid them, which it did in 1915 by launching a predatory animal control program in the Biological Survey, an agency within the Department of Agriculture. By this date, there were only isolated populations of wolves, grizzly bears, and mountain lions; by the 1920s, when wolves were all but eliminated, the coyote had become the "archpredator" in the West.[25] Obviously, coyotes represented the potential for economic loss, though how much loss was—and still is—very hard to determine. One Forest Service official estimated in 1915 that the average sheep loss on national forests for a year hovered around 3 percent, or a total of about one million dollars.[26] Sheep ranchers in the same period claimed that, for the whole West (and not just the national forests), the industry was losing as much as 12 percent of its stock or around fifteen million dollars' worth.[27] Late-nineteenth-century cattlemen remained primarily concerned with wolves, but as they were exterminated and as cattle ranchers used less hardy breeds of cattle, they, too, joined the chorus against coyotes, who were known to prey on calves.

Ranchers' writings also indicate that they were concerned with carving out a danger-free zone of domesticity, as they supported government hunting of wolves and coyotes by decrying in particular the animals' "savagery." The purple prose of A. C. Gage's "To You, Mr. Coyote" captured this notion in the extreme:

> To You, Mr. Coyote: Whose existence is a menace to all productive animal life; whose slithering jaws, in rabid passion of the kill, have relentlessly decimated peaceful, grazing flocks and torn the flesh of tender kids and lambs; whose course through field and forest is bloody with wanton slaughter; . . . to you, whose pups are littered only to perpetuate the vicious activity of the bedlam-dogs that went before; you skulking, dismal-voiced, marauding, predatory anathema; you morbid, mangy mournful malefactor! To you, Mr. Coyote: UNENDING VENGEANCE — AND WARFARE TO EXTERMINATION![28]

As Gage did in this piece, ranchers spotlighted several central aspects of what they perceived to be coyotes' brutal nature. First was the animals' supposed lust for killing, typically phrased as a "blood lust." Coyotes killed because they simply loved to kill, and they violated ranchers' sense of nature, as they often left uneaten large portions of lambs, sheep, and calves. In other words, they were wasteful killers. Second, and perhaps most pervasive, ranchers continually noted that coyotes (and wolves) often began eating their prey before the downed animal was actually dead.[29] They therefore made their prey suffer a slow death. Finally, it was the kind of prey that most provoked ranchers' fury: coyotes and wolves naturally targeted calves and lambs, the most "innocent" of the domesticated animals. While certainly such a response has very deep cultural roots, something more historically specific was at work as well. The early decades of the twentieth century saw ranchers in a process of "domesticating" their industry: they were taking seriously the introduction into the business of less hardy, purebred cattle that were more vulnerable to wolves and coyotes. Ranchers were "settling down" their operations and providing more care for their animals.[30]

At the representational level, especially around the issue of predatory animal control, this domestication involved the human domestic realm itself. Gage's marauding coyote quickly goes from tearing "the flesh of tender kids and lambs" to "terroriz[ing] the children of the settler on new lands."[31] Of course, the fear of *wolves'* preying on small children is one with a long history, but Gage pushes the comparison by asserting that a coyote could "terrorize" small children. In addition, one would not have found such a description thirty or forty years before, as the range was largely regarded as a purely masculinized space few children inhabited and where the coyote and the wolf represented manly challenges. The domestication of the West, however, repositioned both the animals and the men: the latter were now husbands and fathers, designated protectors of their domiciles; the coyote, as the archpredator, became configured as the villain in a melodrama, a form of dramatic "excess" that, in Peter Book's words, involves "a mode of high emotionalism and stark ethical conflict."[32] The starkness of that ethical conflict was, of course, dependent on the existence of a domesticated space for men to protect.

But the domestic sphere would widen still. By the 1930s, ranchers were consistently making the argument that coyotes deserved to be hunted down because they killed wild game such as elk and deer. This was clearly an attempt to win the support of sport hunters, most of whom supported the predatory animal program with the understanding that coyotes and other predators killed off game that would otherwise be available for human hunting. But it was an ironic turn for ranchers to make, because they had traditionally been nervous and sometimes openly hostile to the presence of game animals on their range, whom they saw as competing with their livestock for forage. While that anxiety never went away entirely, ranchers and supporters of the industry began casting themselves—and the government—as the protectors of game animals. For instance, in hearings to extend additional appropriations to the Biological Survey for killing wolves and coyotes, Wyoming senator and rancher John Kendrick argued that "if there is no other reason for the destruction of predatory animals it should be done solely for the protection of wild game. Either we must destroy the predatory animals or they will destroy the game." The program gave livestock producers protection, and indeed this "protection" was "just as vital," wrote one westerner to the Senate Committee on Agriculture and Forestry, "to our game animals."[33]

In firsthand accounts of western ranching in the late nineteenth century, game animals certainly were not perceived as needing protection, although they played an integral part in those narratives: most ranching reminiscences describing this period pause to note the presence of game and other wild animals, some at considerable length. Theodore Roosevelt's ranching escapades in the western Dakotas are perhaps the best and most widely known; indeed, one might reasonably believe that Roosevelt experimented with ranch life as much for the opportunity to hunt as to engage in the busi-ness. His 1888 book *Ranch Life and the Hunting-Trail*, for instance, was struc-tured precisely as the title suggests: for Roosevelt, the "primitive industry" of ranching inevitably involved the pleasures of the hunt, and he included sev-eral chapters about specific game animals—elk, bighorn sheep, and moun-tain goats. Livestock and game occupied a similar geography, and the former were expected to fend for themselves like any other grazing animal.[34] By the 1930s, however, livestock and game in the West were expected to be *managed*, and ranchers' land stood as the centerpiece for both, as the secretary for the Montana Stock Growers Association argued in 1938:

> [The stockman] appreciates the importance of game on his property, and, when numbers are held within reason, . . . he is vitally interested in seeing that no game program is adopted that will jeopardize the health of wild life. He recognizes a close similarity in a good game management program and a good live-stock operating program.[35]

Management embraced both wild and domesticated animals in ranch-ers' discourse, and by the 1940s ranchers consistently claimed that they were the protectors of wild game. The president of the Wyoming Wool Growers Association spoke for many when he noted that "long before our wild life friends awakened to the need of winter feeding in the interest of perpetuat-ing wild-life on the range, [the ranchman's] meadow and grain fields were doing a widespread job of preservation, as they have done ever since."[36] And in case anyone doubted the sincerity of ranchers' affection for game animals, the *American Cattle Producer* featured a child's photograph of a fawn on its September 1942 issue—an astonishing transformation for a magazine that routinely featured photographs of cowboys riding the range and handling cattle. Clearly, the popularity of the film *Bambi,* only recently released, reached the cattle industry with record speed.[37]

From the perspective of ranchers, then, domestication in the West worked in concentric circles, from the home ranch outward to the vast stretches of public and unpopulated land. Yet to understand more fully why ranchers believed they played a crucial role in caring for game, we must return again to that inner circle of the home ranch and, specifically to the care of cattle for a number of forces in this sphere conjoined to alter ranchers' atti-tudes toward their domesticated animals. Certainly, after the winter of 1886–87, which took such an immense toll and resulted in a nose-dive in beef prices, as cattlemen flooded the market with what was left of their herds, the range livestock industry began to change its methods. No doubt the initial attempts by ranchers to provide winter feed for their cattle were established simply to keep their brood herds alive.[38] But in response to changing con-sumer desires for more tender beef, ranchers throughout the early twentieth century invested more heavily in purer shorthorn or polled breeds.[39] This shift carried important ramifications: ranchers had more of their capital tied up with the animal itself and therefore would suffer a larger economic loss if the animal died. These breeds of cattle, however, put on more weight than the "stringy" range cattle of the late nineteenth century and thus could fetch a good price at market. Ranchers therefore could turn over a tidy profit on each individual cow or steer. The risk and the incentive associated with individual animals was thus greater than with the earlier breeds.

The change in range ranching also involved a widespread shift in emphasis from fattening steers to "cow-calf" operations, although by the mid-twentieth century the majority of ranches in the West combined both. A steer rancher would buy up young cattle, put them on the open range with "relatively abundant forage," and pull them off when it was time for slaughter.[40] Such an operation required no supplemental feeding and very little oversight. In contrast, a cow-calf ranch is in the business of producing calves. While a common notion in ranching was that "every time a cow has a calf she pays for herself," ranchers also recognized that the losses could be great.[41] But this change in emphasis removed ranchers one step further from cattle's "destiny"—that is, slaughter—by making them central at the other end of the life cycle: it involved them intimately not only with death but with birth. How intimately? In a kind of ranching manual for prospective newcomers, and particularly ex-servicemen after World War II, Russell H. Bennett describes how ranchers can tell when a cow was about to give birth: "A cow begins to 'make bag,' that is, her udder begins to swell, shortly before she calves. Parenthetically, you must learn to read a cow's udder before you can call yourself much of a stockman. The cow's udder is your business index, the wallboard graph which the progressive businessman keeps always posted to date." Once the cow is observed "making bag . . . then you watch for a swelling of the vulva; when this occurs her time is near." Although most calves were born with little human intervention, Bennett writes, young heifers birthing for the first time often had difficulty, which typically involved false presentation and required "help by manipulating the calf." Bennett reassured his squeamish readers with the comment that "the need for this kind of help is infrequent."[42]

Perhaps too keenly aware of the "tenderfeet" who might read his book, Bennett was antiseptic at best in noting the occasional need for "manipulation." Even sparing the details, however, Bennett's advice would have been unimaginable in an earlier age of ranching: one can only relish the thought of how Teddy Roosevelt would have reacted to hearing that a rancher must "watch for a swelling of the vulva." A contemporary chronicler of ranch life, and herself born and raised on a Wyoming ranch, Teresa Jordan writes more graphically about ranchers' "intimacy with cows" during calving season: "We come in each evening splattered with mud and milk and manure,

AMERICAN
CATTLE PRODUCER

THE NATIONAL LIVESTOCK MONTHLY   SEPTEMBER 1942

A FAWN THAT GRACED THE COVER OF THE *American Cattle Producer* IN SEPTEMBER
1942. COURTESY OF McGRATH LIBRARY, UNIVERSITY OF MINNESOTA.

stained with blood and amniotic fluid, stinking of afterbirth. It's hard to convey the sheer satisfaction of it all."[43] Antiseptic or graphic, such descriptions
of birthing calves belie the very masculinized image of ranching and shift the
locus of vision from the roundup—where cowboys physically coerced animals into corrals for branding or for shipping to slaughter—to (in Jordan's
words) "a maternity ward with eight-hundred patients who can't speak."[44]
Domestication has begun, again, to look like domesticity.

But there are cracks in this picture, of course, because the "maternity
ward" in range country is not a building, but an unsheltered space. And
unlike many ranchers and former ranchers who have written books, Jordan
acknowledges the multitude of moral tensions in the ranching industry:

> In this business of cattle raising, we exert our will. We take a calf off a
> poor cow and graft it onto a good one. We hobble a reticent cow until

she lets her calf suck. We midwife these calves into existence, we care for them, sometimes we even risk our lives for them, and they are ultimately slated for slaughter. In this fact lies the essential irony of our work. No one forgets that a live calf is money in the bank. And yet a reverence remains. . . . Day in and day out we confront the messiness of the business of living; if we live with slaughter, we also live with nurture, with seasons and cycles, with birth and death.[45]

"Reverence" may not have been the first word to come to mind to many ranchers before World War II (and it is impossible to know how many would agree with Jordan today). Nonetheless, ranchers in the business of producing calves inhabited the ironic stance Jordan describes. Russell Bennett's book from 1946 is again instructive and bears closer scrutiny. He tells his audience, for instance, that "[y]ou will not be long in range country before hearing the maxim: 'First look after your cattle, then after your horse, and then after yourself.'" But, he notes, such a maxim does not necessarily convey "affection": most cattlemen he knows feel only "pleasure" when they finally sell off their cattle. This seems to him a "paradox," because when a ranchman has to "sell a saddle horse, he may really grieve over the parting," even though he might have "risk[ed] the neck of that horse—and his own— not once but many times when the business demand[ed] it." He reasons that perhaps this "peculiar attitude" stems from the fact that the cow "is at once a capital item and an item of merchandise. In her youth and maturity she is a producing unity; in her old age she becomes, after a preliminary fattening period, a piece of merchandise on the shelf awaiting sale." His final analysis betrays even further the ironic position of the rancher:

> All your hope of reward thus centers about [the cow]; without her all your grass, all your hay, and all your fences become worthless. Pride and profit and a long tradition all demand that you take all possible care of your cattle, from the time the calf gets up on its wobbly legs until the car doors slam upon it as it goes to the stockyards.[46]

Indeed, he admits several pages later, "The cows and calves on their summer range form the pleasantest sight of all to the rancher's eye . . . I take endless satisfaction in the summer scene, with the calves gathered in a nursery under the supervision of the matron-of-the-day . . . and the good green grass underfoot."[47] Bennett continually reinstates the ironic extremes of the industry, in part because they trap him in the moral quandary in which all ranchers found themselves: they had taken "all possible care" of their cattle, spied on them while they were nursing, and yet saw them off to slaughter. They enjoyed watching a calf stand on wobbly legs, but also profited when the cattle-car door slammed behind the animal.

Ranch men and women have never resolved this tension between guardianship and the market, but where that tension has received comment, it has come largely from women. One early memoirist who admitted to qualms about branding, for instance, was Agnes Morley Cleaveland who, in *No Life for a Lady*, describes growing up in the territory of New Mexico, where she began tending cattle as a child on her parents' isolated ranch. Much more so than her male counterparts, she reflects on human-animal relationships. Speaking of her childhood with her brother, she writes, "Cattle became the circumference of our universe and their behavior absorbed our entire waking hours. . . . As youngsters we learned to recognize the individuals among the cattle as though they had been people, and we watched for their coming with the same interest we would have had in the arrival of personal friends."[48] It is not surprising, then, that Cleaveland admitted to not taking part in burning animal flesh: "The one phase of life, however, which I refused to face directly was the branding itself. However much of an accessory to the crime I may have been in the matter of rounding up or even roping the calf, when it came to the actual applying of a hot iron to sentient flesh, I couldn't do it."[49] Cleaveland's admission is unusual for both ranch men and women, and yet contemporary women writers about ranch life, like Teresa Jordan, also pause longer than men to consider the emotionally complicated relationships between humans and animals. To take another example: over the last several years, the National Cattlemen's Beef Association has published running diaries on its website from western ranch families. Written mostly by women, the entries have also revolved much around animals. In one of the more poignant pieces, Kim DesEnfants from Wyoming describes the shock of losing nearly a quarter of their calves in an early spring blizzard. "It's so hard to know you did all you could and find dead calves lying around," she wrote in April 1997. "It's even harder seeing calves with frozen feet and knowing there is nothing you can do to make them better."[50]

DesEnfants's comment underlines the fact that, while catastrophes such as the winter of 1886–87 are rare in ranching, the industry nonetheless remains one constituted by the caring for animals as well as the pain inflicted on them. Scholars can only speculate on the reasons why ranch women have been more able to remark on this difficult tension than ranch men. Perhaps, as Jane Tompkins has written, the Western as a genre has taught ranch men only too well "to scorn the expression of sympathy for pain" because "the interdiction against sentimentality" is necessary both for the business of ranching and for the "image of manhood" that the ranching industry embraces.[51] But expressing emotions per se has not been the problem: ranch men who wrote about the threats of predatory animals in the early twentieth century let loose a torrent of words and an excess of emotion that cannot be chalked up to mere venality against the wolf and coyote. Rather, their responses suggest that the "war" against these animals emphasized not a masculinity of raw vigor and vitality, but one of patriarchal protection—over children, over flocks and herds, and even over wild game animals—at the moment when the industry was indeed settling down and domesticating the range in a multitude of ways. And yet if men represented the figureheads of the ranch as a domestic space, they were also the ones who were responsible for sending their animals to the slaughter-house; especially in the case of cattle, ranchers were protectors who ultimately did not protect. Ranchers did not simply banish all feelings of sympathy to align themselves with a particularly virile image of manhood, as Tompkins's argument suggests. Rather, their sense of duty and obligation as men was profoundly rent in two directions—between caretaking, about which they were able to speak, and the killing required for profit, about which they seemingly could not. The very occasion when they gained profit as the heads of their households—that is, when they sold their cattle—was the very moment when they abandoned their roles as domestic guardians.

Notes

This essay evolved from a paper first presented at the Shelby Cullom Davis Center for Historical Studies at Princeton University. I would like to thank the seminar participants, and especially Gregg Mitman, for their comments and criticisms. Laura McCall and Martha Umphrey also gave generously of their insights and advice.

1. Edward Abbey, "Something about Mac, Cows, Poker, Ranchers, Cowboys, Sex, and Power . . . and Almost Nothing about American Lit," in *Northern Lights: A Selection of New Writing from the American West,* ed. Deborah Clow and Donald Snow (New York: Vintage Books, 1994), 156. Abbey did not believe that cattle had much of a place on the range. "Shoot them all. Get rid of the cattle" (154).

2. "A real man, I would say, is quiet. He's not a loudmouth like me. A real man is quiet, thoughtful, strong, courageous, resourceful, and he is also kind, considerate, and loving. A real man is a gentle man, though not necessarily a gentleman." This being Abbey, he ends with the wonderful, table-turning line, "Or, in short, a real man has the same virtues as a real woman" (156–57). One might also retort, however, that a "real man" in Abbey's view is Owen Wister's Virginian.

3. On the shift to a more settled industry, see Karen R. Merrill, "Whose Home on the Range?" *Western Historical Quarterly* 27 (winter 1996): 433–51.

4. Susan Lee Johnson, "'A Memory Sweet to Soldiers': The Significance of Gender," in *A New Significance: Re-envisioning the History of the American West*, ed. Clyde A. Milner II (New York: Oxford University Press, 1996), 255 and 257; and Owen Wister, *The Virginian: A Horseman of the Plains* (1902; reprint New York: New American Library, 1979).

5. John Springer, "Inaugural Address," *Proceedings of the National Stock Growers' Convention* (Denver: New Job Printing Company, 1898), 22.

6. Jane Tompkins, *West of Everything* (New York: Oxford University Press, 1992), 120–21.

7. Lucia B. Mirrielees, ed., *Pioneer Ranching in Central Montana: From the Letters of Otto Maerdian, Written in 1882–1883* (Missoula: State University of Montana, 1930), 7, 11, and 14.

8. Maerdian wrote that he only had a revolver with him and that without a rifle he could not even kill an elk. Having a rifle would also have meant that he "would not need to fear Indians or bear." See Mirrielees, 12.

9. William French, *Some Recollections of a Western Ranchman* (New York: Argosy-Antiquarian, 1965), 29.

10. Quoted in Terry G. Jordan, *North American Cattle Frontiers: Origins, Diffusion, and Differentiation* (Albuquerque: University of New Mexico Press, 1993), 217. Jordan notes that in addition to these feral cattle from "earlier, departed Mexicans," the Anglos in Texas also stole some domestic herds.

11. Terry G. Jordan, 210–13.

12. See, for example, the description of catching "mossheads" (six- or seven-year-old steers) in Cordia Sloan Duke and Joe B. Frantz, *Six-Thousand Miles of Fence: Life on the XIT Ranch of Texas* (Austin:

University of Texas Press, 1961), 15. One cowhand noted that the cowboys "would catch these mossheads and cut the cords of one of their front legs, which would then keep the steers on their home ranges and keep them from wandering."

13. French, 132–33.

14. Terry G. Jordan, 236.

15. Frank Wilkeson, "Cattle-Raising on the Plains," *Harper's New Monthly Magazine* 72 (April 1886): 793.

16. Quoted in Ernest Staples Osgood, *The Day of the Cattleman* (Chicago: University of Chicago Press, 1929), 221.

17. Dixon Merritt, "World's Greatest Animal Criminal Dead," in *War against the Wolf: America's Campaign to Exterminate the Wolf,* ed. Rick McIntyre (Stillwater, Minn.: Voyageur Press, 1995), 243.

18. The story of the extermination of the wolf from the West has been well told before, but suffice it to say that the impetus behind this program came from livestock producers. Certainly, for most of this period, their motivations were completely in line with societal views of the animals; but ranchers' and cowboys' viciousness against the wolf, and also against the coyote, would be used by later environmentalists to prove ranchers' antipathy toward animals. As Lynne Jacobs writes in her extensive antiranching tract, "Probably no aspect of public lands ranching stirs such emotions or has induced such a plethora of publicity as its brutal predator 'control' effort. Though surely not the most environmentally harmful of the industry's general activities, it is considered by many to be the most disgusting." Lynn Jacobs, *Waste of the West: Public Lands Ranching* (self-published, 1991), 254. Jacobs focuses in particular on the public lands used in western ranching because, like many environmentalists, she believes they have been squandered for ranchers' personal use, although they belong to all the people in the country.

19. Colorado was the first western state to create a bounty law, in 1869. By 1893 the state of Wyoming paid eight dollars for each wolf killed. See "Wolf Bounty Laws in Wyoming Territory and State," in *War against the Wolf,* 118–120.

20. "Montana Wolves and Panthers," a reprint from an 1886 *Forest and Stream* magazine report, in ibid., 85.

21. Elbert F. Bowman, "Wolves: Being Reminiscent of My Life on an Eastern Montana Ranch," in *War against the Wolf,* 106–7. Rarely did the hunters admit to any ambivalence about this task, though Bowman remarked, "I have done it many times before and since, but I have never had to do anything that goes against the grain much more than to kill the pups at this stage. Potential murderers they may be, and as cruel as man himself after they are grown, but at this time they are just plump, friendly little things that nuzzle you and whine little, pleased whines." While Bowman "felt somewhat ashamed and guilty," he also noted that "it was duty." Bowman then describes the typical wolf-hunter's technique of tying one live pup near the entrance to the den, near where he had also concealed wolf traps. The hope was that the pup would draw in the other adult wolf in the pair.

22. Theodore Roosevelt, "Wolves and Wolf-Hounds," in *War against the Wolf,* 112.

23. Duke and Frantz, 14–25.

24. Charles Russell, *More Rawhides* (1925; reprint Pasadena, Calif.: Trail's End Publishing Co., 1946), 5.

25. Thomas R. Dunlap, *Saving America's Wildlife* (Princeton: Princeton University Press, 1988), 48. The term *archpredator* came from Biological Survey biologist E. A. Goldman in a speech he gave before the American Society of Mammalogists in 1930, "The Coyote—Archpredator," ibid., 57. Certainly, the Biological Survey was killing with gusto: by the mid-1930s government hunters were killing 35,000 coyotes a year, and that figure would rise to over 100,000 annually after the war (49). See J. Frank Dobie, *The Voice of the Coyote* (1949; reprint Lincoln: University of Nebraska Press, 1961), 44. See also Mike Finkel, "The Ultimate Survivor," *Audubon* 101 (May–June, 1999), 52–59.

26. "Sheep and Wool Conference," *American Sheep-Breeder and Wool-Grower* 34 (June 1914): 377.

27. Hugh Sproat, "The Wild Animal Toll," *American Sheep-Breeder and Wool-Grower,* 35 (January 1915), 66.

28. A. C. Gage, "To You, Mr. Coyote," *The National Wool Grower* 11 (November 1921): 1.

29. This focus has been remarkably consistent. In the 1931 hearings about the control of predatory animals, the representative of the National Wool Growers Association said, "[T]here is nothing so vicious in its cruelty as the method employed by the gray wolf in destroying his prey. His prey is literally eaten alive, its bowels torn out while it is still on its feet in many cases." U.S. Congress, Senate Committee on Agriculture and Forestry, *Control of Predatory Animals,* Hearings pursuant to S. 3483, 71st Cong., 2nd and 3rd Sess. (1930, 1931), 6. On his family's page on the website for the National Cattlemen's Beef Association, Doug DesEnfants writes, "I do know all animals have their place on this earth. I ranch because I love animals, but coyotes do brutal things to calves. They don't normally eat the calf outright— they just eat the hindquarters." http://www.beef.org/inddiary/des0397.html. The disgust was not aimed only at coyotes and wolves, although they were the objects of most of it. Agnes Morley Cleaveland tells about a bear that had been hunted down and attacked by bear hounds: "I wanted to feel sorry for the

bear, until I remembered what the carcass of one of our milk-pen calves had looked like when we found it one morning, too far from home, with bear tracks all around it." Cleaveland, *No Life for a Lady* (Boston: Houghton Mifflin, 1941), 209–10.

30. While I've focused here on the cattle industry, this domestication was also true of the sheep industry, which at the turn of the century was made up of many "nomadic" operations.

31. Gage, 1.

32. Peter Brooks, *The Melodramatic Imagination: Balzac, Henry James, Melodrama, and the Mode of Excess* (New York: Columbia University Press, 1984), 12.

33. *Control of Predatory Animals,* 11. The latter quotation comes from a letter from E. E. Brownell, who claimed he had a degree in medicine from Johns Hopkins, and who had spent most of his life "in the stock business" and was very interested in wild animals.

34. "The truth is, ours is a primitive industry, and we suffer the reverses as well as enjoy the successes only known to primitive peoples." Theodore Roosevelt, *Ranch Life and the Hunting Trail* (1888; reprint Lincoln: University of Nebraska Press, 1983), 79.

35. "Anti-Forest Grazing Agitators Answered," *National Wool Grower* 28 (July 1938): 7.

36. J. A. Reed, "Coordinated Land Management," *National Wool Grower* 34 (May 1944), 23.

37. On the Bambi phenomenon, which overtook the country in 1942, see Matt Cartmill, *A View to Death in the Morning: Hunting and Nature through History* (Cambridge, Mass.: Harvard University Press, 1993), 163–82.

38. This is Peter K. Simpson's conclusion in *The Community of Cattlemen: A Social History of the Cattle Industry in Southeastern Oregon, 1869–1912* (Moscow: University of Idaho Press, 1987), 123–24.

39. Reginald Aldridge noted in his 1884 book on ranching that his cattle "were pretty well 'graded up.' They had mostly descended from Texas cows, but these had been crossed with shorthorn bulls, so that the breed had been considerably improved." Given their use of the Texas system, however, ranchers such as Aldridge had to be careful when cross-breeding, because "by continually using shorthorns the breed appears to lose the hardy nature necessary for standing the severities of range life." Aldridge, *Life on a Ranch: Ranch Notes in Kansas, Colorado, the Indian Territory, and Northern Texas* (1884; reprint New York: Argonaut Press, 1966), 83 and 202. Aldridge's comments confirm what Terry Jordan has written, that by the time Aldridge would have been writing the longhorn presence on the plains "was never as pervasive as the mythmakers would have us believe." Terry G. Jordan, 232.

40. Marion Clawson, *The Western Range Livestock Industry* (New York: McGraw-Hill, 1950), 209.

41. Edmund Randolph records a portion of a conversation between a steer rancher and a cow-calf rancher in the mid-1940s. The steer rancher (who controlled the largest area of land around the Crow Indian Reservation in southeast Montana) waxed on and on about the benefits of fattening up steers quickly on his "cheap grass." The cow-calf rancher concurs that "[w]e've both gone broke on cows and calves. Remember the Hard Winter? Remember pouring hay and oil cake into cows all winter, and then having them die in the spring, with their calves inside?" Randolph, *Beef, Leather, and Grass* (Norman: University of Oklahoma Press, 1981), 14–15.

42. Russell H. Bennett, *The Compleat Rancher* (New York: Rinehart and Company, 1946), 35–36.

43. Teresa Jordan, *Riding the White Horse Home: A Western Family Album* (New York: Vintage Books, 1993), 100.

44. Ibid., 98.

45. Ibid., 108.

46. Bennett, 34–35.

47. Ibid., 41. He adds parenthetically that "for the more practical headed," perhaps the "pleasantest sight" is that of "a drove of fat steers heading for the railway in the fall."

48. Cleaveland, 104 and 110.

49. Ibid., 110–11.

50. Kim DesEnfants, http://www.beef.org/inddiary/des0497.html.

51. Tompkins, 121. Of course, Tompkins does not speak specifically about the ranching industry. Nevertheless, her book makes large claims about the way Westerns have taught "us" generally about everything from language to landscape to animals. The "image of manhood" the ranching industry projects continues to be a very complicated one. On the one hand, it holds itself up to be a place where cowboy-ranchers still thrive, with the model of the Virginian ever present. On the other hand, it very much embraces the image of the ranch family as the arid analogue to the farm family.

Man-Power

Montana Copper Workers, State Authority, and the (Re)drafting of Manhood during World War II

Matthew Basso

I realize that I am a soldier of production, whose duties are as
   important in this war as those of the man behind the gun.
I will do my work well and efficiently and will stay on my job,
   producing to the best of my ability, until my shift ends.
I will carry out my duties in accordance with instructions.
I will think before I act.
I will endeavor to save material by avoiding mistakes and spoilage.
I will be careful of my health and prevent accidents, to avoid loss
   of time.
I will keep my working place tidy and in order.
All to the end that we may succeed in our efforts to increase produc-
   tion and attain the goal set as necessary to carry us to the final
   decisive victory over our treacherous enemies who now are threat-
   ening the homes of our children and the liberty of our nation.
                              —*World War II Union Pledge*[1]

On December 7, 1941, as Japanese planes bombed Pearl Harbor, Lewis
Hershey rode through the Mountain West on the Union Pacific rail line from
Salt Lake City to Boise. Hershey was a major figure during World War II:
from 1940 to 1945, in his role as director of the Selective Service System, he
oversaw the induction of well over ten million men into the Army and Navy
and the classification and deferment of another ten million men. For all of these
men, for their families, and for their neighbors, Lewis Hershey and the draft
occupied a prominent place in discussions about citizenship, service, and masculine duty.[2] While the draft touched residents of every region in the country, it
was particularly fitting that Hershey was traveling through the West at the

moment when the United States officially entered the war. Western congressional representatives, led by Montana's Burton Wheeler, had provided some of the strongest opposition both to the draft and to U.S. involvement in the conflict prior to Pearl Harbor.[3] Yet after the country's official entry into the war, the highest per capita voluntary enlistment rates among men came from Western states such as Montana, Idaho, and Utah, and by the close of hostilities New Mexico and Montana had the two highest death rates in the nation.[4] Although seemingly contradictory, neither fact should come as a surprise in light of the traditional isolationist politics championed by the populist-minded West and, of course, the region's reputation for producing hypermasculine men. But what will come as a surprise, especially to those familiar with scholarship on the history of manhood in the United States, is that World War II caused a great number of western men to be anxious about their place in society.

While scholars interested in the gender dynamics of U.S. society have certainly written about male anxiety, they see World War II as anything but an anxious era. In his influential and encyclopedic *Manhood in America: A Cultural History*, Michael Kimmel writes that "reports of battlefield heroism provided some sorely needed manly templates. . . . But war proved again to be only a temporary respite." Peter Stearns argues that World War II provided an opportunity for twentieth-century men to return to the more stable elements of the nineteenth-century gender regime. Like most other scholars who have written on the topic, Stearns and Kimmel see manhood during World War II as centered on those men who entered the armed forces and in relation to the more obvious crisis periods that preceded and followed it. The war helped redress the harm done to the male psyche by the Great Depression, when many men lost their ability to fulfill the breadwinner role. Memory of wartime male deeds also proved at least a moderate anchor as corporations created emasculated "organization men" during the 1950s, and as women demanded greater equality during the 1960s.[5]

The wartime experiences of the primarily Irish, Cornish, Finnish, and southeast European men who worked in Anaconda, Butte, and Great Falls, Montana, as hard-rock miners and smeltermen—occupations that before the war had been considered the ultimate in manly labor—indicate the problems with Kimmel's and Stearns's narratives of wartime manhood. For Montana's miners and smeltermen, Pearl Harbor actually denoted an end to a short period of stability marked by full employment, a moment when working-class men for the first time in a decade had easily met the fundamental, historically specific requirements of hegemonic masculinity: providing for one's family.[6] Once the U.S. officially entered the war, the standards of hegemonic manhood changed radically. No longer did serving as the family's primary breadwinner comprise the essential element of manhood. In a republic like the United States, the sociologist of military "manpower" David R. Segal notes, popular ideology dictated that in times of war male citizens defend the nation in uniform.[7] Thus, despite government propaganda that labeled homefront workers as "soldiers of production" equal to soldiers on the battlefield, men not in uniform during World War II were not meeting the full requirements of wartime manhood.[8]

Women's entry into the armed forces and into homefront industrial work further complicated matters for homefront men. Historians of wartime women have cataloged in remarkable detail the complex changes the war brought for women in various sectors of the population.[9] While traditional attitudes toward women and work did not change during the first months of Franklin Delano Roosevelt's "Arsenal of Democracy" buildup, Pearl Harbor had an explosive effect. Industry suddenly needed and wanted female laborers; within seven months employers decided that women were fit for 55 percent of defense industry jobs.[10] From handling cargo to operating drill presses, women responded to the many opportunities for work. All told, over six million women took jobs, increasing the female labor force by 50 percent. Wages leapt, unionization grew fourfold, and the number of married women who were working doubled.[11] Many homefront men viewed this dramatic sea change warily. In Anaconda, Butte, and Great Falls, men plainly saw it as a threat.

In addition to ignoring the challenge that women's entrance into industrial work represented for homefront men, historians of American manhood have by and large failed to consider the role of class in wartime masculinity.[12] The wartime crisis in manhood hit working-class men more than middle-class men, because women for the first time held previously all-male factory jobs and because manhood was more tightly tied to masculine job status among these men than among middle class men. Working-class men faced the additional anxiety that employers would use women's entry into the workplace as a precedent for a two-income family wage—something many working-class men and women had fought long against.[13]

Working-class men and women at the national and especially the regional level, fully cognizant of these various new tensions surrounding gender roles, created complex psychic mechanisms to deal with wartime anxiety. They also instituted elaborate local codes for judging whether a man was doing his duty and where men fell on the spectrum of masculinity. But for men after Pearl Harbor, whether married or single, whether they wanted to go to war or stay home, the ideal masculine wartime role, one that women could not fill, was inescapably that of combat soldier. Thus, although men working in Montana's copper industry were "in there swinging every day," as one Butte native put it, the war meant dramatic changes in the community's hierarchy of masculine status.

The hypermasculine nature of hardrock mining in the West and its role in providing status for men in the region made the wartime crisis in manhood more severe and consequently more visible in places like Anaconda,

Butte, and Great Falls. The federal government, far from realizing this unique regional dynamic, exacerbated it, revealing the critical role played by the state in the creation of western manhood and invoking the recent debate over the important role of the state in the development of the West.[14] The citizens of Anaconda, Great Falls, and Butte saw the state power that emanated from Washington, D.C., as coming from the 'East.' Their perception of themselves as on the periphery rather than at the center of national life, for good or ill, constitutes a defining aspect of "western-ness" for many westerners. Evidence drawn from wartime Montana—firsthand accounts of entering the armed forces, short stories about the homefront, government-sponsored propaganda, and union transcripts detailing concerns about the draft—confirms the state's role in the shift in standards of manhood produced by the country's official entry into the conflict and highlights the anxiety homefront men felt about their masculine status throughout World War II. These sources also suggest the implications of this anxiety for the relationship between western industrial workers, liberalism, and postwar society.

The story of one man from Butte, William T. Paull, who, unlike most, did rush out and enlist on the day after the bombing of Pearl Harbor, illustrates the almost immediate change in homefront perceptions toward soldiering and manhood.[15] Like many young men, military service as presented in Hollywood's romantic, patriotic fare fascinated Paull. He clearly remembers being bewitched by the 1935 movie *Shipmates Forever,* starring Dick Powell as a suave Annapolis midshipman who successfully courts the "sweet young ingenue," Ruby Keeler. Years later he still recalled Powell crooning to Keeler, "Shipmates stand together, / tho' it's a long, long trip; / fair or stormy weather, / we won't give up, / we won't give up the ship." *Shipmates Forever* prompted Paull, the son of a Butte miner and admittedly no star in school, to apply for an Annapolis appointment, which he received in 1936 from Butte-friendly Democratic senator James Murray.[16] Paull's bubble burst when he failed to pass the Annapolis physical because of hypertension. Dejected, he applied and received admission to the School of Mines in Butte, but when the Fuller Paint Company offered him a full-time job earning seventy-five dollars a month he bought a hot little Chevy coupe with a rumble seat and started work.

Paull's lukewarm response to the draft five years later seemingly contradicts the gung-ho attitude he displayed in applying to Annapolis. He writes, "When the draft came along, I felt smug. I knew I had high blood pressure and wouldn't pass the physical." Like many captivated by celluloid's romantic and patriotic images of military service, when push came to shove, when service meant going to war instead of just wearing starched dress whites while crooning to a beautiful girl, Paull's excitement disappeared. But his notoriously fickle blood pressure read just fine on the day of his physical and Selective Service classified him 1–A. Thus on December 8, 1941, knowing he would be called soon and not wanting the army to "get him," Paull and a friend went down to the recruitment office and enlisted in the Marines.[17]

Paull's description of his friends and family "huddled" around him on the train platform next to others "surrounding their departing heroes" while "clouds of hissing steam from the locomotive, and an over-all somberness" pervaded Butte's Union Pacific Depot, aptly conveys the national mood and the focus on men departing for the services in early 1942 and, with only slightly less drama, throughout the war. To the people on that platform, it did not matter that Paull and many other men were less than enthusiastic draftees or enlistees; once in uniform and on their way, they were heroes doing a man's duty during war.[18]

Even prior to Pearl Harbor, when Selective Service was still drafting only a small number of men each year for twelve-month tours of duty, tension surrounded standards of manhood, as homefront men felt pressured to defend themselves against expectations that they belonged in the service. Working-class men traditionally derived masculine status both from the physicality of their work and from their ability to provide for their families. "Hot Metal," an essay written in late spring 1941 by Edward B. Reynolds for *Men at Work*, a fascinating anthology compiled by the Federal Writers' Project but never published, champions this traditional definition of industrial work against the already considerable status given service in the armed forces. A strange hybrid of ethnography, folklore, and autobiography, the narrator's description of his bona fides in "Hot Metal" also serves as a statement to the audience of Reynolds's own credentials for commenting on the working world of the smelter. The narrator proclaims, "I was born on the smelters. I been breathing sulphur gas as long as I can remember. I use arsenic in my tea and I drank copper water instead of milk." As a resident of Anaconda, a trained observer, and a friend to many of the smeltermen, Reynolds' knowledge of social concerns in Anaconda equaled his shop-floor expertise.[19]

Reynolds opens "Hot Metal" by defending smeltermen against the charge of being "yellow" because they were in the plant instead of the plane, tank, or battleship:

> Certainly, I'm registered for the draft. What do you think? Anytime Uncle Sam needs me he knows where I am. But I've got a hunch he's going to need me a lot more right where I'm at. . . . Why, I'm working in the hot metal at the Anaconda Reduction Works. That's where they smelt the copper out of the ore from the Butte mines. . . . No, I'm not afraid people will think I'm yellow. I told you I work in the hot metal, didn't I? People that are yellow just don't work there.[20]

Reynolds's choice to make his narrator a laborer in the smelter's hot metal section, and the narrator's contention that "[p]eople that are yellow just don't work there" reveals that an elaborate hierarchy of manhood operated within the smelter, just as it did in the Great Falls refining plant and in the Butte mines where, as one miner put it, compared to the others underground, men who worked in the "raises" were the "elite."[21] These hierarchies, in moments of stress, could label some men as more manly than others by implying that in Anaconda, for example, men working in other sections of the smelter might reasonably be called yellow. Certainly smeltermen and community members discussed among themselves the relative manliness of particular jobs prior to the wartime emergency and accorded a type of status to men working in places like the hot metal and arsenic sections, but these discussions about relative worth did not become critical until the draft and deferment.

Status, though, did not accrue solely through performing dangerous work, as the narrator's invocation of his father's career in the smelter reveals. "One of the earliest things I can remember as a kid," the narrator offers, "was when they brought my old man home from the hospital. . . . He worked in the hot metal, too. . . . They told me he was wearing gauntlet gloves and some hot calcine spilled in. That's why you don't see me wearing gauntlets now. I got a good memory. Anyway, when the old man came back his hand was shriveled like an overdone pork roast. It was almost a year before he could use it again." Not only is the narrator not yellow, but he also belongs to a family of tough men willing to do the most dangerous work—and to pay for the consequences. Seemingly, the hard-won lesson provided by the father is not to avoid the dangerous work of the hot metal section, but rather to avoid gauntlet gloves. However, the father's story is not over. Continuing, the narrator informs the reader of how his father regained the use of his "overdone pork roast" of a hand. "He probably never would have been able to use it again because he thought it was paralyzed. But my mother knocked it up in the air to show him it wasn't. The old man almost fainted, but he got the idea."[22] His mother's "idea," one shared by many in the community, was simple: masculine status for dangerous work meant little if a man could not provide for his family.

Such a construction complicates the question of what constituted masculine duty as a nation prepared for war, a question that obviously courses through the opening of "Hot Metal," and that defined the national conversation in the summer of 1941. Working men might have proposed, during those contentious months, that some men from the local community actually desired to serve their country in uniform to avoid working in the mines. They might have been willing to gamble that their number would not come up, or that they would do just fine in the armed forces if it came to that. The majority of men during World War I did not serve as combat soldiers and the same trend appeared likely for World War II. The odds of coming home seemed pretty good. Many men, it is important to remember, were not so sure they would make it out of the mines. Hardrock mining was some of the most dangerous work in the country. The fatality statistics in Butte staggered the mind: one man a day died of tuberculosis or miner's consumption, one man a week died in a mining accident.[23] While not as overwhelming, the number of injuries and deaths caused by the smelter and refining plant was imposing. There is no doubt that men were well aware of these facts. Which, then, was more manly, mine work or soldiering? The way World War II started ended such debates.

On December 7 and 8, 1941, when Lewis Hershey was in Boise and William Paull enlisted, at least seven Montana men died in Japanese attacks on U.S. bases in the Pacific. Three were from Butte. The news of their status as missing in action, and then of their deaths, circulated by word of mouth and the media, highlighted the costs of war and the dangers of soldiering. Each article that appeared in Butte's local paper about these deaths referred to the men as heroes. Each also noted the subject's relationship with Butte, family members still in the area, and even the deceased's former place of residence in town.[24] The story of Private First Class (PFC) Leroy Carpenter and the recollections his relatives later shared about him are indicative of how these deaths were understood in Butte, Anaconda, and Great Falls.

When his family learned that the Army Air Corps had sent Carpenter to the Philippines, they were relieved. The Pacific Islands seemed like a backwater, the sort of place where war would come late if at all. Moreover, Carpenter had enlisted in the Air Corps as a mechanic. In doing so he became part of the large majority of men serving in uniform whose job was service and support of the actual war fighters. And like many others in this category, when he arrived in the Philippines his assignment removed him even further from what was considered frontline duty. Carpenter became the chauffeur for his commanding officer, ferrying him around base, taking him to meetings, the briefing room, and onto the flight line so that the commander could talk to the men who would fly into harm's way. On December 8, 1941, the day after Pearl Harbor and only two months into his tour in the Philippines, a bomb fragment from a Japanese air strike against Clark Air Force Base hit and killed PFC Carpenter. He was twenty-three years old.[25]

Carpenter, who had enlisted in August 1940, was well liked in Butte. His cousin described him as "a mild-mannered man . . . so full of fun," but added that "he could be tough as nails, too." She remembered, smiling, that he was "pretty popular with the girls." Leroy Carpenter was also a talented boxer who had won several amateur bouts.[26] He was the classic Butte boy.[27] In the first six months of the war, Butte, along with Anaconda, Great Falls, and other towns across Montana and the country lost many PFC Carpenters. They all wore the uniforms of the army, air corps, navy, or marines. But unlike World War I, in which air power, with its ability to cause havoc on

troops and civilians far in the rear, was still largely a novelty, and trench warfare, defined by mustard gas and machine guns, produced an enormous percentage of the casualties, fighting in World War II was not isolated to combat
troops. Just like PFC Carpenter, a significant number of those who died in
World War II did not serve on the front lines. Men who had once pointed
out that only a small percentage of those in uniform were in danger could no
longer make that argument convincingly.[28] This new reality, with its implications for families of servicemen and for the manhood of copper men, settled in on Butte, Great Falls, and Anaconda at the same time the government
was putting its homefront propaganda campaign into high gear.

In the wake of Pearl Harbor, propaganda found its way into almost every
facet of homefront culture. Historians, long fascinated by the government's
recruitment of advertising experts to run the World War II propaganda
machine, have written extensively on the subject. Most characterize wartime
propaganda as "constantly [seeking] to generate an appreciation for the
American way of life," but in so doing they tend to assume a generic national
audience and thereby fail to consider how particular affinity groups like western copper workers might have concentrated on a different message of the
propaganda campaign.[29] Scholars have also tended to privilege propaganda in
national media such as movies or mass-circulation magazines over those found
in distinctly local forums. One such local medium, the twice-monthly newspaper *Copper Commando*, produced by the Victory Labor Management
Committee of Montana's copper towns, won praise locally and nationally.[30]
The Victory committee, comprised of members of management from the
Anaconda Copper Mining Company and union representatives from Butte,
Great Falls, and Anaconda, sent a copy of the *Commando* to every worker and
his family and to every former worker serving in the armed forces.

From its inception, the *Copper Commando* featured messages urging
increased production from the nation's civil and military leaders to Montana's
copper workers in virtually every issue. Lieutenant General Brehon
Somerville, commander of the War Department's Services of Supply, set the
tone for these communiqués in the very first *Commando*. Speaking directly to
the miners, millers, and smeltermen of Butte, Anaconda, and Great Falls,
Somerville called on their manhood to see America through the emergency:
"Our soldiers, fighting for our right to live as free men, depend on you . . . on
every last one of you men of Montana no matter what your job . . . to get out
the copper they must have." In the next paragraph, Somerville played both on
notions of fraternal citizenship and on the guilt he apparently felt these men
must harbor for not actually risking their lives in defense of "the right to live
as free men." "I know you will not fail them. They are your men," he wrote.
Continuing, he noted that "[a]round the world Montana boys face the most
cruel and ruthless armies of all time. They cry for copper . . . more and more

copper. No matter how much you produce, it cannot be too much."[31] His request, endlessly higher copper output, was impossible to meet, but it served the needs of both the country and the Anaconda Copper Mining Company. It did nothing to reinforce the self-worth of the worker, making it difficult at best for the man on the homefront to feel he had fully done his manly duty.

Comparing the life of soldiers to homefront workers also emerged as a staple of the guilt-producing genre of homefront propaganda. For instance, the *Commando*, in its September 5, 1942, edition, published a column titled plainly "Boys Away From Home." Flanked by two large photos of men cleaning weapons, writing letters, eating, and performing other chores in the tents that comprised their new homes, "Boys Away from Home," proposed that "[l]ife isn't very sweet for men in the fighting forces." The article suggested that workers on the homefront too often took soldiers for granted and failed to realize that lack of production at the very minimum "handicaps" men on the front lines, who because of absenteeism on the homefront "don't have the tools with which to work." A "soldier cannot lie down on his job. No matter how poor his tools may be, he must still stay at work," the editors argued. While homefront men have the privilege of rejoining their families and resting when they're off shift, men on the front lines "work twenty-four hours a day at their jobs."[32] A half-page story two pages later added the weight of authority and status to the emotional appeal of "Boys Away from Home." With a dateline of Labor Day 1942, and entitled "Chiefs of Four Top War Agencies Appeal to Metal Miners to Remain on Jobs," the article abstracted letters from Donald Nelson, Lewis Hershey, W. H. Davis, and Paul McNutt to union, business, and civic leaders in nonferrous mining and refining towns. Each leader urged miners and smeltermen to continue their critical work, increase output, and not be lured away by other employment.[33]

The sentiments of "Boys Away from Home," although heavy-handed, did in fact echo the beliefs of a significant percentage of workers. Besides those men who served on the Victory committees, men like "Tubie" Johnson, a Butte native who first began working for the company in 1927 and whose prose found its way into the *Copper Commando*, expressed a common perspective. Like the pledge written by working men that serves as an epigraph for this chapter and the illustrations by local artist John Powers that went into every man's pay envelope each week of the war, Johnson's message in "Remember our Boys" stressed the superior sacrifices being made by soldiers.[34]

"Now beyond vast bodies of water
In distant climes across the sea,
An American flag is ever flying
A sacred symbol of our liberty.
Wherever that banner is waving,

Two of the over one hundred and fifty cartoons drawn by Butte miner John Powers during World War II. These examples are from 1942. Courtesy of Montana Historical Society Archives.

On frontiers of white ocean foam,
Remember our own are right there
And keeping invaders from our home.
They pledged their lives to defend us
And we workers cannot let them down—
In our unity, might and strength lies,
In those efforts, true security found.

To battle stations, prepare workers,
You, in factories, mines or mills,
Keep that war production rolling
All wartime orders must be filled.
Those boys of ours, our very own,
Need planes, arms, mechanical mounts.
Work hard the day and have no delay,
Remember every precious second counts.

So unite and pledge to do your job
Because the sacrifice made is small
Compared to our boys way over there
Who are fighting and giving their all."[35]

Tubie Johnson's September 1942 plea for hard work on the homefront also dovetailed with the speech Lieutenant Marion Beatty gave in August 1942 in each copper town. One of the soldiers the OWI and War Department employed to travel to work sites urging homefront men to avoid absenteeism and act honorably toward their enlisted brothers serving in the line of fire, Beatty stood in Butte on a platform with a large sign just over his left shoulder that read "112 employees were absent from war production yesterday!" and then asked, "Were you?" Dirty but respectful miners listened to Beatty talk at the collar of a mine shaft about the importance of miners' working every shift. He told them, "A few thousand extra tons of copper in 1942 and 1943 can possibly end this war a few months sooner and save a million American lives. One miner staying away from his job one day means 5,000 fewer cartridges for some American soldiers somewhere on the firing line."[36] Beatty called on miners and managers to work "all-out every day," but the tone of the rest of Beatty's speech belied such evenhandedness and indicated that the inclusion of management as part of the production bottleneck was only an empty gesture. Beatty, by way of concluding his speech, did not spare the guilt: "You must not send these men against the enemy in a hopeless or helpless condition. When the enemy attacks and pours out tons of burning hell from planes and tanks and guns they must have the means with which to defend, resist and counter-attack." Men in uniform "are fighting to keep us and our way of life from being pushed off the face of the earth," he enthused. And then, returning to a now familiar statistic, he concluded: "A million or more [soldiers] will probably lose their lives in doing so. We cannot fail them. We must get the 'stuff' to them."[37]

The *Commando* reinforced such messages, and in fact ran a war-long campaign against absenteeism. As Beatty was touring Montana's copper production centers, the *Commando*, opting for the carrot instead of the stick, reported that three men at the St. Lawrence mine had struck "good blows" against the Axis powers by not missing a single shift during July's five-week contract period. Ernest Tambling, born in Cornwall, England, in 1878, had come to Butte in 1920 and had worked in the mines continuously since then. Thomas Perez, a native of Spain, came to the United States in 1919 and to Butte in 1936. William Koniw, who emigrated from Austria in 1913 entered the mines in 1922.[38] These three men, who each received a twenty-five-dollar war bond, depict well the strong immigrant presence in Butte and the other copper towns during the war. Moreover, the rhetoric of the article, which highlighted the migration and work histories of these three men, signifies the prevalence of the "Americans all" theme that historians Barbara Savage, Philip Gleason, and Gary Gerstle show to be a pervasive part of wartime ideology.[39] Reinforcing this message, in a photo that ran with the article, the *Commando* had Tambling, Perez, and Koniw pose holding a giant "Buy a Share in America" war poster. And while its stated purpose was to acknowledge the good work of these three miners, the article implies a second equally powerful message: only three men at the St. Lawrence worked all their shifts during July. The *Commando*'s closing point, its desire "to be able to congratulate many more [men] in the future who [by working all their shifts] are helping to win the war," was difficult for the copper men to misinterpret.[40]

But the miners, millers, and smeltermen resisted the implication that unless they marched in lock step with the government and company's wishes they were traitors. Copper men had fought for decades to gain a semblance of control over the pace of the work. Some workers saw the wartime production pace as dangerous. Others felt miners, millers, and smeltermen had not just the prerogative to skip a shift, but the duty to do so as a necessary exercise of worker autonomy that would help maintain equality with management during the no-strike pledge era.[41] Still others felt that the company and its managers, along with middle-class propagandists in Washington, D.C., had failed to make an equal sacrifice to what they demanded of the working men.[42] For these workers, showing independence in the face of company and government power, much as they had done during the 1930s, was essential both to their sense of manhood and to a work culture that empowered working men and their unions and thereby provided stability for workers' families.

In Edward Reynolds's perfectly titled "Blood and Bread," another short story he submitted for *Men at Work*, the Depression does indeed appear to be a crucial framework for understanding the meaning of the war and manhood on the suddenly vibrant American industrial stage. Submitted in the summer of 1941, "Blood and Bread" uses stronger language than Edwards's "Hot Metal" to argue that providing for one's family was as crucial to manhood as wearing the uniform: "Butte and Anaconda were booming and we all had jobs. Far down underground in Butte men were digging ore from the veins of the 'richest hill on earth' and over in Anaconda men were boiling that ore down into molten copper that glowed a bloody red. 'Sinews of war,' the editorial writers call it; 'bread and butter,' say the miners and smeltermen." Elaborating on the copper men's mindset, Reynolds writes: "'Yes,' they agree, 'war is hell. But work is hell, too, and starving to death is a damn sight worse.'"[43]

Reynolds captured an essential element of what the dawning war meant to many men on the homefront. The war, Reynolds's workers believed, would be nasty business, but it would put them back to work, allowing them to provide for their families. Military production meant full employment and that meant security and good wages, but only until working men got drafted or the war ended. After that, because corporations had once more begun to dominate government, a scramble for far fewer jobs, and perhaps another depression seemed inevitable. In "Blood and Bread," working men, "[s]odbusters from North Dakota, cow hands from Eastern Montana, Okies from the dust bowl, boomers from the southland and the west—and home town boys, too, who were given first preference," chose not to talk about the losses the war might bring; instead, their focus was on having jobs, on stability, on being able to provide for the first time in a decade.[44] Unlike the more politically progressive workers George Lipsitz profiles in his excellent study *Rainbow at Midnight: Labor and Culture in the 1940s,* Reynolds's collective protagonists seemingly had given up on the revolutionary potential of the New Deal.[45] They no longer expected that FDR's liberal government would genuinely strive to make full employment its primary social and economic goal. Corporations, having poured leaders into Washington to staff key government jobs in the burgeoning wartime bureaucracy, had triumphed over a model of government that might have made workers equally powerful. Propaganda, national and local, and community pressure to serve like Leroy Carpenter and those other local men who had already given their lives collided with the ideology evident in "Blood and Bread." The product of this clash was the anxious, sometimes contradictory manhood of the wartime industrial West. For the last eighteen months of mobilization and the first year of the war, one issue became the central and most contentious site for negotiating between the ethos represented in "Blood and Bread" and the new standards of manhood that forcefully emerged after Pearl Harbor: the draft.

With its status as an official government program and with its access to regional and national decision makers, Montana's copper workers used the Victory Labor Management Committee as their primary conduit for raising concerns about the draft.[46] In August 1942, the initial month of the committee's full operation, Joe Marcille and Fred Grey, two longtime copper workers who came to represent men wanting protection from the draft, were the first to ask why workers in the Anaconda Company's employ were not being deferred by Hershey's Selective Service System while men from other parts of the country were getting deferments and then coming to Anaconda and Butte to work. Marcille felt that skilled copper workers had more worth in the workplace than as soldiers, and that the committee should make it a priority to figure out how to get deferments for copper workers.[47] Besides more generally signifying anxiety about homefront workers' masculine status, Marcille and Grey's comments evoked the four major themes that typified copper men's interaction with Selective Service and FDR's wartime administration: uncertainty about the draft apparatus, concern over other men "beating the system," the precept that copper work because of its difficulty, danger, and importance to wartime industry held special worth within the national production system, and fear about postwar economic and social security.

A month passed before the Victory committee again officially addressed Marcille and Grey's concerns about the draft. Much research and discussion among the copper men had occurred in those thirty days. Bert Riley, a leader of the Butte Miners' Union (BMU), reported that the head of the deferment board in Helena had agreed that miners and other essential workers deserved deferments if they continued to labor in the copper industry. His remarks considerably cheered the Victory Committee, but instead of celebrating with his colleagues Riley revealed what would become one of the central perplexing factors to these three communities and, thus, the committee's consideration of the draft. He noted there would be some men who would not consider deferment a good deal and others who would fight to be deferred even though their work was not considered essential by Selective Service. For instance, Riley asked, "what about oilers and other men like them: Are they going to take them? They might have to take the place of an engineer should he die."[48] Riley's stress on the danger of copper work echoed Edward Reynolds's narrator in "Hot Metal." But now, eighteen months after Reynolds wrote convincingly about the mood of smeltermen toward the draft, the issue of looking yellow for many workers clearly had been joined by a desire to stay on the homefront rather than to serve wherever Uncle Sam wanted.

Riley concluded that the Victory committee's number one priority regarding the draft and deferment should be to see "that everyone is given the privilege of going into the Army or working in the mines as he wishes." But the committeemen all knew that the issue involved more than just doing one's masculine duty on the homefront or on the front lines. Both union and management were concerned that those who stayed at home would be considered shirkers, draft-dodgers, less than manly.[49] It was the arrival of men to the Anaconda, Great Falls, and Butte copper works who had recently moved from other jobs in town or actually moved to Montana to work in copper, an industry that would provide them the means to avoid the war, that complicated the miners' and smeltermen's ability to negotiate community values regarding deferment. Producing copper had always been considered the epitome of men's work and copper men reveled in the psychological wage provided by that status. Now not only had soldiers like William Paull, who prior to the war worked for a paint company, supplanted copper men, but men were coming to the mines and smelters in order to dodge what was perceived as their masculine wartime duty—soldiering.[50] The miners, millers, and smeltermen, already bombarded with a propaganda that questioned whether they were doing their utmost, felt that their own manhood was being besmirched in the process.

Two workers spoke to the issue of outsiders avoiding the draft during the September 2, 1942, meeting of the Victory committee. The first commented that within the community "[t]here has been a lot of doubt as to the attitude of men who have transferred from other industries into our industry." He continued, "I have heard rumors criticizing a man who never worked for the company, who was working up town and went to work in the mines." The second elaborated on the situation: "I have heard of two, the Harkins kid and Chappelle. The two of them worked a few days in the mines and both quit already. One of them is now working in the iron works as a welder and Harkins is back on the old man's truck. They worked four or five days, possibly a week. I did not see [Harkins], but heard a lot of comments on him. When Harkins went to deliver they would ask if it was from Harkins, and he would be told not to deliver it."[51] That the working men of Montana's copper communities would not tolerate what they perceived as draft-dodging by men like Harkins and Chappelle at the same time that they also wanted to choose where they risked their own hides says much about manhood on the homefront.[52] The workers on the Victory committee applauded E. S. McGlone, the manager of the mines, when he responded to the Harkins and Chappelle situation by saying that the company would make every effort to keep the men in the mines and not be satisfied with replacements from out of state or with local men who tried to beat the system.[53] McGlone understood the men's quandary.

The copper men themselves, in an effort to construct their own manliness in opposition to others on the homefront, openly considered many men—not just Harkins and Chappelle—who continued to work in nonproduction jobs throughout Anaconda and Butte as shirking their manly responsibilities. An exchange that revolved around Victory committee–sponsored Pledge Cards, meant to be a visible symbol of copper workers pledging their all for wartime production, demonstrated the copper men's desire to reestablish themselves as better than other men. It also showed that while there were strict codes of masculine conduct in these western communities, the world of manhood after Pearl Harbor was nonetheless confusing, and often what appeared as a clear-cut issue—men not going immediately into the armed forces should take production jobs and not dally in less meaningful service-sector jobs—was actually befuddling. One union representative told his fellow committee members that the pledge cards should be given not only to miners, millers, and smeltermen, but also to the dealers at the local gambling halls: a category of men who to the copper workers seemed obviously not to be fulfilling the wartime obligations of manhood. To this suggestion a company representative on the Committee replied that "some of [the dealers] have taken the position that if they applied for a job [in the copper industry] they would be considered as draft dodgers." In other words, taking a production job could actually label a man as less manly than simply staying in a nonessential position and waiting to be drafted.[54]

The BMU leader, Bert Riley, said he found the dealers' position contradictory. He asked why, if these men were afraid of being labeled draft dodgers, they did not just enlist in the armed services.[55] Riley, however, knew that the choices afforded men during this trying time were not so simple. A man like William Paull was the exception. Even among the most patriotic copper workers, few wanted to enlist directly, knowing they would be leaving their families, like PFC Carpenter did, for a less than certain proposition. The opportunity to be shot at or to be the target of an enemy bombing mission was not especially attractive to anyone, no matter his nationalist proclivities. It was even less attractive for older men who had greater familial attachments and obligations. Moreover, Riley's own situation did not mirror the dealer's predicament. As a miner he had an essential production job in a protected industry. There was virtually no chance he would be drafted out of that job. Nor would he be labeled a draft dodger because he did not have to move from an unprotected position to one that would likely be considered a deferment job for the length of the war. His criticism—"I don't think that is the right attitude for [the dealers] to take. We have signs right in our [union] hall welcoming them"—constructed the copper men as the only patriotic males within the local community.[56]

Yet the move by Riley and other workers to construct, from the bottom up, copper men as "soldiers of production" equal to men in uniform veils the reality that even a considerable number of men working in the copper industry shared the dealers' predicament. No matter the measures Hershey took to make the system "so simple that even the crooks will say, 'I'll be patriotic and register just like all the other guys,'" the draft and especially deferment were complex issues often misunderstood by the general populace.[57] Virtually every man felt that the government might draft him. Even though some men already in uniform fit this profile, for older men with families, and especially those with sons in the service, such an action was highly unlikely.[58] The odds rose considerably for men under forty.[59] Thus in Anaconda and Butte, determining which jobs the government deemed essential and thereby which workers would be deferred because of the "essential" role they played, quickly became a hot topic. The power of the state over an individual's life visibly emerged as a major theme in these and other draft conversations.

Under Lewis Hershey's signature, Selective Service issued "Occupational Bulletin No. 12" on July 28, 1942, to clarify which jobs within the mining industry it considered as essential to the war effort. The bulletin stipulated that draft boards would judge whether a job required enough skill and training to make the replacement of men on that job so difficult that it took six months or more of training. If it did, then the man holding that job should gain a deferment. Because the list did not specifically enumerate every job classification recommended for deferment, it allowed (and forced) employers and employees, in the words of the memorandum, "to point out to local draft boards the parallel between the degree of training, qualification or skill required for occupations not specifically listed and some of those included in the critical list." Those arguing for deferment who held jobs not listed should make sure local draft boards understood that the Bulletin was "not a direct order" but merely a guide and "should not be considered ground for refusing deferment," the Mining Congress advised.[60]

Thus "Occupational Bulletin No. 12" did not end debates about who should receive deferments. For example, after being asked about certain surface jobs around the mines, McGlone, the Butte Mines manager, indicated that many of the men working on the copper tanks would not be protected. Bert Riley, continuing to play a major role in these discussions, openly disagreed with his boss: "The day we were over in Helena we were told you can get deferments for men on the copper tanks." McGlone responded that it was not that easy. Earning a deferment from the board, he reiterated, "depends upon the skill of the job and the length of time required to train new men to take his place." Tellingly he summarized, "A man is a man with us now." For men who had staked so much of their self-worth and manhood on their experience and expertise these were very hard words to hear. They had been respected figures in the culture of the workplace and the culture of the community. They did not believe that "a man is a man." Men had to earn their manhood in the copper industry. They were not replaceable cogs. But influenced by new wartime realities, McGlone and the government were saying otherwise. McGlone elaborated, "If you were working as a surface laborer and Harry here was a handicapped man and could do your work, and we could not sign an affidavit that you could not be replaced when he was available, you would be out of luck." One of Riley's coworkers countered with the position of the surface workers—men, it is worth noting, whose work typically required less skill and drew less pay. He did not mince words: "The fellows are very dissatisfied on the proposition."[61] He was right.

The feelings of the surface men, gleaned from suggestions sent to the Victory committee, add detail to the changing picture of wartime manhood by outlining how intimately the issues of manhood and class were tied to deferment. Five workers, James L. Barnicoat, John Lasky, William Rozenski, Martin Kovacich, and Pete McDonald wrote, "In regard to having all young top men go underground to work and replacing them with older men on top, we (the top men) are willing to accept such changes in order to aid in production for the war effort, but on certain conditions," to wit:

> We want only old Butte miners to replace us in our present jobs, and we want all "special watchmen," who are as physically fit as we, to give their jobs to old Butte miners also, and accept underground work. If these men who are composed of salesmen, etc., and who, for the most

part, never worked in a mine and many not even at a mine before, are willing to accept such terms, we will go underground gladly but otherwise we will protest.[62]

With the choice of these words, these five men were informing management of the worker value system. Barnicoat, Lasky, Rozenski, Kovacich, and McDonald did not want to go underground. Working the mines was the occupation holding the most masculine prestige in Montana's copper communities, but it was also the most dangerous. These men believed in the code of manhood, but also knew that being considered a real man meant nothing if you were not around to support your family. Going into the mines was risky and, in their eyes, a sacrifice. These five wanted other men who at least nominally held white-collar positions to make an equal sacrifice, to risk their comfortable and stable positions, no matter their class. Barnicoat, Lasky, Rozenski, Kovacich, and McDonald also wanted to make sure that only men who had earned status and proven their manhood—old Butte miners—replaced them on their surface jobs. With this demand these five men made a final claim for their own masculine and class worth. They wanted the company and everyone else to know that special watchmen and salesmen did not have equal masculine status to surface men. Such white-collar workers were not good enough to warrant replacing the surface men at their jobs.[63]

Unlike enlisting, transferring underground did not guarantee that a copper worker could stop worrying about the perception of his manhood in the community. After the release of "Occupational Bulletin No. 12," another worker on the Victory Committee remarked that "the laborers of the copper tanks think if they transfer underground or anything else, they would be considered draft dodgers."[64] A company representative responded that this was the very reason that the head of the local deferment board came out with a statement noting men who transferred to war industry jobs from those in nonessential fields were not dodging their duty. But he underestimated the importance of long-held local working-class ideals about manhood within these western industrial towns. The opinion of the head of the draft board in Helena did not necessarily match that of the community. A man's masculine image was not guaranteed by the edict of a bureaucrat, but rather by following the local value system that labeled certain actions as draft dodging.[65]

The miners' and smeltermen's number one antidote against being grouped with draft dodgers and other slackers was to promote the old idea that copper work was much more difficult than other occupations and thus copper men deserved special advantages and recognition. Most evocative of this effort was the "Meat for Copper Production" drive, one of the most labor intensive and well received of the Victory committee's activities throughout the war. Dennis McMahon, a BMU man and a member of the rationing subcommittee responsible for procuring more meat for the working men, reported to the Victory board that the subcommittee had aided in a mass rally at Butte's Fox Theater. An estimated one thousand people attended this event in support of the "Meat for Copper Production" drive: "Residents of the community were asked to send cards to Washington representatives, pointing to the need for more meat for copper workers." "We figure that upwards of five thousand cards have already been sent to Washington," added McMahon, "and it is our hope that we may reach the figure of twenty-five thousand within the next week."[66] Besides the rally, the previous Saturday evening, John Claxton, chairman of the Victory committee, had appeared on a radio broadcast with Paul Fall of the Miners' Union to discuss the drive. The simple purpose of the campaign was to get a larger weekly meat allowance from the government for the hard-working men of the copper communities. The drive and its remarkably popular support, besides being emblematic of the everyday concerns of homefront America, also showed the opinion this community had of itself and its importance to the war cause. In addition, it indicated that the community, at least subconsciously, knew that the men who remained behind as soldiers of production needed to be reassured of their own worth to the enclave. The philosophy behind the drive—men need meat, the more manly the work the more meat, the more meat allotted the worthier the man—manifests one of the strategies employed by copper workers to reassure themselves of their masculine worth.[67]

The Victory committee's push for special certificates of recognition for the men of the mining industry had a reasoning parallel to that of the meat drive and also required turning to the state for assistance. Indeed, the effort to acquire special certificates from the federal government best represents the unusual relationship between western industrial manhood, the draft, and the state during World War II. Deferred men living in the region's copper communities wanted not just reassurance but physical proof that they were considered equal, both in future worth and current manhood, to their comrades like William Paull serving in the armed forces. Major Walter Mendelsohn of the Manpower Division in Washington, D.C., wrote in response to one of the committee's letters on this matter that "since the discontinuance of voluntary enlistment, however, the fact that a man is not in uniform should be no reflection on his patriotism." The working men forcibly deferred by the government agreed fully with this sentiment, but their experience indicated that others on the homefront did not. It is unlikely, however, that they agreed with Mendelsohn's following point: "If he is in business clothes or in overalls, it is probably because the Government wants him that way. The entire effort is now to get the right worker into the right war job, and that war job may be either in uniform or civilian clothes."[68] Perhaps such a formulation, which equated men in business clothes with men in overalls, made sense in Washington, D.C., but as was evident from the earlier acerbic observation by James L. Barnicoat, John Lasky, William Rozenski, Martin Kovacich, and Pete McDonald regarding "salesmen," it did not carry weight in the industrial West.

Not surprisingly, the bureaucrats in the nation's capital did not see the need for the identification cards for copper workers requested by the Victory Committee. The draft system had already solved the problem in the government's view. As Major Mendelsohn wrote, "Every man now registered has a registration card as evidence that he has presented himself for service, whether he was accepted, rejected, or deferred." "Selective Service," the Major continued, "has been described as an act of volunteering en masse, and as people come to comprehend the basic good sense and philosophy of this statement, the situation which promotes the desire for insignia should cease." The men of management and labor quickly agreed that the fellows in Washington were far removed from the reality of being a worker and a man in the West. As one Victory committee member put it, "Young fellows . . . working in the mines . . . were deferred and for that reason they couldn't join the armed forces if they wanted to. These young fellows were called slackers at different times." Another member of the committee responded that "all the people are not as well informed about these things as selective service is. The fact is that it is not so well known here."[69]

By issuing cards, a powerful central government could potentially heal the wounds and solve the problems of working men. After all, local standards of right and wrong were in some ways being superseded by a federal model. Could such a reengineering include ideas of manhood? Should it? The problems of federal control and standards were also readily apparent to these men. One Victory committee member spoke for the rest. He noted the seemingly automatic and rote dismissal of the committee's request for recognition cards: "It seems to me it is more or less a blanket answer to anything along that line." The committee was worried that in the postwar scramble for jobs, with a depression quite likely, homefront workers, deferred for legitimate reasons or not, would be considered second-class citizens in comparison to those soldiers who actually fought. Riley noted, "We have seen the time when, if you didn't have a certificate of discharge from the last war, you were just out of luck." Yes, a certificate from the company would carry some weight locally, but as McGlone realized, "it will not suffice to get a job if [a worker] applies at Hoover Dam, for instance"; only federal recognition could do that. Yet even when government authority was recognized and sought, it was not always considered a benefactor of the working man. Many on the Victory committee felt that the government itself was "the worst offender," when it came to recognizing the work of men on the homefront. The government said "that ex-service men shall be preferred" over workers tied to the production line, noted another worker.[70] He knew that Lewis Hershey among others had stated his belief that returning soldiers deserved preference for jobs over homefront men. Working men found themselves relying on a government more interested in assuring benefits to veterans than protecting "soldiers of production."

The anxiety surrounding the draft and the ambiguous role of state power in assuaging that anxiety proved to be only the beginning of a crisis in manhood for working-class men in these copper towns. Through newsreels, movies, and other forms of popular culture highly influenced by the government during the war, the white ethnic copper men of Montana learned that women and minority men in other parts of the country were making remarkable government-sponsored social and economic advances.[71] Those changes, and the threat they posed to men who felt they had only recently started to solidify the privileges of whiteness, came home, so to speak, when in late November 1942, on the heels of the draft crisis, the government, with the blessing of the Anaconda Company, sent a regiment of black soldier-miners from the South to help fill the labor shortage in Butte's mines.[72] White miners, already reeling from their loss of masculine status to soldiers, were now being told that black men were their equal and should be allowed to work next to them. The parents of the Irish and southeastern European men who formed the majority of Butte's miners had come to maturity in a time when immigrants from such locales were often considered nonwhite and even black. Some of the miners had likely encountered similar conditions. In America being black meant getting the worst pay for the worst jobs. It meant almost constant oppression. Most European immigrants quickly adopted racist ways to distance themselves from such a connection. Now the connection might be made again. Butte's white miners feared this association, and their racism made them abhor the idea of large numbers of black men, soldiers or not, in their city. En masse the miners walked out of the mines, refusing to work next to black men. The government backed down, but any trust between the liberal state and working men in these towns— who had already witnessed a New Deal administration that seemed more interested in pleasing corporations and rewarding enlisted men than aiding white male homefront workers—virtually evaporated.

Like their resistance to black workers, copper men also quickly drew the line against new government-sponsored roles for women. Two articles in the first *Commando* summed up local men's attitudes toward women and war work in Butte, Anaconda, and Great Falls, and signified exactly in what roles copper men felt comfortable seeing local women. Noting that the Women's Auxiliary of the Butte Miners' Union had agreed to find six hundred women to work as daytime wardens, the column reassured readers that while each female warden would be trained in first aid, in handling victims of a gas attack, and in fighting incendiary and fire bombs, "the work is not as strenuous for women as for men wardens." "Every woman has been looking for a place in war work that she is capable of filling. . . .[but] Not all of us can do active work in defense," the article stressed. Women in Montana's copper communities should not consider doing active work in defense industries, but rather should tend to their "natural" duties as housewives. The *Commando* chose a parable to make this point unambiguous: "There was a woman in a small town in England who wanted to do something for the cause. She was told to keep a kettle of water boiling on her stove at all times. She did—and when the village was attacked, her kettle was the only source of sterile water in the town! The women of Butte can keep their kettle boiling by being wardens."[73]

In another assertion of women's domestic role, the *Commando* proposed that homefront women should also busy themselves making sure the copper men were well fed. In an article plainly titled "Thoughts for Food," Mrs. Smith and Mrs. Johnson talk over a common problem—what to put in the lunch bucket. "But my John won't eat vegetables. He wants meat," begins Mrs. Johnson. "That's just it—" replied Mrs. Smith, "neither will Bill and the boys. But Mrs. Griffith says we can put them in and teach them to like them. They need the energy and the right food so that the extra hours and the extra effort they're putting out won't be so hard on them."[74] But these images of wartime did not represent the mainstream; the copper men were fighting a losing battle against the expansion of women's roles.

In 1943 managers at the Great Falls facility hired women to work in what had previously been exclusively male occupations. The government and company's efforts to introduce local women and men of color as a solution to a 1944 labor shortage in Anaconda's smelter cemented the working men's new perspective on the liberal administration. Now the government and the company seemed intent on having women demean copper workers' masculine status and men of color demean the miners' and smeltermen's racial privilege.[75] Homefront men working in western industrial communities like Butte, Anaconda, and Great Falls felt as if they had lost their power in the liberal state. Even though by and large they continued to back liberal candidates for office, their dissatisfaction with a liberalism that did not support their masculine status nor their white privilege continued into the 1950s.[76] Eventually, what began in World War II ended in firm resistance to the civil rights and women's movements of the 1960s and thereby laid the groundwork for a mass defection of a later generation of western industrial workers to Ronald Reagan's Republican party, a party willing to champion the cause of white working-class men.[77]

Notes

Many fine folks have helped me find sources for, conceptualize, and write this essay and offered encouragement along the way. I'd like to thank Janet Finn, David Emmons, Mary Murphy, Laurie Mercier, Bob Clark, Angela Murray, Brian Shovers, Jodie Foley, Ellen Crain, Robert Vine, Elizabeth Crockett, Elaine Tyler May, Lary May, Dave Roediger, David Noble, Jennifer Pierce, Gary Gerstle, Dee Garceau, Laura McCall, Ilene Alexander, Derek Krissoff, Julia Mickenberg, Andrea Sachs, Robert Frame, Deirdre Murphy, Robin Hemenway, Kim Heikkila, Rachel Martin, and Angela Smith. I've tried to do justice to their insights and suggestions, but in those spots where I have fallen short the fault, of course, is mine alone.

1. This pledge was sent to President Roosevelt by 613 workers at the National Transit Pump and Machine works in Oil City, Pennsylvania. The managers and workers on the grievance committee that met in an effort to iron out any problems that might cause a strike deemed the pledge important enough to be read twice at their August 1942 meeting in Butte. Tellingly, the *Butte Daily Post* also printed the Oil City pledge in its editorial section, and the union went so far as to post it for the duration of the emergency on union bulletin boards throughout the company area. *Report to Donald Nelson,* Victory Committee Records, Anaconda Copper Mining Company Collection, Montana Historical Society Archives (MHSA), Helena, Montana. Hereafter, documents from this source will be abbreviated: Victory.

2. George Q. Flynn, *Lewis B. Hershey, Mr. Selective Service* (Chapel Hill: University of North Carolina Press, 1986), 7 and 84.

3. Significantly, the strongest proponents for peacetime conscription came from the East. See Flynn, 66–69; on Wheeler and the West-East dynamic see J. Garry Clifford and Samuel R. Spenser, Jr., "New York: The National Emergency Committee," chap. 5 in *The First Peacetime Draft* (Lawrence: University Press of Kansas, 1986), 70–82 and 180.

4. Michael P. Malone, Richard B. Roeder, and William L. Lang, *Montana: A History of Two Centuries* (Seattle: University of Washington Press, 1991), 309.

5. Michael Kimmel, *Manhood in America: A Cultural History* (New York: The Free Press, 1996), 223; and Peter N. Stearns, *Be a Man! Males in Modern Society* (New York: Holmes and Meier, 1990), 161. For another general history of manhood that paints the war similarly see Peter Filene, *Him/Her/Self: Gender Roles and Modern America* (Baltimore: Johns Hopkins University Press, 1998). Although women made definite inroads, especially in the arena of leisure, in Montana depression assistance was meted out to support the existing masculine gender regime. Montana's working men felt that the government was on their side, as Montana was second among states in per capita federal spending on assistance during the 1930s. On this trend see Laurie Mercier's excellent *Smelter City: Labor, Gender, and Cultural Politics in Anaconda, Montana, 1934–1980* (Ph.D. diss., University of Oregon, 1995); and Mary Murphy, *Mining Cultures: Men, Women, and Leisure in Butte, 1914–1941* (Urbana: University of Illinois Press, 1997). On industrial Montana in the postwar period see Mercier and Janet Finn, *Tracing the Veins of Copper, Culture, and Community from Butte to Chuquicamata* (Berkeley and Los Angeles: University of California Press, 1998).

6. R. W. Connell, to whose work on gender I am heavily indebted and from whom I borrow the term *hegemonic masculinity,* also argues that gender is a process. The theorist Antonio Gramsci stresses that hegemony is nothing if not a process defined by constant challenge. Crisis moments, such as World War II, often provoke multiple challenges to hegemonic formations including the gender regime. R. W. Connell, *Masculinities: Knowledge, Power, and Social Change* (Berkeley and Los Angeles: University of California Press, 1995), 76–81. Antonio Gramsci, *Further Selections from the Prison Notebooks*, Derek Boothman ed. (Minneapolis: University of Minnesota Press, 1995).

7. David R. Segal, *Recruiting for Uncle Sam: Citizenship and Military Manpower Policy* (Lawrence: University Press of Kansas, 1989). Segal goes on to contend that World War II was the last war that made such service part of the obligations of U.S. citizenship.

8. The reality of U.S. manhood during the war is, of course, far more complex than this. Differences in age, marital status, class, race, region, and religion all complicated expectations. I address this more fully in the first chapter of my dissertation (in progress): Matthew Basso, "From Progressive Unionists to Soldiers of Production," in *Metal of Honor: Montana's World War II Homefront, Movies, and The Social Politics of White Male Anxiety.*

9. It's also worth noting that feminist scholars have taught us that the reformation of gender identity, a social and cultural category with material realities, occurs through interaction between people of like and different sexes at the level of social practice and social structure. As both practice and structure changed in profound ways for women in the first half of the 1940s, it is really no surprise that the same happened for men.

10. William H. Chafe, *The Paradox of Change* (New York: Oxford University Press, 1991), 121–22. See also Sherna Berger Gluck, *Rosie the Riveter Revisited: Women, the War, and Social Change* (Boston: Twayne, 1987); Karen Anderson, *Wartime Women: Sex Roles, Family Relations, and the Status of Women*

during World War II (Westport, Conn.: Greenwood, 1981); and Susan M. Hartmann, *The Home Front and Beyond: American Women in the 1940s* (Boston: Twayne, 1982).

11. Chafe, 128–31. Contemporary commentators cited patriotism to explain women's enthusiastic response to defense industry openings. Undoubtedly this was a contributing factor. More importantly, Chafe insists, such jobs provided a safer, healthier, and more pleasant environment coupled with considerably higher pay. Women working in war industries typically made over 40 percent more than their peers in consumer goods factories. See also Maureen Honey, *Creating Rosie the Riveter: Class, Gender, and Propaganda during World War II* (Amherst: University of Massachusetts Press, 1984).

12. Early on, Clyde Griffen argued that scholars needed to pay more attention to the intersections between manhood and class and to manhood among working-class men specifically. Mark Carnes and Clyde Griffen, eds., *Meanings for Manhood: Constructions of Masculinity in Victorian America* (Chicago: University of Chicago Press, 1990). Ruth Milkman's research is particularly noteworthy on this issue. Milkman incorporates labor market segmentation theory with a subtle understanding of workers' agency in her study of the electrical and auto industry during the war. In doing so, she rejects notions of pure labor market segmentation, which presume that male workers have an interest in class unity and thus would support class-based gender equality. Ruth Milkman, *Gender at Work: The Dynamics of Job Segregation by Sex during World War II* (Urbana: University of Illinois Press, 1987).

13. This, of course, is what eventually happened in the U.S. economy. On the relationship between the postwar economic transition and masculinity, see Susan Faludi, *Stiffed: The Betrayal of the American Man* (New York: William Morrow, 1999).

14. Historians of manhood have been slow to follow political scientist Theda Skopol's call in the 1970s for further research into how the state influences everyday life. On the state and the West see William Deverell's discussion of the ward state dialectic in Clyde Milner, ed., *A New Significance: Re-envisioning the History of the American West* (New York: Oxford University Press, 1996), 29–55; and Karen R. Merrill, "Whose Home on the Range?" *Western Historical Quarterly* 27, no. 4 (1996): 433–51.

15. Paull's story and all quotes are drawn from William T. Paull, *From Butte to Iwo Jima: The Memoirs of William T. Paull* (www.sihopecom/%7Etipi/marine.html, 1996).

16. Ibid. Murray apparently ignored the fact that Paull's family was staunchly Republican.

17. Ibid.

18. Ibid. William Paull further learned of this new public attitude on the long train ride to San Diego for Marine boot camp. When the conductor threatened to kick him and the other freshly minted servicemen off the train because of their drunken and obnoxious behavior, Paull watched as "the other passengers forced the conductor to calm down." For these passengers, just as for the people on that platform in Butte, and for the vast majority across the country, men in uniform "were gallant young heroes going off to save the world." The train's passengers willingly tolerated rowdy masculine behavior from the new standard bearers of American manhood.

19. Edward B. Reynolds, "Hot Metal," 1, WPA Records, MC 77, box 18, folder 6, "Men at Work, 1940–1941," MHSA. Hereafter, WPA Records. Actually born and raised in Anaconda, Reynolds began "rustling" at the smelter on weekends while still in high school and eventually worked in virtually every department of the massive plant. Edward B. Reynolds, "Sketch Autobiography," WPA Records.

20. Reynolds, "Hot Metal," 1.

21. Interview with Joe Navarro by Laurie Mercier, March 25, 1983, Oral History 485, MHSA.

22. Reynolds, "Hot Metal,"1–2.

23. For statistics on injury, disability, and death see David Emmons, *The Butte Irish: Class and Ethnicity in an American Mining Town, 1875–1925* (Urbana: University of Illinois Press, 1989), 148–59. Statistics are an average for the three decades prior to the 1930s when a large number of mines shut down. See also Michael Malone, *Battle for Butte: Mining and Politics on the Northern Frontier* (Seattle: University of Washington Press, 1981).

24. Tracy Thornton, "Butte Man First to Die in State," *The Montana Standard*, December 7, 1991; "LeRoy Carpenter of Butte Is First Montana Soldier Killed in Action" (source and date unknown); "Cited Posthumously [Norman J Fetherolf]," *Montana Standard*, April 2, 1943; "Honored Posthumously [James M. Gill, Jr.]" (source and date unknown); "Additional List of Prisoners Issued," March 7, 1943 (source unknown). It's likely that each unknown article is from the *Montana Standard*. Each citation found in "Montana in the Wars" clippings file, Butte-Silverbow Public Archives (BSBA).

25. Ibid.

26. Ibid.

27. On Butte miners as a type see Murphy, 106–35.

28. David Emmons points out that just prior to the United States official entry into World War I the navy used advertisements to recruit Butte miners that argued that navy jobs were safer and held considerably more benefits than working in the mines. Emmons, 167.

29. Allan M. Winkler, *Homefront U.S.A.: America during World War II* (Arlington Heights, Ill: Harlan Davidson, 1986), 29. For a different view see Michael C. C. Adams, *The Best War Ever: America and World War II* (Baltimore: Johns Hopkins University Press, 1994), 73–75.

30. The Victory Labor-Management Committee of the Anaconda Copper Mining Company served as the group responsible for representing the concerns of the men of Butte and Anaconda about the draft to various federal agencies including Selective Service. So-called Victory committees existed in many war industries. The transcripts of their meetings remain an underappreciated window into wartime labor relations. "Development and Progress of Victory Labor-Management Committees at the Anaconda Reduction Works—Anaconda Copper Mining Company, Anaconda, Montana," memo included in the *Report to Donald Nelson, Chairman War Production Board, Victory Labor-Management Committees at the Anaconda Reduction Works—Anaconda Copper Mining Company, Anaconda, Montana*, June 27, 1942, Victory, 1.

31. *Copper Commando*, August 22, 1942, 2. A complete set of the *Copper Commando* can be found in BSBA.

32. *Copper Commando,* September 5, 1942, 13.

33. Ibid., 15.

34. The WPB regulated the business of war production through a network of subagencies like the Non-Ferrous Commission. For a fuller explanation of the WPB and other wartime agencies see John Morton Blum, *V is for Victory: Politics and American Culture during World War II* (New York: Harcourt, Brace, and Jovanovich, 1976).

35. *Copper Commando*, September 19, 1942, 7.

36. *Copper Commando*, August 22, 1942, 18.

37. Ibid.

38. Ibid.

39. Philip Gleason, *Speaking of Diversity: Language and Ethnicity in Twentieth Century America* (Baltimore: Johns Hopkins University Press, 1992); Barbara Savage, *Broadcasting Freedom: Radio, War, and the Politics of Race, 1938–1948* (Chapel Hill: University of North Carolina Press, 1999); and Gary Gerstle, *Working Class Americanism: The Politics of Labor in a Textile City, 1914–1961* (New York: Cambridge University Press, 1989).

40. *Copper Commando*, August 22, 1942, 18.

41. On the no-strike pledge and wildcat strikes during the war more generally, see Martin Glaberman, *Wartime Strikes: The Struggle against the No-Strike Pledge in the UAW during World War II* (Detroit: Bewick, 1980).

42. On the equality of sacrifice concept see Mark H. Leff, "Politics of Sacrifice on the American Home Front in World War II," *Journal of American History* 77, no. 4 (March 1991): 1296–1318.

43. Reynolds, "Blood and Bread," WPA Records, 1.

44. Ibid.

45. George Lipsitz, *Rainbow at Midnight: Labor and Culture in the 1940s* (Urbana: University of Illinois Press, 1994). I would argue that Lipsitz's workers, who were also interested in bolstering the inter-racial character of the CIO, were in the minority nationally. Interestingly, Mine-Mill's president, Reid Robinson, held the same progressive beliefs. On Robinson and Mine-Mill's interracial organizing in the South see Robin D. G. Kelley's *Hammer and Hoe: Alabama Communists during the Great Depression* (Chapel Hill: University of North Carolina Press, 1990). I draw my understanding of labor's perception of the revolutionary potential of the New Deal primarily from Lisabeth Cohen's remarkable study of Chicago: *Making a New Deal: Industrial Workers in Chicago, 1919–1939* (New York: Cambridge University Press, 1989).

46. On these committees nationally see Nelson Lichtenstein, *Labor's War at Home: The CIO in World War II* (New York: Cambridge University Press, 1982), 89–93.

47. *Report to Donald Nelson,* August 1942, Victory, 2.

48. *Meeting Transcripts*, September 3, 1942, Victory, 1 and 5–6.

49. Ibid.

50. Paull, the son of a miner, could well have been steered away from the mines by his father. Many Butte miners hoped their sons would not have to work in the dangerous mines, but many boys imbibing the masculine culture of the mines and seeking the high pay of miners followed their fathers into the shafts anyway. Oral histories of Butte miners express this dynamic well and also talk about the manly nature of mining. See the Navarro interview, for example.

51. *Meeting Transcripts*, September 3, 1942, Victory, 6.

52. That is not to say the homefront was inherently safe. Industrial accidents and disease were commonplace during the war.

53. *Meeting Transcripts*, September 3, 1942, Victory, 6.

54. *Meeting Transcripts*, October 15, 1942, Victory, 14–18.

55. Ibid.

56. Ibid.

57. Flynn, 77.

58. Most older servicemen had enlisted, but they had a high profile and certainly added to the sense of guilt homefront men experienced.

59. Clifford and Spenser, 74–75.

60. "Occupational Bulletin No. 12," Selective Service System, July 28, 1942, forwarded by the American Mining Congress, Washington, D.C.; and "Memo from the American Mining Congress to Metal and Non-metallic Mine Operators, Re: Deferment Order—Metal and Non-metallic Mines" (signed by Julian D. Conover, Secretary), August 3, 1942, Anaconda Company Records, MC 169, box 70, folder 4, MHSA.

61. *Meeting Transcripts*, October 15, 1942, Victory, 14–18.

62. Ibid.

63. Ibid.

64. Ibid.

65. In fact, although he led a massive federal agency whose purview touched virtually every citizen, male or female, young or old, Hershey's sense that federal government should play the smallest of roles in the everyday life of ordinary working people closely matched that of many westerners. His biographer writes that Hershey felt that "the key to America's republicanism was decentralized government. In the local community people learned and practiced the virtues of cooperation and assumed the responsibility of citizenship." The Selective Service System, with its reliance on local judgment, embodied for Hershey "an application of practical democracy." Flynn, 60 and 77.

66. *Meeting Transcripts*, June 22, 1943, Victory, 2.

67. *Meeting Transcripts*, August 3, 1943, Victory, 6–8.

68. *Meeting Transcripts*, June 22, 1943, Victory, 3–8.

69. Ibid., 4–5.

70. Ibid., 5–7 and 11.

71. Matthew Basso, "'Effect by Contrast': White Male Audiences and the Reading of World War II Newsreels and Feature Films as a Unified Text," *Columbia Journal of American Studies* 4, no. 1 (2000): 128–42.

72. This incident, and those mentioned that occurred in Great Falls and Anaconda, are fully explored in my dissertation in progress.

73. *Copper Commando*, August 22, 1942, 18.

74. Ibid., 15.

75. On operation of white skin privilege see Cheryl I. Harris, "Whiteness as Property," *Harvard Law Review* 106 (1993): 1709–91; and David Roediger, *The Wages of Whiteness* (London: Verso, 1990).

76. Expanding on work by Bruce Nelson and Thomas Sugrue among others, I am arguing that World War II, not the years just after the war, saw the earliest signs of a post-Depression working-class race-based conservatism. Bruce Nelson, "Class, Race, and Democracy in the CIO: The 'New' Labor History Meets the 'Wages of Whiteness,'" *International Review of Social History* 41 (1996): 351–374. Thomas J. Sugrue, "Segmented Work, Race-Conscious Workers: Structure, Agency, and Division in the CIO Era," *International Review of Social History* 41 (1996): 389–406. Regarding the dating of working-class race-based conservatism, Sugrue, supported by the equally groundbreaking research of Arnold R. Hirsch, asserts that the "local politics of race and housing in the aftermath of World War II fostered a grassroots rebellion against liberalism and seriously limited the social democratic and egalitarian possibilities of the New Deal order." Thomas J. Sugrue, "Crabgrass-Roots Politics: Race, Rights, and the Reaction against Liberalism in the Urban North, 1940–1964," *Journal of American History* 82 (September 1995): 552. See Arnold R. Hirsch, *Making the Second Ghetto: Race and Housing in Chicago, 1940–1960* (New York, 1983).

77. Electorally, Republicans made sporadic inroads in Montana from the 1950s through the 1970s, with 1976 hinting most broadly at the change about to take place. Ellis Waldron and Paul B. Wilson, *Atlas of Montana Elections, 1889–1976* (Missoula: University of Montana Publications in History, 1978), 278.

On the Road

Cassady, Kerouac, and Images of
Late Western Masculinity

Craig Leavitt

I walked back in with crazy Dean; he was telling me about the
inscriptions carved on toilet walls in the East and in the West.
  "They're entirely different; in the East they make cracks and
corny jokes and obvious references, scatological bits of data and
drawings; in the West they just write their names, Red O'Hara,
Blufftown Montana, came by here, date, real solemn . . . the reason
being the enormous loneliness that differs just a shade and cut hair
as you move across the Mississippi."
                                          —*Jack Kerouac,* On the Road[1]

In 1947, when a young writer from Massachusetts named Jack Kerouac set
off on a journey to parts west, the United States stood at a crossroads. The
Euro-American civilization of the Atlantic had just exerted itself in world
war; with renewed strength it would soon sweep across the American continent in a wave of economic growth that would everywhere replicate the
tamed and subdued East. Interstate freeways sliced across the Great Plains
and through the vast spaces of the West, bringing with them the homogenized culture of American capital and conformity. Franchised hamburger
stands replaced rickety roadhouses. Large-scale commercial farming and
ranching transformed the independent man of the West into an anachronism, a caricature safe for mass consumption in Hollywood movies.
Television beamed the official, sanitized American culture into every home.
Sprawling suburban tract housing arose from coast to coast, obliterating any
sense of place. The virility of the mythical western man would be neutered,
shrunken to fit into the emerging plastic, prefab postwar world—a world too
small and too civilized to contain his vast, violent energies.

The Old West had essentially disappeared long ago, but its magnetic power continued to draw men like Kerouac, who sought to find some of its mythic flavor and energy. "I'd been poring over maps of the United States in Patterson for months, even reading books about the pioneers and savoring names like Platte and Cimarron," he wrote.[2] He wanted to rediscover something about his country, and about himself, by going west. It was a philosophical quest of sorts: "Somewhere along the line I knew there'd be girls, visions, everything; somewhere along the line the pearl would be handed to me."[3]

The man who handed it to him was Neal Cassady. When Kerouac met his friend and guide, the latter was a footloose youth from Denver, a sometime rancher who had recently been released from a Colorado reformatory and had drifted eastward. Cassady's youth, beauty, keen intellect, and especially his boundless energy inspired much of Kerouac's true-to-life fiction, and thereby the Beat movement.[4] He represented an authenticity Kerouac found lacking in his intellectual New York circles, where he saw his friends "in the negative, nightmare position of putting down society and giving their tired bookish or political or psychoanalytical reasons," but Cassady "just raced in society, eager for bread and love."[5] Philip J. Deloria notes, "Because those seeking authenticity have already defined their own state as inauthentic, they easily locate authenticity in the figure of an Other...the quest for such an authentic Other is a characteristically modern phenomenon."[6] For the urban, eastern, introverted Kerouac, Cassady became this more authentic Other and an idealized image of an alternate Self. The Easterner's literary efforts, including the posthumously published *Visions of Cody* (1972) and especially the highly influential 1957 best-seller *On the Road*, would turn Cassady into a new icon of masculine western freedom and sexual power, an archetype for the Beat and hippie movements, one of the last authentic cultural heroes to emerge from the Wild West.

"With the coming of Dean Moriarty began the part of my life you could call my life on the road," wrote Kerouac, using the character name he had given to the portrait of his friend, Cassady. "Dean is the perfect guy for the road because he was actually born on the road, when his parents were passing through Salt Lake City in 1926, in a jalopy, on their way to Los Angeles."[7] Cassady was indeed fated for a restless and roaming life. Some of his childhood was spent with his mother in the slums of Depression-era Denver. For much of the rest he tagged along with his alcoholic father, a classic western hobo, on his seasonal ramblings in search of warm weather and drink. Watching his father and his companions, young Neal studied a distinct culture of manhood.

In *The First Third*, a partial autobiography published posthumously in 1971, Cassady himself wrote about learning the empty, ritualized language common to a certain brand of uncultured western man:

Their conversation had many general statements about Truth and Life, which contained the collective intelligence of all America's bums. They were drunkards whose minds, weakened by liquor and an obsequious manner of existence, seemed continually preoccupied with bringing up short observations of obvious trash, said in such a way as to be instantly recognizable to the listener, who had heard it all before, and whose own prime concern was to nod at everything said, then continue the conversation with a remark of his own, equally transparent and loaded with generalities. The simplicity of this pattern was marvelous, and there was no limit to what they could agree on in this fashion, to say nothing of the abstract ends that could be reached.[8]

This hobo's dialectic reveals the origins of Cassady's own virtuoso verbal style, which Kerouac marveled at and portrayed with great care. But unlike the vagrants and their anti-intellectual western forefathers, young Neal did not scorn book learning. He craved it, managing to give himself a fair education as he survived on the streets of Denver with the father who could not care for either of them properly. "In the West he'd spent a third of his time in the poolhall," Kerouac wrote, "a third in jail, and a third in the public library."[9] Cassady asked Kerouac to teach him to write, but Kerouac would later insist that Cassady's rambling letters inspired his own free-flowing prose style. One of these, written to a mutual friend from reform school before Cassady and the Massachusetts writer crossed paths, charmed Kerouac with its intellectual ambition. "I was tremendously interested in the letters because they so naively and sweetly asked Chad to teach him all about Nietzsche and all the wonderfully intellectual things."[10] Biographer William Plummer notes that young Cassady's favorite writers included "Schopenhauer and Proust: the philosopher who portrayed man as a creature of will and desire rather than intellect; the novelist who fabricated a world of sensation and pure consciousness, who measured time not by the clock but on the pulse."[11] Cassady's energies turned back from the closed frontier to the project of entering the great body of world knowledge, albeit in his own highly informal way. But as Kerouac would show, Cassady was most at home not in a library, but behind the wheel of a fast car.

As machine-driven industrialized civilization strengthened its grasp on the American West, the old symbols of virility and power changed. One of Kerouac's contemporaries, author Edward Abbey, portrayed the decline of the horse, once an all-important extension of the cowboy's physical presence, in the opening pages of his 1956 novel *The Brave Cowboy*. When his anachronistic hero tries to ride into town on a mare named Whisky, man and beast find their way blocked by a bustling highway built for trucks and automobiles. Whisky "recoiled at the touch of pavement"; the barriers to horsemanship presented by the burgeoning postwar highway system were such that "though he rode for years he would find no end to it; the track of asphalt and concrete was as continuous and endless as a circle or the walls of a cell."[12]

Like the horse, the six-shooter no longer reigned supreme as phallic projector of western masculine power; the automobile took its place as well. It was no longer necessary for the Euro-American to battle Native Americans to dominate the wide-open spaces of the West. That deathly work had been done, and now the postwar white male could "reconquer" the West for himself with the car. A fast and powerful automobile became the ultimate symbol of manhood in postwar America, especially in the West, where the machine gives man power and dominance over the once daunting geographical expanses. Wolfgang Zuckermann notes that the "sexual symbolism equating the automobile with masculinity is well-known," and is often exploited by car advertisers who play upon the fragile self-images of young men who feel constant pressure to reaffirm their masculinity.[13]

"I stole my first automobile in 1940," Cassady wrote, "by '47 when swearing off such soul-thrilling pleasures to celebrate advent into manhood, I had had illegally in my possession about 500 cars—whether just for the moment and to be taken back to its owner before he returned (I.E. on Parking lots) or whether taken for the purpose of so altering its appearance as to keep it for several weeks but mostly only for joyriding."[14] As a Denver teenager, Cassady regularly stole a car in the afternoon, went by East High School as classes were letting out to pick up girls, and, if he was "lucky," drove one up to the mountains for a sexual encounter before returning girl and car to the city limits in the evening. In *On the Road*, in one of the several cross-country trips, an older Cassady leaves his friends to wait while he uses a borrowed Cadillac to pick up a waitress for a quick score:

> From where I stood in the door I saw a faint flash of the Cadillac crossing Cleveland Place with Dean, T-shirted and joyous, fluttering his hands and talking to the girl and hunching over the wheel to go as she sat sadly and proudly beside him. They went to a parking lot in broad daylight, parked near the brick wall at the back (a lot Dean had worked in once), and there, he claims, he made it with her, in nothing flat. . . . Thirty minutes and Dean roared back, deposited the girl at her hotel, with kisses, farewells, promises, and zoomed right up to the travel bureau to pick up the crew.[15]

Auto and libido were synonymous throughout Cassady's life, and the natural symbolism of car as cock was irresistible to the novelist Kerouac. He portrayed Dean Moriarty as "the greatest driver in the world," a force of nature who terrified good citizens with his frightening speed and recklessness behind the wheel.

Dean came up on lines of cars like the Angel of Terror. He almost rammed them along as he looked for an opening. He teased their bumpers, he eased and pushed and craned around to see the curve, then the huge car leaped to his touch and passed, and always by a hair we made it back to our side as other lines filed by in the opposite direction and I shuddered. I couldn't take it any more.... All that old road of the past reeling dizzily as if the cup of life had been overturned and everything had gone mad.[16]

In *On the Road*, the automobile takes on a metaphysical quality, projecting its occupants beyond ordinary time and space into a realm of mythic freedom and power. "Ah, man, what a dreamboat," Moriarty says as he and Kerouac's self-styled narrator, Sal Paradise, hurtle through the Nebraska night at 110 mph in a borrowed car.

"Think if you and I had a car like this what we could do. Do you know there's a road that goes down Mexico and all the way to Panama?—and maybe all the way to the bottom of South America where the Indians are seven feet tall and eat cocaine on the mountainside? Yes! You and I, Sal, we'd dig the whole world with a car like this because, man, the road must eventually lead to the whole world. Ain't nowhere else it can go—right?"[17]

Cassady would have not only the world, but all its women. Observable throughout Kerouac's literary reckoning with the West is an implicit recognition of a culture with much looser sexual mores than the relatively staid and civilized Massachusetts of his youth. Cassady embodies this freer sexuality. Kerouac takes pains to show the titanic virility of his hero asserting itself in early adolescence, writing that "ever since thirteen Cody [another pseudonym for Cassady] was able to handle any woman and in fact had pushed his drunken father off Cherry Lucy Halloween night 1939 and taken over so much that they fist fought like rivals and Cody ran away with the five dollar stake."[18] Cassady himself wrote of his sexual initiation at age nine. Young Neal accompanied his father to the home of a drinking buddy, "a feeble-minded German drunkard," who lived with his wife and no less than twelve children in an old barn in southwest Denver. "Here, made freer by watching the numerous brothers unselfconsciously smoke, cuss and fight together on outlaw forays through sparse neighborhood between creekbed and field, I soon followed the leader in screwing all the sisters small enough to hold down—and those bold enough to lead."[19] This scene of debauchery, incest, and rape, while only a sample of the bizarre environs of Cassady's childhood, sheds much light on the sexual ethics, or lack thereof, of the mature man. Under the eyes of his own inebriated father, who should have represented authority and discipline in the boy's life but who in fact knew nothing of such things himself, Neal learned about sex in an orgy in which the line between pleasure and force was blurred, and any female was a potential sex object. Plummer comments, "It was no wonder that in full maturity, Cassady was never able to fully credit the idea of rape."[20]

Early in *On the Road*, Dean steals a young Denver beauty named Camille from a friend and keeps her ensconced in a hotel room while he pursues his all-night kicks with male buddies and other women. Camille tries to establish when he will return to her:

> "Well, all right, Dean, but please be sure and be back at three."
> "Just as I said, darling, and remember not three but three-four-teen. Are we straight in the deepest and most wonderful depths of our souls, dear darling?" And he went over and kissed her several times. On the wall was a nude drawing of Dean, enormous dangle and all, done by Camille. I was amazed.[21]

In fiction and in reality, Cassady's life was an impossible tangle of connections to different women. He sometimes had two wives at once, and much of the travel portrayed in *On the Road* involves racing back and forth between them. Each woman served a temporary purpose in his ongoing quest for "more"; all were ultimately expendable. But despite—or perhaps because of—its amoral quality, the ecstatic, open-ended sexuality of Moriarty and *On the Road* appealed to readers and foreshadowed the coming rejection of traditional sexual mores by many young American women and men in the 1960's.

Cassady, however, was not all speed and phallic projection and dominance. His was a deeply wounded and nuanced sexuality. Unlike the cowboy tough-guy, Cassady represented a masculinity that was interested in self-knowledge. Reading and jazz helped develop his sensitivity to the human condition. His aggressive sexuality aside, Cassady loathed violence. During the months spent in a Denver tenement with his mother and her family, Cassady's older half-brother Jimmy bullied him and his feeble, alcoholic father mercilessly and forced Neal to fight other boys in the neighborhood. Jimmy and his friends also enjoyed drowning or thrashing stray cats to death, horrifying the young Neal. The negative example of Jimmy's brutality influenced Neal's sensibilities greatly. As a child, "Neal was always the youngest and smallest in a volatile world of desperate men and men-children," and he soon learned that "competition with others was unavailing: it only brought on potentially violent situations."[22] This stance is at wide variance with the traditional western attitude, in which manly skills and manhood itself had to be frequently tested and proved, often through violent means.

Another dramatic change from the older western model of masculinity was Cassady's propensity for enthusiastic self-expression. Western heroes of the past were not known for being extraordinarily articulate; seldom did the lone gunman ride into town, belly up to the bar, and pour out his soul to his peers. In Jack Warner Shaefer's *Shane*, a novel that represents "a kind of archetype, exhibiting with remarkable purity all the basic components of the classical Western,"[23] the hero for whom the story is named enters the community as a total stranger—"he has no family, no friends, and no ties."[24] At the conclusion of the tale, after Shane has vanquished the villain and saved the community, he disappears again into the wilderness without having revealed much of his own story; he remains a mystery to the community he has rescued.

The Cassady image of western masculinity takes the opposite tack: in the Beat milieu it is manly to tell all. Cassady enters the community, represented by Kerouac and his New York circle of friends, and ignites the Beat movement by awing the easterners with his endless tales of life in the West. He tells about the adventures and deprivations of childhood on the street, about his highly unconventional sex life, about the pain and isolation of his lonely condition. In so doing, he helped other men come out of themselves as well. As the last road trip of *On the Road* begins, Dean Moriarty, Sal Paradise, and their friend Stan Shephard hurtle south from Denver toward Mexico. Kerouac shows the power Cassady had to help other men bring their inner lives into the open:

> We all decided to tell our stories, but one by one, and Stan was first. "We've got a long way to go," preambled Dean, "and so you must take every indulgence and deal with every single detail you can bring to mind—and still it won't all be told. Easy, easy," he cautioned Stan, who began telling his story, "you've got to relax too." Stan swung into his life story as we shot across the dark. He started with his experiences in France but to round-out ever-growing difficulties he came back and started at the beginning with his boyhood in Denver...Stan was nervous and feverish. He wanted to tell Dean everything. Dean was now arbiter, old man, judge, listener, approver, nodder. "Yes, yes, go on please."[25]

The far-ranging self-disclosure of Cassady's confessions to Kerouac, the basis of both *On the Road* and *Visions of Cody*, mark a watershed for the western male: a celebration of his ability to reveal self and soul to another man.

Cassady was also bisexual, in dramatic counterpoint to the rigidly heterosexual traditional cowboy masculine ideal. *The First Third* records several homosexual assaults on Neal as a child. The beginning of his friendship with Allen Ginsberg, gay poet and giant of Beat literature, was marked by a sexual affair that continued on and off for months. "My soul melted, secrecy departed, I became / Thenceforth open to his nature as a flower in the shining sun,"[26] gushed Ginsberg in a poem about the first night of the affair. Cassady's heart was not in it; like so much else in the drifter's life, sex with another man was an experiment. Ginsberg, however, was smitten with the handsome young Cassady, and even persuaded him to kneel by a Texas roadside and take improvised vows of eternal spiritual union. Later Ginsberg acknowledged, "By hindsight I realize he was obviously just being nice to me, humoring me."[27]

In *On the Road*, Cassady tries to use his flexible sexuality for strategic gain with a man who has offered the travelers a ride. The more conventional, eastern Kerouac distances himself with homophobic language:

> In the hotel room, Dean tried everything in the book to get money from the fag. It was insane. The fag began by saying he was very glad we had come along because he liked young men like us, and would we believe it, but he really didn't like girls and had recently concluded an affair with a man in Frisco in which he had taken the male role and the man the female role. Dean plied him with businesslike questions and nodded eagerly. The fag said he would like nothing better than to know what Dean thought about all this. Warning him first that he had once been a hustler in his youth, Dean asked him how much money he had. The fag became extremely sullen and I think suspicious of Dean's final motives, turned over no money, and made vague promises for Denver. . . . Dean threw up his hands and gave up. . . . "Offer them what they want and they of course immediately become panic-stricken." But he had sufficiently conquered the owner of the Plymouth to take over the wheel without remonstrance, and now we really traveled.[28]

Cassady's openness to the full range of human experience was one of the qualities Kerouac admired most in him. In a short essay entitled "America's New Trinity of Love: Dean, Brando, Presley," Kerouac discusses the expanded emotional capabilities of a new kind of ideal man: "Up to now the American Hero has always been on the defensive: he killed Indians and villains and beat up his rivals and surled. He has been good-looking but never compassionate except at odd moments and only in stock situations. Now the new American hero...is the image of compassion in itself. It is as though Christ and Buddha were about to come again with masculine love for the woman at last."[29] The new ideal clearly extends to and is indeed embodied by Keroauc's new western hero.

Once dismissed by the intellectual establishment, Kerouac is now the subject of growing posthumous popularity and respect. In 1998, the *Atlantic Monthly* proclaimed his "full ascension to academic respectability."[30] *On the*

Road is indisputably the major foundation of his reputation. So why did a rambling narrative about the travels of a college dropout from Massachusetts and his promiscuous, fast-talking friend from Colorado become an important cultural document? Its impact on American culture in the late 1950s and the 1960s was considerable. "Especially for young males, *On the Road* was something far more than an apology for hipsterism," writes Plummer. "They felt in their marrow what was classically American in Kerouac's book. . . . Like so many American tales, *On the Road* is about escape, about lighting out for the perpetually receding territory ahead."[31] The "escape" many young people wanted to make in the 1950s and 60s was from what they saw as a restrictive and repressive middle-class American culture. Conformity was king and personal expression was frowned upon. Plummer writes, "As Dean Moriarty, [Cassady] was hugely attractive to countless alienated and emotionally hamstrung young men and women."[32] To understand why Cassady became an icon of western masculinity with a national profile, it is helpful to consider certain components of American masculinity and their development over the years.

American masculinity reached another of its perpetual crisis points in the years after World War II.[33] The sweeping triumph of technological capitalism made the strong back of the American worker irrelevant. For upper- and middle-class white men, the rise of corporate office culture created a vast divide between fathers and sons. When a boy grew up working with his father in the fields of the family farm or at an old-style trade such as blacksmithing or shoemaking, the day-to-day physical closeness and the transmission of expertise from father to son usually created deep sympathy and love. Even the factory labor that engaged so many American men in the twentieth century was relatively rich in fraternal camaraderie and filial sensibility. But what happened when a father worked away from his children in the stereotypical suburban corporate commuter arrangement that took hold in the postwar years and beyond?

> When a father, absent during the day, returns home at six, his children receive only his temperament, not his teaching. If the father is working for a corporation, what is there to teach? He is reluctant to tell his son what is really going on. The fragmentation of decision-making in corporate life, the massive effort that produces the corporate willingness to destroy the environment for the sake of profit, the prudence, even cowardice, that one learns in bureaucracy—who wants to teach that?[34]

Even more distance was created in the 1960s between young men and the society of their fathers by the Vietnam War. American militarism after World War II increasingly served an unjust, oligarchic capitalism, yet perversely dressed itself in the rhetoric of an idealized democracy that did not really exist in the segregated and unequal United States. The military masculine model was tarnished for a whole generation, and the unfulfilled democratic ideal unmasked. "The older men in the military establishment and government did betray the younger men in Vietnam, lying about the nature of war, remaining in safe places themselves, after having asked the young men to be warriors and then in effect sending them out to be ordinary murderers."[35]

Just as Cassady was coming of age, the emergence of new musical forms into the mainstream of American life further contributed to the distance between old and young. Jazz, rhythm and blues, and later rock and roll became available to whites on a mass scale due to radio and phonograph technology, and they excited middle-class white youth with their passion and sexual energy, qualities not welcomed by the "polite" Anglo-American establishment.

Changes in the culture of work, and disagreement over the meaning of American democracy and how its interests were best served, coupled with the growing influence of provocative African-American music, served to alienate young, white, middle- to upper-class men from the ideas of masculinity held by their fathers. Many sought a new cultural paradigm that would allow them to make sense of the world and their place in it, a way of being male that would permit more freedom from conformity and would allow for greater expression of masculine passions. The result was the "existential hero."[36]

Anthony Rotundo, author of *American Manhood*, notes a change in the male relation to self in the twentieth century. "Middle-class Americans of the 1800's often viewed the inner movings of the self with Calvinistic suspicion," he writes.[37] Self-expression was considered dangerous. Masculine passion, originating in the self rather than in society, was to be carefully controlled. The self was to be manipulated to other ends, generally economic in nature and derived from the salient "Protestant work ethic." But Rotundo perceives a change. "Where nineteenth-century views had regarded the self and its passions suspiciously as objects of manipulation (self-control, self-denial), twentieth-century opinion exalted them as the source of identity and personal worth (self-expression, self-enjoyment)."[38]

But, paradoxically, most American men in the 1950s lacked true outlets for their passions. Consumerism, mainstream society's major means of creating and measuring identity, was utterly unsatisfying for many. Social roles grew more constrained just as the pressure on masculine identity grew stronger. Rotundo argues that in this tumultuous period, the existential hero represents a new "strategy for establishing a relationship between male passion and modern life." In a formulation that summarizes the Beat mystique as rendered by Kerouac, he asserts that "this ideal grows out of a belief that there is, in fact, no proper place for true masculine impulse within modern society. The hero who lives by this belief is suspicious of authority, wary of women, and disgusted by corrupt civilization. If he would be true to the purity of his male passions and principles, he must—and can only—live at the margins of society."[39]

Rotundo cites such popular figures as Humphrey Bogart, Ernest Hemingway, and John Wayne as existential icons in this mold. He also points to the American cult of the entrepreneur, the economic renegade who powers advances in capitalism by taking risks in speculative ventures without the collective safety of the corporation. Rotundo, however, steers clear of examining the real existential movement in America: the counterculture. His profile of the existential hero is more accurately personified by rebellious postwar personalities like James Dean, Bob Dylan, and Jack Kerouac, though none fits the type better than Neal Cassady. Under the pressures of a shallow and materialistic culture, middle- and upper-class American men looked to the ostracized poor and minority cultures for models, for modes of living that would allow a man to live passionately, true to himself in a larger culture that seemed anything but genuine. The African-American blues singer was one such model; the attitude affected by every rocker from Elvis Presley on owes much to the existential pose of the traveling blues singer who lives on the margins of society. Kerouac jolted American literature in much the same way Presley did music, by bringing the new existential hero to the fore. Cassady represents a white, Western version of this passionate, alienated masculine persona. As portrayed by Kerouac in *On the Road*, Cassady was a breath of fresh air to readers who admired his uninhibited sexuality, sly philosophical humor, and most of all his total commitment to personal freedom. He was one of the first western icons of the American counterculture, and would later, after parting ways with Kerouac, preside over the flowering of a uniquely western counterculture that endures to this day.

One of the most striking connections between Kerouac's vision and that of the traditional western writer is his use of what scholar Max Westbrook would call "sacrality."

> Certainly a substantial number of Western writers believe that Western experience…is the nation's best chance of healing the wounds caused by the Puritans when they made us feel ashamed of our bodies, afraid of the voice that comes from our dark and inner selves, apologetic for our worldly ambitions. Western writers have thus faced anew the ancient and sometimes American hope—the effort to discover the unity of body, soul, and land.[40]

Westbrook gives this acceptance of the spiritual quality inherent in the material world, in the flesh and its desires, the name *sacrality*: an "other way of thinking—a belief in the possibility of knowing through the unity of thought and things."[41] Within such a paradigm, virile masculinity can be celebrated without Puritanical hesitation or guilt. Sacrality is perhaps the major theme of *On the Road* and Dean Moriarty one of its staunchest champions in American literature. Puritanical shame was unknown to him; the record of his exploits in Kerouac's books served as an important volley in the counterculture's assault on the barrier between soul and body in American culture. "To him, sex was the one and only holy and important thing in life," Kerouac wrote, "although he had to sweat and curse to make a living and so on."[42] Kerouac and Cassady believed that through sex, as well as through travel, meeting and "digging" different people of all kinds, through sheer intensity of experience, they could reach the truth about themselves and the world. "'Everything is fine,'" Moriarty proclaims from behind the wheel, "'God exists, we know time. Everything since the Greeks has been predicated wrong. You can't make it with geometry and geometrical systems of thinking. It's all this!' He wrapped his finger in his fist; the car hugged the line straight and true."[43] And yet the acceptance of the holiness of life did not solve the problem of living. For all their philosophical acumen, the heroes of *On the Road* found no lasting satisfaction, no resolution to their yearnings, no place where they were content to hang their hats for long. Instead, they wandered on.

For Cassady, the desperation and isolation of his troubled life redoubled his masculine sexual need. Camille Paglia could have been referring to Cassady when she wrote, "Male sexuality is inherently manic-depressive. Men are in a constant state of sexual anxiety, living on the pins and needles of their hormones. In sex and in life they are driven *beyond*—beyond the self, beyond the body. . . . But to be beyond is to be exiled from the center of life. Men know they are sexual exiles. They wander the earth seeking satisfaction, craving and despising, never content."[44] The male heterosexual mania to reenter the woman, to regain the center, has shaped and indeed dominated the lives of many men. Kerouac writes of hearing his friend make love to his wife in the next room: "I could hear Dean, blissful and blabbering and frantically rocking. Only a guy who's spent five years in jail can go to such maniacal helpless extremes; beseeching at the portals of the soft source, mad with a completely physical realization of the origins of life-bliss; blindly seeking to return the way he came."[45]

Neal Cassady, "exiled from the center of life" with no family, no fixed home, and little stake in the world of money-making and consumerism, had nowhere to go but "beyond." Like the mythic cowboy, he was outside of society, outside of the law. The protagonists of *On the Road* circle endlessly, looking for but never quite finding the center of America, the world, themselves. This sense of lonely wandering and isolation from community is one of the many links between Kerouac's book and the tradition of Western books and films, from which the American culture derives its image of western masculinity. As Will Wright explains, the primary theme of the Western is the relationship between an independent heroic figure and the society he defends—an often difficult and ambiguous relationship. Wright shows that early Westerns, using what he calls the "Classical" plot, generally featured a lone hero with special talents (usually for violence) entering a community to which he is a stranger, defeating a villain or other evil that threatens this community, then becoming an accepted citizen of the grateful town, often sealing this new status by marrying a woman from the rescued population. But as time went on, Wright notes, more and more Westerns presented heroes who rejected membership in the communities they had delivered from evil. Some heroes seemed unwilling to give up their special independent (existential) status, or simply deemed the community in question unworthy. This change reflects the growing existential suspicion of society and its values in the post–World War II decades.

In such an era, Neal Cassady made a natural hero for a generation of disaffected youth. His special talent was not for gun-fighting but for passionate living: lovemaking, drug-taking, spontaneous action without regard to social norms. While often these are highly debatable behaviors, they were in fact the core values of the '60s generation's counterculture. Alienated by the materialism and rigidity of the dominant culture, many took to the Beat vision described by Kerouac and personified by his wandering hero.

This juxtaposition between "hip" and "square" resonates in the Beat worldview and reflects the Beats' perception of a large gap between virile, independent Western settlers and their "softer" eastern contemporaries. "Luxury," wrote Mody C. Boatright of the eastern way of life resisted by protagonists of the earliest, genre-setting cowboy fiction, "had...created an effete society, governed not by natural human relationships but by convention, which tended to deprive men of their masculinity and women of their natural social role."[46] There was nothing effete about Neal Cassady. Kerouac waxed eloquent when writing about just how far on the outside of all convention, social respectability, and protection the young Cassady really was:

> Have you ever seen anyone like Cody Pomeray?—say on a street corner in Chicago, or better, Fargo, any mighty cold town, a young guy with a bony face that looks like it's been pressed against iron bars to get that dogged rocky look of suffering, perseverance . . . poor pitiful kid actually just out of reform school with no money, no mother, and if you saw him dead on the sidewalk with a cop standing over him you'd walk on in a hurry, in silence. Oh life, who is that? There are some young men you look at who seem completely safe, maybe just because of a Scandinavian ski sweater, angelic, saved; on a Cody Pomeray it immediately becomes a dirty stolen sweater worn in wild sweats. . . . It is a face that's so suspicious, so energetically upward-looking like people in

passport police lineup photos, so rigidly itself, looking like it's about to do anything unspeakably enthusiastic, in fact so much the opposite of the rosy Coke-drinking boy in the Scandinavian ski sweater ad, that in front of a brick wall where it says *Post No Bills* and it's too dirty for a rosy boy ad you can imagine Cody standing there in the raw gray flesh manacled between sheriffs and Assistant D.A.'s and you wouldn't have to ask yourself who is the culprit and who is the law.[47]

Cassady did indeed have trouble with the law. His poverty, orphanhood, and Beat cultural orientation made him a target for the police throughout his life. As a teen, he spent much time answering to the authorities due to his predilection for stealing cars. In 1958, just after the success of *On the Road* had given him some modicum of fame, he was arrested and served more than two years in prison for giving two joints of marijuana to undercover policemen who picked him up in their car, offering him a ride to his job on the railroad. Friends suspected the authorities had singled him out because of his counterculture notoriety. Ginsberg and other prominent writers attended Cassady's legal proceedings and agitated for his release, painting him as a martyr of antidrug and anti-Beat hysteria. Marijuana, something of a totem for the existential counterculture, signified the user's rejection of corrupt material society and commitment to a new idea of personal freedom, the all-important western value.

Cassady's letters to his wife Carolyn, compiled in *Grace Beats Karma: Letters from Prison 1958–1960*, show a man struggling to maintain his masculinity and self-respect despite the humiliation of prison life. He became heavily involved in a Catholic prayer practice and excelled in courses in comparative religion while behind bars. Nonetheless, jailing a man of Cassady's independence and boundless energy took its toll. Being deprived of the ability to care for his wife and children (for after all his wandering and adventure, he had settled down and tried to content himself with family life for several years as he worked on the railroad in California) was particularly painful. He wrote to his wife that upon release, "I want to work myself to death, seriously, a kind of legitimate suicide."[48] But after Cassady's release from jail in 1960, the marriage soured. Carolyn had refused to put up the house for Neal's bail money, fearing he would take to the road and leave his family in the lurch. In addition, she made plans to travel overseas at the expense of a male friend whom she hinted would make a good father and provider for the children. Cassady's resentment over this perceived betrayal smoldered. He lost a good job on the railroad due to his long incarceration. Now in his mid-thirties, Neal faced the extinction of work, home, and family; things he craved deeply but which were ultimately incompatible with his freewheeling nature.

Cassady's relationships with women had always been passionate, unstable, even dangerous. The tremendous need Neal felt for women had a dark underside. Though he was much more likely to abandon a woman than to physically harm her, the latter was not out of the question. Kerouac reports: "Marylou [LuAnne, Neal's first wife] was black and blue from a fight with Dean about something; his face was scratched."[49] A fair "fight" between the teenage LuAnne and her muscular husband was impossible. Second wife Carolyn also reported moments of brutality: "He was a raging animal; this could only be lust, not love. . . . The only way he was not able to do it was when I was offering or willing. It had to be rape. Until finally I only submitted because I was afraid of him. At last, then, I said, 'I can't stand it anymore, kill me or whatever,' and much to my surprise he was very nice about it, he seemed to understand."[50] The links between young Neal's bizarre sexual initiation in the German drunkard's barn, his adult desire to dominate women, and his proclivity for flight from commitment are hard to miss.

"It was equally his motif, as it was his father's," writes Plummer about twenty-two-year old Neal learning of Carolyn's first pregnancy in 1948, "to dismantle 'families,' to flee and disappoint his loved ones at precisely the moment he felt the pressure of their expectation. Now, confronted with fatherhood and weighed down by assorted failures, he could not shake the feeling of 'ennuied hysteria.'"[51] His work hours cut due to a slow-down in railroad traffic, unable or unwilling to cope with the pressure, Cassady took the family savings, bought a '49 Hudson Hornet, picked up first wife LuAnne, and raced cross-country to find Kerouac for one of the rounds of traveling recorded in *On the Road*. Beat writer and friend William Burroughs was harsh in his assessment: "Wife and child may starve, friends exist only to exploit for gas money. Neal must move."[52] True to Rotundo's profile of the existential male hero, Cassady was more committed to the fulfillment of his fickle passions than he ever could be to a particular woman. Kerouac wrote uncritically about his friend's cavalier attitude toward women; he intimated that the moral fallout and emotional debris created by Neal's wild twists and turns were a fair price to pay for the freedom thus gained.

But not even in the decidedly masculine world of *On the Road* could a man avoid the wrath of women scorned forever. One scene places Dean on the hot seat in front of a group of women led by Galatea Dunkel, a tarot-card reader whose husband, Ed, has been lost to her for months due to Dean-inspired wanderings. Dean's thumb has grown infected from an injury sustained in a fight with Camille [Carolyn], who has just kicked him out the house, and he paces in a nervous sweat as his crimes against women and humanity in general are enumerated:

It wasn't anything but a sewing circle, and the center of it was the culprit, Dean—responsible, perhaps, for everything that was wrong. . . ."I think Camille was very, very wise leaving you, Dean," said Galatea. "For years now you haven't had any sense of responsibility for anyone. You've done so many awful things I don't know what to say to you." . . . They all sat around looking at Dean with lowered and hating eyes, and he stood on the carpet in the middle of them and giggled—he just giggled. He made a little dance. His bandage was getting dirtier all the time; it began to flop and unroll. . . . "You have absolutely no regard for anybody but yourself and your damn kicks. All you think about is what's hanging between your legs and how much money or fun you can get out of people and then you just throw them aside..." Then a complete silence fell over everybody; where once Dean would have talked his way out, he now fell silent himself, but standing in front of everybody, ragged and broken and idiotic, right under the lightbulbs, his bony mad face covered with sweat and throbbing veins, saying, "Yes, yes, yes," as though tremendous revelations were pouring into him all the time now, and I am convinced they were.[53]

Kerouac's invocation of mysticism to defend Cassady's irresponsible behavior is at best only partially satisfying. The existential strategy comes with enormous costs; it represents a reaction to society, but not a new model upon which societies can be built. The generation inspired by *On the Road* would learn this the hard way as their movement collapsed under the weight of drugs and sexual chaos in the late '60s. Kerouac probably understood this well, but favored the freedom of the individual at whatever cost.

The Massachusetts author was transformed by his travels with the charismatic Westerner. By the end of *On the Road*, the narrator has absorbed the lonely wandering persona of his drifting friend, if not all of his monstrous energy. A deep feeling for the great wide-open spaces west of the Mississippi emanates from his flowing prose. He offers his own melancholy cowboy song as he rolls across the darkened plains on a midnight bus to Denver:

Home in Missoula,
Home in Truckee,
Home in Opelousas,
Ain't no home for me.
Home in old Medora,
Home in Wounded Knee,
Home in Oglalla,
Home I'll never be.[54]

The success of the book did little to give Kerouac peace. In the '60s, he grew increasingly reclusive; he was living with his mother, drinking heavily, reading Buddhism, and writing, but with greatly diminished energy. Cassady's achievements as a writer were slim; he lacked the focus and discipline to get much done at the typewriter. Kerouac would come to see this as a virtue. In one of his last and best books, *Big Sur* (1962), the eastern observer praised Cassady's commitment to worldly action over literary abstraction: "I can see from glancing at him that becoming a writer holds no interest for him because life is holy for him there's no need to do anything but live it, writing's just an afterthought or a scratch anyway at the surface."[55] Kerouac's writings about Cassady, among other things, represent the detached eastern intellect romanticizing the vigorous Western masculine principle. Though Kerouac eventually got off the road, Cassady could not stay off it for long. He knew no other way.

Independently of his friend Jack, Cassady became a leading figure in a uniquely western branch of the emerging American counterculture. On October 13, 1955, the San Francisco Poetry Renaissance began with a much-heralded poetry reading at the Six Gallery in the city by the bay. Beat poets from the East Coast symbolically linked arms that night with a circle of talented San Francisco writers, including Gary Snyder and Lawrence Ferlinghetti, effectively expanding the province of Beat literature from a small New York cabal to a national movement. Easterner Ginsberg organized the Six Gallery event and used it to introduce his best-remembered poem, "Howl." After *On the Road*, "Howl" is the most famous document of the Beat movement and, like Kerouac's book, took Neal Cassady as its major inspiration and archetype: "N.C., secret hero of these poems, cocksman and Adonis of Denver."[56] Cassady attended the reading in his railroad brakeman's uniform and is reported to have enjoyed himself immensely.

After his turn-of-the-decade jailing and final break with Carolyn, Neal was on the road again. Another hip young novelist, Ken Kesey, took Cassady under his wing. Cassady became part of Kesey's "Merry Pranksters," a communal cult based in northern California and bound by psychedelic drugs and a determination to unmask the empty social role-playing "games" Kesey felt dominated the American culture. The main weapon in Kesey's quixotic campaign to free America from itself was LSD. Mid-'60s "acid test" parties brought together literary figures with groups as disparate as pacifist rockers The Grateful Dead and aggressive motorcycle gang the Hell's Angels in a freeform atmosphere in which the now stereotypically Californian[57] values of freedom, individuality and free love were the common denominator. Neal's celebrity was used as a draw to lure the curious into the bacchanalias of drugs and amplified guitar music; his monologues entranced roomfuls of people at a time. Grateful Dead lyricist John Barlow describes the advanced state of Neal's verbal abilities: "He would carry on five different conversations at once and still devote one conversational channel to discourse with absent persons and another to such sound effects as disintegrating ring gears or exploding crania. To log into one of these conversations, despite their multiplicity, was like trying to take a sip from a firehose."[58] "Cassady's raps," as they were known, were rhapsodic monologues in which the Denver hobos' empty, self-concealing drone-chatter about "Truth and Life," as described in *The First Third*, exploded into a singular art form of deeply felt and exhaustively articulated self-expression. For all their psychedelic wit, the Cassady raps retained the flavor of the dusty West. Novelist Robert Stone called Neal's epic musings "Forties stuff. . . old-time jail and musician and street patter." "American-Denver talk," Plummer surmises, "what Kerouac liked to think of as Okie drawl, but with free-lancing Proustian detail."[59]

Cassady's stint with Kesey sealed his image as a titanic, larger-than-life icon of western masculinity. At the age of forty, his physique was rock-hard; his favored pastime flipping a small sledgehammer endlessly to maintain and display his chiseled torso in the California sun. The sexual conquests continued unabated. The burgeoning West-coast hippie scene and Neal's unique celebrity ensured a steady stream of willing women. "Neal would take his women through a whole lifetime of relationships in about an hour," reported Grateful Dead bandleader Jerry Garcia. "He would keep them up for about a week and they'd all become sort of blank from the intensity of the relationship."[60]

Best of all for Cassady, he was given the driver's seat on "Furthur," a converted 1939 International Harvester school bus that Kesey bought to drive the Merry Pranksters around the country for a series of acid-inspired publicity stunts. The bus' very name, deliberate misspelling notwithstanding, indicates a continuation of the *On the Road* motif of motor vehicle as instrument for conquest of both physical and psychic terrain. The bus journeys as well as the California acid parties were recorded by Tom Wolfe in *The Electric Kool-Aid Acid Test* (1968). Though several notches below Kerouac's road book as literature, the popular success of the latter tome did repeat and fix the image of Cassady as existential helmsman of the highway. The road trip has since become an enshrined institution of American youth, a favored rite of passage for thousands of young men and women who travel the roads each summer, often simply for the sake of movement itself.

But not even Cassady could keep moving forever. The years of nonstop drugs, sex, wandering, and kicks took their toll. Friends reported a growing sense of blankness, a loss of the once inexhaustible sense of fun. In a last desperate visit to Carolyn in 1967, Neal confessed he was losing his ability to perform, to play the role of existential acid-cowboy that friends and strangers alike expected from him. Everyone "expected him to be Superman, and he couldn't."[61] The titanic masculine image, first created by Kerouac's earnest observations of a Colorado kid being himself, had grown so heavy and burdensome that the man who inspired it could no longer carry its considerable weight. "Kerouassady," he jokingly called himself; by then he was an amalgam of himself and a mythic hero invented by another man. In February 1968, Neal died from an overdose of alcohol and pills while walking a long stretch of railroad near a town called Celaya in Mexico, traditional retreat of Western heroes.

Notes

1. Jack Kerouac, *On the Road* (New York: Viking, 1957), 267.

2. Ibid., 12.

3. Ibid., 11.

4. John Holmes defined the Beat generation as "A cultural revolution . . . made by a post–World War II generation of disaffiliated young people coming of age into a Cold War world without spiritual values they could honor." Introduction to Anne Charters, ed., *The Portable Beat Reader* (New York: Viking Penguin, 1992), xx. Beat Literature was characterized by its rebellious attitude toward the social order, its embrace of sexuality, drugs, and spirituality, and by its focus on the unique visions and experiences of the individual.

5. Kerouac, *On the Road,* 10.

6. Philip J. Deloria, *Playing Indian* (New Haven: Yale University Press, 1998), 101.

7. Kerouac, *On the Road,* 3.

8. Neal Cassady, *The First Third* (San Francisco: City Lights, 1971), 48.

9. Keouac, *On the Road,* 7.

10. Ibid., 4.

11. William Plummer, *The Holy Goof: A Biography of Neal Cassady* (New York: Paragon House, 1981), 24.

12. Edward Abbey, *The Brave Cowboy* (New York: Dodd, Mead, 1956), 26.

13.. Wolfgang Zuckermann, *End of the Road: The World Car Crisis and How We Can Solve It* (Post Mills, Vt.: Chelsea Green Publishers, 1992), 59–60.

14. Cassady, 170. All text from Beat writers is here reproduced as it stands in the original works; misspellings, unorthodox grammar and punctuation, and invented words are not uncommon.

15. Kerouac, *On the Road*, 225.

16. Ibid., 233–34.

17. Ibid., 230.

18. Jack Kerouac, *Visions of Cody,* (New York: McGraw-Hill, 1972), 56.

19. Cassady, 133.

20. Plummer, 21.

21. Kerouac, *On the Road,* 44.

22. Plummer, 21.

23. Will Wright, *Sixguns and Society: A Structural Study of the Western* (Berkley and Los Angeles: University of California Press, 1975), 33.

24. Ibid., 20.

25. Kerouac, *On the Road*, 269.

26. Allen Ginsberg, "Many Loves," in *Selected Poems, 1947–1995* (New York: HarperCollins, 1995), 65.

27. Barry Miles, *Ginsberg* (New York: Simon and Schuster, 1989), 90.

28. Kerouac, *On the Road*, 209.

29. Various Artists, *Kerouac: Kicks Joy Darkness* (compact disc; Ryko 10329; 1997).

30. Douglass Brinkley, "In the Kerouac Archive," *Atlantic Monthly,* (November 1998), 49.

31. Plummer, 55.

32. Plummer, 9–10.

33. For more about changing masculine roles in America, see Elizabeth H. Pleck and Joseph H. Pleck, *The American Man* (Englewood Cliffs, N.J.: Prentice-Hall, 1980); Jane C. Hood, ed., *Men, Work, and Family* (Newbury Park, Cailf.: Sage Publications, 1993); Edward Klein and Don Erikson, eds., *About Men: Reflections on the Male Experience* (New York: Poseidon Press, 1987); Perry Garfinkel, *In a Man's World: Father, Son, Brother, Friend, and Other Roles Men Play* (New York: NAL Books, 1985); and Harvey Deutschendorf, *Of Work and Men* (Minneapolis: Fairview Press, 1996).

34. Robert Bly, *Iron John: A Book about Men* (Reading, Mass.: Addison-Wesley, 1990), 96–97.

35. Ibid., 95.

36. For more about changing social attitudes in the post–World War II decades, see John Patrick Diggins, *The Proud Decades: America in War and Peace 1941–1960* (New York: W. W. Norton, 1988); Irwin Unger and Debby Unger, *America in the 1960s* (St. James, N.Y.: Brandywine Press, 1988); and David Reisman with Nathan Glazer and Reuel Denney, *The Lonely Crowd* (New Haven: Yale University Press, 1961). For more about the Beat reaction to their contemporary social and historical context, see Edward Halsey Foster, *Understanding the Beats* (Columbia: University of South Carolina Press 1992).

37. Anthony Rotundo, *American Manhood: Transformations in Masculinity from the Revolution to the Modern Era* (New York: Basic Books, 1993), 280.

38. Rotundo, 6.

39. Ibid., 286.

40. Max Westbrook, "The Western Esthetic," in *Critical Essays on the Western American Novel*, ed. William T. Pilkington (Boston: C. K. Hall, 1980), 73.

41. Ibid., 78.

42. Kerouac, *On the Road,* 4.

43. Ibid., 120.

44. Camille Paglia, *Sexual Personae* (New York: Vintage Books, 1990), 19.

45. Kerouac, *On the Road,* 132.

46. Mody C. Boatright, "The Beginnings of Cowboy Fiction," in Pilkington, ed., *Critical Essays on the Western American Novel,* 42.

47. Kerouac, *Visions of Cody,* 48.

48. Neal Cassady, *Grace Beats Karma: Letters from Prison 1958–1960* (New York: Blast Books, 1993), 158.

49. Kerouac, *On the Road,* 133.

50. Plummer, 82.

51. Ibid., 49.

52. Ibid., 64.

53. Kerouac, *On the Road*, 193–95.

54. Ibid., 255.

55. Jack Kerouac, *Big Sur* (New York: Farrar, Straus and Cudahy, 1962), 141.

56. Allen Ginsberg, "Howl," in Ann Charters, ed., *Reader,* 65.

57. For more about Beats in California, see John Arthur Maynard, *Venice West: The Beat Generation in Southern California* (New Brunswick, N. J.: Rutgers University Press, 1991).

58. John Barlow, "Cassady's Tale," *http://www.charm.net/~brooklyn/Topics/BarlowOnNeal.html.*

59. Plummer, 129.

60. Ibid., 142.

61. Ibid., 155.

"All the Best Cowboys Have Chinese Eyes"

The Utilization of the Cowboy-Hero Image in Contemporary Asian-American Literature

Steven M. Lee

Pete Townshend's 1982 rock album *All the Best Cowboys Have Chinese Eyes* combines two disparate discourses. On the one hand the title evokes the appealingly enigmatic figure of a cowboy hero squinting into the sun as he surveys his domain, the perilous West. On the other it simultaneously raises the negative image of the inscrutable "Oriental" whose suspicious character is stereotypically symbolized by his slanty "Chinese eyes." Is Townshend reformulating a derogatory racial metonym into a positive characteristic of one of America's most popular and important cultural constructions? While such speculation might be a generous interpretation of the intent behind this possibly racist moniker, Townshend's *All the Best Cowboys Have Chinese Eyes* evokes the very juxtaposition that is the subject of this essay.

Since the 1880s, one of the most powerful symbolic figures to occupy what Lisa Lowe calls the "terrain of culture" essential to the construction of an American identity has been the cowboy hero.[1] Through over a century of mass marketing and media production, the cowboy hero (and his forerunner the frontiersman) has materialized as a conspicuous embodiment of the national ideal. Indeed, the cowboy is so ubiquitous in the culture, so ingrained in the collective consciousness, that Americans might not even realize the extent to which this image is both cause and effect of a nationalism both racialized (white) and gendered (masculine). Cowboy historian William W. Savage, Jr., attributes much of the cowboy's mass appeal to the fact that "it is an experience easily had." The sheer simplicity of donning the appropriate western attire "contributes to the idea that *anyone* can be a cowboy."[2] Yet Savage's pat assertion that "anyone" may "put on history" and "play an imagined part in some contemporary drama that owes its inception to the past" by merely dressing the part fails to consider the complexities involved when the subject does not easily "fit" the multiple converging discourses inherent in the wardrobe.³ In particular, the authoritative symbolic capital of race, gender, and nationality imbued in the single image of the cowboy creates a compelling contrast to the historical representation of Asian-American men as racially inferior, sexually emasculated, and perpetually foreign.

Three contemporary Asian-American male writers—David Mura, Frank Chin, and John Yau—employ the cowboy image in a distinct manner and for different artistic and/or political aims.⁴ In so doing, each "disrupt[s] the myth of national identity by revealing the gaps and fissures" that in the theoretical terminology of Lowe constitute "immigrant acts":

> The universals [such as the American cowboy] proposed by the
> political and cultural forms of the nation precisely generate the
> critical acts that negate those universals. "Immigrant acts" names
> the agency of Asian immigrants and Asian Americans: the acts
> of labor, resistance, memory, and survival, as well as the
> politicized cultural work that emerges from dislocation and
> disidentification.⁵

Excluded from and disillusioned by the "myth of national identity," these Asian American artists explore and exploit the disparity between the discourses inherent in the cowboy image and the various sociohistorical forces that seek to control and define Asian-American men. As such, they provide alternatives to masculinity in the American West by either reifying or challenging alternatives to the western male trope.

Savage describes the close relationship between the composite cowboy image and the maintenance of American nationalism. He notes how "popular history describes the cowboy as 'a truly unique American type'" and analyzes how the status of this image, associated with the "nebulous concept of a western heritage," is considered by some to be the "last sentinel on the parapet of Americanism. . . . If the cowboy functions as spokesman for the people, he is in a real sense First Citizen of the Republic," in large part because the cowboy possesses and demonstrate values Americans hold dear.⁶ Analyzing the characteristics of popular cowboys in fiction and film, Savage concludes that the cowboy hero survives (both in fictionalized accounts and in the hearts of audiences) because of his pragmatism and common sense— virtues that echo respectively the founding philosophy of Benjamin Franklin and the title of Thomas Paine's famous revolutionary pamphlet.

Following the logic of Lowe, whereby "national culture" is the medium through which an individual "invents lived relationships with the national collective . . . becomes, acts, and speaks itself as 'American,'" one might deduce that subjects imagine themselves as citizens by identifying with the allegorical figure of the cowboy.⁷ Savage adds that "[t]ruth, honor, justice, preparedness, righteousness, free enterprise, and a great many more noble nouns are of a piece in the commonly accepted system of values Americans believe separate them from other people, and the cowboy hero stands squarely in the middle of it all. Not by accident is the cowboy most commonly announced as the *American* cowboy."[8] Although the origins of the mythological American cowboy date back to the second half of the nineteenth century, the lasting significance of this national myth continues to the present day—particularly in national politics.

The notion that the cowboy ought to hold the office of "First Citizen of the Republic" has been repeatedly realized by the election of several presidents, the highest representatives of nationalism, who fit this western mold. During his presidential campaign at the beginning of the twentieth century, Theodore Roosevelt marketed himself as "the Cowboy President" and the "the Rough Rider."[9] Melody Webb writes that Lyndon Johnson "was a Texan, complete with drawl, Stetson hat, and cattle ranch" and emphasizes that "his old-fashioned patriotism, unwavering loyalty, belief in people, love for the land, and celebration of hard work came from the frontier."[10] More recently, Ronald Reagan's astonishing popularity was very much based upon his exploitation of the frontier myth—"our oldest and most identified myth . . . always associated with territorial expansion, of violent conflict, and of resultant spiritual regeneration, often expressed through patriotism" and western symbolism.[10] Commenting upon the renewed national pride during Reagan's presidency, Garry Wills contends, "Reagan does not argue for American values, he embodies them. . . . He renews our past by resuming it."[12] Significantly, Reagan chose to "embody" these values in the guise of the cowboy. A former Hollywood actor who starred in six Western movies, hosted a television program entitled *Death Valley Days* and enjoyed spending time "in the saddle on his ranch in Santa Barbara," Reagan forcefully reinscribed the traditional association between the cowboy and nationalism into America's consciousness.[13]

The image of the cowboy hero also plays a significant role in a larger racialized discourse that, through popular representation, defines the orthodox hero in a very narrow manner: American, male, and white. Susan Lee Johnson, for example, asserts that the frontier itself has been constructed as "a sort of preserve for white masculinity . . . no place has been so consistently identified with maleness—particularly white maleness—as the region imagined as the American West."[14] Although historical photographs occasionally reveal the presence of black, Mexican, and Indian cowboys, the construction, mass marketing, and popular reception of the cowboy is of an exclusively white hero.[15] This definitive image will prevail in the minds of most persons despite any contrary claims by historians, whose pronouncements "that cowboys came in colors other than white may be revelations to the undergraduate, but they cannot negate the lessons learned from a lifetime of exposure to comic-book, radio, motion-picture, and television cowboys."[16]

The restrictive racial composition of the cowboy image is not surprising given its historical function of embodying and propagating a nationalism founded upon an ideology of white supremacy.[17] In "Racism and Nationalism," Etienne Balibar theorizes upon the constitutive relationship between all nationalisms and racism. He states that "in the historical 'field' of nationalism, there is always a reciprocity of determination" between nationalism and racism and that "[t]his reciprocity shows itself initially in the way in which the development of nationalism and its official utilization by the state transforms antagonisms and persecutions that have quite other origins into racism in the modern sense (and ascribes the verbal markers of ethnicity to them)."[18] Balibar's broad analysis of nationalism and racism is particularly germane to understanding how the "production of the 'people' as a political community" in a U.S. context has resulted in the historical marginalization and periodic exclusion of Asians from America.[19] The belief that Americans of Asian descent are "perpetually foreign" and either unable or unwilling to assimilate into dominant society and the body politic is an effect of a racialized nationalism.[20] Although Gail M. Nomura emphatically declares that "Asian American history begins in the U.S. West," she also refers to Roger Daniels's notion of a "defensive frontier psyche" against the "Yellow Peril" to describe the anti-Asian sentiment that was a constitutive element in the construction of the West.[21] The consequence of this ideology at the institutional and personal level has been that a "[s]ustained and systematic violence against Asians in the American West is an indisputable part of the historical record."[22] Gary Okihiro describes the significance of yellow perilism: "The fear, whether real or imagined, rose from the fact of the rise of nonwhite peoples and their defiance of white supremacy. And while serving to contain the Other, the idea of the yellow peril also helped to define the white identity, within both a nationalist and an internationalist frame."[23] In the realm of representation, it is clear that in the overlapping discourses of nationalism and masculinity, Asian American men and the cowboy hero are constructed by the dominant culture as diametrically opposed.

If the cowboy hero has evolved in popular imagination into a specifically white righter of wrongs and a white guardian of American values, a parallel history of cultural representation constructs Asian Americans in opposition to such ideals and as a threat to national interests. William F. Cody invented and introduced the first popular cowboy, William "Buck" Taylor, in his 1880 version of his Wild West pageant. Coincidentally, "[b]y the mid-1880s, hundreds of garishly illustrated and garishly written dime novels were being disseminated among a wide audience," perpetuating common stereotypes of Chinese as deviant, corrupt, and criminal.[23] More recently, the "television

Western is a genre that is constituted at its core by racial conflict: white set-tlers versus Indian marauders, for example, or white Christians versus the "'heathen Chinese.'"[25]

In contrast to the cowboy hero's undeniable American masculinity, the most prevalent "authorized performances of identity" for Asian-American men have been as the evil and effeminate villains epitomized by Fu Manchu, the cowardly but loyal Asian sidekick, and the clever but nonthreatening caricature of Charlie Chan. Concurring with Chinese-American writers Frank Chin and Jeffrey Paul Chan, Elaine H. Kim asserts: "Stereotypes of both 'bad' and 'good' Asian men as not being manly are a reflection of a white male perspective that defines the white man's virility."[26] Asian-American men have not been completely excluded from the privileged cow-boy narrative and the landscape of the West, however. In one of its most popular manifestations, the television series *Bonanza*, the Asian character Hop Sing served as a cook and foil for an entire band of white cowboys.[27] Hop Sing's subordinate position and feminized occupation relative to the other characters is historically consistent. During the Gold Rush in California and the West, many Asian-American men filled the labor positions tradi-tionally considered "women's work" due to a lack of other work opportuni-ties. Yen Le Espiritu notes, "The existence of the Chinese houseboy and launderer—and their forced 'bachelor' status—further bolstered the stereo-type of the feminized and asexual or homosexual Asian man."[28] Furthermore, the "ideology motivating the dissemination of these stereo-types of Asian American males" effects a "symbolic castration."[29]

The cumulative psychological repercussions of these gendered, national-istic, and Western constructions upon an Asian-American male subjectivity appear in David Mura's 1996 memoir, *Where the Body Meets Memory: An Odyssey of Race, Sexuality, and Identity*. Mura admits how the existence of such representations provoked a rage in him toward Asian men "for being like me, invisible, laughed at like Hop Sing cooks and . . . servants groveling before the white mistress and master."[30]

David Mura is a *sansei* (third-generation) Japanese-American poet and writer whose major works include a collection of poems entitled *The Color of Desire* and a previous memoir, *Turning Japanese* (1991). In *Where the Body Meets Memory*, Mura recalls how, when he was a boy growing up in the Midwest during the 1950s, popular representations of cowboy figures formed and deformed his young conception of self. In the second chapter, significantly and ironically entitled "All-American Boy," Mura recalls that his childhood role models and idols were the "classic American icons of the fifties" portrayed in television series such as *"Have Gun—Will Travel, Sugarfoot, Maverick, The Gene Autry Show, The Lone Ranger, Cheyenne, The Rebel."*[31] Mura recollects physically mimicking these icons by "snarling" his mouth "with a bravado and toughness I evince only as a pose or when alone, walking down the dark steps of our apartment building out to the street."[32] He declares, "I wanted what all little boys wanted. To be a hero. To ride horses . . . kill the enemy and never die."[33] Mura adopts (both physically and psychologically) a very specific gendered personality that echoes the correlation between the cowboy, patriotism, and violence articulated by Theodore Roosevelt.[34] An earlier passage reveals another aspect of the cowboy hero's influence upon Mura's emerging sense of masculinity. In this memory, Mura describes not only the extent to which the Wild West infused his boyhood imagination, but also illustrates his savage reaction to his younger sister's affront to this budding manhood:

> At night there are horses rippling beside his bed, great herds of buffalo glide through his room, robbers in masks. His Davy Crockett rifle hangs on the door, his cowboy hat and six-guns guard the foot of his bed. Cattle stampede in the gully between his bed and his sister's. He hears murmurs, perhaps raised voices, his parents arguing down the hall, then only the muffled TV, Shane stepping into the dusty street. Suddenly, his younger sister begins to taunt, You can't hurt me, you can't hurt me.
>
> Who can explain where this chant begins? Or why the brother then hit his sister?[35]

Whereas Mura wonders at the cause of this vicious and gendered outburst, his fantasy is filled with the masculine (and violent) symbols—"robbers in masks," "Davy Crockett rifle," "cowboy hat and six-guns," "Shane"—of the mythic West. Interestingly, Savage comments on this very point:

> We see time and time again the testimony of nostalgic males to the effect that the movie cowboy hero taught manliness, which means that in addition to providing instruction in the arts of fisticuffs and gun-slinging he also taught all those little boys how to deal with women. There is evidence to indicate that the cowboy hero merely reinforced juvenile prejudice against women.[36]

Although Mura's use of the third person establishes a discursive distance from this particular episode, the aggressive masculinity inherent in the cowboy hero affected Mura's psychological development, particularly given the disturbing sexism manifested elsewhere in the memoir. Yet despite Mura's mimicry of the cowboy movements and his reenactment of cowboy values, he is remarkably blind to the physicality of his own racialized body.

The extent to which Mura's early racial identification, his "hallucitory whiteness," is related to his worship of the cowboy is manifest in his description of a poem he wrote as an adult. Mura pictures himself as a young boy in "gunfight delirium, wearing the black cowboy hat and cocked steely gaze of Paladin, who'd leave his calling card, 'Have Gun, Will Travel,' everywhere he went."[36] Mura's fascination with the white cowboy character played by Richard Boone is so thorough that he does not even remember seeing an Asian character named Hey Boy in Boone's television series *Have Gun—Will Travel*. He states:

> When a Japanese Canadian playwright, Rick Shiomi, read the poem, he remarked, "Do you remember what happened at the beginning of that show? This Chinese guy with a pigtail would come running into the hotel lobby shouting, 'Teragram for Mista Paradin, teragram for Mista Paradin?'"
>
> I don't remember this Chinese messenger at all, whose name, Rick informs me, was Hey Boy. All I see is Richard Boone striding down the stairs, the epitome of cowboy cool, his pencil-thin mustache and tight glinting gaze.[38]

Although Mura's affection and identification with the cowboy hero is only one factor in his overall development, the inclusion of these anecdotes demonstrates the powerful effects of the cowboy discourse upon Mura's subjectivity. Mura's broad project (as stated in his prologue) is to articulate the personal and psychological trauma he faced following his disillusionment that he could never be the cowboy hero (that is, white, masculine, unequivocally American). One might speculate that the reason he explicates this disenchantment by introducing these anecdotes through a description of old photographs: "AT THE AGE OF FIVE, in every picture of me, I've got a pair of six-guns cinched about my waist."[39] As a medium for memory, these photographs symbolize the inevitability of the author stepping outside his childhood imagination and being compelled to recognize the incongruities between his Asian physical features and the ideal cowboy hero.

Interestingly, Mura does not make any further references to the cowboy hero in his memoir. Mura does not return to the cowboy hero because the image is incompatible with the central ambition of this "autobiographical manifesto": to contest the historical desexualization of Asian American men and to recover Asian American manhood by reappropriating the body from mainstream constructions.[40]

Playwright, essayist, and novelist Frank Chin is perhaps the most controversial and prolific writer on Asian-American masculinity and a pioneering figure in Chinese-American literature. Unlike Mura, whose visual consumption of popular cowboys contributes to his illusory identification with white heroes, Frank Chin's critique of the mainstream cowboy discourse in his 1975 play *The Chickencoop Chinaman* derives from an absence of mainstream Asian heroes that compels the main character, Tam Lum, to imagine the Lone Ranger he hears on the radio as a Chinese figure: "I heard JACK ARMSTRONG, ALL AMERICAN BOY fight Japs, come outa the radio everyday into our kitchen to tell me everyday for years that ALL-AMERICAN BOYS are the best boys, the hee-rohs! the movie stars! that ALL-AMERICAN BOYS are white boys everyday, all their life long."[41] Spinning the radio dial searching for "ANYBODY, CHINESE AMERICAN BOY . . . doing anything grand on the air," Tam discovers the "masked man" and imagines that various facets of the Lone Ranger's outfit signify his Chinese origins. For example, in Tam's juvenile mind, the Lone Ranger has black hair like everyone in Chinatown because that is how he appears in the Sunday funnies, wears a mask to "hide his Asian eyes," wears a "red shirt for good luck," rides a white horse "cuz white be our color of death," and shoots "silver bullets cuz death from a Chinaman is always expensive. Always classy. Always famous."[42] Tam convinces himself that the Lone Ranger on the radio is the "CHINESE AMERICAN BOY" he had longed for. One scene consists of a dream sequence in which the two young Asian-American characters, Tam Lum and his friend Kenji, actually encounter the Lone Ranger and Tonto. Similar to Mura's story, the drama of this scene focuses upon the disillusionment of Tam when he discovers his marginalization from this national narrative.

Chin's parody of the Lone Ranger character subverts the nationalist discourse embodied in the exceptional cowboy figure. Within mainstream culture, the Texas Rangers have traditionally been revered as mythic patrollers of the frontier and protectors of America's borders. Américo Paredes writes, "The Rangers have been pictured as a fearless, almost superhuman breed of men, capable of incredible feats. It may take a company of militia to quell a riot, but one Ranger was said to be enough for one mob. . . . To the Ranger is given the credit for ending lawlessness and disorder along the Rio Grande."[43] As evident in Tam and Kenji's fascination with the masked man, the legend of the Texas Ranger was infused into the nation's consciousness long after the West was "civilized" via the far-reaching medium of radio. However, rather than the awe-inspiring, authoritative archetype created for mass consumption, the Lone Ranger whom Tam and Kenji meet in *The Chickencoop Chinaman* is so old and frail he requires Tonto to shoot him up with a *"hypo"* midway through his performance.[44] Chin imagines the Lone Ranger as *"a legendary white racist with the funk of the West smoldering in his blood. In his senility, he still loves racistly, blesses racistly, shoots straight and is cuckoo with the notion that white folks are not white folks but just plain folks."*[45] Chin reveals and mocks the Lone Ranger's racist standpoint in his interaction with both his sidekick Tonto and Tam and Kenji. The Lone Ranger is so absorbed in the narrative of his own legendary status, that he comprehends Tonto only when he speaks in character; that is, in the degrading monosyllabic speech of the stereotypical Indian.

Despite Chin's comic portrayal of the Lone Ranger and Tonto, he does not discount the dubious effect these characters have upon the identity formation of the two Asian-American boys. The deleterious influence of the Lone Ranger upon Tam's masculinity is symbolized by the Lone Ranger shooting the aspiring young writer in his hand. Elsewhere Chin has expounded upon his belief that creativity is a constitutive element of manhood and advocated a "backtalking, muscular, singing, stomping full blooded language loaded with nothing but our truth."[46] In their influential and controversial introduction to *Aiiieeeee!: An Anthology of Asian American Writers*, Frank Chin, Jeffery Chan, Lawson Inada, and Shawn Wong state, "The white stereotype of the acceptable and unacceptable Asian is utterly without manhood. . . . At worst, the Asian American is contemptible because he is womanly, effeminate, devoid of all the traditionally masculine qualities of originality, daring, physical courage, and creativity. . . . Stunt the tongue and you have lopped off the culture and sensibility. On the simplest level, a *man* in any culture speaks for himself."[47] Thus, in order to be a man, the Asian-American writer must recover Asian-American history and culture, but first and foremost he must recover his voice. In Chin's *Chickencoop Chinaman*, the Lone Ranger would rather have the "China boys" "preservin [their Oriental] culture," and thus remaining voiceless and unmanly, than creating a new vital Chinese-American culture through writing.

The lasting influence of the cowboy discourse that would deny Asian men their masculinity by denying them their voice reveals itself at the end of Chin's scene, when Kenji's response to Tam's wounded hand is to call him a "lucky dog" and declare enviously, "Yaaahhoooh! Hah ha ha. You was shot in the mitt with a silver bullet, ol compadre!"[48] Similar to the fantasy that blinded David Mura to his degraded status in this discourse, Kenji impulsively sides with the Lone Ranger by enthusiastically applauding the mutilation of his compadre's masculinity. Conversely, a disabused Tam now states, "The masked man . . . I knew him better when I never knew him at all. The Lone Ranger ain't no Chinaman, children. . . . He'd deafened my ear for trains all my boyhood long."[49] Throughout the play, the distant "trains" Tam could not hear as a child symbolize the lost history of Chinese Americans in the West, who were excluded from the dominant discourse of nationality. The tragedy in Chin's work is not only that Tam and Kenji have privileged the mainstream lore of the West via the Lone Ranger radio serial transmitted into their living rooms, but also that they failed to realize the racist nature of this discourse during their formative years. However, despite Chin's humorous deconstruction of the Lone Ranger in this work, he actually finds much to admire and appropriate in the cowboy hero and the West.

In his satiric essay "This Is Not Autobiography," Chin claims the West from mainstream discourse and declares the frontier his own: "And the American west is mine. The US Interstate Freeway system. The railroad."[50] Chin expounds at length upon the resemblance between the Lone Ranger and his construction of a "Chinaman" hero. The Lone Ranger's secret persona and penchant for revenge make him "a very Cantonese kind of hero."[51] Although the Lone Ranger falls short of Chin's standard of manhood because "the mask is, in the Chinese universe, a sissy touch," the "Lone Ranger could almost ride into pages of THREE KINGDOMS and THE WHITE [sic] MARGIN" because the Lone Ranger stands for ideals that transcend nationality:

> Kingdoms rise and fall, you know. There's no need to conceal your identity, in a universe where personal integrity and honor is the highest value, the center of morals. *Nations come and go.* But two guns. Red shirt. White horse. A faithful companion and ally. Obviously the Chinaman is neither white European nor Asian American in your universe. But obviously, from inside the white and Chinese bias, nothing about the Chinaman is obvious.[52]

In "Confessions of the Chinatown Cowboy," Chin actually unveils this hybrid figure epitomized by his character Ben Fee, "a bare knuckled unmasked man, a Chinaman loner out of the old West, a character out of Chinese sword-slingers, a fighter."[52] David Leiwei Li remarks upon this "alternative hero" who simultaneously supplants a stereotypically meek and deferential Chinese American masculinity and challenges the privileged heroism of the Ranger: "With one bold, contrastive stroke, Chin immediately erects his ideal not as someone who apes the Western hero but an alternative hero, a hero from the fighting tradition of ancient China but who belongs to the frontier of America."[54] In this regard, unlike Mura's, Chin's utilization of the cowboy does not stop at a mere critique of the traditional nationalist narrative; rather he appropriates and transforms the cowboy for his own creative and political purposes. Such a move fits nicely within what Lisa Lowe describes as "immigrant acts." For Lowe,

> Asian American culture is the site of more than critical negation of the U.S. nation; it is a site that shifts and marks alternatives to the national terrain by occupying other spaces, imagining different narratives and critical historiographies, and enacting practices that give rise to new forms of subjectivity and new ways of questioning the government of human life by the national state.[55]

The "different narrative and critical historiographies" Chin imagines consist of his conception of the Chinaman and more specifically the Chinatown cowboy, as "new form[s] of subjectivity." The Chinatown cowboy is a masculinist construction, a rebel and outlaw, "neither white European nor Asian American," that confronts dominant culture through an alternative culture.[56] Chin's cultural nationalist standpoint and immense imagination facilitate this unproblematic appropriation of the cowboy image.[57] In contrast, the work of John Yau engages the seemingly oxymoronic site of the Asian cowboy in order to display the disturbing, and perhaps irreconcilable, predicaments of a very different Asian-American subject.

Known primarily as an accomplished poet and art critic, John Yau chooses the Pacific as the site for his short story "Hawaiian Cowboys," which details the mixed-race narrator's struggle to reconcile the complex relationship between his equally ambiguous national and ethnic identities. As the story unfolds, it is evident that this midway point between Asia and the U.S. mainland is important as the narrator partially retraces the diasporic journey of his parents, who migrated from China to the American continent via Hawaii. Comparing his uncertain sense of heritage to that of his white wife, the narrator comments,

> Janet was as proud of her heritage as I was confused about my Dutch father and Chinese mother. Maybe that's why I was ready to come to Hawaii. Janet wanted to relax, but I wanted something else, though I didn't know what. It wasn't detective novels, but being a detective. I was looking for answers, though I would probably be the last to admit it.[58]

Hawaii's location is also important in contrast to the couple's traditional vacation spot, Martha's Vineyard. The proximity of Martha's Vineyard on the eastern seaboard of the United States, the fact that this site is a common destination for an established WASP elite, and the fact that the narrator and Janet traditionally vacation with Janet's parents all underscore a connection between this family practice and a genealogy that originates in western Europe. Janet is able to proudly trace her lineage to the English pilgrims. In contrast, on the "Big Island," the narrator observes that he and Janet live in a house adjacent to a Japanese graveyard, a detail that lays claim to an Asian-American history on the island as well as symbolizing an ancestral presence and cultural practice that speaks to a migration from Asia counter to the dominant discourse of European pilgrimage to the New World. Significantly, however, the narrator does not conceive of Hawaii as part of the West, despite its diplomatic, geographic, and historic connections to the American West.[59] Thus, while the narrator's distinct sense of place facilitates his emerging ethnic consciousness, it also belies his mainland and mainstream sensibility.

In addition to its geographic symbolism, Hawaii is important to the narrator's exploration of his identity because of its racial composition. Hawaii is an exceptional state in that persons of Asian ancestry comprise a majority of the population. In particular, the narrator is comforted by the fact that he witnesses many interracial couples who mirror both his parents' relationship and his own marriage: "In Honolulu I kept looking at the couples, marveling at how many of them seemed, like Janet and me, to be made up of people

from different races and cultures. At times I wondered why my parents did-
n't stop here, why they decided to continue on their trip to America, why
they thought they should go to the mainland."[60] An environment that fosters
such mixing is central to the narrator's personal detective work. Due to both
its symbolic and actual significance, the narrator expresses a strong affinity to
Hawaii: "We've been here for nearly a month, and, for different reason[s],
each of us feels as if the place is tugging at us, asking us to stay."[61]

Prior to this vacation, the assimilated narrator has never seriously contemplated or articulated his position in a racialized society. His admission
that as an adult he was suddenly "looking for answers," coupled with Janet's
wary reaction to his apparent change in character (she refers to his heightened sensibility as "getting morbid"), suggests that in the past, the narrator
functioned from a mainstream standpoint that ignored the import of race
despite his mixed-race background.[62] Living in Hawaii allows the narrator
the opportunity to question the subordination of one's ethnic or racial identity to a national identity. The narrator, for example, rejects an unconditional
patriotism when he recalls how angry he became after a Japanese cab driver
in Honolulu insisted he ought to take Janet to visit Pearl Harbor. He vehemently declares to his wife,

> A Japanese man in his early sixties tells me that I should go to Pearl
> Harbor. For what? Does that mean he's more American or something?
> Does it mean that I'm not, because I haven't gone and don't intend to?
> What am I supposed to say? That I like going to the Bishop's Museum
> more, that I'd rather look at all the specimens of extinct birds, that I
> like looking at the feathered robes, that I like learning about who and
> what were here before any of us arrived.[63]

By refusing to visit the Pearl Harbor memorial, the mixed-race narrator
demonstrates a pan-Asian-American sensibility, implicitly acknowledging
both the mistreatment of Japanese-American citizens by the U.S. government and the harmful effects of this nationalist discourse upon all Asian
Americans. This critique of nationalism foreshadows the narrator's
encounter with the Hawaiian cowboys.[64]

Despite the narrator's adamant position following this incident, his sense
of self in the story remains shifting and ambiguous. Having grown up on
Manhattan Island, he takes comfort in the fact that "we all came from different islands," a heterogeneous conception of society that does not privilege
nativism. He is simultaneously enamored by a search for Asian origins (manifest in his keen interest in the local history), and curious about the cultural
hybridity inherent in Hawaii. However, the narrator's mercurial self-
exploration reaches a point of crisis when he and his wife discover "a small
town that looks like something you'd see in Wyoming or Texas, or maybe a

movie of the west."[65] If the narrator-as-tourist is able to reconcile the com-modified manifestation of this "cowboy country" (he notes the "stores selling fancy cowboy boots, western style shirts and belts, a large storeroom full of shiny Harley Davidsons, and a huge lot full of brand new pickup trucks" in the middle of the South Pacific), he is shocked and ultimately disturbed to find a saloon full of Hawaiian cowboys.[66]

Overcoming his initial astonishment, the narrator observes how "[m]ost of the men are dressed like cowboys, and almost all of them are Asian or Hawaiian. Chinese, Japanese, Filipino, Polynesian, and Samoan. They're all sizes and shapes. Some are thin and wiry, while two are as big and thick as stone fireplaces."[67] His keen interest in distinguishing the diversity of these cowboys once again underscores his attempt to embrace a pan-Asian American sensibility. Such heterogeneity appeals because it both validates and counters his own sense of displacement both in Hawaii (because he is a tourist) and on the mainland where, despite his apparent assimilation, he feels isolated: "The fact is, on Hawaii, all the creatures, whether man, animal, or insect, came from somewhere else. Flora and fauna too. Everything floated, swam, flew or was carried here from there, wherever there was. . . . This was something I kept mulling over, something I found comforting to remember. All of us are from different islands."[68] The narrator further displays his enthusiasm for this heterogeneity in inquiring about the kind of iced tea served at this establish-ment when he declares: "You know, the iced tea. I'm just wondering if it will be American or Chinese, plain teabag or sweet jasmine, cowboy or instant, red zinger or honeyed essence of green hummingbird? I'm wondering if they give you those kinds of choices. If they don't, they ought to."[69] Whereas this speech clearly celebrates an all-inclusive heterogeneity, the status of hybridity in rela-tion to the narrator's sense of self is more complicated.

Upon closer inspection, the list of teas consists to a large degree, of mutu-ally exclusive dichotomies between items "American or Chinese." Janet singles out and corrects the narrator's hybrid invention, "cowboy tea," by reasserting the irrefutably American cultural creation of the West, "cowboy coffee":

> Janet looks me at me oddly, as if she is afraid that I might be slipping off into what she calls my morbid phase.
>
> "Cowboy tea? Don't you mean coffee, cowboy coffee?"
>
> "Yes, that's what I meant," I whisper, nodding and smiling, as if to reassure my wife that I'm not about to get moody on her, and that I now realize I've just told her a bad joke.[70]

The narrator's reference to "cowboy tea" as a "bad joke" demonstrates the incompatibility of these two cultural symbols: "cowboy" as metonym for American culture; "tea" as metonym for Asian culture. Yet the narrator's whispered agreement and reassuring smile suggests that his acquiescent reiteration of Janet's mainstream discourse that upholds the purity of cowboy culture is an empty gesture intended to convince his wife he will not "get moody" by once again asserting a racialized identity that would taint this product of the traditional West. Though at first intrigued by the existence of Hawaiian cowboys, the narrator quickly becomes uncomfortable and feels a sudden desire to leave the island.

Upon seeing the cowboys, however, the narrator recalls his childhood attempts to mimic Western heroes: "I remember a photograph of me when I was a child, dressed up like Hopalong Cassidy, and the Davy Crockett hat I begged my mother to buy me for Christmas. This was before I realized I could never be Wyatt Earp, Jesse James, or Daniel Boone."[71] Similar to episodes in Mura's memoir and Chin's play, this passage reveals the narrator's childhood desire to assume the persona of the cowboy by donning a Davy Crockett hat as well as an intrinsic belief in the viability of this fantasy. He soon realizes, contra Chin and Mura, that he "could never be" any of his Western heroes due in large part (if not exclusively) to his racial composition. As in Mura's portrayal of the disenchantment generated by boyhood images of himself dressing the part, the narrator's own disillusionment emerges from a "photograph of me when I was a child" that bears the innocence of boyhood fantasy as well as the grown-up realization of racialization.

Despite the diversity of the Asian and Hawaiian men in the saloon, all have adopted a common "American" cowboy identity; the narrator's account suggests that the Hawaiian cowboys recognize no disparity between their western attire and their respective ethnicities. The narrator remarks upon the unself-conscious sincerity these men exhibit: "I look around and see men in fancy alligator boots, silver belts, and embroidered shirts. Others are in dusty dungarees, leather chaps, sweat stained shirts, and bandanas. None of them are pretending, like I was when I was a child."[72] On a symbolic level, these men have essentially appropriated the nationalism inherent in the cowboy image. Given the mixed-race narrator's anxiety over his own interstitial location between the dominant culture and a marginalized and ambiguous Asian America, why does he not derive satisfaction from the Hawaiian cowboys and see them as the desirable fruition of cultural mixing? Although the narrator is intrigued by this cultural hybridity, his discomfort is symptomatic of his realization that such a phenomenon is only possible because the isolated and insulate "western" town filled with Hawaiian cowboys is an "island within islands."[73] An Asian man donning cowboy apparel in Hawaii, where such coalescing is not contested by dominant cultural norms is less problematic than a similar construct on the mainland due to the different racial and cultural contexts. In this regard, the cowboys force the narrator to concede that in "looking for answers" it is not enough that he is part Asian— he is not "local." He feels an alienation from the Hawaiian cowboys due to his failure to comprehend and adopt a local sensibility. Moreover, despite the narrator's earlier attempt to grasp a pan-Asian-American consciousness equating his island origins in Manhattan with the Hawaiian islands, his inescapable and myopic mainland sensibility inhibits a reconciliation of the cultural hybridity or appropriation of the Hawaiian cowboys with his own ethnic identity.

Although the narrator's first reaction to seeing the Asian cowboys is surprise, he is quickly overcome with the curiosity of a "nosy neighbor who wants to see who's living on the other side of the fence."[74] Ironically, the narrator's eager eavesdropping echoes the earlier anthropological stance of his wife.[75] He demonstrates this inquisitive but dubious position in relation to these exotic natives by stating, "I try to see what has been embroidered on their denim shirts, a bird-of-paradise flower or a hummingbird, perhaps. I imagine a black Hawaiian shirt with bright red flower, like the one Georgia O'Keeffe painted when she was here, green cacti, saddles and horseshoes."[76] The narrator's comparison between the ornamentation he *imagines* adorns the cowboys' shirts and the paintings of a mainland artist suggests that, like O'Keeffe, his perception (gaze) of the local landscape (including the cowboys) is also refracted through such a continental lens.[77] Drawing this comparison provokes mixed emotions as he considers the fusion between "nature" and the importation of culture and offers further insight into the narrator's relation to the cowboys: "Nature mixed with things that might have been brought here a hundred years ago, in the days when the West was still being won by some and lost by others. I feel dizzy and exhilarated, sad and uneasy."[78]

This ambivalent declaration lends itself to many interpretations. The narrator feels "dizzy and exhilarated" because of the degree of cultural hybridity the Hawaiian cowboys symbolize. Throughout "Hawaiian Cowboys," the narrator's struggle to find solace and meaning in the notion of hybridity proves futile. The cowboys superficially represent the boy in the photograph all grown up. However, the narrator's contextual comment to this "mixture" occurring "in the days when the West was still being won by some and lost by others" raises the specter of colonialism and acknowledges the inequitable outcome of this past. Given the history of Hawaii and the role of the frontier myth in this process of colonization, the surprising discovery of cowboy culture on the island underscores the extension of "the West" beyond the natural borders of the Pacific Ocean and provides an ironic comment upon Hawaii as a colonized land—forcibly conquered by the United States in 1893, achieving territorial status in 1900, but not acquiring statehood until 1959. Thus these men, who unlike the narrator "aren't on vacation," signify that hybridity is not an even process to be simply celebrated but a reality that belies underlying relations and structures of power.[79] Similarly, in *Immigrant Acts*, Lisa Lowe argues that "[h]ybridization is not the 'free' oscillation between or among chosen identities," but is rather the formation of cultural objects and practices that are produced by histories of uneven and unsynthetic power relations; for example, the racial and linguistic mixings in the Philippines and among Filipinos in the United States are the material trace of history of Spanish colonialism, U.S. colonization, and U.S. neocolonialism. Hybridity, in this sense, does not suggest the assimilation of Asian or immigrant practices to dominant forms but instead marks the history of survival within relationships of unequal power and domination.[80]

The narrator might feel "sad and uneasy" because, in his mind, the Hawaiian cowboys symbolize not only the "material trace" of colonial domination but also his own (Asian-*American*) complicity in such endeavors.[81] This connivance complicates the narrator's notion of nationality, because throughout this story he has made gestures toward defining his Asian-American heritage in contradistinction to an Americanism founded upon this colonialist drive. The presence of Hawaiian cowboys reveals a degree of Americanization that shatters the narrator's fantasy of discovering a "pure" or "innocent" Asian-American consciousness. Thus, the Asian cowboys not only embody an inaccessible self-possession, they also expose the narrator's degree of investment and complicity in the dominant culture, as well as the futility of his endeavor to find an ethnic "lifeboat" in the unique West of Hawaii.[82] The narrator's final evaluation of Hawaii offers an irresolute resolution, because he is unable to reconcile his place in the conflicting and converging discourses of race, ethnicity, and nationality. Hawaii is "an island that's growing bigger each day, but it's also sinking into the sea."[83]

Exploring the works of David Mura, Frank Chin, and John Yau reinforces Lisa Lowe's concept of "immigrant acts." Although their respective engagements with the racialized masculinity represented by the cowboy yield different outcomes, each cultural production is political because it "emerges from dislocation and disidentification" and exploits the disparity between the exclusive national mythology embodied by the cowboy and the marginalized site of Asian Americans.[84] Although Mura and Chin effectively deconstruct this signifier of white masculinity in order to elevate the status of Asian-American manhood, neither author is able to transcend traditional conceptions of hypermasculinity inherent in the cowboy. Moreover, as the analysis of John Yau demonstrates, a simple appropriation of the cowboy in the context of a noncultural nationalist examination of Asian-American subjectivity is also fraught with complexities. The representation of the cowboy hero lends itself to such oppositional manipulation by Asian-American male artists because of the interrelated discourses of nationality, race, and gender that define the image and confine the man.

Notes

I would like to thank Matthew Basso and Laura McCall for their insightful criticism and generous assistance in revising htis essay.

1. Despite the fact that real cowboys derived from colonial interracial contact between British settlers, African and African-American slaves who worked the cowpens, and Spanish rancheros, I locate the advent of the cowboy image in the late nineteenth century because 1880 is the year in which William F. Cody introduced and mass marketed as a national symbol the first cowboy in his Wild West pageant.

2. William W. Savage, Jr., *The Cowboy Hero: His Image in American History and Culture* (Norman: University of Oklahoma Press, 1979) (emphasis mine).

3. Ibid., 53.

4. Whereas it is important to recognize the different ethnicities of Mura, Chin, and Yau (Japanese American and Chinese Americans respectively) within the pan-ethnic signifier *Asian American,* their artistic response to the common racial subordination of Asians in America contra the cowboy ideal is of greatest interest here.

5. Lisa Lowe, *Immigrant Acts: On Asian American Cultural Politics* (Durham, N.C.: Duke University Press, 1996), 9.

6. Savage, 152, 15, and 20.

7. Lowe, 3.

8. Savage, 151.

9. Janet R. Fireman, "Ronald Reagan and the Mythic West," *Journal of the West* 34 (April 1995): 93.

10. Melody Webb, "Lyndon Johnson: The Last Frontier President," *Journal of the West* 34 (April 1995): 73.

11. Fireman, 93.

12. Garry Wills, *Reagan's America* (New York: Penguin, 1988), 5, quoted in Fireman, 95.

13. Ibid., 96.

14. Susan Lee Johnson, "'A Memory Sweet to Soldiers': The Significance of Gender," in *A New Significance: Re-envisioning the History of the American West,* ed. by Clyde A. Milner III (New York: Oxford University Press, 1996), 255.

15. Jack Weston, *The Real American Cowboy* (New York: Schocken Books, 1985), 136. See also Richard W. Slatta, *Cowboys of the Americas* (New Haven: Yale University Press, 1990), 203.

16. Savage, 4.

17 See Tomás Almaguer's discussion of white supremacy and the founding of the nation in *Racial Faultlines: The Historical Origins of White Supremacy in California* (Berkeley and Los Angeles: University of California Press, 1994), 12. See also Richard Slotkin, *Gunfighter Nation: The Myth of the Frontier in Twentieth-Century America* (New York: Atheneum, 1992), 86.

18. Etienne Balibar, "Racism and Nationalism," in *Race, Nation, Class: Ambiguous Identities*, ed. Etienne Balibar and Immanuel Wallerstein (New York: Verso, 1991), 52.

19. Ibid., 48.

20. Sucheng Chan, *Asian Americans: An Interpretive History* (Boston: Twayne, 1991), 187.

21. Gail M. Nomura, "Significant Lives: Asia and Asian Americans in the U.S. West," in Milner, ed., *A New Significance*, 141.

22. Darrell Hamamoto, *Monitored Peril: Asian Americans and the Politics of TV Representation* (Minneapolis: University of Minnesota Press, 1994), 52.

23. Gary Okihiro, *Margins and Mainstreams: Asian American History and Culture* (Seattle: University of Washington Press, 1994), 138.

24. Yen Le Espiritu, *Asian American Women and Men: Labor, Law,s and Love* (Thousand Oaks, Calif.: Sage Publications, 1997), 89.

25. Hamamoto, 58.

26. Elaine H. Kim, "Asian Americans and American Popular Culture" in *Dictionary of Asian American History*, ed. Hyung-chan Kim (New York: Greenwood Press, 1986), 108. Many critics (including Kim and Espiritu) have examined the significant role of sexuality in defining Asian American masculinity, particularly in contradistinction to "the white man's virility." The stereotypical representations of Asian-American male sexuality are complex and somewhat contradictory. At times, Asian-American men are constructed as sexually threatening (particularly to white women). Gina Marchetti provides an analysis of this construct in relation to depictions of interracial romance in Hollywood films from silent cinema to contemporary productions. See Gina Marchetti, *Romance and the "Yellow Peril": Race, Sex, and Discursive Strategies in Hollywood Fiction* (Berkeley and Los Angeles: University of California Press, 1993), 2–4.

Asian American men are also portrayed as effeminate, emasculated, and/or asexual. For an analysis of this phenomenon see Richard Fung, "Looking for My Penis: The Eroticized Asian in Gay Video

Porn," in *Asian American Sexualities: Dimensions of the Gay and Lesbian Experience*, ed. Russell Leong (New York: Routledge, 1996), 181–98.

27. For an extensive and nuanced examination of the depiction of Asians in television Westerns see Hamamoto, esp. chap. 2, "Asians in the American West," 32–63.

28. Espiritu, 34.

29. Josephine Lee, *Performing Asian America: Race and Ethnicity on the Contemporary Stage* (Philadelphia: Temple University Press, 1997), 11.

30. David Mura, *Where the Body Meets Memory: An Odyssey of Race, Sexuality, and Identity* (New York: Anchor Books, 1996), 170.

31. Ibid., 57.

32. Ibid., 56.

33. Ibid., 60.

34. In the following passage, although Mura does not directly evoke the cowboy image, although he does reveal the nationalistic influence of famous cowboy actor John Wayne upon his young conscience: *"He'll never be taken prisoner of war. He dies so gallantly, so dramatically, like John Wayne's buddy at Iwo Jima. He believes in the flag, the anthem of the Marines"* (52). In the context of the wartime movie alluded to here, the enemies are Japanese soldiers. In the context of many Westerns, the enemy is typically the demonized Native American. In both instances, American heroism is defined by vanquishing an ethnic villain.

35. Mura, 53 (emphasis in original).

36. Savage, 99.

37. Mura, 57.

38. Ibid., 56–57. The Chinese messenger Hey Boy was played by Kam Tong.

39. Ibid., 56.

40. Sidonie Smith devises the concept of "autobiographical manifesto" in her study of women's autobiography *Subjectivity, Identity, and the Body: Women's Autobiographical Practices in the Twentieth Century* (Bloomington: Indiana University Press, 1993). Although Smith defines the model of analysis in relation to emancipatory women's texts, it is particularly pertinent to Mura's project. Autobiographical manifestos are political acts of self-writing that attempt to "restag[e] subjectivity" and contest "the old inscriptions, the old histories, the old politics, the *ancien regime*" (157; emphasis in original). Smith distinguishes seven significant aspects of the autobiographical manifesto: to appropriate / to contest sovereignty; to bring to light, to make manifest; to announce publicly; to perform publicly; to speak as one of a group, to speak for a group; to speak to the future (157–63). In Mura's test these seven functions overlap and work in conjunction to achieve his political aims.

41. Frank Chin, "The Chickencoop Chinaman," in *The Chickencoop Chinaman and The Year of the Dragon: Two Plays by Frank Chin* (Seattle: University of Washington Press, 1981), 31.

42. Ibid., 32.

43. Américo Paredes, *"With His Pistol in His Hand": A Border Ballad and Its Hero* (Austin: University of Texas Press, 1958), 24.

44. Chin, 34.

45. Ibid., 3 (emphasis in original).

46. Frank Chin, "Frank Chin: Backtalk," in *Counterpoint: Perspectives on Asian America,* ed. Emma Gee (Los Angeles: UCLA Asian American Studies Center, 1976), 557.

47. Frank Chin et al., "An Introduction to Chinese- and Japanese-American Literature" [1974], in *Aiiieeeee! An Anthology of Asian-American Writers*, ed. Frank Chin et al. (New York: Mentor, 1991), 14–15 and 37 (emphasis mine).

48. Chin, *Chickencoop*, 33.

49. Ibid., 38.

50. Frank Chin, "This Is Not An Autobiography*," Genre* 18 (1985): 116.

51. Ibid., 116.

52. Ibid., 117. *The Romance of the Three Kingdoms* and *The Water Margin (or All Men Are Brothers)* are classic Chinese novels that figure prominently in Chin's conception of a heroic Chinese culture as well as his notion of the Chinaman hero. Kuan-chung Lo, *San kuo, or Romance of the Three Kingdoms* (c. 1330–1400; reprint, New York: Kelly and Walsh, 1925). Shih Nai-an or Lo Kuan-chung, *Water Margin* (c. 1290–1400; reprint New York: The Commercial Press, 1937).

53. Frank Chin, "Confessions of the Chinatown Cowboy," *Bulletin of Concerned Asian Scholars* 4, no. 3 (1972): 58.

54. David Leiwei Li, "The Production of Chinese American Tradition: Displacing American Orientalist Discourse," in *Reading the Literatures of Asian America*, ed. Shirley Geok-lin Lim and Amy Ling (Philadelphia: Temple University Press, 1992), 324.

55. Lowe, 29.

56. Chin, "Autobiography," 117.

57. "Unproblematic" concerns Chin's own mind; many critics have found Chin's constructions very problematic, particularly with regard to the sexism inherent in much of his work. See, for example, King-Kok Cheung, "The Woman Warrior versus the Chinaman Pacific: Must a Chinese American Critic Choose between Feminism and Heroism?" in *Conflicts in Feminism*, ed. M. Hirsch and E. F. Keller (New York: Routledge, 1990), 234–51.

58. John Yau, "Hawaiian Cowboys," in *Hawaiian Cowboys* (Santa Rosa: Black Sparrow Press, 1995), 98.

59. John Whitehead, "Hawaii: The First and Last Far West?" *Western Historical Quarterly* 23 (May 1992): 177.

60. Yau, 97.

61. Yau, 98.

62. Ibid., 93.

63. Ibid., p. 94.

64. Ibid. p.87.

65. Ibid., 99.

66. Ibid., 99–100.

67. Ibid., 100.

68. Ibid., 92.

69. Ibid., 101.

70. Ibid.

71. Ibid., 100.

72. Ibid.

73. Ibid., 102.

74. Ibid., 100.

75. Throughout the story, Janet's actions allude to those of the colonizer. For example, Janet is preoccupied with studying maps of the island and planning the route for the couple's expedition (87–88). Midway through their excursion, Janet sits upon a large rock to list everything they have seen. This note-taking is reminiscent of the western anthropologist's mission to record the habitat and native specimens in "exotic" locations. The destructive nature of this enterprise (both historically and within the context of this story) is symbolized by Janet's last entry, "Twenty-seven road kills" (97). However, the seeming critique of this colonialism is complicated by the fact that the mixed-race narrator participates in this endeavor. Not only does he share in the driving duties but he remarks with satisfaction how they have "documented" their journey by taking three rolls of photographs: "I kept looking at the shacks, tilting and tumbling, glad that much of this had been documented on three rolls of film. We didn't take many pictures in Honolulu, but standing here, by the side of a dusty road, I think that maybe we should have" (97). Interestingly, the narrator attempts to position himself in the role of the native informant, particularly in relation to Janet's colonizer. Whereas Janet takes great pains to map out a route around the island and record everything she sees, the narrator submerges himself in learning local history and indigenous facts and communicating them to his wife.

76. Yau, 101.

77. Yau, 94 and 98.

78. Yau, 101.

79. Yau, 100. See also Whitehead, 160.

80. Lowe, 82 and 67.

81. The history of cowboys in Hawaii predates the colonization of the islands by U.S. forces and can be traced back to the presence of *paniolos*.

82. Yau, 102.

83. Ibid.

84. Lowe, 9.

"I Guess Your Warrior Look Doesn't Work Every Time"

Challenging Indian Masculinity
in the Cinema

Brian Klopotek

In literature and film, painting and photography, science and history, and sports and advertising, whites manipulate the symbolic Indian to perform innumerable tasks.[1] The Indian—distinguished here from the Native American person—is a stock character in the non-Native psyche, a metaphor rather than a fully functioning human. Non-Natives historically have used the Indian as a symbol to make statements about themselves and their place in the world, letting it serve as a foil to critique or herald their own values and habits. The thousands of Indians in Hollywood films and TV series over the years have lacked key human traits, not to mention the many tribal characteristics that were absent. However, Native people—through growing political clout and direct participation in movie making— have begun to influence on-screen portrayals much more over the last thirty years than previously, which has led to the arrival of identifiably Native American images in several recent efforts. By directly challenging the hypermasculinity of the symbolic Indians, Native Americans have accomplished some of the most significant revisions of Indian representations to date.

For at least the last century, hypermasculinity has been one of the foremost attributes of the Indian world that whites have imagined.[2] With squaws and princesses usually playing secondary roles, Indian tribes are populated predominantly by noble or ignoble savages, wise old chiefs, and cunning warriors. These imagined Indian nations comprise an impossibly masculine race. Because of such perpetually outlandish representations of Indian gender, masculinity has become a crucial arena for contesting unrealistic images of Indians and introducing Native American perspectives into films. Filmmakers have both played on and repudiated the forms that Indian masculinity assumes, creating such characters as Native American nerds and struggling fathers, and they have strengthened female characters to some extent, without emasculating Native American men, creating much more convincing portraits of Native life than earlier works.

At the risk of oversimplifying a full century of Indian images in cinema, a brief review of classic Indian roles will delineate some of the standard manipulations of masculinity and establish the context from which recent Native American film depictions are emerging.[3] Following the review, I will discuss three recent films that demonstrate the capacity new representations of Native American masculinity have for dismantling stereotyped, racist images of Indians.

The noble savage, the good Indian, is a virtuous, dignified, stoic, hard-working man. He provides for his people, though he is sometimes portrayed without any connections to a living family or tribe. He believes in personal responsibility and loyalty, and he bravely answers calls to arms for noble causes. One with nature, he is free of the corruptions industrial society places on a man's character, yet he embraces the causes of "civilization" and white Americans. He is physically superb, animal-like in his athletic abilities. In many ways, he embodies the ideal traits white society ascribes to manliness. Some classic examples of the noble savage include Chingachgook from *The Last of the Mohicans* (1991), Tonto from *The Lone Ranger*, Squanto, and Iron Eyes Cody in the "crying Indian" commercial from the 1970s.[4]

The ignoble savage, the good Indian's redundantly named evil twin, embodies many of the flaws of normative white masculinity. Representing the wicked potential of masculine strength gone wrong, he is cruel and barbarous, killing and raping in unprovoked rage. He is drunk and lazy, deceitful and treacherous in his essence. He is never portrayed as having any family, except when he has a drudge of a wife whom he works like a mule to compensate for his laziness. A godless hindrance to civilization, he embodies the wild, threatening side of nature, and he obstructs the Manifest Destiny of the United States. Like the noble savage, he is physically powerful. These traits combine to fashion both a cautionary figure, and a figure against whom the superiority and righteousness of the heroic white man— or even the noble savage— is evident. Magua in *The Last of the Mohicans* and Scar in *The Searchers* (1956) are good examples of the ignoble savage, though just about any indian in a John Ford film will fill that role as well.[5]

Good and evil Indians have been used for various ends in white American culture. As a substantial body of scholarship shows, Americans at times identified themselves with the noble savage to emphasize the unique character of their new nation, as they struggled to distinguish themselves from European cousins whom they viewed as morally bankrupt.[6] In other instances, whites portrayed Indians as ignoble savages in order to justify colonial policies and mask the painful truths of American acts of genocide.[7]

The effect of these representations in countless movies is to erase sympathy for Indians (and thus, Native Americans), implying that they deserved the brutalities committed against them. Further, ignoble savage depictions link heroic white masculinity and American nationalism to killing Indians, tying the ignoble savage to the American foundational myths of regenerative violence on the frontier.[8] At other times, whites entirely erase Native Americans from their history so that the blood of conquest does not stain the national myth of righteous pioneers populating an empty North American continent.[9] In their presence and absence, hypermasculine indians have been particularly significant in American nationalist myths.

Indians are usually imagined only in the past, which is part of the reason they are so important to myths of nation-building. Indians never made it out of the national expansion era of the 1800s. Through the centuries, it has proven easier and safer for whites to write romantically about past battles between Natives and whites than to write about current situations in which audiences might be culpable.[10] Further, trapping indians in the past has meant that Native Americans of today feel pressure to certify their ethnic identity by resembling the hypermasculine white construction of the Lakota of 1860 through 1890, currently popular culture's favorite tribe and time period. This allows white people to dictate the terms of modern tribal identities even while Native Americans try to escape wholesale adoption of American culture by returning to ancestral traditions.[11] Hypermasculinity, combined with the tendency to keep Indian stories set in the past, has made indians particularly manipulable in national myths, a characteristic especially obvious in Westerns, movies with masculine nationalist myths of rugged individualism and regenerative violence at their very core.[12] Being trapped in the Western genre inextricably links indians with masculine myths of nation-building, making masculinity absolutely central to American constructions of indians.

Hollywood has also produced a string of Indian sympathy Westerns, such as *Broken Arrow* (1950), *Cheyenne Autumn* (1964), and *Dances with Wolves* (1990), in which Indians are drawn as tragic victims of certain segments of the white population.[13] These movies typically contain plots suggesting the predictable demise of Indians at the hands of a few corrupt pioneers or government types unless a white hero saves them from doom. The white good guy not only validates heroic white masculinity, but also provides a safe surrogate for white viewers, a person with whom they can identify to relieve the guilt they might feel if all whites were depicted wickedly.

Directors of some sympathy Westerns intended the indians in their films to be metaphors, at least in part, for other abused groups. They use Native American histories to make moral statements about race relations in general, a technique that has contradictory effects. On the one hand, it reminds people of the brutalities Native Americans have endured in their interaction with the United States, but on the other, it diminishes the significance of the original story by reducing it to the status of a metaphor for some other, more immediate problem. For example, in *Little Big Man* (1970), Arthur Penn intended his film to critique the Vietnam War as a continuation of American imperialism. As the film was shooting in 1969, news of the U.S. military's 1968 massacre of several hundred Vietnamese civilians at My Lai, Vietnam, leaked to the public. By the time the public saw *Little Big Man*, its depiction of Custer's slaughter of more than one hundred Cheyenne on the Washita River in 1868 came to stand as an indictment of the My Lai massacre more than of the Washita massacre.[14] Certainly the two incidents are products of the same U.S. imperialist agenda, but in a sense the allusion also diminishes a tragic event in Native American history to a metaphor for injustice instead of an actual injustice.

From Indian sympathy films emerged the wise old chief character, a variation on the noble savage. Vine Deloria describes this character type as one who "contains the classic posture of mysterious earth wisdom. He speaks primarily in aphorisms and rarely utters a word that is not wise and sentimental. He is always in favor of love and understanding and never advocates that we take up violence against those who have wronged us."[15] As a direct descendant of the noble savage, the wise old chief follows the time-honored tradition of embracing the causes of the "good" white men. He has grown in popularity over the last thirty years, having first been embraced by the hippies, and now the New Agers and men's movement groups as they riffle through world religions looking for inner peace.[16]

One scholar suggests that the spirituality of the wise old chief removes his political threat by feminizing him.[17] In that sense, the function of the wise old chief is not only to reassure white audiences that it was indeed their Manifest Destiny to own the continent, but also to restate the link between white masculinity and national expansion. The wise old chief's passivity links Indian-ness to subordination and femininity while simultaneously linking whiteness and masculinity to the right to own the land. This diversion from the hypermasculinity of earlier images reveals that the success of recent Native American efforts to reform male images is not as simple as toning down Indian masculinity, but that it involves removing Indians from the discourse of white masculinity altogether.

Portrayals of Indian women in films have been scarcer than images of Indian men, but they, too, have said more about white American masculine myths than about Native Americans.[18] In fact, perhaps the most obvious feature of images of Indian women in film is that they are far outnumbered by hypermasculine images of Indian men. This could be said of cinematic images regardless of race, but this imbalance cuts to the heart of the reason that

Native American filmmakers lately have deployed gender images so successfully to create more recognizable cinematic images of themselves.

Over the last thirty years, Native people have found ways to influence and manipulate the images of themselves that non-Natives see on the big screen and on television. A transformation began when Native American actors such as Dan George in *Little Big Man* and Will Sampson in *One Flew over the Cuckoo's Nest* (1975) played significant Indian characters. Their characters were symbolic, to be sure; as Old Lodge Skins, George played the wise old chief adopting the white guy and imparting all the knowledge of his people upon him, while Sampson's Indian character, Chief Bromden, at least partly symbolized a free spirit trapped by the rigid expectations of American social norms. But each of these actors cracked through the Indian shell, bringing Native American mannerisms, gestures, and faces to the roles—traits that were absent when white actors played Indians. While *Little Big Man* follows the tired stereotype of the wise old chief, it also plays on that cliche by injecting humor, fallibility, and anguish into George's character, making him more human and more Native American than any previous movie Indian. Sampson impressively portrays a patient in a psychiatric hospital pretending to be deaf and mute. Since beads, feathers, and mysticism are absent, and the movie is set in the present, the symbolism of his ethnicity is barely evident. The net effect is that Sampson comes off as a human in a human situation rather than as a cardboard cutout.

White authors created Old Lodge Skins and Chief Bromden, and both of the movies were also directed by whites, revealing that collaboration between whites and Native Americans can produce effective portrayals.[19] Without the talents, knowledge, and—yes—genetics of George and Sampson, though, the characters whites created would have been incomplete. White actors playing Indians always seem so busy trying to be Indian that they cannot develop other facets of their characters. Not so with George and Sampson, whose unstrained ease and comfort in roles as Native Americans allowed them to focus their efforts on separate aspects of their identities. In these movies, Native American actors began to reveal fully human, three-dimensional Native American men whose function was not merely to validate white American masculinity or nationalism. And more importantly, Native people recognized themselves in these characters.

Released in 1989, *Powwow Highway* is the first feature film that could reasonably be called a Native American film, rather than an Indian film. It takes steps toward presenting new gender images, especially in Gary Farmer's portrayal of Philbert Bono, but unfortunately it also reiterates some of the old stereotypes about Indians and Indian gender. The movie is based on the novel by Huron author David Seals,[20] and the main actors are Native

American, but nearly everything else in the movie was assembled by non-Natives, creating a fragmented, almost schizoid final product.

Perhaps the strongest appeal of *Powwow Highway* is that it features late-twentieth-century Native Americans as main characters who deal with modern issues and have at least partially Native American perspectives. A road buddy/action/adventure flick about two Cheyenne men on a multipurpose quest, it is packed with jokes, character traits, and themes that are not readily intelligible to a person unfamiliar with modern Native America. It addresses the issue of mining on reservations, the collusion of the federal government with mining interests, the history of the American Indian Movement (AIM) on Pine Ridge, the importance of teaching Native children their cultures, "rez cars," suburban migration, powwow culture, water contamination on reservations, and mixed receptions of traditionalism among tribal members. These are themes that most of white America would not even notice, but they are (or were, at least) refreshingly meaningful to Native American viewers.

The road buddy format allows *Powwow Highway* to address the split and convergence between competing notions of ethnic identity embodied in Buddy Red Bow, the glamorous militant political activist who shuns the cultural aspects of Cheyenne identity, and Philbert Bono, the nerdy traditionalist who never participated in the activism of the 1970s. As with all road buddy movies, the divergent characters come together in the end, resolving the conflict as they each combine aspects of the other's identity with their own.[21] The intersection of their identities echoes AIM history: urban Native militants and certain traditional reservation Natives allied with one another in the turbulent 1970s, though the movie polarizes the two characters more than Seals's novel does. An examination of the contrasting characters reveals interesting messages about Native American masculinity.

Buddy Red Bow is presented as strong, smart, confrontational, and potentially volatile in the same tradition as Hollywood action heroes such as Mel Gibson in the *Lethal Weapon* series. In other words, he is on a testosterone overload, as demonstrated in several scenes of indignant rage. Racism and government treachery always provoke these rages, making Buddy seem justified in his actions. No one gets killed, but the fisticuffs, knife-throwing, jailbreaks, and exploding cars all end up helping the protagonists toward their goals, so that in the final analysis, the American myth of regenerative male violence is confirmed by Native Americans.

There are moments of subversion of this myth, though, and more than one layer of meaning to Buddy's warrior image. From one perspective, his Vietnam veteran status makes him a walking cliché. As Ted Jojola notes, the story of the Indian vet out for justice was crusty by the time *Powwow Highway* was made because of the long string of movies with that storyline dating back

PHILBERT AND BUDDY ON THE ROAD. *Powwow Highway*. COURTESY OF THE ACADEMY OF MOTION PICTURE ARTS AND SCIENCES.

to the 1960s.[22] Beyond that, Vietnam vets seeking justice were a favorite theme in mainstream cinema since the 1970s in such movies as *Gordon's War* (1973), *First Blood* (1982), and *Out for Justice* (1991). Buddy's veteran status can be read as affirmation of his masculine strength, a shorthand way of saying he is one tough customer with a political chip on his shoulder. Such a rendering confirms earlier stereotypes about the hypermasculinity of Indians. Being a Vietnam veteran, however, has more significance than simply adding to his hypermasculine persona when the story is viewed from a tribal perspective.

Many Native American cultures, including the Cheyenne, afford veterans substantially more prestige within the community than non-Native American cultures do, so Buddy's status as a vet with three Purple Hearts takes on more meaning in a Native American context. In most Native societies, tradition holds that the more experience men gain in war, the higher a status they achieve (though it must be noted that warfare is not the only way for a man to raise his status). Add to this the fact that Native Americans have perhaps the highest military participation rates of any ethnic or racial group in the twentieth century,[23] and it becomes evident that Native American viewers might have a perspective on Buddy's veteran status and its relation to his masculinity and stature that would not be obvious to non-Natives. Being a veteran makes him a man of status and a potential leader. So although the film certainly manipulates the renegade vet image in standard ways, it may also be read as a product of a Native American author manipulating Cheyenne warrior traditions and their associations with modern veterans when he wrote the book on which the movie was based.

The two other Native vets in *Powwow Highway,* Jimmy Campbell and Wolf Tooth, offer a different perspective on Vietnam vet status than Buddy's. Jimmy Campbell was a POW in Vietnam who, Wolf Tooth tells us, "spent thirty-one months in a tiger's cage. He finally escaped, but he had to slit four throats to do it. He's got just about every medal there is." Jimmy's knife-throwing skills save Buddy from an attack by political enemies, which would ordinarily make him a tough guy. Instead, he is portrayed as an emotionally and physically disabled shell suffering from post-traumatic stress disorder. On one level, Jimmy is a critique of the tragedy of American colonialist wars and their effects on the many Native American vets and Native peoples in general. But on another level, his experiences inflate his own and Buddy's masculinity by glamorizing the conditions they endured and escaped. The layered, almost contradictory meanings simultaneously confirm and disrupt the hypermasculine Indian image, making many critics love and hate *Powwow Highway* at the same time.[24]

Like Buddy, Wolf Tooth is a veteran of both Vietnam and the American Indian Movement, yet he does not embrace the hypermasculine ethic in the same way as Buddy. He and his wife, Imogene, live on the Pine Ridge reservation, but they move away in the course of the movie because of political intimidation and violence there. With Imogene pregnant, she and Wolf Tooth decide that they must leave their home to find a safer, more stable life. Buddy criticizes the decision to move, to which Wolf Tooth replies, "You wanna fight every day of *your* life, *you* live in Pine Ridge. I had enough of that shit in Nam." With these words, Wolf Tooth challenges Buddy's confidence in the potential regenerative value of violence, and thus temporarily undermines the hypermasculine Indian image for the viewer. In fact, the image is undermined repeatedly in the movie by all the Native men aside from Buddy, but the movie also continues to glamorize Buddy's hypermasculinity. The scene in which Buddy throws a plate of glass from Philbert's wonder-car at a police cruiser in pursuit, magically making it flip onto its roof, illustrates the fragmented nature of the images. In mid-throw, Buddy mystically changes from a denim-clad activist throwing a Buick window at a cop to the noble savage, dressed in buckskin and feathers, throwing a stone hatchet. This heavy-handed attempt to link past and present battles affirms the old Indian images that Native Americans have been trying to overcome.

Philbert Bono, on the other hand, is neither a veteran of the Vietnam War, nor of Wounded Knee 1973, and his character counters the hypermasculine Indian image more than any other feature of the movie does. Philbert is a tubby, simple-minded outcast in the beginning of the movie. Flashbacks show that he was a nerd in grade school, ostracized by cool Native boys like

Buddy. In fact, the only reason Buddy associates with Philbert in the movie is because Philbert has a car he can use to give him a ride to Santa Fe to bail out Buddy's estranged sister, Bonny. Toward the beginning of the movie, Philbert decides that the time has come for him to become a warrior, and throughout the rest of the movie, he is "gathering medicine," collecting four "tokens" that will signify approval of his quest from spiritual powers. Along the way, he has several visions and continually gains spiritual power, finally receiving his fourth token. Buddy mocks Philbert's warrior quest and his spirituality at first, but gradually comes to embrace it, as the road buddy format demands. Similarly, Philbert comes to share Buddy's taste for resisting the enemy.

Philbert has little masculine prowess in the way it is typically portrayed, and in that aspect, he begins to undermine the standard hypermasculine portrayals of Indian men. That is not to say that Philbert's character is stereotype-free. His big vulnerable teddy-bear image, combined with his passionate, occasionally hokey spirituality makes him verge on becoming a New Age mystic mascot rather than a real person. Seals wrote an irreverent, coyote-style spirituality for the novel's Philbert, while the movie's Philbert is a more closely white version of Indian spirituality. In addition, Philbert's visions in the movie tend to confirm the stereotype that the only real Native Americans were warriors in nineteenth-century buckskin clothes, diminishing the advances the movie makes by showing Native Americans in a modern setting. What is new and appealing about Philbert, though, is that he is neither cool nor tough. He steals money from the police and pulls the bars out of the window of the jail cell that is holding Buddy's sister, but he does not throw punches or swing hatchets like Buddy. He dresses badly, eats too much junk food, and has no social skills. Philbert develops a fatherlike relationship with Bonny's young daughter, Skye, to whom he teaches aspects of Cheyenne culture. He relates more to her innocence and fascination with Cheyenne culture than to the manliness and political aggression of Buddy Red Bow. In these ways, he is a character who cannot be easily subsumed into the old hypermasculine images. Philbert almost slips into the "dumb buck" indian role, but he is redeemed by his mentoring relationship with Skye, his compassion, his generosity, and the cunning he reveals in solving the central dilemmas of the plot. He successfully relies on Cheyenne stories and Cheyenne values to save the day, but he is also an unpopular, irksome oaf, making it difficult for the viewer to link his Cheyenne identity to hypermasculinity.

Powwow Highway's depiction of Native American women brings it back to the old Indian masculinity, though, since the sole function of the women is to demonstrate the masculine heroism of the two buddies. The only Native woman with any meaningful role in the movie is Bonny, who is portrayed as an Indian princess—blameless, pure, and in need of rescue by the dashing warriors. The movie implies that she is arrested falsely in order to get Buddy away from the reservation during a crucial vote on a mining referendum. Bonny in the movie is shown as a helpless, innocent victim, but David Seals wrote Bonny as a more complicated character. While the federal government did target her for arrest to get Buddy away from the reservation, she was also a drug dealer and part-time hooker in the novel.[25] In portraying her as a princess, the movie *Powwow Highway* not only missed an excellent opportunity to push images of Native American women beyond stereotypes, but it forced Philbert and Buddy into clichéd roles as manly protectors of the virtuous woman.

When it was released, *Powwow Highway* provided a glimpse of Native American lives on screen, but it was riddled with inconsistency. It produced mixed messages about Native American masculinity, sometimes reiterating the old hypermasculine warrior images, and sometimes liberating Native American characters from them. The lasting value of the movie lies in the scenes in which it deflates the myth of the regenerative value of male violence, and in its portrayal of a human, oafish Native American hero. Such images begin to chip away at the white Indian and provide recognizably Native American characters.

An HBO production aired in the summer of 1996, *Grand Avenue* is notable for two important achievements. First, it features modern Native Americans living in an urban setting. Since a majority of Native Americans are now urban dwellers, it is important to address and represent the lives of urban Natives instead of always sticking to stories about reservations. Second, and perhaps more important, it overrides the standard Indian representation of hypermasculinity by presenting realistic and dynamic images of Native American women. Anyone familiar with Native Americans knows that in many Native communities, women hold an extraordinary amount of power and assume a variety of leadership roles. This reality had never been adequately portrayed on film prior to *Grand Avenue,* because whites usually do not imagine that Indians live in female-centered, family-based communities.[26] The Native American men in the movie are not portrayed as weak or hapless because of the focus on the strength of the women, though, as the emphasis is placed consistently on building the strength of the community as a whole. *Grand Avenue* is the most successful collaboration between Native Americans and whites in terms of its consistent Native American perspective, a fact which is likely traceable to the amount of creative control Miwok tribal member Greg Sarris exercised as author of the teleplay and co-executive producer.[27]

Grand Avenue tells the stories of an urban community of interrelated Pomo tribal members. This gritty rendering addresses gang violence, teenage sex, urban migration, spirituality, uneasy views of tribal traditions, alcoholism, fathers' responsibilities, kinship, interracial relationships, intertribal relationships, labor conditions, and cultural conceptions of illness and healing.

The story begins with a middle-aged widow, Mollie, moving with her three children to Santa Rosa, California, after the family of her recently deceased husband forces her to leave his reservation. She shows up at the door of her cousin Anna, who helps her find a one-bedroom house to rent up the street. Mollie does not realize that Steven, the unknowing father of her oldest daughter, Justine, lives on the block, too. In addition, an old basket-maker/healer named Nellie, who is related to all three households, lives a few doors away. *Grand Avenue* examines family and community dysfunction in several of its manifestations. Mollie is an alcoholic who has faced a life of adversity. Anna hides her failing marriage behind a veil of pride, while her daughter, Jean, is slowly dying of brain cancer. Justine lacks boundaries and lashes out at her mother in typical "bad girl" ways. Mollie's fourteen-year-old daughter, Alice, feels the burden of responsibility for her family's care. Incest lurks in the shadows when Steven's son, Raymond, begins dating Justine without knowing they are related.

While the movie does not delve into the concept of "poison," which is defined as culturally central to the community's dysfunction in the novel,[28] it indicates that community health can be restored through proper family relations and a return to Pomo spiritual traditions. In that way, it gives the Pomo people the capacity to fix their own problems, rejecting the "tragic victim" image of Indians, in which a white man would save them. The community's growing reliance on their kin and Pomo traditions saves the families from destroying themselves, and it is Pomo women such as Alice and Nellie who provide the impetus and strength behind this regeneration. Men do not rush in to save the women; women save themselves and therefore the community, implying their centrality to its survival.

As stated earlier, the Native American men in this movie are not portrayed as weak or hapless because of the strength of the women. Rather, they also are defined in terms of their relationships to the whole, to the community. The two main Native men in the movie are Steven and his son Raymond. Steven is a handsome man in his late thirties married to an Apache woman named Reyna. Raymond is his son from a previous marriage whom he has raised mostly on his own. He got Mollie pregnant when they were seniors in high school, but he never took responsibility for his daughter Justine and Mollie never asked him to help. In fact, he forgot about her pregnancy until Mollie moved back into his neighborhood. Only Mollie and Steven know that he is Justine's father. When Steven sees impending romantic involvement between his two children, Justine and Raymond, the threat of incest— the ultimate improper kin relationship— moves him to tell both Raymond and Justine that they are siblings. His actions cause rage and pain for his children, as well as for Mollie, who did not want to deal with Steven or let him into Justine's life. He wallows in self-pity, wondering if he has done the right thing, until Nellie arrives and tells him to quit pitying himself. Nellie reminds him that he made a mistake, as people are liable to do, but he will be redeemed because he took responsibility and established proper kin relations. Telling the truth about his relation to Justine turns out to be an incredibly painful act for all involved, but it is also redemptive. In a parallel plot, Steven intervenes to prevent fellow tribal members from selling a tribal cemetery, a temporarily unpopular move that eventually establishes proper relations between the Pomos and their ancestors. In each case, his actions relieve the stress, deceit, and bickering that caused great rifts in this little community that should have been so close.

While Steven develops into a strong person as *Grand Avenue* progresses, he begins the movie as one of the weakest of the characters, according to Sarris, even though he has all the characteristics that make him a successful man in white society—the house, the income, the pretty wife, the well-muscled body. Yet he cannot face his emotions or his responsibilities even as well as Mollie; at least she does not abandon her children.[29] He learns from Mollie and gains strength through facing the truth, and that adds another layer to Sarris's new interpretation of Native American gender identities. *Grand Avenue* shows men becoming stronger and more confident in their masculinity by learning new behaviors from the women.

Through *Grand Avenue*, Sarris suggests a new, more complex image of Native men. Steven clearly avoids the hypermasculinity of the old images, yet neither is he idealized as the noble savage or the wise old chief. As with Dan George's character in *Little Big Man,* Steven's fallibility makes him more realistic, more human. He causes pain even as he restores community health through humility and personal responsibility to kin, contrasting him with one-dimensional Indians created by white filmmakers.

While many cinematic images depict Indian masculinity as violent, even if that violence is justified, Sarris chooses to completely avoid that image, finally bringing Native American men into roles that have been available to people of other races for decades. He disregards any notion that Steven could be a perfect father, too, which is an aspect of the noble savage imagery that the mythopoetic men's movement embraced in the early 1990s.[30] Steven's virtue lies in his eventual confirmation of the importance of appropriate kin relations and his confirmation of Mollie's strength. He is not heroized by such actions; rather, his adherence to Pomo traditions is validated. The ability to fight has nothing to do with his role as a man in the Pomo tribe. Rather, the movie suggests that his humility, his newfound willingness to confront his emotions, and his responsibility to his kin through all adversity are ideal virtues for him as a Pomo man. To say that these are exclusively Pomo values would be misleading, but these certainly are values Sarris believes modern Native men need to embrace. His characters bring Native American men up to date in that regard.

Similarly, Raymond's character moves images of Native American masculinity away from the established hypermasculine Indian in that Raymond avoids involvement with the violent neighborhood gangs. Sarris includes youth gangs in the community he portrays, but the only gang-affiliated Native American in the movie is Justine.[31] It might have been realistic to show young Native men as gang members, considering the extent of the problem among Native communities, but Sarris chooses a different route. Young Native men already have enough pressure to prove their identity because of movie images; instead of producing new images of violent, tough-guy Indians to live up to, Sarris made Raymond a whitewashed, city version of a Native American who, like his father, had to learn what it means to be Pomo through interaction with Pomo women. Justine had to teach Raymond how to be responsible enough to confront his family problems.[32] By arranging the representations of these characters in such a way, *Grand Avenue* offers a modern Miwok's vision of Native gender roles.

Raymond demonstrates Sarris's vision of Native masculinity in other ways, as well. He is a gentle, straight-laced sixteen–year-old who likes playing sports. In a time and place where being a thug is the definition of cool, Raymond is a nerd. He is not a nerd in the pocket-protector, allergies, and thick glasses sense, but he is a straight arrow, a goody two shoes. He excels in school and baseball, and likes to play the decidedly unmacho sport of tennis. He is awkward around young women. He does not drink or smoke. He stands in stark contrast to the violent young gangsters in the movie. Their dysfunctional masculinity reveals the models of masculinity available in his neighborhood, and shows that Steven has raised Raymond differently. Like Philbert in *Powwow Highway*, Raymond is a nerd when compared to the boys around him. He does not participate in macho activities or try to be a tough guy. His clothes are not flashy. He is handsome enough, but his *Leave It to Beaver* nerdiness removes the potential for the romantic allure of a macho persona.[33]

The nerdiness that comprises one aspect of Raymond's identity counters the stereotypes non-Natives created for Indians. It takes him out of the white gender discourse that makes indians into noble and ignoble savages. He is not menacing or wicked, like the ignoble savage. He is a decidedly modern figure, not an anachronism like the noble savage. He is a human, with human foibles, not a mythical figure. Contrasting with the savage motif, Raymond's social awkwardness is a cross-cultural phenomenon, which makes it easier for non-Native audiences to understand him as a real person. Raymond dresses in blue jeans and button-down shirts, lacking the primitive appeal of the noble savage, so he will not be quickly coopted by New Agers, European Indianists, or the men's movement. Making Raymond a little bit nerdy is a simple way to make sure Raymond is a Native American and a person, not an Indian.

Spokane/Coeur d'Alene author and filmmaker Sherman Alexie uses a classically nerdy character in *Smoke Signals* (1998) to even greater effect. Alexie wrote the screenplay and the book upon which *Smoke Signals* is based, and he exerted considerable influence on the movie in his role as coproducer with Cheyenne/Arapaho director Chris Eyre.[35] Being the first full-length feature film written, directed, and coproduced by Native Americans to receive a major distribution deal makes it a particularly important milestone because of its potential for presenting Native American perspectives on film to a wide audience.

As with much of Alexie's work, *Smoke Signals* is in perpetual dialogue with popular white constructions of Indians, and like *Powwow Highway*, the movie uses the road buddy format to address Native American identity and its relation to Indian images. Thomas Builds-the-Fire, the nerd of the movie, stands in contrast to Victor Joseph, the cocky basketball star, and as expected in the road buddy genre, they come to a new understanding of each other's perspectives by the end of the movie.

The film begins with a flashback to a bicentennial Fourth of July house fire that killed Thomas's parents. Baby Thomas was thrown from a second-story window by his parents just before they perished, and Victor's father, Arnold Joseph, caught him. Thomas never finds out that it was Arnold who accidentally started the blaze in a drunken fireworks mishap, so he "adopts" Arnold as a father figure out of admiration for the heroic man who saved him. Arnold buckles under the burden of years of secret guilt for starting the fire, and it is one of the factors that eventually pushes him to leave his family on the reservation when Victor and Thomas are still boys. He dies in Phoenix, where his neighbor, Suzy Song, calls Victor's mom to see if someone wants to come down and claim his remains and his beat-up pickup truck. Victor does not have enough money to make it to Arizona, so Thomas offers to chip in if he can join him on the trip. Victor reluctantly agrees, unexcited by the prospect of spending several days with a chatty nerd in a secondhand three-piece suit. So their journey begins similarly to the *Powwow Highway* journey, with the macho man turning to the meek man for a ride.

As they proceed, Victor's conflicted relationship with his father becomes a bone of contention between him and Thomas. Through flashbacks and dialogue, the audience sees that Victor loved his father ferociously, but that his father's inconsistent expressions of love and volatile behavior— both results of his alcoholism—caused Victor untold pain. In one scene, for example, just as young Victor was feeling close to his father, Arnold hit his son and scolded him for spilling a beer, creating confused and conflicting emotions in the boy. The effects of Arnold's alcoholism and self-hate haunted his son. When he left home for good, Arnold finally broke Victor's heart. Throughout the rest of the movie, Victor's resentment and love mingle in a dysfunctional morass that finds expression only in anger, self-pity, and arrogance.

Thomas, on the other hand, idolizes Arnold Joseph. To him, Victor's father was the man who saved him from the fire that took his parents, the man pictured on the cover of *Time* magazine in a poignant political moment in the 1960s, the man who took him out to breakfast at Denny's. Thomas never experienced the pain and abandonment that Victor associates with Arnold. On a trip loaded with emotions and memories, Victor snaps as Thomas begins to tell another eulogic tall tale about Arnold:

> VICTOR: I'm really sick and tired of you telling me all these stories about my dad like you know him.
> THOMAS: But I did know him.
> VICTOR: What do you know about him, Thomas? Did you know he was a drunk? Did you know he left his family? Did you know he beat up my mom? Did you know he beat me up?
> THOMAS: Your dad was more than that. Just let it go, Thomas. He's nothing but a liar.[35]

An earlier conversation between Suzy Song and Victor evokes the same discordant views of Arnold Joseph, views that should be understood both literally and figuratively.

First, Alexie is examining the actual problems of father-son relationships among Native Americans. The problems are common enough to people of all cultures, but this should not be interpreted solely as an attempt to bridge cultural differences by stating that, at root, all humans have the same problems. While it is true that the father-son relationship in *Smoke Signals* is humanizing, understanding it solely through that lens fails to account for the Native American context. The movie discusses the localized impacts of colonialism on Native American men and the people in their worlds. It depicts a Native American family coping with the dysfunction caused by rampant alcoholism on reservations, and a Native American man whose life and family were destroyed by a celebration on the U.S.'s bicentennial, subtly indicating the role that the creation of the United States had in the family's misery. So while there are universal themes present, this story specifically contemplates Native American fathers and their families in a colonized nation at the end of the twentieth century.

Second, the conflicting interpretations of Victor's father are not solely about his literal father. The varying perspectives people had on Arnold mirror the internal conflicts Native Americans sometimes face when coming to terms with the legacies of their ancestors (or forefathers, to make the connection explicit). Thomas, the storyteller, embraces and embellishes Arnold's memory without contemplating his faults. Victor, wounded by the effects of colonialism on his father, spurns his memory and focuses only on his faults. Suzy Song, who says Arnold was "like a father" to her, knew him as a complicated man who had his faults, but who was also honorable in his intentions. Thus Arnold's three "children" understand his legacy, and, metaphorically, the legacy their forefathers left them. By communicating with each other, Victor and Thomas metaphorically develop new understandings of their ancestors by the end of the movie that are more in line with Suzy Song's. Colonialism tripped up their forefathers, and sometimes they tripped themselves up, but they were worthy, if flawed, individuals. Again, this can be seen as a universalizing move by Alexie and Eyre in that all people must grapple with the legacies of their ancestors, but it should be understood primarily as a critical issue that Native Americans need to address. Native Americans face shame, poverty, and high rates of suicide and substance abuse as direct consequences of colonialism and racism. Sometimes it feels as though these problems have been passed down through the generations like unholy heirlooms, since Native Americans today seem to grapple with the same demons as their ancestors did. Still, their ancestors' resistance and cultural survival are sources of great strength and pride that Native Americans draw on to overcome obstacles in the present. *Smoke Signals* poignantly addresses that conflict between romanticization and rejection of ancestors.

Another strength of the depiction of Arnold is that it does not directly engage white understandings of him. The perspectives on Arnold, at least, are strictly Native American. This represents quite a change in cinematic history, in which even Indian sympathy films have nearly always involved interaction or conflict with whites in some way. This is a significant accomplishment in both *Grand Avenue* and *Smoke Signals*. Even *Powwow Highway*, though it was grounded in the stories of two Native American men, was propelled by conflict with whites. *Smoke Signals* and *Grand Avenue* reveal certain aspects of Native American lives that largely exclude white people. It is not that Native Americans do not normally interact with whites or that whites do not have an impact on the lives of the characters, but that there are times when white people are irrelevant to the story being told. The depictions of Arnold reveal to the audience that Native Americans have internal worlds separate from whites.

While Arnold's image is insulated from white cultural constructions,

Thomas and Victor certainly are not. They directly engage popular white constructions of the Indian to great effect, through both dialogue and character development. Alexie establishes Thomas as an "antiwarrior."[36] He intends the hypomasculine nerd to directly combat the images of hypermasculinity into which Indians have been locked throughout the history of the white American imagination. Thomas wears a three-piece suit and thick glasses that keep sliding down his nose. He is small, skinny, and unathletic. He wears a frilly apron while cooking for his grandma, who is his closest companion.

Evan Adams, the actor portraying Thomas, added significantly to the antiwarrior image by playing Thomas as if he were an old woman from his reservation.[37] Alexie loves this androgynous aspect of Thomas that Adams brought to the screen, and he wishes he had thought to write him that way in the first place, so pleased was he with the result.[38] Thomas's ambiguous gender identity opens the possibility for audiences to interpret him as gay, as well, which furthur erodes white constructions of Indian men. Together, Adams and Alexie introduced a character who counters the ability of the Indian icon to circumscribe Native American male identities.

In a scene in which Thomas and Victor are on the bus to Phoenix, Victor confronts Thomas about his failure to adhere to the warrior image that movies created for them, and chides him for trying to be a different kind of white version of an indian.

> VICTOR: Why can't you have a normal conversation? You're always trying to sound like some damn medicine man or something. I mean, how many times have you seen *Dances with Wolves?* A hundred, two hundred?
> *Embarrassed, Thomas ducks his head.*
> VICTOR: Oh, jeez, you have seen it that many times, haven't you? God. Don't you even know how to be a real Indian?
> THOMAS: I guess not.
> VICTOR: Well, shit, no wonder. Jeez, I guess I'll have to teach you then, enit?
> *Thomas nods eagerly.*
> VICTOR: First of all, quit grinning like an idiot. Indians ain't supposed to smile like that. Get stoic.
> *Thomas tries to look serious. He fails.*
> VICTOR: No, like this.
> *Victor gets a very cool look on his face, serious, determined, warriorlike.*
> VICTOR: You got to look mean or people won't respect you. White people will run all over you if you don't look mean. You got to look like a warrior. You got to look like you just came back from killing a buffalo.

THOMAS: But our tribe never hunted buffalo. We were fishermen.

VICTOR: What? You want to look like you just came back from catching a fish? This ain't *Dances with Salmon,* you know? Thomas, you got to look like a warrior.

Thomas gets stoic. He's better this time.

VICTOR: And second, you got to know how to use your hair.

THOMAS: My hair?

VICTOR: Yeah, I mean look at your hair, it's all braided up and stuff. You've got to free it. *(He shakes his hair out and runs his fingers through it)* An Indian man ain't nothing without his hair. *(Pause)* And last, and most important, you've got to get rid of that suit, Thomas. You just have to.[39]

This self-reflexive, even postmodern,[40] scene crystallizes the ramifications of white portrayals of Indian men in films. Whether a hypermasculine warrior or a mystic medicine man or even an Indian princess, these images taunt young Native American people as they try to live up to the movie image of the Indian. There is no small amount of irony in the fact that in portraying Native American men in a realistic manner on film, Alexie felt he needed to have them grapple with and even accidentally adopt white images of Indians from films. No clearer statement could be made about the need for Native Americans to be in control of Native American cinema.

Not only does Thomas's nerdiness undermine interpretations of him as a warrior, it also thwarts potential interpretations of him as a medicine man or wise old chief. An Indian medicine man should be solemn and wise, but Thomas is goofy and socially irksome. Director Chris Eyre notes that a non-Native American "would've made Thomas into a shaman in two minutes. I'm not making Thomas into a shaman and prostituting him that way."[41] So when Victor denounces Thomas's affection for the Indian medicine man image, he effectively ends the potential for comfortable interpretations of him as a modern mystic in the Indian tradition.

While Victor's embrace of the warrior image is half sarcastic, Alexie and Eyre quickly undermine it as well. At a bus stop, Thomas changes out of the suit into jeans and a "frybread power" T-shirt, takes off his nerd glasses, stiffens his jaw, and lets his hair blow free in the wind, giving him that warrior look following his lesson from Victor. He walks across the parking lot in slow motion, striking the warrior's pose, convincing the audience that he has transformed into the hypermasculine stud Indian Victor tries to be. As he nears the bus, he puts his glasses back on and grins sheepishly at the posturing he has just done, revealing that the warrior image is a joke to him.

The work of devaluing the warrior ethic is not over yet, though. When they get back on the bus, they find two rednecks have taken their seats.

THOMAS: THE NERD AS ANTIWARRIOR. *Smoke Signals* (1996). COURTESY OF
MIRAMAX PICTURES.

Victor tries to intimidate them out of the seats with his warrior look, but one
of them says calmly, "Now listen up. These are our seats now. And there ain't
a damn thing you can do about it. So why don't you and Super Indian there
find yourself someplace else to have a powwow, okay?" A staredown ensues,
which Victor loses, and he dejectedly pulls Thomas to the remaining seats in
the back of the bus, near the washroom.

> THOMAS: Jeez, Victor, I guess your warrior look doesn't work
> every time.
> VICTOR: Shut up, Thomas.[42]

And with that, the warrior ethic is deflated and defused. Alexie and Eyre
will not allow their characters to become cardboard cutouts of Indian men.

The film's intent, according to Eyre, is "to personalize [Native
Americans]. It's supposed to deconstruct the icon [Indian] and let you get to
know Victor and Thomas as people. It's an invitation to come see Thomas as
[a Native American] and as a person."[43] "It could have been about two guys
in Croatia, but the sensibilities are specific. They are Native American, about
us representing ourselves."[44] Even though Alexie and Eyre were aware that
a large part of their audience would be non-Native, the movie was made
largely with the Native American audience in mind. They find the most satisfaction in the reactions Native Americans have to seeing people they rec-

ognize as Native American on the screen. Helping non-Natives understand Native Americans as human beings, with hometowns, families, and foibles is certainly important, but it is not the only benefit.

The depictions offered in the three movies discussed here should not be understood as providing new, singular definitions of Native American masculinity. "Native American" encompasses hundreds of different cultures with varying conceptions of masculinity, and even within each tribal culture, different people will have different ideas about the virtues, faults, and responsibilities of manhood. A Miwok and a Coeur d'Alene tribal member cannot be expected to share the same ideas about masculinity, just as two Miwoks should not be expected to agree on the traits of manhood. Some Native Americans view violent defense of their rights as a positive tribal characteristic,[45] while others view violence as an affliction. Many Native American teenagers would cringe at the thought of being associated with the nerd, Thomas Builds-the-Fire, while others see him as their hero.

These films cannot define what a "real" Native man is. They reject the hypermasculine image that whites gave indians. They offer a vision of what a Native man can be, and what he certainly is not; they have been moderately successful at bringing more Native women characters into central roles, thereby countering the white tendency to imagine whole tribes comprised of men. Their greater success, however, has come through redefining Native men. As nerds, struggling fathers, veterans, wounded sons, husbands, and activists in Native American communities, the new Native American male characters undermine the hypermasculinity of the white construction of the Indian, thereby undermining one of the most consistent characteristics of white indians. This has allowed recent depictions to emphasize the humanity and diversity of Native men and women. In confronting and discarding the hypermasculine portrayals of indians, Native actors and filmmakers wrench the power to define Native Americans away from non-Natives, and successfully establish Native American perspectives in the cinema.

Notes

Thanks to Shadiin D. García for her support and theoretical contributions, to the editors of this volume as well as Carol Miller and Paul Pfeiffer for editorial suggestions, to Eric Buffalohead and Kirk Crowshoe for provocative discussions of Native American films, to Greg Sarris, Evan Adams, and Sherman Alexie for talking with me about their work, and to Matt Basso for soliciting this essay.

1. I combine the thinking of Gerald Vizenor and Robert Berkhofer in distinguishing between *Indians* and *Native Americans* in cinematic imagery. In real life, Native Americans call themselves by many names, including Indians, American Indians, First Nations people, and Native Americans, to name a few, or by their tribal names. The purpose of making the distinction between Indian and Native American in writing is to emphasize the extent to which the Indian is truly a construction of the white imagination, having little resemblance to Native Americans. Of course the concept of any universal term or category for all the indigenous nations of the Americas is itself deeply rooted in colonialism, but such terms— for

better or worse—have become more meaningful at the beginning of the twenty-first century. Gerald Vizenor, *The Everlasting Sky: New Voices from the People Named the Chippewa* (New York: Crowell-Collier Press, 1972); Robert F. Berkhofer, Jr., *The White Man's Indian: Images of the American Indian from Columbus to the Present* (New York: Vintage Books, 1978).

2. For a more complete discussion of the early development of this trend, see David Anthony Tyeeme Clark and Joane Nagel, "White Men, Red Masks: Appropriations of 'Indian' Manhood in Imagined Wests," this volume, 109–30. Prior to this time, images of Indians were sometimes feminized to suit colonial interests, but the masculine noble and ignoble savages were already typical representations. See Philip J. Deloria, *Playing Indian* (New Haven: Yale University Press, 1998).

3. It is not my intention here to reiterate the entire history of Indian images in film and popular culture. Several volumes have already tackled that task, and I direct anyone interested in more work in that direction to S. Elizabeth Bird, ed., *Dressing in Feathers: The Construction of the Indian in American Popular Culture* (Boulder, Colo.: Westview, 1996); Peter C. Rollins and John E. O'Connor, eds., *Hollywood's Indian: The Portrayal of the Native American in Film* (Louisville: University of Kentucky Press, 1998); and Robert F. Berkhofer's work, cited above. Readers should understand that the introduction here is presented rather simplistically for the purpose of brevity. Reception of these characters varied from individual to individual, as a body of recent scholarship reveals. Many Native American youths, for example, loved Tonto when he first appeared on television in the 1950s because he was a famous good guy played by an identifiably Native American actor, Jay Silverheels. Steven M. Lee's essay "'All the Best Cowboys Have Chinese Eyes': The Utilization of the Cowboy-Hero Image in Contemporary Asian-American Literature," (this volume, 231–49) addresses audience response superbly.

4. See also Sally L. Jones, "The First but Not the Last of the 'Vanishing Indians': Edwin Forrest and Mythic Re-creations of the Native Population," in *Dressing in Feathers*.

5. A large number of essays have discussed the ignoble savage imagery of Indians in film. Any of the books cited here will have some reference to such imagery, though the introduction to *Dressing in Feathers* by S. Elizabeth Bird specifically shows a good example of the "drudge of a wife" imagery (6). Also on the relationship between ignoble savages and their wives, see Frank Goodyear, "The Narratives of Sitting Bull's Surrender: Bailey, Dix, and Meade's Photographic Western," in *Dressing in Feathers*, esp. 37.

6. See Deloria.

7. While no one has ever admitted to creating ignoble savage imagery for these purposes, dime novels, Western movies, and Wild West shows certainly achieved this end. Sally L. Jones discusses a telling example of this phenomenon from the South in the 1830s. Theatergoers there were outraged by portrayals of Indians as people worthy of sympathy because they were, at the time, trying to remove all tribes near them to lands west of the Mississippi, justified to some extent by assumptions of Indian savagery even among the so-called civilized tribes. Jones, 17. See also C. Richard King, "Segregated Stories: The Colonial Contours of the Little Bighorn Battlefield National Monument," in *Dressing in Feathers*; and Ken Nolley, "The Representation of Conquest: John Ford and the Hollywood Indian, 1939–1974," in *Hollywood's Indian*. For a broader discussion of the ways the United States has written imperialism out of its history, see Amy Kaplan and Donald Pease, eds., *Cultures of United States Imperialism* (Durham, N.C.: Duke University Press, 1993), esp. "Introduction," by Amy Kaplan.

8. See Pat Dowell, "The Mythology of the Western: Hollywood Perspectives on Race and Gender in the Nineties," *Cineaste* 21, nos. 1–2, (winter–spring 1995), 6ff; Richard Slotkin, *Regeneration through Violence: The Mythology of the American Frontier, 1600–1860* (Middletown, Conn.: Wesleyan University Press, 1973); Clark and Nagel, this volume; and Lee, this volume.

9. See Ward Churchill, *Fantasies of the Master Race: Literature, Cinema, and the Colonization of the Americas*, ed. M. Annette Jaimes (Monroe, Maine: Common Courage Press, 1992); and Bruce Greenfield, *Narrating Discovery: The Romantic Explorer in American Literature, 1790–1855* (New York: Columbia University Press, 1992).

10. See Joel W. Martin, "'My Grandmother Was a Cherokee Princess': Representations of Indians in Southern History," in *Dressing in Feathers*; Renato Rosaldo, "Imperialist Nostalgia," in *Culture and Truth: The Remaking of Social Analysis*, (Boston: Beacon Press, 1989); and Johannes Fabian, *Time and the Other: How Anthropology Makes Its Object* (New York: Columbia University Press, 1983).

11. Gerald Vizenor's parable of Tune Browne satirically critiques this predicament. "Socioacupuncture: Mythic Reversals and the Striptease in Four Scenes," in *Crossbloods: Bone Courts, Bingo, and Other Reports* (Minneapolis: University of Minnesota Press,1990). See also Ward Churchill, in "Indians Are Us?" *Indians Are Us? Culture and Genocide in Native North America* (Monroe, Maine: Common Courage Press, 1994).

12. See, for example, *Drums along the Mohawk* (1939), *The Searchers* (1956), or *How the West Was Won* (1962). See Lee, this volume, for an excellent discussion of the ways white cowboy masculinity frames American nationalism.

13. Angela Aleiss discusses certain forgotten films from the silent era that qualify as Indian sympathy films, such as *The Vanishing American* (1925) and *Frozen Justice* (1929). She recovers very important information about Native American involvement in cinema in this era, but there is little analysis of film content in this article. Angela Aleiss, "Native Americans: The Surprising Silents," *Cineaste* 21, no. 3 (summer 1995): 34. Also accessible at: http://www.lib.berkeley.edu/MRC/NativeAmericans.html.

14. *Soldier Blue* (1970) has similar political intentions. John O'Connor, "The White Man's Indian: An Institutional Approach," in *Hollywood's Indian*, 37; and Margo Kasdan and Susan Tavernetti, "Native Americans in a Revisionist Western: *Little Big Man*," in *Hollywood's Indian*.

15. Vine Deloria, "Foreword: American Fantasy," in *The Pretend Indians: Images of Native Americans in the Movies*, ed. Gretchen Bataille and Charles L. P. Silet. (Ames: University of Iowa Press, 1980), xi.

16. With apologies to those who are shocked to learn that people are offended by white attempts to make aspects of other people's spiritual traditions their own. The problems come when white people believe they are experts in the given tradition, and pronounce themselves authorities. Because of unequal power structures between whites and nonwhites, many people absurdly grant white "experts" more credence than the people whose traditions they study, at which point white people have stolen the ability of a people to define their traditions for themselves. See Churchill, *Indians Are Us?*

17. See Dowell.

18. See Rayna Green, "'The Pocahontas Perplex': The Image of Indian Women in American Culture," *Massachusetts Review* 16, no. 4 (autumn 1975): 698–714.

19. Thomas Berger, *Little Big Man* (New York: Dial, 1964); Ken Kesey, *One Flew over the Cuckoo's Nest* (New York: Viking, 1962). Arthur Penn directed *Little Big Man*, and Milos Forman directed *Cuckoo's Nest*.

20. David Seals, *The Powwow Highway* (New York: Plume, 1979).

21. See Steven Cohan and Ina Rae Hark, eds., *The Road Movie Book* (New York: Routledge, 1997).

22. Ted Jojola, "Absurd Reality II: Hollywood Goes to the Indians," in *Hollywood's Indian*.

23. See Tom Holm, *Strong Hearts, Wounded Souls: Native American Veterans of the Vietnam War* (Austin: University of Texas Press, 1996).

24. See Eric Gary Anderson, "Driving the Red Road: *Powwow Highway*," in *Hollywood's Indian*.

25. Tasunkanupa's website, May 30, 1997. Site no longer available; essay in possession of the author.

26. Maggie Eagle Bear (Sheila Tousey) moved in this direction in *Thunderheart*, as a fictional representation of the assassinated Micmac AIM activist, Anna Mae Pictou Aquash, but since she is killed before the end of the movie, the permanent presence and value of female leadership is never fully realized. Instead, the men save the day in this two-hour testosterone bath of a movie. Like *Powwow Highway*, though, *Thunderheart* is a conflicted mix of Native American and white influence. On the one hand, it values traditional Lakota spiritual practices, uses Lakota language, informs the audience of dire circumstances on South Dakota reservations, condemns the history of federal abuse of Native lands for uranium mining, and tries to portray some of the violent political turmoil of Pine Ridge in the 1970s. On the other hand, it suggests that an FBI agent came in and saved all the traditional Lakotas, that the uranium mining was stopped, and that the general public would not have accepted a brown-skinned hero. This is not to imply that collaborative efforts cannot work in movies, because certainly *Grand Avenue* provides proof that they can. Rather, it suggests that collaboration is not an easy thing to master.

27. I do not want to diminish the role of director Daniel Sackheim, who also directs TV's *NYPD Blue* and *Law and Order*. His considerable skill in directing dramas certainly raised the quality of this production to a high caliber, though I doubt he was the key to the successful presentations of Native American perspectives in the movie. Greg Sarris deserves the lion's share of commendations in that regard, though the very talented Native American cast (yes, A. Martinez is Piegan) certainly contributed to the final product as well.

28. The teleplay is based on Sarris's excellent novel of the same name. Greg Sarris, *Grand Avenue* (New York: Penguin, 1994).

29. Greg Sarris, conversation with the author, January 19, 2000.

30. See Sherman Alexie, "White Men Can't Drum," *New York Times Magazine*, October 4, 1992, 30–31.

31. By making Justine a gangster, he reaffirms the strength of Native American women, and he eventually shows that she is strong enough to leave gangster life behind.

32. Sarris, conversation with the author.

33. On the romantic allure of indian men, see Peter van Lent, "'Her Beautiful Savage': The Current Sexual Image of the Native American Male," in *Dressing in Feathers*.

34. Sherman Alexie, *Smoke Signals: A Screenplay* (New York: Hyperion, 1998). Screenplay based on Alexie's collection of short stories, *The Lone Ranger and Tonto Fistfight in Heaven* (New York: Atlantic Monthly Press,1993).

35. Alexie, *Smoke Signals*, 109.

36. Alexie, conversation with the author, May 4, 1999.

37. Evan Adams, personal correspondence, May 16, 2000; Evan Adams, conversation with the author, June 12, 2000.

38. Alexie, conversation with the author.

39. Alexie, *Smoke Signals*, 61–63, with minor adaptations.

40. By calling the film self-reflexive and postmodern, I mean that the movie alludes to the fact that it is a movie. The filmmakers are aware of the historical relationship between Native Americans and the cinema and the role that the current film has in changing that history, and they incorporate that relationship into its content.

41. Bob Ivry, "From the Reservation of His Mind," *The Record* (Bergen, N.J.), June 28, 1998.

42. Alexie, *Smoke Signals*, 65.

43. See Ivry.

44. Michael Fleeman, "'Smoke Signals': Doors May Be Swinging Wide Open," *The Standard-Times* (New Bedford, Mass), July 4, 1998.

45. See, for example, Karen Blu, *The Lumbee Problem: The Making of an American Indian People* (Cambridge, Mass: Cambridge University Press, 1980); 144–60.

Tex-Sex-Mex

American Identities, Lone Stars, and the Politics of Racialized Sexuality

José E. Limón

At the heart of this essay is an extended consideration of John Sayles's film *Lone Star* (1996). Sayles's masterpiece provides both the impetus and part of the content for my argument concerning recent and hopeful changes in certain American identities. Before film became their primary mode of discourse, these identities and the politics of racialized sexuality they reflect were first fully articulated in nineteenth-century dime novels of the West, many of which were, like *Lone Star*, set in Texas. A now very distant discursive cousin of the Sayles film, called, in fact, *Little Lone Star* (1886) and written by one Sam Hall featured, for example, Anita, "a physically precocious" young Mexican woman living on a Texas hacienda "whose passions and complexion are compared to the red-hot volcanoes of her native Mexico." She is being threatened with rape by Caldelas the Coyote, a vicious, degenerate Mexican bandit, until she is rescued by a strong, clean-cut, fair-haired Anglo-Texan cowboy named William Waldron. Anita reciprocates the sexual interest of the "fair-haired hero."[1] Identities like Anita's, Caldelas's, and Waldron's were on display again and again throughout the late nineteenth and twentieth centuries in fiction, film, song, and even television advertising. Who can forget the Frito Bandito, cartoon cousin of Caldelas the Coyote? From them we have inherited a potent and perduring American cultural iconography of Anglo-American–Mexican relations that because of its demographics and history has a special intensity in Texas, but certainly resounds in other parts of the U.S. West.

In this essay, I take up the intertwined theoretical spheres of postcolonialism, race, and sexuality to reexamine this iconography in the conflicted social histories of these two peoples, and suggest that this iconographic relationship goes beyond simple mutual stereotyping; it has politically critical ambivalence. I explore this concept first by offering an analysis of the iconographic representation of Anglo and Mexican manhood and womanhood in popular literature, songs, and ballads, and then by considering the ambivalent nature of these icons, particularly as seen in the classic film *High Noon*. Because cultural texts like songs, pulp fiction, and movies often work in unison to reinforce particular images, I will treat them together rather than as singular entities. Finally, I contend that Sayles's *Lone Star* offers a radical revision of the traditional iconography and its inherent ambivalence, a revision consistent with a major shift in the social relations between Anglos and Mexicans, at least in Texas, in the 1990s.

The male Anglo icon is a tough, swaggering, boastful—sometimes taciturn—hard-drinking, hard-riding, straight-shooting cowboy. He is also usually tall, strong, lean, handsome, and of course white figure—John Wayne in any of his Westerns. These bodily attributes contrast with a fat, slovenly, dark, mustachioed, and often drunken, deceitful, and treacherous Mexican male with whom our Anglo cowboy is usually at personal and political odds—for example, the Mexicans in *Little Lone Star* and in Sam Peckinpah's *The Wild Bunch* (1969). The figure of a Mexican woman brought into close sexual conjunction with the cowboy mediates these two. She is usually an upper-class, very attractive, light-complected, often "Spanish" senorita, such as Alejandra in Cormac McCarthy's otherwise subtle, "modernist" *All the Pretty Horses* (1992)[2] or Selena, the "Mexican girl" in Marty Robbins's popular song "El Paso" (1959), which memorably begins, "Out in the west Texas town of El Paso, I fell in love with a Mexican girl." While attractive like the Spanish señorita, this "girl" Selena has a distinctively darker sexual semiosis. She is, characteristically, a bar-girl, or prostitute, and sometime lover to the song's cowboy hero, like *Little Lone Star*'s Anita. This figure of "darker" and lower-class illicit sexuality—usually positioned on the real and figurative border—is more common in the popular imagery than is the senorita. Robbins's cowboy narrator, Gary Cooper's Will Kane in *High Noon,* and McCarthy's John Grady Cole might be attracted to, have sex with, and even fall in love with such a figure, but usually these relationships are not culturally meant to last, as we see in a nineteenth-century cowboy song:

Me and Juana talkin' low
So the "madre" couldn't hear—
How those hours would go a-flyin',
And too soon I'd hear her sighin',
In her little sorry tone—
"Adios, mi corazon" . . .

Never seen her since that night;
I kain't cross the Line, you know.
She was Mex and I was white;
Like as not it's better so.[3]

More often than not, our cowboy must take up romantic permanency with his own racial-cultural kind:

I'm free to think of Susie—
Fairer than the stars above—
She's the waitress at the station
And she is my turtle dove. . . .

I take my saddle, Sundays—
The one with inlaid flaps—
And on my new sombrero
And my white angora chaps;
Then I take a bronc for Susie
And she leaves her pots and pans
And we figure out our future
And talk o'er our homestead plans.[4]

Yet another song fills out the spiritual dimensions of this female figure:

You wonder why I slicks up so
On Sundays, when I gits to go
To see her—well, I'm free to say
She's like religion that-a-way.
Jes sort o' like some holy thing,
As clean as young grass in the spring.[5]

In these songs and in other cultural texts of the time, Anglo women are represented, on the one hand, as religious, virtuous, faithful, hard-working housewives or potential housewives pretty, if sometimes a bit homey. For example, in *High Noon* the "prim and proper" schoolmarm, Amy, just such an Anglo woman, does not forsake Will Kane on his wedding day.[6] On the other hand, we have the image of the tough-talking, somewhat sexually available, take-charge Anglo woman who can drink—Miss Kitty of the old television series *Gunsmoke* (1955–75). A related version is the older woman-in-charge, such as Jordan Benedict's feisty unmarried sister, Luz, in Edna Ferber's *Giant,* as both novel (1952) and film (1956).[7] Susie in the cowboy song embodies this type as does more recently the ex-prostitute Anglo character, Lorena, in Larry McMurtry's *Streets of Laredo.*[8]

This cultural complex attracted significant analytical attention in the 1960s, even as early as 1958, with Américo Paredes's *"With His Pistol in His Hand": A Border Ballad and Its Hero.*[9] In the 1960s Chicano and Chicana cultural critics offered a critical reading of its iconography, although Anglo scholars generally share the view as well. All unequivocally implicated these recurrent images in the history of Anglo conquest and the quasi-colonialism of Mexican communities, not only in what later became the Southwest, but in Mexico as well. Casting Mexican women, in particular, as sexually promiscuous made them morally available within a code of racism ratifying and extending the right of Anglo conquest to the realm of the sexual. By taking "his" woman, the Anglo colonizer further diminished the already desexualized Mexican male even as the Anglo male body was sexually affirmed. Anglo males thus extracted not only economic surplus value from Mexicans but also what Chicano Marxist critic Guillermo Flores calls "racial-cultural surplus value."[10] In their extensive review of American literature treating this subject, Alfredo Mirande and Evangelina Enriquez conclude,

> The progressively bleak picture we have presented . . . reveals a pathetic series of depictions of the Chicana in American literature. From the coquettish senorita to the lusty whore . . . a series of portrayals unfolds that pays little tribute to Mexican femininity. Underscoring this series, which recedes into negativity, is the theme of an encounter between two very different cultures which produces a pattern of initial attraction that quickly gives way to rejection, seduction, and finally, relegation to inferior status of one by the other.[11]

Otherwise highly critical of such representations, Mirande and Enriquez offer one ambivalent passage that, as early as 1979, began to lead me away from my own former view that this iconography simply reproduced colonialist dominance: "Although their [Mexican women's] deficiencies are cited as frequently as their attractions, it is noteworthy that their exotic qualities often triumph when they are compared with their American sisters."[12]

The very persistence and predictability of the iconography, together with the advent of certain strains of postcolonial theory and the passage of time and change of circumstance, now lead me in a direction that lends full valence to the exotic and erotic character of these figurations, even as it restores a part of the iconography often left out of such analyses: hard-working, faithful, religious, sort of pretty Anglo Susie and the somewhat later "Latin lover." An intriguing passage focused on Texas, in Arnoldo De Leon's 1983 *They Called Them Greasers: Anglo Attitudes toward Mexicans in Texas, 1821–1900,* further encouraged this new direction:

The image of Mexicans as irresponsible and promiscuous laid the foundation for another important theme in nineteenth-century Texas—the sexual desire of white men for Mexican women. White men took Mexican senoritas to bed, perhaps more often than can ever be known. But the sexual relations were not just something that naturally came to be: on the contrary, they occurred only after the physical drive of white men wrestled with the discriminating psyche that resisted such relations.[13]

Charles Ramirez-Berg has also taken a similar perspective, though framed in Lacanian theoretical terms: in such images, he says, "the Other is (temporarily) idealized as the path back to wholeness, until what always happens does happen—the subject realizes that the Other is lacking. In terms of Hispanic stereotypes, it might be speculated that the stereotypes have persisted in cinema—since the earliest years of this century—because they fulfilled a need of the Anglos."[14]

The alternative reading of this iconography conceptually departs from De Leon's perhaps unintended double entendre on the Anglo "discriminating psyche."[15] The Anglo male's struggle is not so much between his psyche and something distinct called the physical; rather, it is deeply intrapsychic even as it is social. The problem of "discrimination" is not confined to external social relationships; it is a struggle to discriminate between deeply internalized political relationships and allegiances. Needed also relative to Ramirez-Berg's Lacanian thesis is a historicization of an otherwise quite persuasive psychoanalytic insight that informs my own argument as well. One must account for these complexities of desire with greater historical specificity as to social change and conditions that might be loosely termed colonialist.[16]

Homi K. Bhabha's recent theoretical work on race, sexuality, and colonialism provides a further catalyst for taking this new direction. Robert J. C. Young explains how Bhabha exploits a somewhat repressed distinction that Edward Said made in his now famous formulation of Orientalism as the discursive project through which the West came to fashion its inherently denigrating view of the colonized cultural Other. Employing a psychoanalytic perspective, Bhabha pursues Said's brief notice of a latent as well as a manifest Orientalism, or what Young terms "an unconscious positivity of fantasmatic desire."[17] By emphasizing the extent to which the two levels fused, Bhabha shows "how colonial discourse of whatever kind operated not only as an instrumental construction of knowledge but also according to the ambivalent protocols of fantasy and desire."[18] Bhabha moves us away from a rigid, univocal understanding of such cultural constrictions toward *ambivalence*: "To recognize the stereotype as an ambivalent mode of knowledge and power demands a theoretical and political response that challenges deterministic or functionalist modes of conceiving of the relationship between discourse and politics. The analytic of ambivalence questions dogmatic and moralistic positions on the meaning of oppression and discrimination."[19] Bhabha shifts us from "the ready recognition of images as positive or negative, to an understanding of the *processes of subjectification* made possible (and plausible) through stereotypical discourse." Rather than simply judge such a construction as the sexy señorita as a "bad" image, he proposes that one "displace" it, by engaging with its "effectivity; with the repertoire of positions of power and resistance, domination and dependence, that constructs colonial identification subject (both colonizer and colonized)" in forms of difference that are racial and sexual. "[S]uch a reading reveals . . . the boundaries of colonial discourse," Bhabha believes, and "enables a transgression of these limits from the space of that otherness."[20] "In making ambivalence the constitutive heart of his analyses," Young explains, "Bhabha has in effect performed a political reversal at a conceptual level in which the periphery—the borderline, the marginal, the unclassifiable, the doubtful—has become the equivocal, indefinite, indeterminate ambivalence that characterizes the centre."[21]

Bhabha's work raises a number of critical questions regarding the subject of this essay. How, for example, can ambivalence provide an understanding of the cultural iconography in which, against a degenerate Mexican male, the Anglo cowboy seeks a Mexican woman, even as Susie waits ready to homestead with her pots, pans, and religion? How can students and scholars now rethink the relationship of this expressive complex to quasi colonialism in the Southwest, especially Texas—a quasi-colonialism that included land usurpation and physical violence, but also, more significantly, the daily extraction of labor power and racial-cultural gratification and status within a code of racial segregation often enforced through the power of the state, which prevailed well into my own lifetime? In the summer of 1962, I drove back to south Texas with other angry, disappointed working-class Mexican guys, on a senior trip to Anglo-dominated central Texas, after we were refused admission to the wonderful swimming areas in a town named San Marcos, fed by three rivers—named in the seventeenth century as the San Antonio, the Guadalupe, and the Medina. We listened to Robbins's "El Paso" on the car radio. What did it mean not only to listen to such a song with some pleasure but actually to sing along in chorus about a heroic but lonesome Anglo cowboy longing for an attractive Mexican bar-girl? What pleasure could segregated Mexican boys, or those who segregated them, take in a musical performance seemingly reproducing their social relationship, a relationship still more viciously dominant in the nineteenth-century Texas of the song? Is this not a case of what Renato Rosaldo calls "imperialist nostalgia," which "uses a pose of 'innocent yearning' both to capture people's imagination and to conceal its complicity with often brutal domination"?[22] Following Bhabha's mapping of ambivalence, for such instances from the Mexican border I want to suggest a more complicated signification.

Frederick B. Pike describes how nineteenth-century middle-class Anglo America conflated sexual repression and control with capitalist expansion. "For the businessmen intent upon building America's economic foundations, thrift seemed a cardinal virtue; and thrift meant establishing strict control over spending—both dollars and sperm. . . . Nineteenth-century defenders of American middle-class respectability assumed that excess spending of male sperm was bad both for the nation's economy and its morality."[23] The lack of this capitalist virtue was then projected onto what later came to be called the Third World, which, for such Americans, meant Latin America and, according to Pike, the American South. Challenges to such a capitalism—in the 1960s, for example—carried with them a sexual practice critiquing repression, along with more instrumentalist political-economic analyses and actions.

The American cowboy, the Mexican female figure of illicit sexuality, and the "prim and proper" Anglo female figure represent a scenario of ambivalence played out in partial and unconscious challenge to the ruling cultural order. Significantly, this scenario's central figure of ambivalence is a cowboy, a figure on the lower rungs of American capitalism at its most expansive moment, working in the West and in Texas, a periphery of the American capitalist culture centered in the East and Midwest well into the twentieth century.[24] A complicated ambivalent resistance to this expansive culture has always been sited on the cowboy. While many such figures represent societal law and order—Matt Dillon in *Gunsmoke*, for instance—loner figures like Clint Eastwood are already at the critical margins of society. When either enters the realm of the sexual Other, however, the critical possibilities are enhanced as the culture gives full valence to the rhetorically sexualized Mexican woman for what this figure might say about the men who so persistently desire her. In the figure of the desiring cowboy we can, indeed, see the colonizing agent—white, tall, strong gunfighter—but we can also detect a fissure in the colonial enterprise, a break with the sexual repression concomitant with the ruling order that desire for the racial Other accentuates. At its most extreme, the agent of colonialism might actually die in his quest for the Other. In the song "El Paso," the Anglo cowboy finally dies in Selena's arms. Recall also, however, her desire for him. Critics often read such a woman's active pursuit as yet another example of colonial dominance—she longs for his domination. However, as bell hooks notes of such racialized Otherness, "within this fantasy . . . the longing for pleasure is projected as a force that can disrupt and subvert the will to dominate. It acts to both mediate and challenge"—although I would add, never wholly undo. [25] Such mutual longing, such ambivalent guerillalike activity, destabilizes the unitary, repressed colonialist capitalist culture at its most primal site of value.

Such a sexualized destabilization without clear victory is the critical value of the film *High Noon*, whose appearance in the early 1950s coincided with the segregation and labor exploitation of Mexican Americans in Texas and throughout the nation. As a Mexican boy growing up in San Marcos, Texas, in the mid-'50s, the well-known poet Tino Villaneuva drew deep racial instruction from the movie *Giant*, while I, in southern Texas, watched Stanley Kramer's *High Noon* in utter fascination. Perhaps more *boy* than Mexican, I, like many other Americans, was wholly taken by Gary Cooper as town marshall Will Kane awaiting, in his small nineteenth-century western town of Hadleyville, gunfighters from Texas sworn to kill him as the clock strikes twelve. But one now sees the significance of Helen Ramirez, the town madam and Will Kane's former lover, played by Katy Jurado. At first, wholly within the tradition of the eroticized Mexican woman, she is inevitably contrasted with Amy, Kane's new bride. A Quaker, Amy will not abide her husband's impending violence and decides to leave him, though later she abruptly changes her mind. Out of her very sexual marginality, however, Helen has forged a distinctive subversive identity within the town's repressive moral and political economy. Her professional sexual practice has led to a "primitive" accumulation of capital, which she has used to convert herself into a "legitimate" and competent businesswoman, owner of a saloon and a store. Her combined sexual and economic power allows her to hold sway over the town's white male community as they make ritual, obsequious visits to her queenly apartment above the barrio to curry favor while their repressed white wives wait at home.

In a long and telling middle scene, Helen and Kane confront each other at the height of Kane's crisis, and it is abundantly clear that Kane has fully experienced her evident passion and still cares deeply for her, as she does for him. Imbedded in their dialogue is a brief but fulsome exchange of deeply romantic words uttered in Spanish, probably lost on the predominantly Anglo audience since they are inserted without any translation and are therefore already subversive. These words speak massive cultural volumes to any native member of the Spanish-speaking world: "Un año sin verte" (A year without seeing you), she says to him as she gazes deeply into his eyes; "lo se" (I know), he answers. He answers in such an informed Spanish that it is clear that he has been interpellated by the language just as he has by her entire sexual-cultural being. Indeed, he knows a great deal, more than he will be willing to admit, but she knows that in their *mano a mano* he has capitulated to the other side. She decides to leave town with their love never permanently fulfilled.

They see each other only once more. Helen is riding to the train station in a buggy with Amy, who is also leaving town; they pass Kane standing in the street awaiting his assailants. Amy looks away from him, but Helen's eyes lock onto Kane's and through her eyes the camera holds him for a full five seconds as he returns her steady parting gaze. So how could this passionate romance have failed? Why does Kane leave Helen for Amy and the life of a small shop-keeper? The implication is quite clear: he has been unable to escape the racism and the sexual and economic repression of the town's capitalist moral economy. Helen comments on this as she gets ready to leave: "I hate this town. I've always hated it, to be a Mexican woman in a town like this." Kane leaves Helen for Amy even though Helen is the superior figure; she even rhetorically forces Amy to assist in his final moment of crisis as the gunfight begins. At the end of the film, he and Amy emerge triumphant heroes over some part of this economy, but it is also clear that they have both derived great strength from the racial-sexual Other—Helen Ramirez—even as Kane denies her claim on his sexual and moral sensibility. She will, of course, lose Kane to Amy and leave town. In her final scene, however, Helen is on the train, and as the camera focuses on her strong, beautiful Mexican face, we clearly sense how she has achieved some large measure of victory in this contest even as the film at the end too quickly erases her strong, sexualized Mexican female presence to make narrative way for the reunited white couple, triumphant heroes of the rising yet repressed bourgeois social order in the later nineteenth century.

One conventional, circumscribed reading of *High Noon* is that the town has morally failed the heroic Will Kane, taking this as a critical commentary on the McCarthyite 1950s, when society failed to act against the "bad men" until it was almost too late. But as a perhaps unintended critical commentary on the Anglo-Mexican racial politics of this period, the film is a local inter-vention often ignored in efforts to nationalize and universalize it. While heroic in one way, Kane fails in another. After their climactic meeting Kane labors with his own racially motivated moral failure to fully respond to Helen's plenitude and to thereby transcend the racialized political-economic moral order. Even as he survives the gunfight and restores his marriage with Amy, it is clear that his petit bourgeois world has been forever destabilized by his prior knowledge of the Mexican sexual Other. Helen's parting gaze rests upon him forever and "un año sin verte" plus many more might never be enough to undo her ambivalent yet powerful incursion into Will Kane's life.

If the Mexican woman in her full sexuality has critical possibilities, what of the clearly despised Mexican male? With none of the exoticism, eroticism, or freer play given that of the Mexican woman, he is a rhetorical construction for which the term *stereotype* is in unforgivingly full force. In this encounter men read other men in a discursive *mano a mano*. Denigration of the Mexican male is conventionally understood as the articulation of colonialism directed specifically at the male body that traditionally offered the greatest opposition, namely the heroic male figures of the Texas-Mexican border ballads, or *corridos*. In the context of the Anglo male's politically and psychologically necessary desire for Mexican women, however, we begin to see here a psychoanalytic relationship of identity and difference, narcissism and aggression. The Mexican and Anglo males narcissistically identify with each other as equally available sexual partners for Mexican women. Indeed, Américo Paredes suggests that the ideal Mexican cowboy, or *vaquero*, quite contrary to the stereotypical image, was more likely to be tall, lean, and dark with green or tawny eyes, more like his Anglo counterpart than not.[26] However, such a Mexican man would still have a cultural advantage over his Anglo mirror image relative to Mexican women, if only by his Spanish fluency. In response, the Anglo, who controls this discursive site, produces a maximum form of difference and aggressivity so as to wholly deny the identity of the Mexican man, which, if it were acknowledged, puts him at a disadvantage in his quest. When it comes to the construction of Mexican males by Anglo males, there can be no rhetorical quarter given, no ambivalence.

Ambivalent toward Mexican women as he is, the Anglo male nevertheless recognizes the limits of his transgression and returns to Susie. And what else is Susie—pots, pans, hard work, religion, and all (likely including a timid sexuality)—but the representative figure of the dominant culture that compels this resolution? In the white "settlement" of the West, such women represented the most effective form of colonialism, bringing with them the daily habitus of households, social etiquette, religion, and schools for the reproduction of fundamental colonial values.[27] The schoolmarm emerges as the ultimate pairing for our cowboy once he is done with his transgressive experimentation at the border. As mothers, such women were also obligated to reproduce Anglo culture, literally, in its numbers, but also through socialization. J. Frank Dobie, an archetypal cowboy, grew up on a Texas ranch in the late nineteenth century and wrote about his very religious mother, who was a schoolteacher in south Texas before she married his rancher father, bore six children, and eventually persuaded him to move the family into town.[28] Giving up his range life for the sake of such civilizing women is another vector of cowboy ambivalence, as "A Cowboy's Son" also suggests:

Whar y'u from, little stranger, little boy?
Y'u was ridin' a cloud on that star-strewn plain,
But y'u fell from the skies like a drop of rain
To this world of sorrow and long, long pain.
Will y'u care fo' yo' mothah, little boy?

When y'u grows, little varmint, little boy,
Y'u'll be ridin' a hoss by yo' fathah's side
With yo' gun and yo' spurs and yo' howstrong pride.
Will y'u think of yo' home when the world rolls wide?
Will y'u wish for yo' mothah, little boy?

When y'u love in yo' manhood, little boy,—
When y'u dream of a girl who is angel fair,—
When the stars are her eyes and the wind is her hair,—
When the sun is her smile and yo' heaven's there,—
Will y'u care for yo' mothah, little boy?[29]

In this cowboy world, the mother, conflated with the "angel fair" girl, exerts civilizing power along with domesticity. Though "fathah" appears as cowboy mentor with horse, gun, and pride, the song never asks the question, "Will y'u care for yo' fathah?"

The Anglo male's ambivalent transgression with the Other as sexualized Mexican woman is usually resolved in the direction of this hegemonic Anglo woman–centered culture, from where such a woman might also recognize her greatest enemy. For we learn again from Dobie's autobiography that his mother had specifically instructed her sons never to "debase themselves by living with Mexican women."[30] Like Will Kane's choice in *High Noon,* this resolution of ambivalence often occurred with nostalgia:

Her eyes were brown—a deep, deep brown:
Her hair was darker than her eyes;
And something in her smile and frown,
Curled crimson lip and instep high,
Showed that there ran in each blue vein,
Mixed with the milder Aztec strain,
The vigorous vintage of Old Spain. . . .

The air was heavy, the night was hot,
I sat by her side and forgot, forgot;
Forgot the herd that were taking rest,
Forgot that the air was close oppressed. . . .

And I wonder why I do not care
For the things that are, like the things that were.
Does half my heart lie buried there
In Texas, down by the Rio Grande?[31]

Whereas the nineteenth-century cultural iconography we have dealt with so far was specifically sited in the western United States, the twentieth century brings another image, broadly Latin American. It began in the early 1920s with the film career of the Italian Rudoph Valentino and his portrayal of the "Latin lover," and developed through the present in a lineage that includes, most prominently, Gilbert Roland, Desi Arnaz (before he loved Lucy), Fernando Lamas, Ricardo Montalban, Zorro, Julio Iglesias, and—in contemporary, funkier versions—Jimmy Smits and Antonio Banderas. How does this strong, slender, suave, sophisticated, slightly accented, slightly dark, simmering, sultry—is it necessary to say sexy?—figure work into this iconography? The "Latin lover" emerged in relation to two factors emerging out of the period between the two World Wars and gained potency after 1945: first, the greater cultural tolerance at the national level for Latin America, especially Mexico, as a result, in significant part, of the latter's enlistment on the Allied side in World War II—what Helen Delpar has called "the enormous vogue of things Mexican"; second, the increasing structural and cultural freedom of Anglo-American women—the presumed desiring audience for this icon. Recall how often in films and TV shows she meets the "Latin lover" while she is on vacation somewhere in Latin America either by herself or with a girlfriend. Ricky came to love Lucy while she was vacationing in Havana with Ethel sometime before 1959, for example.[32] In the relationship of these latter-day Anglo women—now at some considerable distance from Susie and J. Frank Dobie's mother—to this figure of Latin male sexuality, do we not have a relationship similar to the traditional Anglo male–Mexican woman conjunction? Does this relationship not also make a momentary ambivalent claim to greater though transgressive fulfillment, although the Anglo woman also usually finds permanence elsewhere?

In the preceding, I have tried to shift us from a directly correlated, univocal relationship between such iconography and quasi colonialism to one of ambivalence. The colonized thus become a site for witnessing a fissure or decentering within the colonizer, while remaining unequal. A larger realm of freedom for colonized and colonizer required termination of this ambivalence and a revision of the social relations that had sustained it. John Sayles's 1996 film *Lone Star* suggests such a termination by radically revising the history of this iconography.

A murder mystery, *Lone Star* is set in contemporary small-town southern Texas along the U.S.-Mexico border.[33] Through flashbacks it spans the years from the 1930s to the present. In the 1990s Sam Deeds—the young, tough, lean, soft-spoken Anglo country sheriff—is trying to solve the murder of Charlie Wade—the former corrupt, tyrannical, and racist sheriff, whose remains were accidently found in the desert after his mysterious disappearance some forty years earlier. Between these two sheriffs' tenure, the office was filled by Sam's father, Buddy Deeds, said to be the living definition of the epic Texas male. Although Buddy too is now dead, he becomes a prime suspect in Wade's murder. Buddy served as Wade's deputy before becoming sheriff, and they clashed over Wade's corruption. Led by Hollis, the mayor and a former deputy to both Wade and Buddy, the town—Anglo, Mexican, and African American—remains loyal both to Buddy's epic quality and his patronage politics. Revered almost as much as Buddy, his now dead Anglo wife Muriel is said to have been "an angel of a woman." In the course of his investigation, Sam comes upon repressed information that revisits the traditional iconography.

Sam eventually discovers the identity of Wade's killer, but this other knowledge of past and present racialized sexualities gives the story greater significance. It sketches the evolution of Anglo-Mexican relations in Texas and radically revises the traditional iconography. Buddy presided as sheriff in the period roughly from the late 1950s to the early 1970s. Though not a Charlie Wade, he still participated in maintaining a colonialist social order in which the local Mexicans knew their place; he did not, for example, permit his teenaged son, Sam, to date Pilar, a Mexican American, and was livid when he caught them necking at a local drive-in theater. The reason for these strictures turns out to be more complex than simple racism: Pilar is the attractive daughter of Mercedes Cruz, the owner of a successful local Mexican restaurant and herself a beautiful woman in her youth. Mercedes's husband, Eladio Cruz, had died some years previous. While Sam has become sheriff, Pilar has become an activist high school history teacher. As the murder investigation proceeds, Sam and Pilar rekindle their romantic relationship, culminating in a slow romantic dance to jukebox music after hours in her mother's restaurant. Befitting the social forces they come to represent, they dance to the 1960s tune by Ivory Joe Hunter with the refrain, "Since I met you baby, my whole life has changed," sung, however, in Spanish by Freddy Fender.

As late as the mid-1960s, colonial order still prevailed in many parts of Texas, of which the administrations of both Charlie Wade and Buddy Deeds are very accurate representations. Buddy changes the style of administration, however, from one of violent coercion to one in which, in Gramscian terms, the state justifies and maintains its dominance by winning the active consent of the dominated.[34] Buddy, our archetypal Texas male, played out the sexualized cultural politics of ambivalence. While married to an Anglo woman with an appropriately angelic name, Muriel, he completes the traditional constellation of images through a love affair with the beautiful Mercedes. As with Kane and Ramirez, this is an affair that questions the cultural totality of the ruling order, especially since the erstwhile "Mexican" Pilar is *his* daughter and therefore Sam's half sister. It remains for his son Sam and his daughter Pilar to move beyond this dialectic of rule and ambivalence into a greater realm of freedom.

As the film ends, Sam and Pilar are sitting on the hood of a car parked at the now abandoned drive-in theater as Sam tells her all that he has discovered about their mixed parentage. Sam and Pilar, like Will Kane and Helen Ramirez, must make a critical decision. They can go their separate ways, or they can continue and make their relationship permanent through marriage, despite, or perhaps through, this knowledge. The film ends without an absolutely clear resolution. For me, there is nothing now in the social order to prevent the legal and moral consummation of their love. They are free to do what Kane, in his shallow heroism, could not. I am not persuaded that Pilar and Sam will forsake each other on *their* wedding day about-to-be. It is entirely appropriate that this final scene and decision take place in the now decaying drive-in theater where they once made illicit teenage love; the theater and the lovemaking symbolize another era when the colonial order was still in full force (when Mexicans were not allowed to swim in the swimming areas of San Marcos fed by the San Antonio, Medina, and Guadalupe rivers).

"Forget the Alamo," says Pilar, as she and Sam decide to forge a relationship based not on sexually transgressive ambivalence but rather on a clear recognition of their relative equality and the public continuation of their love. A college-educated intellectual, she has social status equalizing whatever cultural capital still accrues to him as an Anglo in the 1990s. As a public school teacher—indeed a teacher of history, the "queen" of the sciences—she revises the image of the Mexican woman (often prostitute) at the sexual and social margins of society. In effect, Pilar appropriates the traditional image of the civilizing Anglo schoolmarm with a critical difference: she is a civilized and civilizing individual while maintaining a full and healthy display of her sexuality. Her initiation in a Mexican restaurant of the sex she will enjoy with Sam revises the iconographic sexual encounter between Anglo cowboy and Mexican woman in a cantina. Not a cantina, this is a socially sanctioned space; the fact that it is not only a Mexican but also a Mexican-owned restaurant testifies to the full emergence of a Mexican-American social class that effectively demands an equal place in society. Other well-educated Mexican-American figures appear who are on the verge of taking over civil and state society, replacing the Hollises and Sams or at least sharing power with them. Represented by clean-cut, earnest young Mexican-American males—a journalist and a mayoral candidate who will replace Hollis and Sam—they are garbed in the coats and ties of civil society. These Mexican-American male figures have no discernible sexual valence in the film, negative or positive; they are a considerable distance from both the rapacious Mexican bandit and the "Latin lover."

PILAR AND SAM GET REACQUAINTED. *Lone Star* (1995). COURTESY OF THE ACADEMY OF MOTION PICTURE ARTS AND SCIENCES.

This implied ending of the colonial order has much to do with the sexualized kinship twist Sales has given his story. The fact that Pilar and Sam are simultaneously lovers and blood brother and sister reinforces their sexually constituted love with the enduring bonds of consanguineous affiliation. Their half-blood relations suggest that these two social sectors are now also united in brother-sisterhood, though still with some, perhaps minimal, social distance.[35] Public equals and in unambivalent love, in semibrother-sisterhood, still aware of their ethnicities, Pilar and Sam are willing, in her words (and it is critical that she say them), to "forget the Alamo." She is a teacher of history, who intends to negate history by moving beyond the colonial, if ambivalent, sexual and social worlds of her parents.

Is *Lone Star* a utopian vision? Perhaps, but the foremost social historian of these matters in Texas, with great sociological supporting data, wrote in 1986, "From the long view of a century and a half, Mexican-Anglo relations have traversed a difficult path, from the hatred and suspicion engendered by war to a form of reconciliation."[36] "[T]his does not mean that ethnic solidarity has become a matter of the past; it means rather that it has become subordinated to the voices of moderation from both communities. The politics of negotiation and compromise have replaced the politics of conflict and control."[37] Negotiation and compromise characterize a good marriage, one beyond domination, inequality, stereotypic iconographies, and ambivalence.[38] Seen in the context of a correlation of social forces now underway in Texas, New Mexico, and perhaps other parts of Mexican America, *Lone Star* is a film that seeks to end the legacy of *Little Lone Star*. It invites us to review this iconographic and social history, and that of the West more generally, even as it seems to propose productive forgetfulness in the name of a larger vision long overdue. Relative to the conflicted history of colonialism, sexuality, and gender and race relations in the U.S. West and greater Mexico that *Across the Great Divide* illuminates, students and scholars need to ask themselves whether John Sayles's 1990s perspective on these matters obscures a history of conflict, contact, and often uneven negotiation, or whether Sayles is truly, in Alan Stone's words, "a prophet of hope" who has accurately forecast the beginning of a new chapter in the story of the West.

Notes

1. Arthur G. Pettit, *Images of the Mexican American in Fiction and Film*. ed. with an afterword by Dennis E. Showalter (College Station: Texas A&M University Press, 1980), 39 and 30. Pettit, the principal Anglo-American scholar, was preceded by Cecil Robinson and his *With the Ears of Strangers: The Mexican in American Literature* (Tucson: University of Arizona Press, 1963). See also Sam Hall, *Little Lone Star; or, The Belle of the Cibolo* (1886).

2. Cormac McCarthy, *All the Pretty Horses* (New York: Vintage, 1992).

3. John A. Lomax, comp., *Songs of the Cattle Trail and Cow Camp* (New York: Macmillan, 1919), 67–68.

4. Lomax, 65–66.

5. Lomax, 72.

6. On this pattern, see Pettit, 205. *High Noon*, dir. Fred Zinneman, prod. Stanley Kramer, with Gary Cooper and Katy Jurado (United Artists, 1952).

7. The film was produced by George Stevens and Henry Ginsburg.

8. Larry McMurtry, *Streets of Laredo* (New York: Simon and Schuster, 1993).

9. Américo Paredes, *"With His Pistol in His Hand": A Border Ballad and Its Hero* (Austin: Unversity of Texas Press, 1958).

10. Guillermo Flores, "Race and Culture in the Internal Colony: Keeping the Chicano in His Place," in *Structures of Dependency*, ed. Frank Bonilla and Robert Girling (Oakland, Calif.: Sembradora, 1973), 194.

11. Alfredo Mirande and Evangelina Enriquez, *La Chicana: The Mexican-American Woman* (Chicago: University of Chicago Press, 1979), 158.

12. Ibid., 143.

13. Arnoldo De Leon, *They Called Them Greasers: Anglo Attitudes toward Mexicans in Texas, 1821–1900* (Austin: University of Texas Press, 1983), 39.

14. Charles Ramirez-Berg, "Stereotyping in Films in General and of the Hispanic in Particular," *Howard Journal of Communications* 2 (1990): 291.

15. Consult Américo Paredes's brief and general yet intriguing assessment of this iconography in his essay "The Problem of Identity in a Changing Culture: Popular Expressions of Culture Conflict along the Lower Rio Grande Border," in *Views across the Border: The United States and Mexico*, ed. Stanley Ross (Albuquerque: University of New Mexico Press, 1978), 43. Reprinted in *Folklore and Culture on the Texas-Mexican Border*, ed. Richard Bauman (Austin: Center for Mexican-American Studies, University of Texas, 1993).

16. For a fine discussion of the history of the concept of colonialism relative to Anglos and Mexicans in the Southwest, see Tomás Almaguer, "Ideological Distortions and Recent Chicano Historiography: The Internal Colonial Model and Chicano Historical Interpretation," *Aztlan: A Journal of Chicano Research* 18 (1987): 7–28.

17. Robert J. C. Young, *Colonial Desire: Hybridity in Theory, Culture, and Race* (London: Routledge, 1995), 161.

18. Ibid.

19. Homi K. Bhabha, *The Location of Culture* (London: Routledge, 1994), 66–67.

20. Ibid., 67.

21. Young, 161.

22. Renato Rosaldo, *Culture and Truth: The Remaking of Social Analysis* (Boston: Beacon Press, 1989), 70.

23. Frederick B. Pike, *The United States and Latin America: Myths and Stereotypes of Civilization and Nature* (Austin: University of Texas Press, 1992), 53.

24. David Montejano, *Anglos and Mexicans in the Making of Texas, 1836–1986* (Austin: University of Texas Press, 1987).

25. bell hooks, *Black Looks: Race and Representation* (Boston: South End, 1992), 27.

26. Paredes, *"With His Pistol In His Hand,"* 111.

27. Sarah Deutsch, *No Separate Refuge: Culture, Class, and Gender on an Anglo-Hispanic Frontier in the American Southwest, 1880–1940* (New York: Oxford University Press, 1987), 63.

28. J. Frank Dobie, *Some Part of Myself* (1976; reprint Austin: University of Texas Press, 1980).

29. Lomax, 88.

30. Dobie, 89.

31. Lomax, 24–26.

32. See Gustavo Perez Firmat, *Life on the Hyphen: The Cuban-American Way* (Austin: University of Texas Press, 1994), chaps. 1 and 2.

33. *Lone Star*, dir. John Sayles, prod. R. Paul Miller and Maggie Renzi, with Kris Kristofferson, Matthew McConaughey, Chris Cooper, and Elizabeth Peña (Columbia Pictures, 1996).

34. Walter L. Adamson, *Hegemony and Gramsci's Political and Cultural Theory* (Berkeley and Los Angeles: University of California Press, 1980), 165.

35. Sayles has to foreclose the possibility of biosocial reproduction, however, so Pilar, for past medical reasons, can no longer get pregnant. Yet Sam and Pilar have nothing to prove on this score; already products of such racialized sexuality, they foretell the shape of the new social order. Admittedly, this is an ambiguous ending, although it is clear that Sayles expected his audience to understand that Pilar and Sam would stay together. See Alan A. Stone, "The Prophet of Hope," *Boston Review* (October–November 1996): 20–22.

36. Montejano, 297.

37. Ibid., 306.

38. This marriage does not involve recent undocumented Mexican immigrants such as those working in the kitchen of Mercedes's restaurant. In her transformation from hostility to some sympathy for this population, Mercedes represents Mexican-American ambivalence toward Mexican immigrants. See Rodolfo O. de la Garza et al., *Latino Voices: Mexican, Puerto Rican, and Cuban Perspectives on American Politics* (Boulder, Col.: Westview, 1992); and David Gutierrez, *Walls and Mirrors: Mexican Americans, Mexican Immigrants, and the Politics of Ethnicity* (Berkeley and Los Angeles: University of California Press, 1995), 207–16.

Contributors

Durwood Ball is associate professor of history and editor of the *New Mexico Historical Review* at the University of New Mexico in Albuquerque. He is the author of *Army Regulars on the Western Frontier* (University of Oklahoma Press, 2001).

Matthew Basso is a Ph.D. candidate in the American studies program at the University of Minnesota. Basso's research and teaching focus on the interplay between popular culture, politics, and ethnoracial, class, and gender identity. His work on wartime films and their audiences has appeared in the *Columbia Journal of American Studies,* and his study of western workers, movies, and the social politics of white male anxiety (1938–1948) is forthcoming from the University of Chicago Press.

David Anthony Tyeeme Clark (Mesquakie) is a graduate minority opportunity fellow in the American studies program at the University of Kansas. His recent work includes "'The Number of Tribes . . . Right for Him or Her': Romancing Imaginary 'Indians' in *On the Rez,*" *American Indian Quarterly*; "Breaking the Iron Bonds: Indigenous Subject-Citizens and the [Il]Logic of Social Life," *American Quarterly* (2001); and with Joane Nagel and Troy Johnson, *Roots of Red Power: American Indian Protest and Resistance, from Wounded Knee to the Chicago Indian Conference* (forthcoming, University of Nebraska Press).

Dee Garceau is assistant professor of history at Rhodes College in Memphis, Tennessee, where she teaches courses on gender and the American West. She holds a Ph.D. in American civilization from Brown University, and founded the Desert Writer's Workshop in Moab, Utah, sponsored annually by

Canyonlands Field Institute and the National Endowment for the Humanities. Garceau is the author of *The Important Things of Life: Women, Work and Family in Sweetwater County, Wyoming, 1880–1929* (University of Nebraska Press, 1997) and has an essay forthcoming in *Sifters: Native American Women's Lives,* ed. Theda Perdue (Oxford University Press, 2001).

Ramón A. Gutiérrez is professor of ethnic studies and history at the University of California, San Diego, and the founding director of the Center for the Study of Race and Ethnicity. He is currently working on two projects: a history of the Chicano movement in the United States and a history of Indian slavery in New Mexico.

Susan Lee Johnson is the author of *Roaring Camp: The Social World of the California Gold Rush* (W. W. Norton, 2000). She teaches U.S. western history, gender/women's history, and the history of sexuality at the University of Colorado at Boulder. She is working on a study that uses Kit Carson's intimate relationship with Arapaho, Cheyenne, and New Mexican women as a window on questions of space, race, gender, nation, and desire.

Brian Klopotek, of Choctaw and Irish-American heritage, is a doctoral candidate in the American studies program at the University of Minnesota. His research interests include all areas of Native American studies in the twentieth and twenty-first centuries. His current research project examines the impact of the federal recognition process on Native Americans in Louisiana.

Craig Leavitt is an independent scholar and novelist who lives in Denver, Colorado.

Steven M. Lee is a graduate student in comparative ethnic studies at the University of California-Berkeley. His research interests center on the study of gender and sexuality in Asian-American literature.

Karen J. Leong is assistant professor in the women's studies program at Arizona State University. She received her doctorate in U.S. history from the University of California-Berkeley, and her dissertation received the 2000 Lerner-Scott Prize from the Organization of American Historians.

José E. Limón, professor of anthropology and English at the University of Texas-Austin, is the author most recently of *American Encounters: Greater Mexico, the United States, and the Erotics of Culture* (Beacon Press, 1999). His academic interests are varied and include Chicano literature, Mexicans in the United States, United States-Mexico cultural relations, and folklore and popular culture. He has been a fellow of the Stanford Humanities Research Center, the National Endowment for the Humanities, and the American Council of Learned Societies. Since 1989 he has also been a member of the National Faculty, working with public school teachers in economically impacted areas of the country. Limón was selected as one of the "Twenty Most Influential Texans" for 1999 by *Texas Monthly*.

Laura McCall is professor of history and member of the honors faculty at Metropolitan State College, Denver. She received her Ph.D. and M.A. from the University of Michigan and her B.A. from Northwestern University. McCall's published works include the coedited *A Shared Experience: Men, Women, and the History of Gender* (New York University Press, 1998); studies of Sacagawea; and literary treatments of sexuality in antebellum America, *Godey's Lady's Book*, and women who committed violent acts on America's fictional frontiers. A community activist, McCall has lectured on gendered attitudes toward the American landscape as well as on individualism versus community in the American West.

Karen R. Merrill is assistant professor of history at the University of California, Irvine, where she teaches western history. Her study of political conflicts over the public range, between ranchers and the federal government, is forthcoming from the University of California Press. She is the editor of *The Modern Worlds of Business and Industry: Cultures, Technology, Labor* (Brepols Publishers, 1998).

Joane Nagel is University Distinguished Professor and chair of sociology at the University of Kansas; her recent work includes *American Indian Ethnic Renewal* (Oxford University Press, 1997), "Masculinity and Nationalism: Gender and Sexuality in the Making of Nations," *Ethnic and Racial Studies* (1998), and *Race, Ethnicity, and Sexuality: Intimate Intersections and Forbidden Frontiers* (Oxford University Press, 2001).

Gunther Peck is associate professor of history at the University of Texas-Austin and the author of *Reinventing Free Labor: Padrone and Immigrant Workers in North America West, 1880–1930* (Cambridge University Press, 2000), which explores the practice and ideology of free wage labor during the peak years of immigration. Peck is currently working on a social and cultural history of white slavery in North America before and after Emancipation.

Permissions

Articles

Gutiérrez, Raymond. "Honor and Virtue," Chapter 6, reprinted from *When Jesus Came, the Corn Mothers Went Away,* by Raymond Gutiérrez, with permission of Stanford University Press. © 1991 by the Board of Trustees of the Leland Stanford Junior University.

Johnson, Susan Lee. "Bulls, Bears, and Dancing Boys: Race, Gender, and Leisure in the California Gold Rush," *Radical History Review,* fall 1994, vol. 60: 4–37. Reprinted with permission of Cambridge University Press.

Limón, José E. "Tex-Sex-Mex: American Identities, Lone Stars, and the Politics of Racialized Sexuality," *American Literary History,* 1997, 9, no. 3: 598–616. Reprinted with permission of Oxford University Press.

Peck, Gunther. "Manly Gambles: The Politics of Risk on the Comstock Lode, 1860–1880," *Journal of Social History,* 1993, 26, no. 4: 701–723. ISSN: 0022-4529.

Photographs

Ball, Durwood. "Cool to the End: Public Hangings and Western Manhood." Photos courtesy of the Arizona Historical Society/Tucson, AHS nos. 28197 and 17667.

Basso, Matthew L. "Man-Power: Montana Copper Workers, State Authority, and the (Re)drafting of Manhood during World War II."

Cartoons reproduced from collections in the Montana Historical Society Archives.

Clark, David Anthony Tyeeme, and Nagel, Joane. "White Man, Red Masks: Appropriations of 'Indian' Manhood in Imagined Wests." *Charles Eastman* courtesy of Dartmouth College Library. *Seton's Tribe* courtesy of the Seton Memorial Library, Cimarron, New Mexico.

Garceau, Dee. "Nomads, Bunkies, Cross-Dressers, and Family Men: Cowboy Identity and the Gendering of Ranch Work." Haircut photo courtesy of the Library of Congress. *Cowboys in Their Camps* photo courtesy of the Colorado Historical Society, no. F-14,800.

Johnson, Susan Lee. "Bulls, Bears, and Dancing Boys: Race, Gender, and Leisure in the California Gold Rush." *J. D. Barthwick's Rendering of a Gold Rush Ball,* no. F865B7, p. 320, and *The Grizzly and His Captors,* no. 1963.002:0049B; both courtesy of the Bancroft Library, University of California, Berkeley.

Klopotek, Brian, "'I Guess Your Warrior Look Doesn't Work Every Time': Challenging Indian Masculinity in the Cinema." *Pow-Wow Highway* (Warner Bros., 1989) photo courtesy of the Academy of Motion Picture Arts and Sciences. Photographic still from *Smoke Signals* courtesy of Miramax Films. All rights reserved.

Limón, José E. "Tex-Sex-Mex: American Identities, Lone Stars, and the Politics of Racialized Sexuality." *Lone Star* (Sony Pictures Classics, 1996) photo courtesy of the Academy of Motion Picture Arts and Sciences.

McCall, Laura. "Introduction." Teddy Roosevelt photos courtesy of the Theodore Roosevelt Collection, Houghton Library, Harvard University.

Peck, Gunther. "Manly Gambles: The Politics of Risk on the Comstock Lode, 1860–1880." *Miners Working thro Gould and Curry Shaft* courtesy of the California Historical Society, George D. Lyman Collection, no. FN-27898.

Index

Black Hills, 110. *See also* Little Big Horn,
    Battle of
Blaine, James G., 143–144
Blasingame, Ike, 160–161, 165
blood, 29–30, 102. *See also* race
"Blood and Bread" (Reynolds), 196–197
BMU. *See* Butte Miners' Union
Boatright, Mody C., 223
body symbolism, 29–30
Bonanza, 235
Book, Peter, 176
Booth, Sam, 131, 146(n1)
Booth, Zack, 101
Borthwick, J. D., 17, 50–51, 60, 65–66
Bowman, Elbert F., 183(n21)
Bowman, Ellen, 174
boys and boyhood, 17, 22(n40), 95(n51), 113,
    140–141, 235–236
"Boys Away From Home" (article), 193
Boy Scouts of America, 112. *See also* Woodcraft
    Indians
branding, 173, 181
bravado, 100, 104, 106
The Brave Cowboy (Abbey), 213–214
Brooks, Mrs. B. B., 150
Bryan, Tom, 164
"Buffalo" Bill. *See* Cody, William Frederick
    ("Buffalo Bill")
bull-and-bear fighting, 64–67, 71(n64)
"Bullard's Wolves" (Russell), 174
bunkies, 154–155, 156(fig), 159, 161(fig), 167(n24)
Burlingame Treaty, 136, 139–140
Butte, Montana, 187–188, 191–192, 195–196,
    198–199, 203, 205, 207(n1). *See also* copper
    workers
Butte Miners' Union (BMU), 198, 200, 205–206,
    207(n1)

California, 9, 17, 45–67, 68(nn 2–3), 70(n37),
    136–138, 147(nn 25, 43)
captivity narratives, 115, 127(n26), 128(n30)
Carillo, Juana, 33
Carillo, Manuela, 28
Carnes, Mark, 81, 94–95(n42)
Carpenter, Leroy, 191–192, 197
Casey, Joseph, 100
Cassady, Carolyn (Camille), 216, 224–225, 229
Cassady, Neal (Dean Moriarty/Cody Pomeray),
    14, 211–230
Catholics, 25, 50, 101, 103. *See also* priests
cattle, 12–13, 19, 149–153, 165, 169–182, 182(n10),
    182–183(n12), 183–184(n29), 184(nn 39, 41, 47).
    See also cowboys
Chan, Jeffrey Paul, 235, 239
Chávez, María Rosa, 36
Cherokee Kid, 157–158
Cherokee people, 17–18
Cheyenne people, 125, 126(n1). *See also* Little Big
    Horn, Battle of; *Powwow Highway*; *Smoke
    Signals*

Chicanos/Chicanas. *See* Mexican men; Mexican
    women; Spanish New Mexicans
The Chickencoop Chinaman (Chin), 237–238
"Chiefs of Four Top War Agencies Appeal to
    Metal Miners to Remain on Jobs" (article), 193
Chileans, 46–47, 50, 57–58, 60, 63–64
Chin, Frank, 15, 235, 237–240, 246, 247(n2),
    249(n57)
Chinese Exclusion Act (1882), 131
Chinese men, 10–12, 46, 81, 84–85, 131–148,
    234–235, 240. *See also* Asian American men
Chinese women, 46, 131–134, 136, 138–141,
    147(nn 37, 43)
Christianity, 101, 103–107. *See also* Catholics;
    churches
Christman, Enos, 56–57, 65
churches, 50–52, 140. *See also* Christianity
citizenship, 131–148, 133, 143–144, 185, 232–233
civil rights, 135–136, 206
class, socio-economic, 9–10, 74–75, 90–91, 136,
    153–154. *See also* middle-class men; mine
    workers; working-class men
Claxton, John, 203
Cleaveland, Agnes Morley, 181, 183–184(n29)
Cleveland Indians (baseball team), 121–123
cockfighting, 80, 94(n36)
Cody, William Frederick ("Buffalo Bill"), 106,
    117–118, 234, 247(n1)
colonialism, 16, 25–44, 275–291
Colorado, 22(n40), 183(n19)
Comstock Lode, 73–96
"Confessions of the Chinatown Cowboy" (Chin),
    240–241
Conley, John, 100, 103
Connell, R. W., 7, 207(n6)
Cooksley, Elsie and Amy, 151–152
coolness, 98–100, 104–107
Copper Commando, 192–196, 205–206
copper workers, 14, 185–210
Córdova, Francisca, 41–42
"A Cowboy's Son" (song), 284
Cowboy Life in Texas (James), 163
cowboys, 149–168, 247(n1)
    and animals, 169–170, 174, 183(n18)
    in Asian-American literature, 15, 235–246
    bunkies, 154–155, 156(fig), 159, 161(fig),
        167(n24)
    cowboy hero/myth, 152–153, 155, 163, 165, 170,
        184(n51), 231–240, 247(n1), 275–276,
        281–283
    cross-dressing, 12, 160–163
    homoerotic feelings, 155–159, 167(n36)
    marginal status, 152–154, 159–160, 162–165
    non-Anglo cowboys, 17–18, 233–234, 242–246,
        249(n75), 284
    property ownership, 163–164, 166(n3), 168(n82)
    tasks, 172, 179, 182–183(n12)
    and women, 12–13, 16, 149–154, 159–164,
        275–277
    See also cattle; ranchers